Advance praise for *Preparing Leadership Educators*

"Jonathan Kroll has interpreted the mammoth body of literature on leadership development with his wisdom and years of experience. The result is this terrific handbook for all leadership educators—whatever approaches to leadership they may prefer—and advances the growing profession of leadership education."—**Susan R. Komives**, *Professor Emerita, University of Maryland; Former President of ACPA, CAS; 2022 Life Time Legacy Award Recipient from the International Leadership Association*

"As someone who teaches courses on leadership and facilitation, I am excited for *Preparing Leadership Educators*. Jonathan Kroll has composed an informative and engaging text that includes both the 'what' of leadership theory and literature as well as the 'how' of facilitation. This combination of theory and practice is essential to the future of leadership education. I'll definitely be adopting this as my textbook the next time I teach!"—**Annemarie Vaccaro**, *Professor and Associate Dean, University of Rhode Island*

"*Preparing Leadership Educators* is a critical text that furthers the conversation around the training and development of leadership educators. The text explores theoretical frameworks as a foundation for practice and empowers leadership educators to dive into the historical, foundational, and paradigmatic influences of leadership education—while reflecting on their own leadership praxis. The impact of the text is two-fold among leaders on college campuses: those who educate students and the students who are identified as emergent leaders."—**Amber Manning-Ouellette**, *Assistant Professor and Coordinator, College Student Development Program, Oklahoma State University*

"*Preparing Leadership Educators* fills a niche need for professionals in leadership education, training, and development, with a resource-rich compendium of facilitative tools. This text builds quickly from knowledge to effective praxis in leadership education spaces and focuses on the ubiquitous dialogical approach integrated across experiential approaches to leadership learning. This is a must-read for leadership educators who are looking to fine-tune their training and facilitation skills or pick up a few new pedagogical strategies for teaching the most common leadership theories and practices."—**Dan Jenkins**, *Professor of Leadership and Organizational Studies, University of Southern Maine; coauthor of* The Role of Leadership Educators: Transforming Learning

"*Preparing Leadership Educators* is a critical resource for leadership educators charged with developing the next generation of leaders. However, it extends beyond the resource gap. Jonathan Kroll illuminates the art and science of leadership education, which makes this text a go-to resource for the training and development industry and growing field of leadership education."—**Katie Friesen**, *Assistant Professor of Education and Director of First-Year Experience, William Woods University*

"This book provides a masterful blend of leadership theories and practices that will equip educators with the knowledge and skills necessary to prepare leaders for an ever-changing world. It is a powerful and important resource for anyone engaged in working with leaders."—**Kari Taylor**, *Assistant Professor and Director, Student Affairs Administration Program, Springfield College.*

"Bridging the gap between theory and practice, this book provides valuable information to those tasked with training future leaders. Throughout the book, Jonathan Kroll shares personal experiences of training leaders, which bring leadership theories, practices, and facilitation approaches to life and allow readers to visualize how they may apply this knowledge in their own praxis."
—*Gudrun Nyunt, Assistant Professor, Northern Illinois University*

"As a result of Jonathan's dedication and vision, we now have a resource to fulfill a role which was envisioned from the founding days of student affairs. Through an unusual breadth of experiences and constant reflection on what worked and didn't work in leadership learning, Jonathan compiled a book of gems to help leadership educators be more effective in facilitating the leadership training and development of their participants. Not until *Preparing Leadership Educators* has there been a resource to help those with responsibility for leadership learning to rise to higher levels of competence in this crucial arena of talent development."—*Denny Roberts, Independent Consultant, New Dimensions in Education; Past President, American College Personnel Association; Former Assistant Vice President for Education, Qatar Foundation*

"In a time where there is such hunger for leadership development, *Preparing Leadership Educators* is both inspiring and practical. If you are responsible for leadership training, then this book is a must-read! It is filled with leadership theories, experiential learning opportunities, and reflective questions that will assist any leadership educator in enhancing both their own knowledge, as well as those they are educating."—*Christine Gravelle, Director of Student Activities, Texas A&M University*

"Jonathan Kroll gets it! Leadership education, while in dire need of a new approach, must also stand on the shoulders of the theory, scholarship, and approaches before it. In *Preparing Leadership Educators*, he does both. Incorporating the importance of identity, efficacy, facilitation, execution, and leadership development, this book is an important resource and guide for leadership educators."—*Daymyen Layne, Director of Multicultural Education and Training, Quinnipiac University*

"*Preparing Leadership Educators* is an amazing leadership tapestry: It weaves together leadership theory, leadership practices, and hands-on facilitation tips. One could use this to not only grow oneself and others as leaders and facilitators themselves, but with the scope of topics covered, could create a tailored and multifaceted leadership curriculum."—*Lisa Slavid, Leadership and Strategy Consultant and Facilitator; (Former Higher Education Executive, 25+ years)*

"A stark reality has plagued our world for far too long: 'Bad leadership kills.' Thankfully, as leadership trainers, there is a way to both treat the suffering that exists at the hands of these leaders as well as prevent subsequent bad leaders from being produced: *Preparing Leadership Educators*. Having studied medicine and leadership my entire professional career I can say that no panacea exists—but this book is a prescription that approaches that ideal. A must-read for leaders, educators, and every person interested in making the world a healthier and happier place."
—*Gary Redfeather, Programme Lead and Senior Lecturer of Clinical Leadership, Education, and Research, De Montfort University; Executive Leadership Coach, ExecOnline*

"Organizations spend around $359 billion per year on leadership development worldwide, with dubious results. Leadership scholar and master trainer Jonathan Kroll has big ideas about how to improve things, and it starts with preparing leadership educators to be more effective with their training and facilitation. His book expertly navigates the whitewater between theory and practice and steers the reader into the clear channels of experiential learning and reflective dialogue. I recommend it highly."—**Doug Kirkpatrick**, *Founder, D'Artagnan Advisors—Global Thought Leader on Leadership and Self-Management*

"In times of uncertainty, the world needs more leaders. Jonathan Kroll has passionately written a foundational must-read for those that are in the business of training and developing leaders. It is packed with resources and exercises to help leadership educators, and anyone involved in developing the next generation of leaders to level up like never before."—**Ethan Huynh**, *Founder and CEO, Acellent Plus*

"*Preparing Leadership Educators* is the go-to guide for all who have the honor to facilitate and hold space for leadership training and development. While this is a great resource for those in higher education, those in the corporate or nonprofit sector can benefit greatly from the depth and ease of this book. By utilizing this text, you will have the knowledge and skills to move participants forward by through the use of experiential learning and reflective dialogue." —**Annalyn Cruz**, *CEO of Grounded In Wisdom, LLC, Leadership & Empowerment Coach/ Instructional Designer/Group Facilitator*

"I am impressed with *Preparing Leadership Educators* because of how it fills a learning gap in my leadership journey! In this book, Jonathan Kroll offers facilitation tools for leaders to hone their training craft through experiential methods that center on personal identities, narratives, and reflections. I am relieved that this resource is finally available for leaders to become exceptional. This book should be essential reading for all leadership educators."—**Elsie Gonzalez**, *Director of Diversity, Equity, and Inclusion, CREC (Capitol Region Education Council)*

"*Preparing Leadership Educators* is an asset for those who facilitate leadership training and development. Jonathan is a masterful leadership educator and facilitator with decades of experience that are illuminated within these pages. This book is accessible and practical and will be of value for folks across industries who want to create structural change within their teams and organizations—through training and facilitation."—**Faustina Cuevas**, *Diversity, Equity, and Inclusion Officer, City of Lynn, MA*

"Jonathan Kroll has an incredible depth of knowledge of leadership that shines in *Preparing Leadership Educators*. This book is an incredible resource for leaders of all organizations— especially nonprofit organizations—because it prepares us to be better leadership educators who can dynamically assist others advance in their leadership journey."—**Michael Cipoletti**, *Executive Director, FNE International*

"In a student affairs division with multiple staff and departments responsible for student leadership development, *Preparing Leadership Educators* is the ideal resource. Jonathan Kroll provides an accessible overview of leadership theories, models, and frameworks that a cross-division team with varying areas of expertise can use to form a shared understanding and approach to leadership education. The detailed and numerous training activities shared in the book are a gold mine of promising practices that are easily adapted to a unique institutional context."—**Dave Stanfield**, *Vice President of Student Affairs, Yale-NUS College (Singapore)*

PREPARING LEADERSHIP EDUCATORS

PREPARING LEADERSHIP EDUCATORS

A Comprehensive Guide to Theories, Practices, and Facilitation Skills

Jonathan R. Kroll

Foreword by Cameron C. Beatty

Afterword by Sarah Kutten

STERLING, VIRGINIA

Stylus

COPYRIGHT © 2023 BY STYLUS PUBLISHING, LLC.

Published by Stylus Publishing, LLC.
22883 Quicksilver Drive
Sterling, Virginia 20166-2019

Library of Congress Cataloging-in-Publication Data
The CIP data for this title has been applied for.

13-digit ISBN: 978-1-64267-276-3 (cloth)
13-digit ISBN: 978-1-64267-277-0 (paperback)
13-digit ISBN: 978-1-64267-278-7 (library networkable e-edition)
13-digit ISBN: 978-1-64267-279-4 (consumer e-edition)

Printed in the United States of America

All first editions printed on acid-free paper that meets the American National Standards Institute Z39-48 Standard.

Bulk Purchases

Quantity discounts are available for use in workshops and for staff development.

Call 1-800-232-0223

First Edition, 2023

To Peter Magolda and Robert Rappaport.

To these two educators who persistently challenged and supported me through my formative years of becoming a leadership educator.

Contents

Foreword

Somebody has to stand when other people are sitting. Somebody has to speak when other people are quiet.

—Bryan Stevenson

Leadership education is an ever-evolving and progressing field. I identify as a leadership educator who has worked in leadership education for almost 15 years. Early on in my leadership educator career, I would always search for activities, team builders, or lesson plans to teach a leadership lesson without fully considering where the theory came from, what skills were needed to facilitate the experiential learning activity and reflective dialogue, and what I believe about leadership—and how will those beliefs showed up through my facilitation. I always felt like I had strong facilitation skills, but I never considered what it meant to continue to develop those skills as a leadership educator. Over time I have noticed how the resources to "put on" leadership programs have shifted from primarily asking, who am I programming for? to also considering who am I as a leadership educator and how does that inform my practice and pedagogy as a leadership educator.

We must be prepared to be leaders beyond just the positional understanding of leadership—beyond roles and titles—to impact change and engage in the leadership process. Engaging in leadership is not only needed in a global community, but also in our local communities that are rooted in equity and justice for all. We want leadership learners—our training participants—to be visionaries and about the business of change through collaborative coalitions. As you dive into this resource, I invite you to reflect on some questions: (a) What have I previously learned about leadership training and development?; (b) What do I need to unlearn about leadership training and development?; (c) Who am I as a leadership educator?; (d) Who do I want to be as a leadership educator?; and (e) How can I continue to develop my facilitation skills as a leadership educator?

What I appreciate about *Preparing Leadership Educators: A Comprehensive Guide to Theories, Practices, and Facilitation Skills,* is that this unique resource offers practical trainer resources for a plentiful array of leadership theories, practices, and contexts. For example, when I was first learning about facilitating training experiences with experiential activities and reflective dialogue, this text would have helped me with the "how" to do this transformational work effectively. I also deeply appreciate that this book offers the foundational theoretical frameworks along with the themes of leadership in the context of gender and culture, justice and equity, and the role of ethics in leadership learning.

As a seasoned leadership educator, I find the final section of the book the most meaningful. Here, Jonathan Kroll offers practical facilitation approaches for experiential learning activities and reflective dialogue. This material is brought to life throughout *Preparing Leadership Educators* with valuable instructions for facilitating specific experiential activities for each and every theory and practice included. As a new professional and leadership educator who was responsible for facilitating diverse training experiences, this text would have been instrumental to my development. Now, as a seasoned professional and faculty member, I found myself excited to consider new approaches to facilitating leadership learning and critically considering how reflective dialogue contributes to the learning process and outcomes.

When considering your own story of becoming a leadership educator, also consider the power of being a leadership trainer in terms of facilitating leadership from an equity and justice lens. This book will support your own reflection and practice with this process no matter if you are just a beginner or have been a leadership educator for years. We as leadership educators have the privilege to share the world we want to see through critical leadership training and development. I'm excited for the journey you are about to embark on with this text and look forward to you reflecting and applying the learning opportunities Jonathan Kroll has created and curated through this book.

Cameron C. Beatty
Assistant Professor and Program Coordinator
Higher Education Program
Associate Director of Leadership Learning
Research Center
Florida State University

Acknowledgments

The greatest thing is to give thanks for everything . . . those who have learned this knows what it means to live. They have penetrated the whole mystery of life: giving thanks for everything.

—Albert Schweitzer

These words, adapted from Albert Schweitzer, from his *Thoughts for Our Times*, are an immensely meaningful way for me to share my gratitude for those who have provided their wisdom, insight, reflections, questions, critique, time, and energy as this book proceeded through its manifestation process. It was through my intimate connections with the Albert Schweitzer Institute at my alma mater (Quinnipiac University) that I ventured to Nicaragua. There, I believe, is where my leadership educator work and identity first, formally, took root.

We know from Margaret Mead that we should never doubt that a small group of thoughtful, committed people can change the world. And from Mahatma Gandhi, that a small body of determined spirits, fired by an unquenchable faith in their mission, can alter the course of history. Thank you to my small group of thoughtful, determined spirits who, through your (healthy) challenge and support, assisted me in ever-so-slightly—in a leadership training and development context—changing the world and altering the course of history. For you, I have immense gratitude.

Specifically, I want to thank my parents, Judi and Lee, for their support in every way manageable and to my brother (Seth), sister-in-law (Nicole), nephew (Louis), and niece (Rose) for being my bubble during the pandemic, when this book was written. You provided me incredible nourishment—and distraction—while I researched and wrote this book.

To the entire team at Stylus and specifically David Brightman—I am immensely grateful for your thoughtfulness and guidance—and patience with a first-time author.

To my colleagues and Leadership Trainer's board directors—thank you for helping bring Leadership Trainer's Narrative Approach, experiential learning activities, and guidance provided in this book to life: Cameron Beatty, Bruce Brown, Michael Cipoletti, Faustina Cuevas, Erika De Jesus, Elsie Gonzalez, Christine Gravelle, Barbara Hetzel, Ethan Huynh, Doug Kirkpatrick, Sarah Kutten, Daymyen Layne, Amber Manning-Ouellette, Gary Redfeather, and Rachel Samuelson.

To those who spent time with my initial drafts and highlighted growth opportunities for this book; to Peter Magolda and Marcia Baxter Magolda, who offered their wisdom and insight as I was developing the idea and prospectus for this book; and to Stacy Blake-Beard, Thulani DeMarsay, Kathy Manning, Amber Manning-Ouellette, Dan McCaffrey, Denny Roberts, Judy Rogers, Emily Sandoval, Isaiah Thomas, and David Blake Willis—you have helped me sharpen my focus and enhance the final product. Thank you for your time, energy, and support as I worked my way through this book.

To my best friends, whose weekly calls provided dialogue of meaning and depth—as well as endless laughter—and for our yearly retreats that are the most nourishing and rewarding parts of my year. Pete Athans, Kevin Bickart, Joe Discepola, Raju Kansagra, Joe Lamendola, Dan McCaffrey, and Joe Villapiano—your friendship is an incredible light in my life. Words cannot express the profundity of my gratitude.

PART ONE

LAYING OUR LEADERSHIP FOUNDATION

I T IS A GOOD day to be a leadership educator. Across the globe, individuals are thirsty for leadership training and development. More, organizations have the resources and are spending billions of dollars on leadership learning opportunities and initiatives. Yet, what is being offered is not as effective or impactful as what is expected. In short, they are not producing the leadership learning outcomes they espouse. There are numerous reasons for this. Based upon my own research and years of experience in the leadership and training and development fields, one critical element is that those who are charged with and responsible for the leadership training and development of others are ill prepared. This book serves as a comprehensive compilation of resources and preparatory materials for those who facilitate the leadership training and development of others.

Plan of the Book

This book is not intended to be read as a novel. While writing, I envisioned this book being utilized as a resource for those who facilitate leadership training experiences. For example, if we are charged with facilitating a training on transformational leadership, we can review that section in chapter 4 to acquire a grounded understanding of the theory as well as a potential experiential learning activity (with instructions) and reflective dialogue questions. Similarly, if we are responsible for a training on communication, as a leadership practice, we can hone in on that section in chapter 9—complete with a potential experiential

learning activity (with instructions) and reflective dialogue questions. The theories and practices are drafted to be overviews—a first taste—of vast material on each of them. Although comprehensive, it is surely not a complete list.

This section, Part One, explores the "what" and "who" of leadership. It is important for leadership educators to understand what leadership is and who leadership educators are. I begin by sharing about myself. I offer a positionality statement as well as my story of becoming a leadership educator. Further, in the first chapter—the introduction—I draft a note to student affairs educators and others who may benefit from this book—namely nonprofit and corporate leaders—to explicitly state why this book will be useful to you. In chapter 2, I explore the leadership landscape as well as what leadership is before differentiating between leadership education, development, engagement, and training. I then describe who leadership educators are. The final element to this chapter and Part One is a model of what is included with every leadership theory and practice included in *Preparing Leadership Educators: A Comprehensive Guide to Theories, Practices, and Facilitation Skills*—a leadership training praxis activity. As a tactical and tangible resource, I hope you utilize this book to inform your leadership training experiences. Included are instructions on how to facilitate experiential activities as well as my go-to reflective dialogue questions.

Part Two takes us on an expedition through the theoretical leadership landscape. We begin by exploring the foundational (industrial) theories, models, and frameworks. These are the original leadership theories that launched the field. We then shift to postindustrial theories, models, and frameworks of leadership. This is when a major transformation occurred that launched a revolution in how leadership was understood and practiced. Contemporary leadership theories, models, and frameworks illuminate the latest thinking and scholarship on leadership. Before moving on to Part Three, we review the intersections between leadership and various themes—including developmental relationships, demographic considerations of gender and culture, the pursuit of justice and equity, and ethics.

Part Three reviews leadership practices, skills, and competencies. These are compiled into four groupings: cognitive leadership practices, emotive leadership practices, cooperative leadership practices, and generative leadership practices. Cognitive leadership practices focus on intentional thinking. With these skills, we get into the right mindset and headspace to intensify our leadership practices. Emotive leadership practices focus on emotional developmental skills for relational connections. When we nurture resonance with others, we magnify our leadership practice. The third grouping focuses on skills to enhance collaborative engagements with others. These are our cooperative leadership practices and are the most outwardly concentrated of the leadership competencies presented in this book. Finally, generative leadership practices explore the healthy leadership habits that enable leaders to personally thrive and assist their organizations or communities in flourishing.

Part Four focuses on training tactics and facilitation techniques. We ground this section in experiential learning and reflective dialogue. Leadership Trainer's Narrative Approach is our methodology to create dynamic and engaging "training stories" and techniques to enhance our facilitation.

Within this text, I offer dozens of experiential learning activities and reflective dialogue questions to support you in implementing the facilitation skills in a practical, relevant, and hands-on manner. As a way to integrate Parts Two and Three with Part Four, at the end of each theory and practice, I provide reflections on what to be cognizant of when facilitating a training on that particular topic. I also include step-by-step instructions on how to facilitate each curated experiential learning activity—crafted specifically for that topic—along with go-to reflective dialogue questions. This is praxis—the integration of theory into practice. Let's get into it!

CHAPTER 1

Introduction

THE EXPLICIT REASON FOR this book is that our organizations and communities need more effective, just, and resonant leaders. This book is not written for *leaders*, though. There are plenty of resources for those who desire to practice leadership more effectively. What has been absent is a comprehensive compilation of resources and preparatory materials for those who facilitate the leadership training and development of others. This book is deliberately designed for *leadership educators*—specifically, leadership educators who facilitate leadership learning and development through intentional *training* experiences.

Leadership educators have an essential role in human becoming. Without us, how can the next generations of changemakers effectively develop the leadership skills and capacities they'll need to navigate the challenges in the decades ahead?

Leadership educators have an elemental role in organizational and community development. Without us, how will our organizations and communities become the holding environments and learning laboratories that empower connections of meaning and depth, embolden courageous exploration, and enable the structural and systemic change we desperately need?

Our charge is to become the exceptional and extraordinary leadership educators the fate of the world needs. It sounds dramatic, I know. Arawana Hayashi (2021) offers insight into our current condition:

> Some say we are now living in a dark age. The global climate crises, heartbreaking social inequality, structural racism, worldwide health threats, and the solidification of political views that do not allow for dialogue or "stepping into the shoes" of others. All of these conditions contribute to a sense of the darkening of human potential. They are signs of a shutting down of the natural brilliance of human beings. (p. xxvii)

If we critically review our current leadership development programs and training opportunities, we'll notice their severe inadequacies. They are not producing the leadership learning outcomes they espouse. Collectively, we are thirsty for leadership development and training experiences that actualize what they claim—to prepare us to be effective, just, and resonant leaders. The type of leaders who can nurture our own and others' brilliance, illuminate human potential, and deeply connect with others in nourishing relationships so we can collaboratively do good in our organizations, communities, and the world. We keep pursuing leadership development and enhancement opportunities because nothing seems to quench this thirst to become the leaders we dream of being.

I do not believe we are born as leaders. Becoming a leader is a developmental process. It is the result of serious and significant churning within the cauldron of lived experience—and the purposeful processing of those experiences. The same is true about becoming a leadership educator. The position we hold, the power we wield, and the prestige we attain are irrelevant to our performance as leadership educators.

Exceptional leadership educators have done the work to earn this identity. More importantly, they have engaged in the priming work to ensure that we perform as leadership-developmental mediums for our participants. Extraordinary leadership educators have engaged in purposeful identity development and self-reflective practices. They have studied and acquired leadership wisdom through a deep understanding of the theories, themes, history, and trajectory of the scholarship and field as a whole. They have intentionally infused healthy leadership habits into their own practice. This enables them to identify transformative leadership developmental opportunities for others—and structure leadership learning experiences that enable others to acquire and implement competencies and skills in their practice. And these notable leadership educators have mastered diverse facilitation techniques—particularly with experiential learning and reflective dialogue. Our training experiences are designed and facilitated so that our participants can *access* the training message and material, *internalize* the leadership learning, and then *apply* that learning to their practices beyond the training bubble.

To be an effective leadership educator, we need to know the *stuff* of leadership. This includes the theories, history, and complexities of the field; the healthy leadership habits that encourage individuals to thrive and organizations to flourish; and the facilitation techniques that enable our participants to access the training message and material, propel them to internalize leadership learning, and then apply that learning in meaningful ways to their own progressive leadership practice.

Archilochus, the Ancient Greek scholar and poet offered, "We don't rise to the level of our expectations, we fall to the level of our training." While we should yearn and strive for lofty expectations, if we want to be the effective leadership educators we dream of being, we must strategically and diligently prepare. With worthy aspirations accompanied by purposeful and persistent training, we will become equipped to accomplish our goals and exceed expectations. This preparatory training should be a threefold approach: mastering the leadership content, cultivating leadership skills and competencies, and acquiring the technical aptitudes to facilitate leadership learning experiences that enable our participants to *access* the training material and message, *internalize* their leadership learning, and then *apply* that learning to their practice.

What I detail in this book is an integration of this triad so that you and other leadership educators can nurture your practice in a way that is (a) informed by theory, (b) imbued with healthy leadership habits, and (c) imparted with time-tested facilitation techniques—particularly experiential learning and reflective dialogue.

Positionality Statement

In addition to the three focus areas noted previously, I would be remiss as a leadership educator by not articulating that we also need to know ourselves. Before we can effectively serve in this capacity, leadership educators must purposefully engage in the challenging construction and recurrent exploration of ourselves. By examining, questioning, reflecting upon, and processing our positionality, sense of self, and beliefs we cultivate deeper levels of authenticity, foster enhanced levels of connectivity with our values, and model a healthy leadership habit.

Our identity is our self-image. It is a self-representation and self-concept that is engrained and informed by our biologies and personal histories. These are the genetic makeups, socializations, values, self-perceptions, and life experiences that endow us with particular ways of making meaning and sense of the world (Day et al., 2009; Silsbee, 2018). Our identity influences the way we perceive our surroundings, our affective responses, and our behaviors (Adriasola & Lord, 2021). Alvesson and Robertson (2016) define it as "a reflexively organized understanding of one's distinctiveness, values, and key characteristics" (p. 9).

Our identity is important because it grounds us in understanding who we are—our goals and aspirations, strengths and growth opportunities, relationships with self and others—and provides the cornerstone for us to successfully navigate the complex challenges in our lives. Understanding our identity is critical as we seek grounded decision-making and interpersonal interactions with diverse others (Baumister, 1995). Furthermore, engaging in identity development empowers us to focus energy and attention on minimizing gaps between our present self and our ideal self—as well as avoiding our nightmare self (Day et al., 2009).

Intentional identity exploration is the core practice and process of self-authorship—the internal capacity to define one's beliefs, identity, and social relations (Baxter Magolda, 2001; Kegan, 1994). Laurent Daloz

(1986), the esteemed adult educator, describes the transformative journey to self-authoring one's identity:

> Traveled with integrity, the way home leads to a fuller and clearer sense of who we are, a new and broader boundary between oneself and the world. The struggle to be something more than the person others have made, to construct and then live to a set of *our own* expectations, is one of the most compelling struggles of our . . . lives. (p. 154)

When we purposefully engage in identity exploration and the pursuit of a self-authored identity, we are better positioned to interpret our experiences, know ourselves, and conduct our lives with authenticity. Doing so enables us to better understand our power and privileges, process how we see the world, and reflect on how others see us.

Specifically for leadership educators, our identities inform our preparation, approach, pedagogy, and performance as facilitators of others' leadership training and development. If we want to be effective in this work, it is imperative we engage in intentional identity exploration. It is through this reflective process, over time, that we gain stability in understanding who we are, open ourselves up to further growth opportunities, and cultivate connections of meaning and depth with our participants.

So, for the sake of transparency—and because it is an important part of my personal leadership educator practice to continually explore, examine, and evaluate my identity—I offer a glimpse of composite factors of my identity.

I am an American who was raised in central New Jersey. I am currently living in Boston, Massachusetts—a city I have considered "home" for the past 15 years (since 2008). I am middle class economically and well educated. I have earned a bachelor's degree, two master's degrees, and a doctorate (PhD). I speak English and barely passable *Español*.

Professionally, I identify as an educator and entrepreneur. I've been working since high school as a bagel shop cashier, camp counselor, university orientation coordinator, student affairs administrator, business cocreator, nonprofit founder, faculty member, and professional leadership educator and trainer.

I am a White (ethnicity), Caucasian (race), heterosexual, single, 42+-year-old, able-bodied, healthy, fit (5'5 and ~150 lbs.) cisgender male. I was raised in a Jewish family but am currently nonidentifying/agnostic. I do not have any children—yet proud to be an uncle and uncle figure to many. In the hierarchy of privilege—and in the words of the professional facilitator Mark Smutney (2019)—I'm located somewhere between "the stratosphere and outer space" (p. 13).

This is me—at least a sliver of how I see and understand myself and the dominant fibers that stitch together the fabric of *Jonathan*. Of course, these are not independent entities. Our identity is a complex composite and intermingling of all the elements that make us who we are. I can't remove my race or height or uncleness from my identity. They are integrated, woven together, to create a unique individual. Who are you? How do you identify?

My Story: Becoming a Leadership Educator

When we offer our personal stories, we reinforce our common humanity (Rego et al., 2019). Here I invite you to read my story of becoming a leadership educator while also encouraging you think about the defining moments of your leadership educator journey.

In the fall of 2005, a few months after I had graduated with my master's in college student personnel from Miami University (Ohio), I independently volunteered in León, Nicaragua, as an English language teacher. I had enough financial reserves to postpone working for a year, and serving at a private, family-owned English language center in the cultural capital of Nicaragua felt like a perfect opportunity. (I have purposefully removed name references to protect the identity of individuals and organizations due to the political situation in Nicaragua. More on the leadership landscape and political condition in Nicaragua can be found in an article I coauthored in the *Journal of Leadership Education*; see Kroll & Moreno, 2022.)

In my mind, this time in Nicaragua was supposed to be light and breezy—plenty of time at the beach, exploring a new and different place, reading interesting nonacademic literature, and teaching a little bit of English. It ended up being heavy on the teaching and light on the "light and breezy." I also started facilitating leadership trainings. I had an interest and skill set, albeit limited, that matched the desire—particularly of young, college-age Nicaraguans—in that local community. As one participant shared, speaking for herself while also on behalf of her generation, "We're *thirsty*" for leadership training and development opportunities.

For context, Nicaragua is the second poorest country in the hemisphere. Basic services are a challenge for most of the population. Approximately 46% of the population lives on less than $2 per day. Although there was sustained economic growth in 2016, 2017, and early 2018, the World Bank expects, due to political and social unrest (since April 2018) and the COVID-19 pandemic, the economy to struggle and forecasts that it will weaken further.

Leadership training and development are perceived as a luxury—if they are even in one's frame of reference—in Nicaragua. They are almost nonexistent. Youth sports programs? Exceedingly rare. Boy Scouts and Girl Scouts and Big Sisters and Big Brothers? Might as well be fictional. Clubs and organizations in community centers, houses of worship, and schools? Not that I ever found.

While many young people in the United States of America attend university where students can explore leadership via academic courses and degrees and cultivate leadership skills through cocurricular involvements such as clubs and organizations, work-study, athletics, study-abroad opportunities, and a multitude of other workshops, conferences, and retreats, these opportunities rarely, if at all, exist for youth and university students in the Global South—Nicaragua in particular.

Professionals, too, in Nicaragua, are not afforded the same leadership development opportunities to which those of us in the Global North are accustomed. Conferences and associations are rare. In-house learning and development departments that focus on leadership training are also scarce.

Over these initial 6 months and the following decade, I would facilitate intentional leadership training experiences for my advanced English language students, the staff at the English language center, university students and faculty, middle managers of a Ford subsidiary, executives of large corporations, owners of local family businesses, nonprofit and nongovernmental organization (NGO) leaders, and others who were interested in particular leadership themes. I loved these leadership-developmental opportunities. I had heard my calling though these experiences.

I needed to do the work, though. I knew little about leadership—especially as an intellectual and professional field with a rich history of research, scholarship, and robust theoretical underpinnings. My only formal learning was a single graduate-level course in my master's program. Although deeply engaging, a one-time, survey-level, semester-long class does not provide the depth of knowledge to *know* leadership. It provided a first taste—a treat—that sparked my curiosity.

I have also been blessed to have mentors who do know this stuff. Our conversations were—and continue to be—provocative, deeply meaningful, and important reflective leadership learning opportunities. Their questions penetrated and pierced the assumptions I held about leadership—all of which were rooted in my experiences as a student leader and the requisite leadership workshops, retreats, and conferences I attended as an undergraduate and graduate student.

One such mentor is Dennis (Denny) Roberts. Denny is a leadership educator trailblazer who established the foundational structures for the intentional leadership learning opportunities and programming of college students in the 1970s. Before this work formally began, Denny was doing it. It was through my relationship with Denny that I realized there was a field of leadership with full-bodied scholarship and real theoretical foundations with which I can inform my knowledge base.

With regard to leadership skills and practices, I also needed to do the work. I knew that my leadership competencies and capabilities were limited. I had little formal practice leading organizations, programs, or projects. I also knew that simply reading the books about cultivating healthy leadership habits wasn't going to magically result in the manifestation of a grounded practice. I, literally, needed to *practice*. It was necessary that I had opportunities to purposefully explore and experiment with leadership. Only by doing so would I be able to enhance my skills, identify and then learn from my leadership gaps and faux pas, and have the breadth of experiences—along with the stories to tell—that could inform my leadership trainings in responsive and resonant ways for my future training participants.

Most of my leadership educator preparation, though, like most leadership educators, needed to come in the form of facilitation techniques. How does one facilitate the leadership learning of others?

The traditional style is to lecture. It is perplexing how many leadership educators root their training experiences in lectures with lengthy sermons or formal presentations laden with PowerPoint *about* leadership. I needed to learn how to create hands-on experiential learning opportunities that enabled participant experimentation and immersive engagement in the material to optimize their leadership learning. I needed to work on enhancing my facilitation techniques—particularly with experiential learning and reflective dialogue.

This worthy work takes time and necessitates intentional effort to be effective. We need to review and process the literature, resources, and others' facilitation techniques; surrender to our own vulnerabilities by stumbling through faulty facilitated experiences as learning opportunities; welcome critical reflections from trusted mentors and guides; and continually repeat this process to master our trainer practice.

In addition to my leadership training experiences in Nicaragua, I had facilitated a healthy amount of leadership and other developmental trainings as a student affairs practitioner. These included the traditional resident assistant and orientation leader preacademic year training week experiences, in-house departmental seminars for colleagues across my institutions, and conference presentations at national and international gatherings. I also cofounded a business with my best friends, iBELIEVE, that shared the power of belief—belief in oneself and belief in one's goals to accomplish the goals that we put our minds to—through facilitated workshops. However, it wasn't until a sunny day in the fall of 2012 that I fully embraced my leadership educator identity.

It was a Monday. October 1, 2012, to be exact. Not an ordinary start to the week in the slightest. On this particular Monday, I was serving as a resident director on an around-the-Atlantic Semester at Sea voyage. The shipboard community of students, faculty, and staff didn't operate in the traditional 5 days of schooling and 2 days of weekend rejuvenation. Rather, courses were only held at sea on an A/B schedule. Classes were offered on either "A" days or "B" days. When we were in port, aside from some academic course-related excursions, we were invited to explore these ports and cities and countries at our leisure.

The context surrounding this Monday was far from ordinary. Per the original itinerary, on this particular Monday, we were supposed to be in Casablanca, Morocco. Weeks prior, though, two American diplomats—Ambassador J. Christopher Stevens and Information Management Officer Sean Smith—were killed at the U.S. Embassy in Benghazi, Libya. Shortly thereafter, the United States of America issued travel warnings for many Muslim countries in North Africa and the Middle East. Morocco was on the list. Semester at Sea decided to heed these State Department warnings and, while in scramble mode, shift our itinerary. On short notice, we extended our time in Cadiz, Spain, and added Las Islas Canarias (the Canary Islands) to our voyage.

For every port of call, Semester at Sea offered extensive, albeit optional, in-country excursion opportunities. These were designed through Semester at Sea's headquarters and facilitated by our onboard field office during the voyage. These excursions were contracted well in advance through a significant vetting process of in-country vendors and tour agencies. Tenerife, the largest and most populated of the Canary Islands, served as our 2-day docking station. Due to the circumstances, official Semester at Sea–sponsored excursion options were limited.

On this particular Monday, I would organize and facilitate a last-minute, half-day leadership retreat. I and the dean of students of our voyage, Lisa Slavid, another incredible and wise leadership educator-mentor, collaborated to design and host a compelling and reflective morning experience. This leadership training was proposed to fill a gap. We wanted to offer something structured and leadership-developmental for the students of our voyage as an alternative to walking the city streets or visiting a nearby beach.

It was a solid program, especially under those circumstances. We prepared and arranged the 4-hour experience in less than 2 days without having a physical location or preplanned experiential activity training materials. We didn't know how many students would actually be interested in participating, nor did we provide any incentives like meals or course credits.

It was this experience, though, that enabled me to truly embody my leadership educator identity. The fact that I could collaboratively organize a spur-of-the-moment half-day leadership training without any resources, predetermined or vetted location, marketing campaign, or incentives for the participants illuminated for me that I had the self-awareness, knowledge base, skill set, and confidence to do this work. After years of facilitating countless leadership training experiences, I became a leadership educator.

A few years after this voyage, in 2015, following earning my doctorate—a PhD in leadership from Fielding Graduate University—I established a non-profit leadership institute, Leadership Trainer. I wanted to increase the impact of what I started in Nicaragua a decade before. For almost 4 years, I split time between Boston and Nicaragua. I facilitated dozens of leadership trainings and launched our flagship program—the Leadership Trainer Certification Program. Over time, it became clear that rather than focus energy and attention on one-time workshop experiences, my gifts are best suited to engage in trainer preparation work and assist others in becoming leadership educators.

A Note to Student Affairs Educators

This book is for you. Prior to founding Leadership Trainer and serving as an academic and administrator in a university leadership studies program, I spent a decade as a student affairs educator. I earned a master's in college student personnel (Miami University in Ohio) and then worked in the field in multiple capacities. I often share that this career empowered me to focus my attention on community-building, reflection initiatives, and leadership development of students. Formally, I served as a resident director, coordinator of spirituality and meaning-making programs, and in a bridge role between academic and student affairs. I've taught first-year introductory 101 seminars and as an adjunct faculty member in a student affairs master's program. I chaired departmental and campus-wide committees and led alternative break trips internationally. I spent hours on duty rotation, supervised student leaders, advised student organizations and living-learning communities, and crafted an award-winning programming series—Common Senses. I've partnered with campus colleagues, managed budgets that were insufficient for the nature and charge of the work, and fulfilled "other duties as assigned" more times than I can count or remember. I've presented at springtime ACPA and NASPA gatherings, regional events, and other professional conferences. I've navigated the campus trauma of student death and joyously celebrated student graduations and other significant accomplishments. Student affairs colleagues as well as former students are considered dear friends. I understand the nature of this work.

I also understand the context of leadership training and development within our higher education institutions—or rather lack thereof. At the time of this writing, of all the 52 colleges and universities in Greater/Metropolitan Boston (my home community), a hub of higher education in the United States of America, as an example, not a single one has a dedicated cocurricular leadership operation. In short, there is no leadership institute, center, or department that exclusively concentrates on student leadership development.

Why is this problematic? The issue is that leadership training and development gets lumped in with all the other responsibilities of student affairs educators—advising, coordinating, event planning, and more. Leadership then becomes secondary or tertiary (or even further down the priority and implementation list). The other concern when leadership is lumped with other offices and responsibilities is that hiring tends to focus on generalists who have broad skill sets. Often, these skills are not focused on leadership training and development.

I wanted to explore this leadership educator preparation conundrum further, so in the summer of 2020 I launched a research investigation into master's-level student affairs preparatory programs. With the support of a graduate research assistant, Joseph Guvendiren, a study was designed to explore (a) how many of our preparatory programs offer leadership courses—and how many of those are a part of the core curriculum or an elective—and (b) what is actually offered in these courses.

Essentially, I wanted to understand how these programs were preparing budding student affairs practitioners to serve as leadership educators. I believe the findings are quite telling, unfortunately. I share a bit of the findings here. More details, findings, and the research methodology can be found in an article published in the *Journal of Student Affairs Research and Practice* (Kroll & Guvendiren, 2021).

The study began by reviewing NASPA's directory of preparatory programs. More than 280 college and university websites were explored to determine if the listed student affairs preparatory program (a) existed, (b) was in fact a student affairs preparatory program, and (c) offered a leadership course. If so, the courses were included in the formal study. If not, these programs were excluded. Of the 285 programs, 214 were included in the study.

The results showed that 38% of master's-level student affairs preparatory programs do not offer leadership courses. To repeat and emphasize, almost 40% of our preparatory programs *do not* offer any leadership course. Of the programs that do offer leadership courses, only 68% offer it as part of the core curriculum—required to graduate. The remaining 32% of programs only offer leadership courses as electives or part of a specialized "track." When combining this data, 57% of these programs do not require their graduate students to study leadership. More than half—almost 60%—of our master's-level preparatory programs do not make available or do not require any formal exploration of leadership.

The content and thematic portion of this inquiry was designed to illuminate what these courses, across our master's-level student affairs preparatory programs, are about. Namely, what are the foci of our master's students' leadership learning in these courses? Three themes emerged. The courses (a) stress leadership practices with minimal engagement with theory or praxis, (b) are often combined with other topics or themes, and (c) are mostly limited to the students' personal understandings of leadership. In summation, these courses focus on preparing students to be leaders, not how to be *leadership educators*.

This should be no surprise for those who are familiar with the ACPA and NASPA (2015) leadership competency. At just the foundational level, our professional associations list an overwhelming 17 distinct outcomes. Of these 17, not a single outcome references leadership theory. The outcomes are exclusively practices.

A deeper exploration of the ACPA and NASPA competencies reveals a discrepancy between the formal competency presentation (ACPA & NASPA, 2015) and the associated assessment rubric (ACPA & NASPA, 2016). Rather than show consistency, the competency presentation and the rubric utilize varying frameworks. This is highlighted by the rubric's utilization of a different structure and headings than the presentation's education, training, development, and engagement framework. Although the word *theory* is included in these headings and descriptive paragraphs, the outcomes are the same—not a single one expressly details the importance of budding leadership educators having any knowledge about leadership theories. Master's-level preparatory programs are supposed to be utilizing these foundational competency outcomes

as a means of informing "minimum expectations for master's level graduates" (ACPA & NASPA, 2015, p. 10). If the outcomes exclusively reference leadership practices and skills, courses are going to singularly emphasize those as well. As part of our graduate curriculum, student affairs practitioners should learn the theoretical constructs, models, and frameworks of leadership—and should be able to infuse that knowledge into their practice.

These leadership courses, as a collective, are not preparing graduates to facilitate the leadership learning or skills development of their students. This is problematic. Entry-level practitioners (recent graduates) typically serve as the foremost leadership educators of traditional undergraduate students due to their proximity and the nature of their roles. Yet they are seemingly ill-prepared to serve as effectively as they could in this capacity.

Others have drafted articles and conducted studies that explore the current problematic nature of student affairs practitioners as leadership educators. Haber-Curan and Owen (2013) speak directly to this. They offer that there is

a dearth of formal leadership education training provided in graduate preparation programs. Because student leadership programs are just one functional area under the larger student affairs umbrella, it is not commonplace for student affairs graduate programs to include substantial curriculum on college student leadership education and development. Some graduate programs include leadership education and development to varying extents within core curriculum, other programs offer elective courses on student leadership, and others may not offer any curriculum at all on the topic. Some students may receive on-the-job training through graduate assistantship or internships, but few opportunities such as these exist. As such, many student affairs professionals enter student affairs and take on student leadership education responsibilities with little theoretical grounding in leadership and without training or education on teaching, learning, and curriculum development. (p. 41)

Teig's (2018a) dissertation study, as another example, explores the leadership educator preparatory nature of master's-level student affairs programs from the lens of graduate students. She indicates that although student affairs practitioners' work often includes expectations for leadership education and development, there exists no formal preparation process or curriculum for master's students in graduate preparatory programs to access learning about becoming a leadership educator. More directly, she details that those who do the work of leadership education (i.e., student affairs practitioners) are undertrained in the scholarship and pedagogy of leadership development. She highlights a relevant implication for student affairs educators: They need more and better exposure to leadership theory, leadership development, and pedagogical tools. *Preparing Leadership Educators* includes all three.

Teig's (2018a) findings and sentiment are mirrored by other scholars. Jenkins and Owen (2016) unabashedly share their surprise at the number of foundational documents for leadership education that fail to address the issue of leadership educator preparedness. And Dunn et al. (2021) posit that although student affairs practitioners are characterized as leadership educators by experts in the field, leadership education is not traditionally part of student affairs preparatory programs.

These studies indicate we have work to do. Presently, our student affairs master's-level preparatory programs are insufficiently (at best) preparing the next generation of practitioners to serve as leadership educators. This has far-reaching implications. It illuminates our inability to effectively prepare the next generation of leaders to navigate the challenges we will all inevitably face. As a professional field squarely at the center of facilitating the leadership development and capacity-building of students, we should be concerned. If, as Denny Roberts (2007) suggests, leadership learning is the primary purpose of higher education, our findings indicate these professional preparation programs are struggling to deliver on this goal. How can student affairs practitioners expect students to develop the leadership skills and capacities they desire and need if preparatory programs offer only limited leadership courses and if the courses that are provided predominantly focus on leader development—rather than leadership educator preparation?

Developing the leadership skills and capacities of university students has been a long-standing aspiration of American higher education (Guthrie & Osteen, 2016)—all the way back to the colonial origins of these institutions (D. Roberts, 2007).

Leadership exploration, training, and development is included in the cocurricular spectrum of services afforded to students (Guthrie & Jenkins, 2018). And currently, more students receive leadership education from student affairs offerings than academic leadership courses (Dunn et al., 2019). We supervise and advise students living in the residence halls; provide programming for student organization officers—including governance groups, fraternity and sorority members, cultural and religious clubs; and host leadership development conferences, retreats, and workshops for the student campus community. *Leadership* has been jointly identified as an essential core competency by our two student affairs professional associations—ACPA and NASPA. The assumption—by university executives and students alike—is that student leadership development is cultivated through training and other experiences provided by student affairs educators. How can our universities possibly develop the leadership skills and capacities of students if our student affairs campus administrators do not have sufficient self-awareness, leadership knowledge or skills, or facilitation aptitude?

My hope is that this book will provide student affairs educators with insights about how to enhance the work with which we are charged. We can use this text to identify the subconscious lenses with which students engage in leadership—sometimes antiquated leadership perspectives rooted in power and position—in order to assist them in developmentally growing in their leadership understanding. Student affairs educators can use this book to enhance their own leadership practice by applying their learning to cultivate healthy leadership habits. Finally, as many student affairs educators are responsible for facilitating diverse leadership trainings throughout the academic year, the facilitation skills they acquire can be applied to ensure impactful training experiences and leadership learning by their student participants. This book includes instructions on how to facilitate various experiential learning experiences that can be infused easily into training programs that take the form of workshops, retreats, or conference sessions.

This book is for you, student affairs educators. It purposefully and strategically integrates leadership theories, leadership practices, and facilitation skills. I firmly believe that, after reading and internalizing this material, it can serve as a catalyst for you to serve as exceptional and extraordinary leadership educators.

A Note to Nonprofit Leaders, Corporate Trainers, and Others Who Are Charged With and Responsible for the Leadership Development of Others

This book is (also) for you. For the sake of transparency, many of the examples provided throughout are directed toward a university administrator (student affairs) audience. Yet the leadership theories, leadership practices, and facilitations skills transcend any one professional field or industry. There is a tremendous amount to be gleaned from this book that can be directly applied to your contexts. How do I know? Because I've lived it too. I founded a nonprofit leadership institute and, prior to that, a business. I've consulted and trained leaders from across these industries, and I've done my homework.

Just like the student affairs preparatory programs mentioned previously, our graduate-level nonprofit management, organizational development, sport coaching, and divinity programs—among others—rarely provide intentional coursework on the vast landscape of leadership. If they do, it tends to be a surface-level survey of the material—and as an elective rather than a part of the core curriculum. These programs tend to focus, appropriately so, on tactical skills for that particular profession, rather than leadership skills. And rarely, if ever, do these graduate students learn how to facilitate the leadership development of others—particularly through experiential learning and reflective dialogue in training contexts.

I've also spent countless hours with professionals from across industries—many with advanced degrees—who are responsible for the leadership development of others. They have continually articulated to me how they are ill-prepared for this role and responsibility. Their leadership knowledge is limited. Their leadership skills need refinement. And their only facilitation preparation has come in the form of observing others.

For example, nonprofit and faith-based organizations—of all sizes and varieties—are often the first medium for leadership exploration or an important avenue for young people's leadership learning. Whether the programmatic focus of the organization is on youth, women, marginalized communities, or others who serve in public, charitable, or religious organizations, we are often responsible for facilitating leadership trainings and development. Yet we are rarely

trained in leadership. Nevertheless, we become primary sources who are expected to develop the leadership skills and capacities of young girls and boys. Or as a frontline employee or middle manager of a community nonprofit, we are charged with the leadership training and development of our constituents. As clergypeople or lay leaders of faith congregations, we are immersed in this work—formally and informally. Yet, across the board, we are not formally trained in leadership—structurally we have not learned about leadership theories, leadership practices, or facilitation skills from our parent organizations or in our educational histories. All the while, we are expected to provide this type of leadership-developmental experience.

How can we expect nonprofit organization participants to gain leadership skills and capacities if our nonprofit leaders are neither knowledgeable and skilled leaders nor dynamic leadership educators?

The corporate training and development space is no different. There may be more resources and dedicated professionals, yet the context is quite similar. In-house trainers rarely have the educational background and theoretical knowledge to inform this work. Seldom do they understand the nuances of facilitation—particularly with experiential learning and reflective dialogue. Research indicates that corporate trainers receive little to no training—even with basic facilitation and teaching methods—and yet each year more than a million people are given first-time responsibilities for training others (Bolton & Bolton, 2016). That more than a million people doing this work are ill-prepared to facilitate the leadership learning and development of their peers is serious cause for concern.

In one of my consulting opportunities, a corporate trainer was completely flabbergasted by the notion of not relying on PowerPoint. He had been conditioned to present trainings as a lecture and formal presentation. Participants were expected to sit and listen and then go do what they were told. Yet we know that is not how leadership learning—or any kind of learning—occurs. To be more effective, he needed to have relinquished control and given more ownership to the participants through experiential learning—and then assist them process the learning through reflective dialogue.

In another corporate leadership training experience, the executive and middle-management participants were absolutely flummoxed when asked to reflect upon and share their leadership "story" and highlight a defining moment in their leadership journey. This was a transformative moment for them. Why was it that the in-house leadership educators hadn't facilitated training experiences for their employees to understand, explore, and glean insights from their own leadership defining moments? The answer is because these corporate leadership trainers only focused on the hard skills, like communication, through formal presentations and traditional training methods.

How can we expect corporate executives, managers, frontline employees, and everyone in between to gain the leadership skills and capacities if our corporate trainers are not knowledgeable, skilled, or dynamic leadership educators?

Additionally, athletics and sports have been touted as ideal forums for leadership learning, skills development, and capacity-building. Unfortunately, research indicates otherwise—simply participating on a sports team does not guarantee the development of leadership skills (Extejt & Smith, 2009). Intentional leadership training is necessary. Yet those who are charged with providing leadership education rarely have expertise in leadership. Sport coaches and athletics administrators at all levels, from youth in community to collegiate—and even professionals—are entrusted by parents and athletes alike to provide tactical sport-specific skills-building in addition to leadership. They are gifted with a remarkable forum for cultivating leadership skills and capacity-building. Yet such practitioners only have an intimate knowledge of their sports and ways to develop their players to perform athletically. Leadership training is not their forte. At the high school and collegiate levels, more and more athletics departments are offering leadership academies and trainings. Often, these are facilitated by team coaches or invited speakers who rarely have the leadership knowledge, healthy leadership habits, or facilitation skills to effectively train athletes in leadership.

To highlight its applicability, think about the traditional go-to practice of choosing team captains.

Captains are often selected because they are the best athletes. This method, based on athletic ability, is closely aligned with the antiquated trait theoretical perspective. Here, the athletic ability—a specific trait—is the driving factor, *not* leadership capabilities. Different leadership theories and approaches can have a more advantageous outcome. For example, selecting captains based on the adaptive leadership model and skills may be more appropriate—as those athletes can effectively navigate the trials and tribulations that come along with a grueling, competitive sports season—during competitions, in the locker rooms, and beyond the sport. (More on adaptive leadership can be found in chapter 5.)

How, then, can our athletes possibly develop the leadership skills they need and capacities they desire if our sport coaches are not prepared?

This book is ideal for nonprofit leaders, corporate trainers, sport coaches, and others who are charged, formally or informally, with leadership training and development. It introduces and synthesizes two dozen leadership theories. It also prepares us to practice healthy leadership habits—enhancing our own skills for the work in our organizations and communities. With the learning gained from this book, we will be capable of training our constituents as well as our colleagues. Together, we can change this culture.

Conclusion

Across industries, for those of us who are charged with and responsible for the leadership training and development of others, we have work to do. In the following chapters, I detail the what and who of leadership, leadership theories, leadership practices, and facilitation skills so that we can design, deliver, and demonstrate leadership training experiences that are both amazing and impactful.

CHAPTER 2

Leadership
What and Who

I F WE ARE GOING to effectively serve as leadership educators, it is imperative that we have a common understanding as to what the leadership industry and landscape is, what *leadership* is, why this work is essential, and who is doing it. In this section, we explore the what and the who of leadership. This chapter provides context and a foundation for everything else that is to come.

The Leadership Landscape

The leadership training industry is worth billions and billions of dollars (Ashford & DeRue, 2012; Ashkenaus & Hausmann, 2016; Ready & Conger, 2003)—although the exact number is difficult to pinpoint. Training Industry (www.TrainingIndustry.com), an organization that promotes itself as the most trusted source of information on the business of learning, compiles financial data on the training industry, broadly. They detail that the total global spending in 2019 on training was over $370 billion. In North America, it was over $169 billion. These billions of dollars spent by companies for training activities do *not* include individual consumer spending for training and development—only organizational spending for employee training experiences. Per Training Industries research, between 2010 and 2020, the training industry grew by $100 billion. The leadership training industry is not only worth billions upon billions of dollars, it continues to grow at a seemingly exponential rate.

These leadership training experiences comprise hands-on opportunities for leadership development, including leadership coaching, conferences, retreats, seminars, webinars, and workshops. There is no shortage of books, magazines, and online resources. Motivational speakers, understanding how hot "leadership" is, exploit this "L" word in their marketing and promotion. Certificates, undergraduate studies, and graduate-level academic programs focusing on leadership—or just strategically utilizing the word—continue to proliferate.

Organizations of all types promote leadership as part of their vision and mission—or an outcome of participation. We would be hard-pressed to identify a university that does not explicitly "develop the leadership capacity" or "prepare students to be the leaders of tomorrow." Similarly, sports programs and nonprofit organizations large and small promote leadership as a primary outcome. Here, I highlight some examples and pull statements that are published on their websites. The Boy Scouts of America suggest "scouting is adventure, family, fun, character, *leadership* and so much more." Strong Women Strong Girls "fosters *leadership* skills, a sense of female community and . . ." Nica Nadadores, a small NGO, uses "the sport of swimming as a tool to empower the next generation of *leaders* in underserved communities in Nicaragua."

The question that I ask all of us, and the industry writ large, is, how can we effectively develop the leadership skills and capacities of others if we do not have the theoretical knowledge, practical abilities, or facilitation skills to do so?

It is my belief that *Preparing Leadership Educators* is a first-of-its-kind book because it purposefully combines leadership theories, leadership practices, and facilitation skills into a single resource. My hope is that with its publication, by bringing together these three entities, you can access the leadership knowledge base, develop healthy leadership habits, and cultivate the tactical and technical facilitation skills to become an effective leadership educator.

What Is Leadership?

Leadership has been practiced for millennia. Even so, when it comes to actually defining *leadership*, we struggle. Today, there is no shortage of literature and resources that offer diverse ideas and understandings of leadership. Just before this book went to print, in late-2022 when searching Google for the term *leadership*, 6,170,000,000 responses emerge in a matter of seconds. This abundance of definitions, descriptions, articles, and news makes it no easier for us to define and understand exactly what is meant by the term *leadership*.

Part of our struggle is that we subconsciously and mistakenly interchange *leadership*, *leader*, and *leading*. For example, when I ask training participants, "What is leadership?," often a response is, "A leader is somebody who . . ." or "A leader has these [fill in the blank] characteristics" or "Leading is when [this or that] happens." The answers are beautiful and brilliant and often the "right stuff"—but to an entirely different question than what I asked. These three terms refer to distinctly separate entities.

Leading is what somebody (i.e., a leader) does. These are the actions in a particular moment of time—dependent on how one conceptualizes leadership.

Leaders are the people who undertake said actions. Leaders do not necessarily need to have a position, role, or title to exercise leadership.

Leadership is a complex relational concept that is utilized to recognize and understand who (i.e., a leader) is doing what (i.e., leading) in a specific time and place.

Another contributor to our *leadership* definition struggle is that leadership scholars—those who do spend their careers exploring, researching, and writing about leadership—have yet to agree on a single, concise, easily understood definition. Joseph Rost

(1993), the late leadership scholar, detailed in the early 1990s that for almost a century (since 1910) over 60% of the authors who wrote about leadership did not define leadership in their works. Those who did failed to "define leadership with precision, accuracy, and conciseness so that people are able to label it correctly when they see it happening or when they engage in it" (p. 6). He goes on to share, which still holds true—and is undeniably magnified almost 30 years after the publication of his *Leadership for the Twenty-First Century* text—that the word *leadership* has come to mean all things to all people.

Try one of these experiments and see for yourself: Conduct a Google search of the word; during your next leadership training ask your participants how they define or understand *leadership*; or listen to the news, a sports broadcast, or political pundits and test how quickly or how often they mention this "L" word. It's everywhere! And everyone has a different definition or understanding of leadership. Rost (1993) elaborates:

> Even worse, *leadership* has increasingly become a very "hot" word since about 1960, with an ability to produce a passionate reaction that draws people to it through an emotional attraction. Leadership has been "in" for so long, I cannot remember when it was "out." University programs, seminars, conferences, speeches, books, training activities, people, products, positions, and many relationships (group, marriage, counseling, teaching, friendship, etc.) are all called *leadership* in order to present a positive image of these phenomena so that people accept them more readily and voluntarily, and to attract people to them for the purpose of selling them, dignifying them by putting them on some kind of pedestal, or pushing them into the limelight when they might not otherwise be able to gain that light. . . . It has taken on a mythological significance. (p. 7)

To highlight our predicament, a selection of leadership scholars' definitions and understandings are offered. Ironically, Rost (1993) contributed to this conundrum by promoting his own definition of *leadership*. I begin with his and follow in alphabetical order:

- an influence relationship among leaders and followers who intend real changes that reflect their mutual purposes (Rost, 1993, p. 102)
- when persons with certain motives and purposes mobilize, in competition or conflict

with others; institutional, political, psychological, and other resources so as to arouse, engage, and satisfy the motives of followers (Burns, 1978, p. 18)

- the release of human possibilities (Jaworski, 1998, p. 66)
- leadership is not about individuals. . . . It is a system in which each of these three parts—leaders, followers, contexts—is *equally* important in which each of these three parts impinges *equally* on the other two (Kellerman, 2018b, p. 123)
- a relational and ethical process of people together attempting to accomplish positive change (Komives et al., 2013, p. 29)
- an interaction between leaders and their followers (Lipman-Blumen, 2005, p. 17)
- conviction in action (D. Roberts, 2007, p. 3)
- sensing and actualizing the future (Scharmer & Kaufer, 2013, p. 110)

Jaworski's "release of human possibilities" is significantly different than the formal-feeling definition offered by Burns. Roberts's definition, "conviction in action," might be the shortest definition of leadership one can discover. Kellerman believes that leadership is a triadic system of "leaders, followers, and contexts." Komives et al. believe leadership is value-laden—that it is about "positive" change—leadership is only for good. Most understand leadership to be a relational enterprise—"an interaction between leader and followers," according to Lipman-Blumen—while others describe it in a more transcendent sense. What exactly does Scharmer and Kaufer's "sensing and actualizing the future" mean?

Even since Rost's (1993) publication, the field has yet to unify around a collective definition and understanding of *leadership*—let alone one with precision, accuracy, and conciseness. As Barbara Kellerman (2018a), a renowned leadership scholar, offered during the question-and-answer segment of a keynote address at the 2018 International Leadership Association Conference, "the leadership field . . . is bedeviled by the issue of language" (56:36–56:39). How can we possibly make sense of and serve as effective leadership educators if even the scholars define and understand leadership in such wildly divergent ways?

Kellerman's (2018a) response to this question was powerful and poignant—it spoke to both the

conundrum we face and autonomy we're allotted due to diversity of theoretical underpinnings and divergent ideas of leadership scholars. It was profound in its simplicity—that this definitional issue is both exhausting *and freeing*. She invites leadership educators, as serious students of leadership, to exercise our freedom to establish our own definitions and understandings of leadership. All we need to do is to share our conceptualization. We can be self-determined and self-authored in how we articulate what leadership is because there will inevitably be supporters and deniers who agree and disagree with our characterization and explanation. Wryly, with a smile, she concluded those remarks with a "Go for it. Feel free to impose your own definitions on the language you use. . . . It is very hard to argue with because there are so many choices" (Kellerman, 2018a, 57:54–58:05).

Personally, I don't argue for or against any one definition. And in this book I do not offer a leadership definition. Rather, it is essential that each of us—every leadership educator—has a laser-sharp focus regarding the assumptions, core features, and parameters of leadership. And, yes, we need to have a solid, grounded understanding of how it has been and continues to be conceptualized. We need to do the work of exploring exactly what we believe leadership to be. We do not need to craft our own definition necessarily, but we do need to think critically about what it is—and what it is not.

Throughout this book, as a placeholder, I generally utilize three terms when discussing what leadership is—either as navigating obstacles, creating change, or accomplishing goals. Without formally defining *leadership*, these three ideas feel the most relevant and resonant as broad conceptions for what happens when leaders are leading.

To be clear, our personal understandings of leadership inform our practice of leadership. If we believe that leadership is rooted in one's position and only those in specific roles can and should lead, in practice, we only seek the guidance, direction, and support of those with specific titles. If our core understanding of leadership is that it is about power and personal reward, our practice of leadership is going to be explicitly focused on acquiring influence and reaping the tangible benefits of the authority we wield.

Fundamental to our role as leadership educators, we need to develop, educate, train, and engage others from an informed stance—a personally understood notion of leadership. If this were a training rather than a book, at this point, I would purposefully pause and facilitate an experiential activity, deep reflection, and dialogue about our personal understandings and notions of leadership. Since it is a text, I'll invite you to consider what you believe leadership to be before continuing on.

Leadership, in the most universal sense, has been perceived in three general ways—as influence, as process, and as outcome.

Leadership as influence views leadership as a relational mechanism to create change. Leadership, when thought of in the context of influence, is about intentionally shaping the beliefs, desires, and priorities of others. Individuals who wield significant social power and authority or hold a formal position can strategically utilize their influence for goal achievement. This shaping of beliefs, desires, and priorities is not tied to a value. Rather, the influence can be for what might be considered good or bad. Influence may take the form of inspiration. Or influence could be rooted in cultivating fear. Leadership scholar Sumru Erkut's (2001) notion of influence is about *persuading* other people.

Leadership as process can be thought of as an activity—those tangible actions that enable change to occur. *Mobilizing* seems to be the process of choice. Burns (1978) and Heifetz (1994) both strategically utilize that term. However, other leadership processes include *developing, directing, educating, engaging, facilitating, guiding, motivating, organizing, orienting*, and dare I say, *training*. Although there is a relational element to this understanding, the focus here is on the actions—the processes—undertaken by leaders.

Leadership as outcome distinguishes leadership by what occurs following the leadership action. With this understanding of leadership, the end result is what matters. Boyatzis and McKee (2005) detail that effective leadership should "build a sense of community and create a climate that enables people to tap into passion, energy, and a desire to move together in a positive direction" (p. 22). As an outcome, leadership is determined by leaders' ability in bringing forth desired change.

These three perceptions are not intended to be absolute or distinctly separated in our minds. It is not that we *only* believe in the notion of leadership as influence—they live within a spectrum. Yet we tend to lean heavier to one over the other two. Often,

subconsciously. The more we can recognize how we understand leadership, the better we can comprehend and appreciate how this understanding informs our practice of it. It is for this reason that I further describe these in Table 2.1 and utilize these descriptions at the end of this chapter for the praxis example.

Before reviewing leadership assumptions, take a moment to review the definitions offered previously and consider with which category (influence, process, or outcome) each one most closely aligns. Do they all have a categorical home? If not, how might you label that leadership understanding? Do some have multiple categorical homes? What might this suggest about leadership understandings being viewed along a spectrum rather than in three distinct and separate spaces? How do the ways you think about leadership fit within these three categories? Which of these three categories most aligns with your understanding of leadership? How does your understanding of leadership guide and sway your leadership practices? These questions can serve as a starting point as we cultivate grounded, personal, and meaningful understandings of leadership.

Antiquated perceptions of leadership continue to inform leadership practices. Leadership is commonly assumed to be intimately connected to position,

TABLE 2.1: A Description of Our Three Perceptions of Leadership	
Leadership as . . .	*Core Focus*
Leadership as *influence*	The focus of one's leadership practice is on *relationships*—collaborating with others in order to do what needs to be done.
Leadership as *process*	The focus of one's leadership practice is on *the work* of leading—acting to do what needs to be done.
Leadership as *outcome*	The focus of one's leadership practice is on *the results*—analyzing and assessing how well we did what needed to get done.

power, and prestige. This promulgates a focus on personal reward—a "what's in it for me" leadership attitude. Corrupt behaviors are frequently the outcome. This is not new. Van Vugt and Ahuja (2011) explain that a major shift in our collective notions of leadership occurred when we, societally, transitioned from hunter-gatherer to agrarian societies.

As hunter-gatherers we made leadership decisions as a group. The collective needed to agree—their lives depended on it literally. If one person wanted to go hunting, the chance of survival against wooly mammoths, saber-toothed tigers, or the elements was slim. Only the group could (potentially) accomplish the hunting objective—and survive.

As agrarian societies developed, leadership decision-making shifted. The group decision-making process was replaced by individual decision-making. The person (or family) who had the most (e.g., land, crops, livestock, etc.) wielded the most power. This power typically afforded them formal positions of authority and brandished the most prestige.

This is the legacy of leadership today—and this is typically how we understand and conceptualize leadership in the first quarter of the 21st century. How do you see it in your organization or community? What about in business? In education? In politics? In sports and entertainment? This notion of leadership is everywhere.

We're up against 10,000 years of deeply engrained leadership culture; we have a long, uphill adventure to generate cultural change around leadership mental frames. If we are to change our own—and our leadership training participants'—thinking about leadership we need to alter what we've been conditioned to believe about leadership—away from position, power, prestige, and personal reward. Rather, we need to emphasize that leadership is about the authentic person and intrinsic purpose for leading.

We need to shift our inherent leadership questions—away from "what's in it for me?"—and toward questions of depth, meaning, and significance. We need to carve out intentional space for reflecting on these questions—and provide detailed, insightful responses. Regarding the authentic person, we can probe about "Who am I?" "What are my values?" "What is my vision?" Regarding the intrinsic purpose, we can postulate about "How can I engage in good, meaningful work?" and "Where do my personal passions intersect with the pressing needs of my organization or community?"

While asking, reflecting upon, and responding to these questions, it is just as important to notice from where our antiquated leadership perspectives and understandings arise. Not surprisingly, they are rooted in severely embedded and widespread assumptions—what we consider leadership myths. I present these myths in Table 2.2 and highlight the comparative truths in the paragraphs that follow to advance a necessary shift in our leadership thinking.

> Truth: *Leadership is experiential.* Leadership is about what we do—rather than the role we hold. Leadership is about the pursuit of change we drive rather than the position attained within our groups,

---

TABLE 2.2: A Description of Leadership Myths and Truths

Leadership Myths	*Leadership Truths*
Leadership is positional.	Leadership is experiential.
Leadership is a singular, personal experience.	Leadership is a relational, collaborative experience.
Extroverts are the best leaders.	Leaders capitalize on their strengths and authenticity.
Leaders are born.	Leaders are developed.
Leadership can be learned quickly without much practice or energy investment.	Leadership is a lifelong developmental journey that requires intentional practice and significant emotional reserves.
There is one universally perfect way to lead.	Leadership is context-based and socially constructed.
Leadership is value-neutral.	Leadership is value-laden.

organizations, and communities' hierarchical structures.

Truth: *Leadership is a relational, group experience.* Leadership is a relationship. It involves the engagement between leaders and followers. We need to move away from the notion that successes and failures are the result of a single, solitary leader.

Truth: *Leaders capitalize on their strengths and authenticity.* Charisma and extroversion are wonderful traits. They do not, however, determine leadership. Effective leaders are those who exploit their strengths and lead from a place of a genuine and self-authored sense of self.

Truth: *Leaders are developed.* Being "born to lead" is a fallacy. This suggests only a few special individuals have the capacity to lead. This is limiting. All of us have the potential to develop leadership skills and capacities.

Truth: *Leadership is a lifelong developmental journey that requires intentional practice and significant emotional reserves.* If we are serious about developing our leadership skills and capacities, we need to dedicate purposeful time and energy—over the course of our lives—to become the leaders we dream of being.

Truth: *Leadership is context-based and socially constructed.* Leadership is context-based and determined by the leaders, followers, situation, and interaction among these three elements in the particular time and place in question. There is no universally perfect way to lead.

Truth: *Leadership is value-laden.* Leadership has value—it is for good. Leadership is about creating positive change. If the work is not oriented toward the virtuous, it is not leadership. It is certainly something. But it is certainly not leadership. (Of course, this raises the important questions of what is good, who decides what positive change is, and how do diverse cultural contexts shape differing perspectives of virtuousness.)

Leadership is defined in an abundance of ways. As leadership educators, no matter how we define it, we can find supporting evidence from the scholarship.

More important than defining the concept, though, is recognizing that our leadership practices manifest in different ways—determined by the ways in which we conceptualize it. Furthermore, by spending time reading the leadership literature—and in purposeful reflection—we can better understand our own truths of leadership.

What Is Leadership . . . Education? Development? Engagement? Training?

Leadership *education.* Leadership *development.* Leadership *engagement.* Leadership *training.* These four terms are often used interchangeably. Yet the importance of their separation and differentiation is argued for by Roberts and colleagues (S. Allen & Roberts, 2011; Anthony-Gonzalez & Roberts, 1981; D. Roberts & Ullom, 1989), as well as Guthrie and Osteen (2016). By clearly understanding the nuances between these four pedagogical strategies for leadership and their particular uses, we can more intentionally facilitate the leadership learning of others.

- Education: *understanding* of leadership knowledge, skills, and values
- Development: *reflection and integration* of leadership knowledge, skills, and values
- Engagement: *application and practice* of leadership knowledge, skills, and values
- Training: *cultivation* of leadership knowledge, skills, and values

Leadership education is the broad understanding of leadership knowledge. When educating in leadership, the approach—whether in formal classrooms or cocurricularly—is subjective in nature. With an education lens, we encourage others to access, acquire, and internalize the wide world of leadership, which includes theories, history, and competencies. In this role, as leadership educator-educators, we ask, What can be learned about leadership that will be useful to your practice?

Leadership development occurs through the intentional reflection and integration of our leadership knowledge, skills, and values. When developing in leadership—through purposeful one-to-one and small-group relational engagements with trusted resources—we are strengthening others' capacities for future potential and possibilities. With a leadership development lens, we engage others in purposeful maturation processes so that they can operate at their fullest potential when called upon. In this role, as leadership educator-developers, we ask, How might you become the leader you envision becoming?

Leadership engagement is the tangible application of our leadership learning. When engaging in leadership, we encourage the infusion of cognitive understandings, healthy habits, and leadership wisdom into real-world practice. With a leadership engagement lens, we craft holding environments so that others can experiment with their leadership learning through practical, hands-on, lived experiences. In this role, as leadership educator-engagers, we ask, How might you respond in a way that leads to the desired outcome?

Leadership training is the cultivation of skills. When training in leadership—often in workshops, conference sessions, or retreats—the focus is on enhancing leadership abilities so we can be more effective when practicing leadership. With a training lens, we support others as they tactically improve the way they lead. In this role, as leadership educator-trainers, we ask, What can I facilitate that will enhance your practice?

Since this book is deliberately written for leadership educators who facilitate developmental experiences in training environments and contexts (commonly referred to as leadership trainers or facilitators), I want to unpack this a bit more. Leadership trainers are charged with and responsible for the tactical leadership training and development of others through a specific type of intervention. We serve as facilitators of leadership skills development and capacity-building through intentional leadership training experiences.

Leadership training is different than formal educational classroom settings as well as typical leadership engagement experiences. Trainings are experiences designed to deepen the knowledge and develop the practical skills of participants so that they can effectively perform leadership (S. Allen & Roberts, 2011). We facilitate this through interventions typically in the form of hands-on and highly engaging workshops, retreats, or conference sessions. In the words of Jonathan Halls (2019), a master trainer who has been engaged in training and development for over 25 years,

We help people do the work of making themselves more skillful and knowledgeable. These new or deeper skills and knowledge help organizations function better and create value for their stakeholders. . . . what we do is noble when exercised professionally and ethically. But it comes with enormous privilege. . . . learners open their minds and allow you to influence their thinking. This is awesome and requires us to do everything we can to be great trainers. (pp. x–xi).

Leadership training is central to leadership learning because of the focus on skill development and competency enhancement (Guthrie et al., 2021). When conducting training experiences for others, we curate experiences that illuminate proven solutions to known problems. Our participants are provided hands-on, immersive, engaging, and dynamic experiences that serve as leadership learning laboratories. It is through their own participation, experimentation, and engagement that our participants experience, reflect upon, and dialogue about the training theme. This is the developmental experience that enables them to access the training material and message, internalize their leadership learning, and then apply that learning to their leadership practice. The compilation of theories, practices, and facilitation skills in this book will provide you with the knowledge, tactics, and tools to frame and facilitate exceptional leadership trainings. This is our worthy work—facilitating continuous and ongoing leader development efforts through intentional training experiences. We have an awesome responsibility.

Day et al. (2009) summarize why our work—that of facilitating leader development training experiences that enable our participants to access the training message and material, internalize learning, and then apply that learning to their practice—is so important:

Being an effective leader means drawing from a repertoire of skills and higher order competencies that require nearly a lifetime of experience, intense practice, and learning to master. This lifelong perspective on leader development explains why continuous and ongoing leader development efforts are especially important. . . . [They] cannot guarantee success, but can certainly raise the odds dramatically. (p. 172)

Who Are Leadership Educators?

In a broad conception, leadership educators are those individuals who intentionally design and foster leadership development (Guthrie & Jenkins, 2018). I agree. Yet we also need to clarify what makes leadership educators *good*. Many professionals can design a leadership workshop. Others can foster leadership development through a coaching endeavor or mentoring relationship. Just because we can design a leadership program or foster a leadership-developmental outcome does not magically make us effective leadership educators. If we want to live into this identity, it is imperative that we engage in critical self-reflection as well as acquire a depth of leadership knowledge, recognize and practice healthy leadership habits, and improve our facilitation of the leadership learning—particularly through experiential learning and reflective dialogue—of our participants.

Corey Seemiller and Kerry Priest (2015, 2017) have been exploring the leadership educator professional identity. Based upon their synthesis of the professional identity literature, they propose a model to better understand the professional identities of those who identify as leadership educators. There are four phases of leadership educator identity development: exploration, experimentation, validation, and confirmation.

In the exploration phase, budding leadership educators explore if, and to what extent, they accept and internalize the leadership educator professional identity. Leadership educators may be perennially in the exploration phase by continually deepening their understanding of self as a leadership educator. As new information emerges through experimentation, validation, and confirmation processes, the reconceptualization and reinterpretation of their leadership educator professional identity is a natural outcome.

In the experimentation phase, the leadership educator tries on the identity. This often occurs by imitating or mirroring those who have more experience self-authoring their leadership educator professional identity. There is a flirtation with leadership educator roles and testing of practices. Taking on the leadership educator identity is pivotal to accelerating the developmental process. In my story, this experimentation phase took place between 2005 and 2015 while serving as a volunteer in Nicaragua as well as a student affairs practitioner in the United States of America.

Next comes the validation phase. Here leadership educators receive external validation as well as self-validate through intentional leadership educator practices. This could be facilitating a successful leadership workshop, retreat, or conference session. It could also be teaching a leadership course or directing a leadership-oriented initiative. From my journey,

validation occurred in the latter half of the 2000s decade as my performance and effectiveness in this capacity improved.

Finally, leadership educators advance into the confirmation phase. This is when the identity is fully internalized and leadership educators confidently recognize themselves as leadership educators. Within this phase, there is also recognition within the leadership education community of practice. In addition to engaging in the practices of leadership educators, these individuals assist in the socialization and leadership educator identity development processes of others.

Seemiller and Priest (2015, 2017) note there are multiple influences that impact one's professional leadership educator identity. These include personal identities, personal agency, context, socialization, and critical incidents—positive or negative moments of significance and meaning in one's life that result in a paradigm shift or intentional and responsive future action. Additionally, credibility plays a factor. If others do not see me—particularly those in my leadership educator community—as a valued and valuable leadership educator, my sense of self as a leadership educator will likely diminish. Competence matters too. Leadership educators pursue lifelong leadership learning opportunities to enhance their knowledge and improve their skills.

Priest and Jenkins (2019) offer a four-part framework for leadership educator professional development. This includes engaging in our own identity development as well as enhancing our own understanding of leadership. The framework also encompasses engaging in praxis—applying theory to practice—in addition to acquiring the aptitude around the design and delivery of leadership programs.

Leadership educators need to engage in purposeful and persistent identity development—exploring the questions

Who am I?
How do I bring myself into the work of leadership education?
What are the implications of my identity on my work as a leadership trainer and developer of others?

Engaging in this type of internal inquiry and exploration is a powerful tool as we make sense of our experiences, confront our assumptions and unconscious biases, clarify our aspirations, and claim our leadership (and followership) identities (Seemiller & Crosby, 2019).

Beyond understanding the "who" of leadership training and development, leadership educators need to have foundational knowledge of leadership. This includes "formal knowledge around the subject of leadership and leadership learning and development: theories, concepts, models, or wisdom of experience" (Priest & Jenkins, 2019, p. 12). Leadership educators also engage in praxis. That is, they integrate that leadership knowledge into practice—serving as scholar-practitioners or practitioner-scholars.

Finally, leadership educators need to harness the energy of "how" (Priest & Jenkins, 2019). This is about the design and delivery of leadership programs. In leadership training contexts, I suggest that this is about having a profound knowledge of and skill in facilitating experiential learning activities and hosting reflective dialogue.

The Council for the Advancement of Standards in Higher Education (CAS, 2020) has developed a set of standards and guidelines specifically for university student leadership programs. As part of these standards, they feature a detailed list of prerequisites for leadership educators. Professional personnel involved in leadership education and development should possess certain knowledge that includes

- history of and current trends in leadership theories, models, and philosophies
- organizational development, group dynamics, change strategies, and principles of community
- pedagogies and instructional design
- how identities and dimensions of diversity influence leadership
- inclusion and its effects on development
- how inclusion, intersectionality, and power influence leadership
- the contextual nature of leadership

As a leadership educator, do you possess this knowledge? What are your growth areas? What are you going to do about it?

Before continuing on to the initial praxis (connecting theory to practice) opportunity in this book, these three questions deserve a moment of reflection. Purposefully pause here to think about your leadership educator knowledge base and how

you might deepen your understanding in any one of those domains—as well as your leadership educator identity. What phase do you see yourself in? And how might you engage in purposeful and persistent identity development?

Leadership Training Praxis (Connecting Leadership Theories and Practices to Facilitation)

Before exploring leadership theories (Part Two), practices (Part Three), and facilitation skills (Part Four), I want to share a few words regarding the purposeful integration of the theories and practices with facilitation. This book is written so that the next generation of leadership educators have the knowledge base and skill set to ensure that leadership training participants can *access* the training material and message, *internalize* leadership learning, and *apply* that learning to their leadership practice beyond the training bubble.

My deepest desire and hope is that this text be utilized as a practical resource. To that end, for each theory and practice presented in the book (45+), I offer insight into how I've utilized experiential learning activities and reflective dialogue questions to traditionally engage and empower participants through leadership training experiences. With each leadership theory and practice, I include a brief overview, a description of the experiential activity (indicated as either a physically engaged or reflective activity), summary instructions on how to facilitate the experiential learning activity, and sample go-to reflective dialogue questions that illuminate leadership learning opportunities for participants. These are the recipes to my leadership training secret sauce.

For effective facilitation of each and every activity listed throughout this text, I offer five guidelines. (Many more details on facilitation—as well as how to craft an effective "training story" utilizing Leadership Trainer's Narrative Approach—are explored in Part Four.)

First, be sure to *provide clear instructions*. We want our participants to be successful. We set them up for success by providing clear and concise instructions. Here, we remove any initial barriers and reduce potential fears by centering their energy and attention on us. We know that listening happens best when distractions are limited. Be sure to call for participants' attention. It is entirely appropriate—and suggested—to wait for everyone's attention before providing the instructions rather than having participants miss information or needing to repeat the instructions several times. Before completing the instructions, we ask participants if they understand the instructions to verify they are ready to begin. We also offer a space for the participants to ask any clarifying questions. Even though we provide clear and concise instructions, we are strategic in what we offer. Often, providing limited details on how to progress through the activity leaves opportunities for participants to think critically, engage collaboratively, and exercise their leadership.

Second, we *give them ample space to take ownership over the experiential learning activity*. Once the activity is live, we let the participants do their thing. Here we step back and engage in ways that make sense for each particular activity. Mostly we observe their performance while letting them work through it. This is an opportunity for us to ensure the safety of the participants as well as to take mental notes for the reflective dialogue to come.

Third, we *monitor the time*. Effective facilitation is all about strategic time management. Some activities are time-limited. That is, training participants need to accomplish the task in less than 1 minute. Or, they have a maximum of 20 minutes to complete the activity. In these scenarios, we need to share timing updates with the participants so they can strategize and make good use of their time. Of course, as savvy leadership educators, we can utilize these updates to raise the level of challenge or reduce it depending on the participants' performance. In general, we monitor the clock because we need to ensure the activity and the training end at the intended, designated time. By being mindful of the time—and potentially manipulating it—we make strategic facilitation decisions to ensure participants' success, engage in robust reflective dialogue, and support their leadership learning.

Fourth, in our observational role, we *assess the level of challenge—and make appropriate adjustments if necessary*. Is the activity intended to be a low-risk, medium-risk, or high-risk activity? Is that how it is playing out? While observing these experiential learning activities, we ensure the level of challenge matches the participants' ability. If alterations are necessary, we intervene by raising or decreasing the level of challenge.

Fifth, we *host a reflective dialogue as a follow-up to the experiential learning activity*. No experiential learning activity is complete without reflective dialogue. Our experiential learning activities are designed to enable participants to access the training message and material. The reflective dialogue empowers our participants to internalize the leadership lesson. It is this personal purposeful processing and socially engaged dialogue that enables their internalization of the material and the practical application of their learning beyond the training bubble. The reflective dialogue is our opportunity to assist participants in translating their experience into leadership learning—and it is what makes the training experience transformative.

As a sample of what is to come in Part Two (leadership theories) and Part Three (leadership practices), I offer a training segment on *What is leadership?* Before facilitating this experiential learning activity—and any others found throughout this book—I highly encourage you to read through Part Four (Facilitating Leadership Trainings) so you have the tactical skills to facilitate these training experiences with dynamism and confidence.

Leadership Educator Praxis Activity

Leadership Theme: What Is Leadership?
Exercise: Four Corners (physically engaged activity)

When exploring the broad concept of leadership with your participants, there are no less than a few dozen directions leadership educators can take. We can directly ask what our participants know about leadership, share a variety of definitions to spark dialogue, or utilize their personal leadership-defining moments to rediscover a leadership experience—and its implications—in their lives. I've utilized this initial praxis example during trainings to explore what we mean when describing leadership. Specifically, this training framework and activity is quite useful when I want participants to think critically about *how* the ways we understand leadership impacts our practice of it.

There are plenty of reflective exercises to engage participants in thinking about leadership. The simplest way is to directly ask them, how do you define leadership? Or invite them to share one thing they believe is a Truth (capital "T") about leadership. Although this is a worthwhile endeavor, the Four Corners exercise enables participants to be physically engaged by literally moving their bodies to one of four corners during each round of the exercise before engaging in dialogue with their peers.

Four Corners Activity

In the Four Corners activity, participants are instructed to move to the corner that most resonates with their beliefs—if they "strongly agree," "agree," "disagree," or "strongly disagree." To make a determination, participants are shown pictures of "leaders." (I place the word *leaders* in quotation marks here because most often these are people in formal positions of power and authority—which is antithetical to leadership being about authentic personhood and intrinsic purpose. When facilitating this activity, it is important to be strategic and purposeful about who is represented visually as leaders—and who is excluded.)

The objective with this activity is not about debating *if* the pictured person is a leader, but about *why* our participants believe the way they do about that individual. What is their underlying rationale? Is it because they believe the leader is influential—or not? Or because the leader is exhibiting a remarkable leadership process—or not? Or did the leader's work result in something transformative—or no impact at all? As the activity moves forward, continually expressing the objective of the activity may be necessary to ensure participants focus less on *if*, and more on *why* they believe this person is a leader.

Because this necessitates critical thinking skills to move beyond if a person is a leader to why, I suggest this activity be utilized with developmentally mature participants. Furthermore, it is wise to avoid politically, socially, and culturally charged individuals as the pictured leaders. When these individuals are utilized as the "leaders," it is often difficult for participants to think critically about rationale when they are emotionally connected to whether the person is a leader—or are diametrically opposed to that belief.

A final note on this activity is be sure to leave time and space for each participant to get a brief understanding of who the pictured person is. For example, I've used Benjamin Franklin and Abraham Lincoln, two well-known historical-political figures in the United States of America. Yet participants from other countries who had limited knowledge of this history knew very little of these two. As a bonus, you may utilize a leader who has various identities. Jessica Alba is an often go-to example of mine. She is known worldwide for her acting, beauty, and Tik-Tok dancing. She

is also a cofounder of ecofriendly household goods, The Honest Company—valued at over $1 billion. Depending on the context regarding how participants know about these leaders, their understanding of the depicted "leaders" will vary.

Materials

- signage: "Strongly Agree," "Agree," "Disagree," "Strongly Disagree" (these are to be posted in four distinct corners of the training space)
- pictures of "leaders"—typically on a slide deck (posters can work well, too)

Instructions

- Begin by providing a picture of a "leader." Participants should be encouraged to make a quick decision and move to the corner that has the most resonance.
- If there is confusion or a lack of knowledge about the pictured "leader," invite a few participants to vocalize something that they know about that person.
- Once in their corners, the participants should be instructed to have partner conversations or small-group dialogue as to why they believe what they do—why they are in that particular corner.
- Following that dialogue, participants should be instructed to identify, based on their "why," how that response connects to leadership as influence, process, or outcomes:
  - Leadership-as-*influence*: The focus of one's leadership practice is on *relationships*—collaborating with others in order to do what needs to be done.
  - Leadership-as-*process*: The focus of one's leadership practice is on *the work* of leading—acting to do what needs to be done.
  - Leadership-as-*outcome*: The focus of one's leadership practice is on *the results*—analyzing and assessing how well we did what needed to get done.
- Once these conversations have elapsed, bring the whole group together and ask for a volunteer from each group to share what was discussed in that corner.

- After the large-group sharing, switch to another "leader" picture.
- Continue this process for several rounds so participants can reflect upon the rationale for how they perceive these "leaders" from multiple perspectives.
- After these rounds are complete, settle energy and shift into the reflective dialogue.

Reflective Dialogue Questions

Our objective is to engage participants in understanding *why* they believe each of those "leaders" are leaders. In the reflective dialogue, we are less concerned whether someone strongly agrees or just regularly agrees—or disagrees at those varying levels. A selection of my go-to reflective dialogue questions includes the following:

- What did you notice about why you believe what you do about these leaders?
- Did you notice if you believed these leaders were leaders because of their influence, processes, or outcomes? (Follow-up: Share more about that.)

- What does this belief mean for how you understand and practice your own leadership? (What do you inherently focus on when leading?)
- What does this belief mean for how you understand the leadership practices of others with whom you engage?
- If, through this exercise, you've become aware that your leadership approach is generally informed by influence, what does that mean for how you engage with others who are informed by leadership as process or outcome?
- Who is missing from these pictures? Who else should be considered a "leader"? (This question does not focus on influence, process, or outcomes, but assists participants in critically thinking about who has been exempt or excluded from the leadership conversation.)
- What can we learn from this exercise that can be applied to our own leadership practice?

PART TWO

LEADERSHIP THEORIES, MODELS, FRAMEWORKS, AND THEMES

LEADERSHIP EDUCATORS KNOW *ABOUT* leadership. We have to. In order maximize and flex this identity, it is imperative that we have a deep understanding of leadership. We need to be well versed in the history, scholarship, and breadth of literature. Leadership has become a field of study unto its own. As informed leadership educators, we ought to perpetually study, work, and live within the depths of knowledge of the leadership theories and themes that underscore our expertise.

Part Two of this book explores leadership theory. Included are two dozen theories and themes that can and should ground our knowledge base and inform our leadership trainings. Each chapter in this section is intended to serve as a theoretical or thematic overview. I include the critical features and core facets that serve as a foundation. This is intended to be comprehensive, albeit not all-encompassing. I encourage you, if something strikes your interest, to pursue the primary sources, referenced articles, and other resources to deepen your understanding.

These theories and themes were selected to provide leadership educators with a sense of the trajectory of leadership research and scholarship over the past century. We begin with industrial leadership theories. These are the original approaches to understanding leadership. Then we explore the first major shift in leadership research and scholarship—what is understood as postindustrial leadership theories.

With these, there is less a focus on surface-level traits, skills, and behaviors, and more of an emphasis on the relationship and transformational potential of leading. The third grouping is our contemporary leadership models and frameworks. These highlight the leadership research and scholarship from the mid-1990s to the present day. This compilation also recognizes a shift—back to the leader—but at a deeper level of authenticity than just surface-level traits, skills, and behaviors. Here, generally, we focus on the internal disposition of leaders. To conclude Part Two, we review a handful of leadership themes that are important for leadership educators to explore. Often, we facilitate on these themes during our leadership trainings. More importantly, these themes deeply inform our own understanding and practice of leadership.

At the end of each theory, model, framework, and theme I provide a praxis opportunity. This links theory to our leadership educator practice by including my reflections on the implications of this material from the perspective of leadership educators in training environments and contexts. Suggestions and considerations are offered regarding how each of these can be structured and infused into the fabric of intentionally facilitated leadership trainings. There I utilize each of these leadership theories, frameworks, models, and themes to illuminate how they merge with experiential learning activities and manifest into tangible leadership learning experiences for our participants.

CHAPTER 3

Industrial Leadership Theories

THE INDUSTRIAL LEADERSHIP THEORIES and approaches provide leadership educators an opportunity to peek into the history of leadership research and scholarship. These are the original, foundational leadership theories that launched the industry. Often perceived as outdated, they are very much infused into our leadership psyche and manifest into our leadership practices today. In this section we will explore the trait approach, skills approach, behavioral approach, situational approach, path-goal theory, and leader–member exchange theory of leadership.

Trait Approach

The trait approach, commonly referred to as the "great man" theory, assumes that leaders are born, not developed. Van Vugt and Ahuja (2011) capture the essence of the trait approach to leadership magnificently. With a trait lens, "leadership is not really a phenomenon in its own right; rather, it seeps out like a cloud of dry ice, from superior beings who are blessed with exceptional intelligence, energy, and moral capacity" (p. 27). Essentially, this understanding of leadership posits that leaders are born with specific traits—unambiguous characteristics that make these select few leaders *great*. The assumption is that regular people, most of us, do not have the natural capacity to lead—leadership is solely reserved for rare, elite, and superior beings. Philosophically, these people are revered as the heroes of our organizations and protagonists of our communities. They have superior leadership abilities,

rising up in times of need to save the day with their special leadership traits.

Great man theories originated in the early 20th century with the first systematic studies of leadership (Northouse, 2021). Scholars were interested in identifying the traits that determined effective leadership. Men of privilege studied other men of privilege. Those who were identified as "great" became the subjects so that the world would know and better understand their innate qualities and characteristics. These traits were not necessarily developed through exposure, experience, or learning (D. Roberts, 2007)—instead, they were perceived as inborn or God-given. Great man theories presumed (and often still presume) that women were not eligible for leadership opportunities—or greatness (Heifetz, 1994).

A survey of these leadership traits—that is, the original surface-level factors and innate qualities that make outstanding leaders—include ambition, attractiveness, extroversion, intelligence, masculinity, and perseverance (Northouse, 2021; D. Roberts, 2007; Van Vugt & Ahuja, 2011).

By simply looking at this list, many of us may be shocked by how this antiquated perspective of leadership still holds significant weight today. To be clear, most contemporary leadership research and scholarship has focused on other interests: leadership for differing situations and contexts; relationships between leaders and followers; new theories, models, frameworks, and approaches to leading; the connection between authenticity and effectively leading; and, most recently, the intersections of leadership with justice and equity. In practice, though, we see an ongoing application of traits and great men as leadership hallmarks. The examples, in diverse contexts, seem endless.

The trait approach is unfortunately widespread in the political arena. Collectively, as citizens, we tend to focus our energy and attention on traits rather than on policies when selecting candidates for office or trusting those who already hold these influential positions. For example, women in politics are often critiqued for their clothing—the color and style of their pantsuits—compared to men. This type of thinking falsely assumes that women are better suited (pun intended) for the runway rather than the Oval Office. Another way the trait approach emerges in the political realm is by our fascination with the age of politicians. During the 2016 Republican primary for president of the United States of America, my grandmother commented—much like many others—that Marco Rubio, the senator from Florida, looked "too young to be president." Yet Rubio had significantly more years of political experience in both state and federal government than President Barack Obama did prior to his own election for the high office. Because of his physical appearance—looking too young—his years of experience were essentially discounted. We saw this in the 2020 Democratic primary too—only the reverse. Bernie Sanders (78), Michael Bloomberg (77), Joe Biden (77)—who was ultimately elected—and Elizabeth Warren (70) would all have served as president at 70+ years of age. (Donald Trump, the Republican nominee for the 2020 presidential election, at 73, can also be included in this group.) Many political theorists, policy wonks, news contributors, and voters wondered if their age—as the sole determining factor—made them irrelevant and out of touch. Rather than exploring their policies, credentials, political accomplishments, health records, and other factors to make a more educated and informed decision, we relied on their age as an innate surface-level trait to make surface-level determinations of their leadership skills and abilities.

In October of 2012, I was visiting Ghana while serving with the Semester at Sea program. This visit, it just so happened, was before an important countrywide election. In the taxi, the driver, Kosi, was commenting that he hoped "we [other Ghanaians] would elect people who just did the right thing." I was profoundly struck by the sense of powerlessness in his voice and statement. Kosi was so disenfranchised due to the corruption in government that

he did not believe he had any role to play in creating change. He did not see himself as a leader or capable of leading—that was solely reserved for an elected official. Leadership was apportioned for a special someone else—a politician who had the traits to swoop into office and make radical and healthy changes desired by Kosi. Although this interaction with Kosi took place in Accra, Ghana, political systems in the Global North celebrate notions that leadership positions and roles are reserved for superior individuals who need to "save the day" or that these singular individuals are the only ones who can bring about the change they desire.

In business and other organizations, we see the strength, lasting impact, and presence of the great man theory. Extroversion is often seen as an important leadership quality. People are hired, propped up, or promoted due to their gregariousness. Yet we know that introverts are just as capable at leading enterprises, projects, and personnel. Masculinity is another trait that often becomes a determining factor in hiring or promotion. We see this most clearly with the glass ceiling and labyrinth that prevent women from attaining jobs or executive-level roles at the same rate as men. This happens, in part, due to the subconscious assumptions we hold about how masculinity is an important and idealized leadership trait.

Within education, teachers and administrators, during selection processes for student leadership opportunities, comment that particular candidates are "born leaders"—assuming that their leadership prowess is from winning the genetic lottery or is God-given—rather than skills that can be developed by any of our students. Or at the end of the academic year, when awards ceremonies are taking place, we praise students for their personality and popularity—associating these traits with good leadership. It would be more appropriate to celebrate the goals the students were able to accomplish or the way they were able to mobilize others to achieve meaningful change on campus. Similarly, our policies around student clubs and organizations promote a hierarchical, positional, and trait-based approach to leadership. When we require clubs and organizations to have formal leadership roles, we institute structures and systems that suggest leadership is only enacted from the position held and the power wielded.

Sports is another avenue where we see the prevalence of the trait approach. Often, team captains are selected for their surface-level athletic abilities. It is never a surprise when the best athlete or most prolific scorer becomes captain. Since when has athletic prowess been synonymous with leadership ability? Sport broadcasters love to talk about the leadership aptitudes of the superstars. When the championship is won, it is seemingly solely because of the leader-as-MVP. In this example, these sport broadcasters are propagating an antiquated perspective of leadership that only a select few heroes—those who visibly lead their teams to victory—are the leaders. Everyone else is a follower (often used in a derogatory way) at best.

We, as consumers of politics, business, education, and sport, usually accept and reinforce these trait-based practices and perspectives of leadership without critically examining how the practice of leadership is being expressed or understood. The previous examples highlight how specific traits (e.g., age, attire, masculinity, outgoingness, personality, and athletic ability) still influence our understanding of what makes good leaders and leadership. We have been conditioned to identify protagonists who can captivate us with their charm and traits—as leaders.

After more than a century of exploration and study, scholars have synthesized hundreds of leadership traits and identified five core leadership attributes for those who want to be perceived as effective leaders (Northouse, 2021). These are the leadership traits that leadership educators should focus on when engaging participants in our trainings. Unlike the traits of long ago, these can be developed by all of us—not just a select few of the privileged leadership classes—and ought to be developed to enhance our abilities to lead effectively:

Determination. Determination is about accepting the challenge, pursuing the goal, and accomplishing the task. People with the determination trait are willing to assert themselves, be proactive, and persevere in the face of obstacles.

Integrity. Integrity is based on the qualities of honesty and trustworthiness. Those who are connected to a strong set of values and principles, and who take responsibility for their actions, demonstrate integrity. People with the integrity trait can be trusted to enact what they espouse.

Intelligence. Intelligence is not just about book smarts. A leader's intellectual ability is about seeing the systems and interconnections that exist as well as reasoning abilities. People with the intelligence trait can perceive what's to come and navigate through challenges effectively.

Self-confidence. Self-confidence is the capacity to be certain and assured about one's abilities. People with self-confidence truly, deeply believe in their powers and skills. In a leadership context, self-confidence is not arrogance, but an inner knowing and strength.

Sociability. Sociability refers to seeking out healthy social relationships. This is not necessarily extroversion, as introverts can master sociability. People with the sociability trait are diplomatic, friendly, hopeful, optimistic, and tactful—and they are sensitive to others' needs.

Leadership Educator Praxis Activity

Leadership Theme: Trait Approach (great man theory)
Exercise: Line Up! (physically engaged activity)

Many, if not most of our leadership training participants may hold fast to the notion that leaders are born—not developed. Or that leaders are identifiable by surface-level innate qualities. Being extroverted, as an example of a surface-level innate trait, assumes introverts do not have the ability to effectively lead. What *we*—knowledgeable leadership educators—may believe as standard-issue understandings of leadership may come as a shock to the philosophical leadership underpinnings of our participants. This is because many of our participants have yet to engage in the critical reflection necessary to understand why they believe what they do about leadership. They hold these antiquated perspectives in their subconscious. This is particularly important for leadership educators to note—especially if we are working in contexts where limited leadership training infrastructures and development opportunities are the norm. Sharing concepts that challenge and confront the held beliefs of participants—and their leadership practices (e.g., hiring extroverted candidates or awarding accolades to individuals for personality traits)—may feel, to them, offensive and agitating. Prior to any training, it will be important to assess our participants' level of understanding of leadership so we can best approach our training experience in ways that have resonance and applicability for our participants. When facilitating a training on the trait approach, I like to highlight, through the Line Up! experiential activity, that leaders, for most of history, were selected or celebrated for traits that ultimately did not determine effectiveness in leading.

Line Up!

In the Line Up! activity, participants are instructed to create a straight line, shoulder-to-shoulder, based upon various characteristics. This activity can also be utilized as an energizer and icebreaker—totally disconnected to the trait approach. To make it relevant to the theory—and to inform a robust reflective dialogue—I suggest we utilize traits that have historically been identifiers for positional leaders, for example, height. Taller people are more likely to be considered leaders than shorter people (Lindqvist, 2012). Age is another example. Older people are considered more qualified for leadership than their younger counterparts. If the participant group is very familiar and seem comfortable together you can dig a bit deeper and utilize economic wealth. Many still hold the age-old belief that those with wealth are "naturally" better leaders.

Materials

- N/A

Instructions

- Participants will be instructed to "line up" shoulder-to-shoulder as quickly as possible—*in silence*. The participants can line up based upon:
  - height—shortest to tallest
  - age order—youngest to oldest
  - alphabetical order—A to Z by first or last name
  - birthday—January 1 through December 31
  - economic wealth—poorest to wealthiest
- Following each lineup, be sure to make a delineation that only the select few, tallest, oldest, and wealthiest individuals are leaders. Everyone else . . . not so much—they are exempt from formal leadership roles, experiences, and opportunities.

- These statements are not intended to be the reflective dialogue. That is to follow. These are just to raise awareness about how, historically and in contemporary contexts, we utilize the trait approach both consciously and subconsciously to determine who is qualified to lead.
- Once the participants have lined up in a variety of ways, enter into the reflective dialogue to process the experience.

Reflective Dialogue Questions

Our objective is to physically engage participants in an activity to help them understand and reflect upon how the trait approach comes to life even in contemporary contexts. A selection of my go-to reflective dialogue questions includes the following:

- How did it feel to be labeled as a leader for your height?
- How did it feel to be labeled as a follower because of your age or wealth?
- How did leadership actually manifest through this experience of lining up?
- What is an "a-ha" moment as we engaged in this activity?
- How else do we see traits and surface-level innate characteristics utilized to determine leadership effectiveness?
- What can we learn from this exercise that can be applied to our own leadership practice?

Skills Approach

Like the trait approach, the skills approach is leader-centric and focused on specific attributes of the leader. The key difference is that leadership skills can, inherently, be developed. Our thinking shifts from those personality characteristics (i.e., traits) that are generally innate and fixed to abilities (i.e., skills) that can be learned and enhanced (Northouse, 2021). This is where we come in. As savvy and skilled leadership educators, we are the ones who are charged with assisting our participants in developing their leadership skills and capacities through intentional, engaging, and dynamic training experiences.

The skills approach was one of the original methods of understanding leadership. The focus, generally, was on the capabilities that make for effective leading. Katz (1955) outlined a three-skill approach that is still heavily utilized today. The three-skill approach emphasizes that leadership skills are arranged into three sectors: technical, human, and conceptual.

Technical skills relate to domain-specific knowledge and proficiency in tactical work tasks (Northouse, 2021), for example, knowing how to utilize a certain type of machinery or computer program. It is assumed that leaders who possess superior technical skills are better equipped to evaluate others' work and provide meaningful feedback (Day et al., 2009). For leadership educators, technical skills relate to our ability to effectively facilitate an experiential learning activity or host an impactful reflective dialogue.

If technical skill is about mastering the use of things, human skill is the ability to understand people—a relational aptitude. These interpersonal skills are necessary to understand and analyze social interrelationships and to effectively employ emotional intelligence (Day et al., 2009). For leadership educators, human skills are aligned with building rapport and connecting deeply with the participants in our training experiences.

Conceptual skills are those abilities to work with ideas. Leaders with high levels of conceptual skills are able to easily internalize and express complex philosophies, beliefs, and visions to others. These individuals are able to understand systemic and structural challenges, generate solutions, evaluate alternatives, and implement action plans. Leadership educators utilize conceptual skills to clearly share theories and practices in ways that can be accessed, internalized, and then applied by our training participants.

More recently, Mumford et al. (2000) illuminated two core leadership skills related, generally, to (a) leader competencies and (b) leader attributes. These competencies are focused on leaders' capabilities in problem-solving, awareness with social judgment, and enhanced knowledge. Problem-solving skills relate to the creativity necessary for navigating challenges and struggles. Social judgment skills, similar to human skills already addressed, convey an understanding of people and social systems. Enhanced knowledge, the third competency, expresses the accumulation of information.

The leader attributes refer to four personal abilities and characteristics of leaders: general cognitive ability, crystallized cognitive ability, motivation, and personality. General cognitive ability relates to the ways in which leaders process information, implement creative thinking, apply reasoning, and control memory. Crystallized cognitive ability is the capacity of leaders to apply the learning from their lived experiences. Motivation is the willingness of leaders to pursue the leadership challenges they face. Personality is concerned with a leader's internal dispositions—and the impact they have on skills development. For example, curiosity and adaptability impact a leader's interest in and navigation of challenges.

Leadership Educator Praxis Activity

Leadership Theme: Skills Approach
Exercise: Trade Me a Skill (physically engaged activity)

As leadership educators, we know that no two participants need to develop the same exact skills. Participants' skills development varies depending on needed technical, human, and conceptual skills, as well as their competencies and attributes. Of course, this is personal and in relationship to their organizational role, current skill set, developmental capabilities, and other factors. We can assist our participants by creating trainings—infused with experiential learning activities and reflective dialogue—that specifically meet the developmental needs of our participants. It is for this reason we need to do the critical discovery work to clearly understand participant dynamics and their skills-development needs. We have a responsibility to assist participants in cultivating the skills that will enable them to overcome obstacles and enhance their performance via tactical abilities, intellectual prowess, and relational faculties. This means we need to center our attention on creating experiences that personally resonate and matter to our participants rather than generic trainings that may only be limitedly impactful. The Trade Me a Skill? activity can empower our participants to self-identify leadership skills that they believe are essential for effective leadership practice.

Trade Me a Skill?

In the Trade Me a Skill? activity, participants are instructed to utilize notecards to draft what they believe are three essential skills for effective leadership. During the activity, participants' task is to engage with others to trade and collect three skills they believe are indispensable for effective leadership.

Materials

- three index cards per participant
- writing utensil

Instructions

- Distribute the three index cards per participant and ensure everyone has a writing utensil.
- Invite the participants to write three essential leadership skills—one on each card. (It is a best practice to have several examples to visibly and verbally share with participants.)
- Once all of the skills are drafted, collect and shuffle the cards.
- Redistribute the cards so each participant has three random skills.
- Instruct them to spend the time allotment (approximately 5 minutes for small groups, 10 minutes for medium-size groups, and 15 minutes for large groups) trading their skills for other participants' skills—based on the cards in their hands.
  - Note, they *do* need to trade—even if none of the skills are preferred over what they currently have. When approached by another participant, each person will select the card they want to relinquish and trade it. Then, each participant will find a new person and continue with this process until the allotted time has expired.
  - Participants do not need to acquire their original handwritten skills. They will keep trading with the intention of acquiring three skills that they believe illuminate premier skills—by relinquishing their least desirable skill with each new encounter.
- At the end of the allotted time, bring the group back together for the reflective dialogue.

Reflective Dialogue Questions

Our objective is to assist participants in thinking about what they believe to be valuable leadership skills. They begin with personal reflection and then widen their scope by learning about what others believe are essential skills through trading opportunities. A selection of my go-to reflective dialogue questions includes the following:

- What were your original leadership skills? Why are those important to you?

- What skills do you have now? Why did you want to keep them? (Follow-up: Are they the same or different—why?)
- Did someone want a skill that someone else was *not* wanting to trade? (Follow-up: How did that make you feel?)
- Did you give away a skill that you wish you had back?
- Which leadership skills seemed to be the most popular or desired? Which leadership skill seemed to be most repeated? What do we take from this?
- Which of the three leadership skills in your hand do you want to spend time developing for your own leadership practice?

Behavioral Approach

The behavioral approach to leadership focuses on what leaders do—not on their surface-level characteristics (traits) or abilities (skills)—when leading and engaging with followers. Although the focus is still explicitly on leaders—their behavior—this understanding of leadership was the first to recognize the relationship and interconnectivity between leaders and followers.

There are two general behaviors of leadership: task behaviors and relationship behaviors. Task behaviors focus on results. What leadership behaviors will allow leaders to work through struggles and accomplish goals? Relationship behaviors focus on people. What leadership behaviors will allow followers to feel comfortable with themselves, with one another, and with the situation in which they are currently immersed?

It is important to recognize these behaviors are not independent entities. Both behaviors—task and relationship—are intertwined. The central purpose of this leadership approach is to recognize the ways in which they are combined so as to dynamically and effectively influence followers to succeed at their endeavors (Northouse, 2021).

Over several decades, Blake and Mouton (1964, 1978, 1985) developed a box grid with two 9-point axes—with concern for people on the left and concern for goals on the bottom. Although there are technically 81 different locales along the spectrum (9 × 9 = 81), they identify five broad spectrum behavioral styles of leadership. Leadership educators can utilize this model—and the behavioral approach to leadership—to help participants think through how they currently engage with followers. The objective with this approach is to assist participants in making strategic changes that can better motivate and mobilize followers to accomplish their goals.

Impoverished. Leaders have a low concern for results and a low concern for people. In this behavioral approach, leaders focus on the minimal amount of follower and goal engagement that will get the desired result.

Authority–compliance. Leaders have a high concern for results and a low concern for people. In this behavioral approach, leaders focus on efficiency and goal accomplishment—typically at the expense of followers' well-being or interests.

Middle-of-the-road. Leaders have medium concern for results and medium concern for people. In this behavioral approach, leaders are only mediocrely paying attention to both followers and results. This typically results in adequate morale and satisfactory results.

Country club. Leaders have low concern for results and high concern for people. In this behavioral approach, leaders intentionally establish a comfortable and friendly atmosphere for followers—sometimes at the expense of achieving goals.

Team. Leaders have a high concern for results along with a high concern for people. In this behavioral approach, leaders foster dynamic relationships of trust and respect while engaging followers in accomplishing goals of significance and magnitude.

Before sharing a praxis activity, I want to stress that many training participants believe team leadership is the best. It is easy for us to assume that we should always be striving for leadership in accordance with high levels of attention toward results *and* followers. While that sounds worthy, without understanding the situation, context, and relationships between leaders and followers, it is difficult to understand what effectiveness is in any one situation. For example, in an emergency or crisis situation, authority–compliance may be the most advantageous leadership behavior to meet the needs of that particular environment.

Leadership Educator Praxis Activity

Leadership Theme: Behavioral Approach
Exercise: Extraordinary Leader (reflective [worksheet] activity)

The behavioral approach to leadership focuses on what leaders do, not on their surface-level characteristics (traits) or abilities (skills). When framing a leadership training around the behavioral approach, I love utilizing the Extraordinary Leader activity. This worksheet-based experiential activity empowers participants to think about their leadership heroes—those who they believe are extraordinary exemplars—as a way to explore and unpack what makes these individuals leadership models.

Extraordinary Leader

With the Extraordinary Leader activity, participants move from thinking about a specific leader-exemplar, to the characteristics that make these individuals extraordinary, to identifying if these characteristics are attitudinal, skills-based, or a gift. We purposefully and strategically guide them through the activity—one step at a time—to ensure everyone stays at the same pace.

In my 100+ times facilitating this activity, except on one occasion, *attitude* has received the most votes, *skills* the second highest, and *gifts* the least identified. When facilitating this activity, I believe you will find that by the end, it becomes clear that leadership is (a) in small part due to capitalizing on our gifts, (b) about maximizing our skills, and (c) significantly influenced by our attitude—the purposeful choices we make to behave in certain ways. I treasure this activity because it enables our participants to initially self-identify a leadership exemplar and then to build awareness that we are all capable of heroic leadership because it is mostly about our attitude and behaviors—not our skills or gifts.

Materials

- worksheet or blank piece of paper

Instructions

- Provide a worksheet or blank piece of paper to each participant.
- In step 1, participants are to think about a model extraordinary leader.
- In step 2, participants are to list a minimum of characteristics.

- In step 3, participants narrow their list to what they believe are the four most important characteristics of their extraordinary leader.
- In step 4, participants are to indicate if each characteristic is an attitude (a), a skill (s), or a gift (g). (Definitions and parameters for each of these should be shared so there is no discrepancy):
  - *attitude*: an intentional choice or decision that they make to think and act in a particular way
  - *skill*: a habit they developed over with time, patience, and hard work
  - *gift*: a trait with which they were born or won the genetic lottery
- As you move through these four steps, leave enough time for participant introspection. This activity should not be rushed. Additionally, in between each step, it is entirely appropriate to invite response-sharing about what the participants wrote. This can be facilitated in pairs, small groups, or in the public domain.
- Once all the participants have indicated an "A," "S," or "G" for each characteristic, they should be individually tallied and shared for a master compilation.
- After the "A"s, "S"s, and "G"s have been tallied from the whole of the participant body, slide into the reflective dialogue.

Reflective Dialogue Questions

Our objective with this activity is to invite participants to reflect upon leadership behaviors (attitudes), skills, and gifts. The brilliance of this activity is that the participants self-identify that a prime factor for extraordinary leadership is one's behavior—rather than being told. This illuminates that leadership is *not* about position, power, or prestige. Extraordinary leadership is grounded in our attitudes—what we do and how we behave. However, if when we are facilitating this activity, there is an occurrence where our participants collectively have more skills or gifts rather than attitude, they did *not* do anything wrong. In this scenario, we celebrate those findings and continue with a robust reflective dialogue to unpack their experience and illuminate their rationale for what makes an extraordinary leader. (If you are interested in seeing a live facilitation of the Extraordinary Leader activity, I include it as part of a no-cost quarterly virtual training.

More details can be found at LeadershipTrainer.org and by searching for the *Preparing Leadership Trainers: Tactics and Techniques for Facilitating Experiential Learning and Reflective Dialogue* workshop.) A selection of my go-to reflective dialogue questions includes the following:

- What can we learn about leadership when, collectively, we have . . . (share the tallied count of attitudes, skills, and gifts) as characteristics of our extraordinary leaders?
- What attitudes (behaviors) do you want to cultivate more of in your leadership practice?
- Who is capable of extraordinary leadership—and why? (Hint: The answer is *all of us*—all of our participants because it is based on attitude and behavior, which we are all in control of).
- What can we learn from this exercise that can be applied to our own leadership practice?

Situational Approach

Context matters. The situational approach to leadership is a slight shift from leadership focused on the leader—specifically the surface-level characteristics, skills, and behaviors—to a focus on the context and the relationship *between* leaders and followers. The philosophical undergirding of the situational leadership approach is that effective leadership shifts and changes depending on the many environmental and relational factors present in any one situation.

The situational approach to leadership was the first leadership model to suggest that there was no single-best, "ultimate" way of leading. Rather, each situation is contingent on many factors. There are two ways to understand—and work within—this leadership framework. To be most effective, leaders need to match their style to the levels of ability and investment of their followers—or be matched to maximize that relationship.

With regard to matching, leaders can adapt their style to fit the needs of the nuances of the situation at that particular moment and time. To effectively embrace this framework, leaders need to be aware of the context and make appropriate adaptations to their leadership practice.

In the other structure—be matched—different leaders excel depending on the nuances of diverse contexts and situations. To effectively embrace this framework, leaders ought to be selected appropriately so that their authentic leadership practice matches the needs of that particular context.

The situational approach to leadership began as a collaborative effort between two leadership scholars in the late 1960s. However, over time, Ken Blanchard and Paul Hersey's notions of situational leadership diverged. Since the late 1970s, they have each further developed their own models of the situational approach to leadership. Before detailing the contemporary differences, I describe the original.

Leadership, when understood from a situational lens, is grounded in the task behaviors (i.e., support) as well as the relationship behaviors (i.e., investment) leaders provide to their followers. To be effective in diverse situations, leaders shift their leadership style based on the skills and developmental maturity of their followers.

Within the original model, maturity was detailed along a spectrum of high to low. Followers with *high maturity* are able to complete tasks on their own and are confident in their ability to it well. Followers with *medium maturity* are either skilled for the task but lacking confidence or have the confidence but are lacking the skills. *Low-maturity* followers lack both skills and confidence to complete tasks. Once it is clear what the skills and maturity level is of our followers, we can enact certain leadership styles.

> *Delegating leadership style.* Leadership situations that call for delegating are those in which leaders need to provide low levels of task support along with low levels of relational investment. This is best employed for followers with high levels of competence and high levels of maturity because it empowers followers to become decision-makers.
>
> *Participating leadership style.* Leadership situations that call for participating are those in which leaders need to provide low levels of task support along with high levels of relational support. This is best employed for followers with moderate levels of competence and variable levels of maturity because it encourages shared decision-making.
>
> *Telling leadership style.* Leadership situations that call for telling are those in which leaders need to provide high levels of task

support along with low levels of relational support. This is best employed for followers with low levels of competence and high levels of maturity because it demands followers to do what they are told—and to respond accordingly.

> *Selling leadership style.* Leadership situations that call for selling are those in which leaders need to provide high levels of task support along with high levels of relational support. This is best employed for followers with some competence and low levels of maturity because it expects followers to "buy into" the ideas of their leaders.

Following a legal battle, Paul Hersey and The Center for Leadership Studies now own the rights to Situational Leadership. They have retained much of the original language, which includes the four behaviors (i.e., delegating, participating, telling, and selling). They have changed, though, the notion of follower maturity to *performance readiness*.

Ken Blanchard and his Ken Blanchard Companies own the rights to SLII. In his book *The One Minute Manager*, Blanchard along with colleagues (1985) described changes including language associated with the four behaviors. They shifted to the terms *competence* and *commitment* to describe the varying levels of follower ability and investment. Here, the behaviors, include delegating (high competence, high commitment), supporting (high competence, variable commitment), directing (low competence, low commitment), and coaching (low competence, low commitment).

From my perspective, it is less important to understand the nuances of these two quite similar frameworks for the situational approach to leadership, and more important to recognize that as leaders, we need to engage our followers in different ways. In order to maximize opportunities for goal accomplishment, we need to assess our followers' levels of ability and investment. This is why it is essential for leadership educators to exercise our belief that there is no one universal, perfect way of leading.

Leadership Educator Praxis Activity

Leadership Theme: Situational Approach
Exercise: The Great Card Race (physically engaged activity)

Previous leadership models posited that impressive leadership was a direct result of leaders—their traits, skills, and behaviors. With those approaches there was limited interest in the environmental considerations or relational nuances between those leaders and followers. Situational approaches to leadership posit that context and interactions matters—and different contexts (i.e., situations) require different ways of leading. Leadership is much more than the individual traits, skills, and behaviors of leaders; it has to do with many factors, including the environment, followers/supporters, culture, pressure of the situation, and so on.

The situational approach is the theoretical cache that we utilize to emphasize there is no perfect way to lead. A universally recognized best way to lead does not exist. When training participants who need that reminder—if, for example, they remark about someone being born to lead—we can (gently) inquire about which context or situation they were given the birthright for . . . and why. Based on their response we can offer different types of situations to both encourage and (gently) challenge them to think a bit more globally about leadership and the differing types of leadership needs based upon diversities in context as well as follower ability and investment levels.

When integrating the situational approach into a leadership training, any activity that invites participants to navigate diverse situations so that they change their leadership approach works. I particularly like the Great Card Race because it has an initially competitive and then collaborative element to the exercise.

The Great Card Race
The Great Card Race begins with participants arranged into two groups—possibly up to four groups if the participant body is quite large. These groups will be competing against one another. The competition is to line up in a very specific order, shoulder-to-shoulder, based upon a selected playing card that each participant collects from a central area. After several rounds of competing against the other group(s), all of the participants need to accomplish the same task, but as one large entity—collaboratively against the clock. Here, we've made a situational and contextual change so that during the reflective dialogue we can illuminate how leadership practices during the activity needed to change—from competitive to collaborative.

Materials
- deck(s) of playing cards so that there are enough cards for each participant to collect one during each round of the activity

Instructions
- Begin by laying out the cards, facedown, in a central area. (The cards should be spread out rather than stacked.)
- The participants should be divided into two, (possibly three or four) groups, and situated on opposite sides so that participants are facing one another—the cards should be in between the two groups of participants.
- Now, you'll share that the participant's objective is to grab a card, find the appropriate space in their group's line, and sit down to indicate their group has completed the task.
- When lining up, the participants are to find their "spot" based on the retrieved card, Ace at one end and King on the other. Once in line, a participant with a "five" should be shoulder-to-shoulder with a participant holding a "four" on one side and "six" on the other. If nobody on the team has a "five," as the facilitator, you can determine if there should be a gap or the "four" and "six" stand shoulder-to-shoulder. If multiple participants have the same number (e.g., five of hearts and five of diamonds), the participants should be standing (and then sitting) one in front of the other.
- Once the participants are lined up, they should indicate their completion by sitting. The first group to be completely sitting is the winner.
- You will then verify they are in the correct order based on the cards of each individual participant. If so, that team wins! If not, by default the other team wins.
- Once the round is complete, the participants can return their cards to the central area—facedown and shuffled—and prepare for another round.
- This activity should be facilitated for several rounds so the participants get comfortable with the competition.
- After those rounds, announce to the group that instead of competing, the whole of the

participant body is to act collaboratively, against the clock.

- As a collaboration, this should also be facilitated several times, each by significantly reducing the time goal to make it a challenge.
- Once the group has had a sufficient amount of rounds as a large group, settle the energy and enter into the reflective dialogue.

Reflective Dialogue Questions

Our objective with this activity is to highlight how leadership needs change based upon situation and context. In the first part of the activity, participants are competing against the other group(s). In the second part, a significant shift occurs and they need to work collaboratively to accomplish the goal. A selection of my go-to reflective dialogue questions includes the following:

- For the group that won the competition, what did you do to make that happen?
- For the group that lost the competition, why do you believe you did not perform as well as the other group?
- How did leadership change as the activity shifted from competition to collaboration?
- What can we learn from this exercise that can be applied to our own leadership practice?

Path-Goal Theory

Leadership is a process of navigating obstacles by motivating followers to accomplish goals—that is, according to the path-goal theory. In this approach, there is an emphasis on the relationship between leaders and followers. Leaders, rather than adapt to the developmental locale and skills of followers, prioritize the motivational influences of followers. Essentially, the fundamental principal of the path-goal theory is that leaders can enhance follower performance and satisfaction by focusing on their factors of motivation (Northouse, 2021).

To effectively implement this theory into leadership practice, it is necessary for leaders to understand the dynamics of motivation—as well as the motivational influences of their followers. Vroom (1964) suggests there are three components of motivation: capability of accomplishing the task or achieving the goal, belief that their efforts will result in an expected outcome, and confidence that there will be a reward or satisfaction once the task is complete (see the section in chapter 9, Motivating Others Toward Goal Accomplishment, for greater detail on motivation and motivational factors).

There are four common types of leader behaviors that influence the motivation of followers: directive, supportive, participative, and achievement-oriented (Northouse, 2021). With directive behaviors, leaders provide explicit instructions and expectations—with limited ambiguity and input from followers. With supportive behaviors, leaders attend to the emotional well-being and needs of the followers—with a particular emphasis in cultivating confidence and a cooperative environment. With participative behaviors, leaders create opportunities for collaboration and shared decision-making—with energy expended on generating and implementing the ideas and opinions of followers. With achievement-oriented behaviors, leaders drive followers to perform at the highest levels—with an expectation of extraordinary standards of excellence.

Follower behaviors are another factor influencing their confidence in achieving desired outcomes (Northouse, 2021). Leaders can strategically respond to these behaviors as a way to engage and motivate followers. Followers have needs for affiliation. Leaders who perceive followers' desire for affiliation can create an environment where they feel included and engaged. Followers have desires for control. Leaders who recognize followers' desire for control can provide opportunities for follower ownership. Followers have perceptions of their own abilities. Leaders who capitalize on followers' perceptions of their own abilities (or lack thereof) can respond in ways that empower followers or raise their level of confidence.

The characteristics of the tasks, projects, or assignments also influence follower motivation levels (Northouse, 2021). Task characteristics include three components: the tasks themselves—the literal work, projects, or assignments—for which followers' level of interest greatly influences their level of motivation; the authority system and the structures (formal and informal) of power that influence level of motivation; and the primary work group—those with whom the followers engage.

Followers become more motivated to navigate challenges and pursue objectives when various elements are present: when the number and kinds of payoffs increase, when the path toward goal accomplishment is clear and easily attainable, when obstacles are removed, and when the work itself is personally satisfying for followers (House & Mitchell, 1974, 1975). Conceptually, we can envision a path-goal leadership process to include four steps (Northouse, 2021):

Defining goals. Leaders—either individually or collaboratively with followers—establish clear metrics of accomplishment.

Clarifying the path. Leaders—either individually or collaboratively with followers—provide instructional boundaries.

Removing obstacles. Leaders—either individually or collaboratively with followers—encourage success by reducing obstructions.

Providing support. Leaders utilize personally relevant and resonant forms of encouragement to engage followers toward goal accomplishment.

Leadership Educator Praxis Activity

Leadership Theme: Path–Goal Theory
Exercise: Pebble in the Shoe (physically engaged activity)

The path-goal leadership theory emphasizes that leaders can effectively serve their followers by understanding and fittingly responding to their motivational needs. It is particularly important to recognize that leader behaviors, follower behaviors, and task characteristics all influence the type and level of motivation necessary to empower followers to work through struggles and toward goal accomplishment. By focusing on this triad, we can assist our leadership training participants in working toward goal accomplishment by tapping into the motivational factors of those with whom they engage. Furthermore, the four-step process (defining goals, clarifying the path, removing obstacles, and providing support) is an accessible progression that can engage leadership training participants in thinking through and actualizing opportunities to motivate themselves and others toward goal accomplishment. This can be facilitated with a printed worksheet, experiential activities, and/or small- and large-group conversations. Each of these engagements are utilized to assist participants in thinking critically and tactically about how they are working toward the results they desire. A leadership training, informed and structured by the path-goal leadership theory, can be arranged as a one-time workshop as well as a programmatic series with each session focusing on a different component of the four-step process. The Pebble in the Shoe activity is an experience that we can craft in our leadership trainings to highlight this progression—with a special emphasis on the obstacle component.

The Pebble in the Shoe

The Pebble in the Shoe is an experiential learning activity that makes participants very uncomfortable physically (yet, in a safe, learning-oriented way). We utilize a marble (in lieu of a pebble) as an obstacle—something the participants first struggle with and then need to remove. We ask participants to place it in their shoe and walk laps while in dialogue with a partner around the training space. This pebble is an obstacle that prevents the participants from staying fully present and engaged in their partner conversations. (For participants who are not able to walk, we invite them to place the pebble somewhere uncomfortable that intentionally disrupts their attention. For example, if a participant is on crutches, they might place the marble between their hand and the grips. If a participant is wheelchair-bound, the pebble might be placed under the participant's rear end or on the joystick of the electric device—so long as it is still safe enough to operate.)

Materials

- one marble per person

Instructions

- Begin by providing each participant a marble.
- While distributing them, make it clear to the participants that it is theirs to keep—because it is going in their shoes. (If comfortable, you can make light of it by referencing the pebble touching their stinky feet or socks.)
- Once each participant has a marble firmly placed in their shoe—or other strategic location—instruct them to find a partner.
- With their partner, their goal is to hold a dynamic conversation while walking laps around the training space. (As the facilitator, you can select a topic—possibly something

leadership-related—or offer to let the participant pairs select the topic. You can also decide if it is best to have one person talk for a certain amount of time and distance and then the other—or for it to be conversational. Another decision to make is to determine if you want the pairs walking and talking for a certain distance (i.e., laps) or for a certain amount of time.)

- Their path is clarified by providing these instructions and engaging with them as they make their way around the training space. You may want to ask questions or make comments about how painful the "pebble" is—to highlight and purposefully draw attention to it.

- Once they have completed their laps or the timer has indicated that they should pause, have them take their pebbles out of their shoes and engage in a second round of walking and talking—without the marble in their shoes.

- Once this second round of conversations is complete, bring the entire group together for the reflective dialogue.

Reflective Dialogue Questions

Our objective with this activity is to illuminate this four-stage process—particularly the marble obstacle—and how leaders can navigate these challenges toward goal accomplishment. A selection of my go-to reflective dialogue questions includes the following:

- With the path-goal theory of leadership, one process is to define goals, clarify paths, remove obstacles, and provide support. How did you see each of these elements during the activity?

- What impact did the marble have on your conversations?

- What impact do real leadership challenges have on our goal accomplishment efforts? What are some of these challenges that we are facing today?

- As a leader, what can you do to remove these pebble-obstacles?

- As a leader, how do you provide support in the face of challenges?

- What can we learn from this exercise that can be applied to our own leadership practice?

Leader–Member Exchange Theory

Leadership is a relational experience. The leader–member exchange (LMX) theory conceptualizes leadership as a strategic and dynamic interaction between leaders and followers. Prior to LMX, leadership scholars solely assumed leadership was something leaders did to their followers. With the emergence of LMX, leadership scholars began to understand and challenge that assumption, eventually shifting their attention to the differences that exist between leaders and their followers—at an individual level (Northouse, 2021).

The initial LMX studies discovered that leader–follower relationships were rooted in two types of experiences: in-groups and out-groups. As can be imagined, followers in leaders' "in-group" are better supported and more compatible. They tend to receive more information and influence than those followers in "out-groups." This is for several reasons—in-group followers may have stronger interpersonal relationships with leaders and are more aligned in terms of work ethic, organizational vision and pursuits, and communication, among other behaviors.

In-group followers, it can be assumed, have high-quality connections with leaders. These are life-giving relationships.

> Like a healthy blood vessel that connects parts of our body, a high-quality connection between two people allows for the transfer of vital nutrients; it is flexible, strong and resilient. In a low-quality connection, a tie exists (people communicate, they interact, and they may even be involved in interdependent work), but the connective tissue is damaged. With a low-quality connection, there is a little death in every situation. (Dutton & Heaphy, 2003, p. 263)

High-quality connections lead to personal and organizational benefits. In other words, the more people in leaders' in-groups, the better—for both individual and organizational reasons. As Dutton and Heaphy (2003) illuminate, with high-quality connections, people are more alive and healthy (physiological benefits); have greater psychological safety and emotional capacity (psychological and emotional benefits); gain clarity on self-purpose and developmental pursuits (developmental benefits); see an expansion of knowledge of self, relationships, and the world (learning benefits); and receive a strengthened flow of information and resource exchanges (interactional benefits).

Based upon what we know of high-quality (and low-quality) connections, in- and out-groups can be easily identified. In-group followers have a significantly stronger depth of relationship with leaders, resulting in vibrant relationships, enhanced opportunities, and a healthy work environment. This is juxtaposed against out-group followers. Their relationship, if not strained with leaders, is disengaged. Furthermore, they tend to be less involved, committed, and passionate about their work.

Leaders should not be satisfied with only some followers as part of the in-group and others as part of the out-group. They should strive to create the conditions for all followers to be part of the in-group—if for nothing else, due to the significant advances in productivity and performance when followers feel include and supported. Although there are numerous factors that contribute to being in the in-group or out-group (e.g., commitment to the work and organization, communication alignment, depth of interpersonal relationships, performance behaviors, and work ethic) Graen and Uhl-Bien (1995) detail a process for leaders to cultivate those high-quality connections and exchanges—what they call *leadership making*.

Leadership making develops over three progressive stages. In the "stranger phase," the interactions between leaders and followers are scripted, rule-bound, and surface-level. These tend to be low-quality connections and relationships directed from the leader to the follower. Motivations are self-directed. In the "acquaintance phase," interactions between leaders and followers are evaluative. This is a testing phase where leaders and followers assess if there can be enhanced responsibilities for the follower and increased social chemistry. Motivations are for the self and others. In the "partnership phase," the interactions between leaders and followers are strong. There is mutual trust, respect, and investment. The relationship has been tested, and they have cultivated high-quality connections and relationships.

Leadership Educator Praxis Activity

Leadership Theme: Leader–Member Exchange Theory
Exercise: Assessment (reflective [worksheet] activity)

LMX is valuable for our work in highlighting the need for participants to craft in-group relationships—especially as they plan to translate their learning into their leadership practice beyond the bubble of the training intervention. It is also valuable for how we facilitate our leadership trainings. When facilitating trainings, we want to be conscious of the in- and out-groups that emerge. If our participants are feeling as though they were out-grouped, we are failing them as leadership educators. By striving to create experiences where each participant feels valued, engaged, and included, we increase the opportunity for our trainings to be developmental opportunities and experiences for each and every one of our participants. Additionally, when facilitating trainings of an organizational group or team—people who work together regularly—we ought to be mindful of the currently existing in- and out-groups. We utilize this information during the training experience to strategically strengthen the bonds between participants while also avoiding any sensitive subjects and relationships.

LMX harnesses the energy between leaders and followers. Specifically, with this approach, leadership is a dynamic interaction between them. Because of that, an assessment (e.g., CliftonStrenghts, DISC, MBTI, True Colors, etc.) is a great place to start. With this type of experiential activity, participants are able to better understand themselves and gain insights on how to maximize engagement with followers.

LMX describes the importance of leaders shifting followers from out-groups to inclusion—in the in-group. With an assessment, participants are able to learn about themselves, learn about their colleagues and collaborators, and—most importantly, through the reflective dialogue—learn how to apply the insights to enhance their leadership practice based on their assessment findings. (Each of these assessments has differing protocols, costs, facilitation techniques, and even certifications to become a credentialed facilitator. A simple internet search can provide details on each of them as well as illuminate free options of similar, less scientific assessments.) Here, I offer instructions on facilitating assessment in a general sense. Each assessment will have specific criteria and nuances.

Assessment
Assessments are not tests. This is important to articulate—especially in the context of facilitating trainings with developmentally younger participants. It is not an exam. It is an assessment. There are no right or wrong answers. It has been designed to assist participants in discovering and understanding themselves.

The insights that can be garnered enable participants to make informed decisions, cultivate synergistic relationships, collaborate more effectively, and ultimately perform better when leading. The reason each of these assessments has its own credentialing and facilitator training experiences (except for the free ones on the internet) is because facilitating them effectively—to reap the greatest amount of benefit for our participants—is not as easy as leadership educators assume. These assessments require skillful facilitation and purposeful hosting of the reflective dialogue. Otherwise, their power is lost and the experience feels more like a game than a serious opportunity for leadership learning. In addition to the assessment credentialing opportunities within each of those brands, Leadership Trainer's Certification Program trains individuals on how to effectively facilitate this type of experiential activity—and many others explored throughout this book.

Materials

- assessment form

Instructions

- Provide one assessment form or the internet link to the participants.
- Deliver the initial instructions for students to read through the questions one at a time.
- Give participants time and space to complete the assessment. (Facilitation tip: Be sure to review it before facilitating to get a sense of how long it might take for participants. It is wise and suggested for you to take the assessment during your preparations to determine how long it might take your participants.)
- Once the assessment is complete, the participants will calculate or electronically receive the results. Usually, this is the time in the training where gasps and guffaws take place. These descriptions are often "spot on" and illuminating for participants.
- Depending on the size of the group, you can invite the participants to engage in pair-sharing or small groups about their findings.
- Now is when we, as savvy leadership educators, can shine. We shift from individual engagement with the assessment questionnaire to reflective dialogue. (Although I provide some questions, the dialogue should

intentionally focus on—from a participant perspective—what can be learned about myself and others to enhance my leadership practice. We should not limit the training experience and leadership development potential of our participants to just focus on learning about one's personality. That is good. A training with this experiential activity can be great if it is structured to explore how this information can be utilized to enrich one's leadership practice—particularly in the context of effective working relationships and in-grouping.)

Reflective Dialogue Questions

Our objective with this activity is to assist participants in gaining insight and clarifying who they are—as well as engage in dialogue about what that information means for cultivating synergistic and deeply collaborative in-group relationships with followers. A selection of my go-to reflective dialogue questions includes the following:

- What did you learn about yourself from this exercise?
- What did you learn about others from this exercise?
- How does this new insight and wisdom impact the way you can engage as a group or team?
- What might you do differently when you engage as a group or team member?
- What can we learn from this exercise that can be applied to our own leadership practice?

Conclusion

These industrial leadership theories and approaches laid the groundwork for what we understand to be the contemporary leadership industry and landscape. Although they are perceived as antiquated, they are very much infused into our leadership psyche and manifest into our leadership practices today. Not only are they ubiquitous, they are often unexamined—leading to unhealthy leadership understandings rooted in power, prestige, position, and personal reward. Rather than skip over these original leadership constructs, leadership educators should purposefully explore and infuse them into our leadership knowledge base.

CHAPTER 4

Postindustrial Leadership Theories

NOW WE ARE GOING to sense a dramatic change in how leadership is understood and practiced. By the 1970s, leadership scholars and practitioners recognized that the surface-level leader characteristics (i.e., traits, skills, behaviors), as well as the surface-level contextual and relational aspects of leading, left something to be desired. With this shift, postindustrial leadership theories began to broach the depth of a leader's personhood as well as their relationships with followers.

Transformational Leadership

Transformational leaders are agents of change—they are empowering and appeal to the deepest parts of our selves. Transformational leaders both inspire and elevate their followers. Often, when we dream of the ideal of leadership, the image is of transformational leaders and their practices.

Today, it is difficult for us to imagine that the epitome of leadership is anything but a synonym for transformational experiences. However, until the late 1970s, when James MacGregor Burns's (1978) germinal text, *Leadership*, was printed, leadership was solely viewed—and acted upon—as a transaction. The leader led. The follower, in response, followed. Followers were rewarded for how well they listened to and heeded the orders of their leader in order to complete tasks. Today, we recognize and align transactional leadership with management. Transformational leadership is something completely different.

Transformational leadership emphasizes goal accomplishment while also focusing on follower development in order to enhance followers' levels of engagement, growth, learning, motivation, and empowerment (Northouse, 2021). This was a significant attitudinal shift—from thinking about leadership as accomplishing goals at any cost to accomplishing goals while also authentically and wholeheartedly believing that leadership is a worthwhile developmental experience for followers. That is, there is a focus on assessing follower motivations, satisfying follower desires, and treating followers with humanity.

This leadership framework was *transformational*. It was a radical departure from the previous ways of thinking about leadership due to the way leaders see and act upon their relationships with followers. The pivot is emphasized by a focus of leaders on providing meaning—rather than just rewards—for followers.

James MacGregor Burns was an American historian and political scientist. He is the forefather of what we know as transformational leadership—what he labeled as *transforming* leadership. It was his original thinking and writing that invited a new generation of leadership theories and models to emerge. This new understanding of leadership celebrated the relationships between leaders and followers—and the ways in which leadership could be used to transform individuals. The following highlights his thinking about leadership—specifically as a force for transformation:

> Transforming leadership, while more complex (than transactional) is more potent. . . . The transforming

42

leader looks for potential motives in followers, seeks to satisfy higher needs, engages the full person of the follower. The result of transforming leadership is a relationship of mutual stimulation and elevation that converts followers into leaders. (p. 4)

[Transformational leadership] occurs when one or more persons engage with others in such a way that leaders and followers raise one another to higher levels of motivation and morality. . . . Their purposes, which might have started out as separate but related, as in the case of transactional leadership, become fused. . . . Power bases are linked not as counterweights, but as mutual support for common purpose. . . . Transcending leadership is dynamic leadership in the sense that the leaders throw themselves into a relationship with followers who feel "elevated" by it and often become more active themselves. (p. 20)

Exceptional leadership may also make a difference in transforming dormant into active followers. . . . Heroic, transcending, transforming leadership excites the previously bored and apathetic; it recreates a . . . connection with the alienated; it even reaches to the wants and needs of the anomic and shapes their motivation. (p. 137)

Leaders can also shape and alter and elevate the motives and values and goals of the followers through the vital teaching role of leadership. This is transforming leadership. The premise of this leadership is that, whatever the separate interests persons might hold, they are presently or potentially united in their pursuit of "higher" goals. (p. 425)

With a transformational leadership approach, leaders are dedicated to the learning and development of their followers. Essentially, leaders seek to transform followers by connecting to their emotions, values, ethics, standards, passions, and goals (Northouse, 2021). If transactional leadership is about nuts and bolts, transformational leadership is about hearts and minds (Van Vugt & Ahuja, 2011).

When thinking about transactional versus transformational leadership, it is not necessarily either–or. A leader's approach to follower engagement falls along a spectrum. On one end of the continuum are transactional approaches. On the other are transformational approaches to leading. On the transactional end, leaders capitalize on their self-interests and the exchange of those things perceived to be of value (e.g., financial compensation) as a way to motivate followers. On the transformational end, leaders are invested in the aspirations, learning, growth, and development of followers—as a mechanism to raise their levels of consciousness, transcend self-interest, enhance performance, and increase productivity (Dugan, 2017).

Following the publication of Burns's (1978) *Leadership*, Bass (1985) expanded upon this leadership paradigm by noting four factors of transformational leadership and also that laissez-faire approaches to leadership should be included in the spectrum. *Laissez-faire*, taken from French, implies that leadership can be completely hands off. In this approach, leaders abdicate responsibility, delay decisions, provide limited instruction and feedback, and engage limitedly to satisfy follower needs or motivate followers.

Bass's (1985) four transformational leadership factors highlight the ways in which leaders can assist followers in improving their performance while developing them to their fullest potential:

Idealized influence. Transformational leaders are purpose-driven role models who provide followers with a vision and sense of mission.

Inspirational motivation. Transformational leaders galvanize followers toward worthy goals through effective communication, storytelling, and emotional appeals.

Intellectual stimulation. Transformational leaders encourage innovation and creativity as a way to navigate challenges and work toward goal accomplishment.

Individualized consideration. Transformational leaders genuinely care about followers' well-being and growth at a personal one-to-one level.

An essential feature and notable shift from transactional to transformational leadership is an emphasis on ethics and moral grounding. Transformational leadership is based on an ethic of care—specifically from leaders toward followers (Kezar et al., 2006). Without an ethical grounding, Burns's original intent of transformational leadership is lost. With the absence of moral grounding, leaders with deleterious and "horrifyingly negative influences on society" (Dugan, 2017, p. 191) would be classified as transformational leaders. (More on leadership ethics can be found in chapter 6.)

Leadership Educator Praxis Activity

Leadership Theme: Transformational Leadership
Exercise: Shrinking Islands (physically engaged activity)

The nature of transformational leadership is the ideal—where leaders are just as invested in the outcome as they are about their people. With a transformational leadership approach, leading is a developmental experience where followers are genuinely encouraged to learn, grow, and develop through the leadership experience and their relationship with the leader. Leadership educators often forget how revolutionary this idea was not too long ago—less than 50 years. Now we see this stark difference between transformational and transactional leadership, which is what we understand as contemporary management. To be clear, both are essential to smooth-operating, successful organizations. At times, situations and followers call for leadership. At other times, situations and followers need management.

Transformational leadership radically shifted the leadership landscape. With this turn, our understanding and practice of leadership adjusted from a transactional experience to one where leaders expressed their sincere care for followers' well-being. The Shrinking Islands activity is an experience that can highlight this shift from participants acting individualistically at the beginning to collaboratively, with care for the others, at the end in order to accomplish the task.

Shrinking Islands

The Shrinking Islands activity is an experiential learning opportunity that engages participants to accomplish a collective goal—to place their feet within the bounds of a designated "island." I like to use brightly colored yarn to designate the islands. At the start of the experiential learning activity, there are plenty of island options (of many sizes and shapes) for our participants—enough so that on some islands there might be just one or two participants. As time progresses through the activity, participants will need to move between islands. In the end, there becomes only one island for all the participants.

With the Shrinking Islands activity, I've found that embellishing the story around the activity is a tremendous way to engage participants. For example, the participants are a community living in the middle of a vast ocean. Due to melting icebergs, the sea is rising and devastatingly impacting their island homes and community. With each round, more ice melts and the sea rises—which is the reason the islands keep disappearing.

For this activity, the way that the objective is described is critical. The trick is to articulate that participants need their *feet* on the "island." This is essential because the final island will need to be too small for all the participants to be standing together. Some will need to sit on the floor with just their *feet* in the island.

Materials

- yarn—to craft islands of different sizes and shapes

Instructions

- Begin by arranging the training space to have multiple islands of varying sizes and shapes with the yarn.
- Provide instructions that participants will need to move about the islands until the time stops (this could be up to 30 seconds). When movement time has ended, the participants need to find an island home and ensure that both feet are on the island.
- After a round or two, remove a selection of the islands—this should take place when the timer is counting down and the participants are island hopping.
- Continue with this process until there is only one island left. This last island should be big enough to accommodate everyone's feet—not their whole bodies.
- After the goal has been accomplished, settle the energy and prepare for the reflective dialogue.

Reflective Dialogue Questions

Our objective with this activity is to offer insight as to how leadership shifted from a transactional (independent) experience to a supportive, caring, and transformational experience. A selection of my go-to reflective dialogue questions includes the following

- How was leadership practiced when there were lots and lots of island options?

- How was leadership practiced when there was only one island option?
- What did we notice about our behavior when comparing these two scenarios?
- What can we learn from this exercise that can be applied to our own leadership practice?

Servant Leadership

If James MacGregor Burns (1978) was the first scholar to explore this shift in thinking about the foundational principle of leading—from being a transactional activity to a transformational experience for followers—Robert Greenleaf (1970, 1977) was the first practitioner. He offered a philosophical reframing of leadership—highlighting what it should be—based upon his experiences as a business executive with AT&T. Greenleaf (1977) emphasized that formal, positional leaders ought to frame and prioritize their work as *servants to followers*. This was a radical turn from traditional notions of leadership where followers are solely dedicated to the service of leaders:

> The servant-leader is servant first. . . . It begins with the natural feeling that one wants to serve, to serve *first*. Then conscious choice brings one to aspire to lead. That person is sharply different from one who is *leader* first, perhaps because of the need to assuage an unusual power drive or to acquire material possessions. . . . The difference manifests itself in the care taken by the servant—first to make sure other people's highest priority needs are being served. The best test, and difficult to administer, is this: Do those served grow as persons? Do they, *while being served*, become healthier, wiser, freer, more autonomous, more likely themselves to become servants? And, what is the effect on the least privileged in society? Will they benefit, or at least not be further deprived? (p. 27)

Although Greenleaf (1970, 1977) promoted this notion decades ago through his own writing and practice, it was only recently that scholars began to clarify this leadership approach and provide a framework for generalized practical application (Liden et al., 2008, 2014; van Dierendonck, 2011). Seven leader behaviors have been identified as critical to infusing servant leadership into one's leadership practice:

Conceptualizing/utilizing conceptual skills. Leaders cultivate a deep and holistic understanding of the leadership environment and context (e.g., organization) so as to effectively support followers as they shift obstacles into opportunities.

Providing emotional healing. Leaders demonstrate sensitivity to the personal concerns and well-being of followers while actively, authentically supporting them in restorative processes and practices.

Putting followers first. Leaders prioritize followers—and their work—above all else. This is the defining characteristic of servant leadership.

Helping followers grow and succeed. Leaders recognize opportunities for personal and professional growth and then proactively provide support and resources for that learning and development to occur.

Behaving ethically. Leaders hold fast to personal and professional ethical principles while treating followers with transparency, fairness, and honesty.

Empowerment. Leaders establish a culture of follower success providing opportunities for them to be included, make decisions, resolve problems, and direct their own work.

Creating value for the community. Leaders expand the sense of responsibility from the group or organization to the community. Servant leaders have a genuine concern for and intentionally give back to their communities.

Leadership Educator Praxis Activity

Leadership Theme: Servant Leadership
Exercise: The Great Balloon Grab (physically engaged activity)

Leadership educators should know that servant leadership is quite popular, in theory. Our leadership training participants may personally identify with the theory because of the value and service orientation. However, in practice, it is quite difficult for leaders to implement. Much of this is due to the need for positional leaders to relinquish their power and control.

There is hesitancy on their part to serve as servants to their followers—specifically in the ways described by Greenleaf (1970, 1977).

Servant leadership is most effective when followers are empowered and have the autonomy to make things happen. This can be a challenge to those in leadership positions because of their desire to command authority over projects and personnel. As leadership educators, we need to recognize the magnetic pull of servant leadership while honoring the reality that many leaders, in their practice, will rebel against the reduction of their power and authority. The Great Balloon Grab activity is a tremendous exercise to highlight the power of servant leadership because it enables participants to see how much more effective we can be—in an intentionally hands-on way—at goal accomplishment when we have a service-oriented leadership practice.

The Great Balloon Grab

The Great Balloon Grab activity takes a bit of preparation but can be exceedingly rewarding at emphasizing the principles of servant leadership. In this activity, each participant is provided three or four balloons. (The balloons should be preinflated prior to the training. As an alternative, if there is time, you can incorporate the blowing up of the balloons into the activity.) Once the balloons are in hand, participants should gently write their names on the balloons. These are then collected, shuffled, and placed in a different part of the training space or room altogether. (Extra balloons should always be available.) The objective will be for each participant to retrieve their balloons— the ones with which they wrote their names. This is a timed activity to see how fast they can accomplish the task. Typically, they begin by each running around the space, focusing myopically on getting their own balloons by themselves. It becomes a competitive frenzy. After this round, we help them to shift perspective, by sharing that there is a way to accomplish the goal quicker by reminding the participants about servant leadership. Future rounds lead to participants supporting one another by sharing responsibility for retrieving and distributing the balloons—with a collective, service-oriented approach.

Materials

- balloons—three or four per participant with extras
- soft-tip markers

Instructions

- Begin by preparing the training space with preinflated balloons.
- Share with the participants the initial instructions—that they will need to gently write their names on the balloons—and then place them in the designated area. (This could be a distinct area of the training space or a separate room entirely.)
- Distribute the balloons and markers. (It is best to share the instructions first, because once the balloons are distributed participants tend to be distracted, and there may be the distracting sounds of popping balloons.)
- Once the balloons are named and in the correct place, bring the group back together and share the second set of instructions—the participants will need to move as quickly as possible to collect their balloons.
- Following this round, which is highly likely going to be an individualistic approach, the balloons are to be shuffled and replaced in their appropriate spot. This is also the opportunity for any popped balloons to be replenished.
- Once the balloons are appropriately distributed, bring the group back together again and express they can be quicker. You should invite participants to brainstorm about how. Hopefully, they raise the servant approach. If not, it is entirely appropriate for this to be shared by you.
- Following the conversation, time the participants during round 2.
- As the group reconvenes, offer the difference in time between rounds 1 and 2.
- As an optional round 3, reduce the time allotment and challenge the participants to go even quicker than the first two rounds.
- After the goal has been accomplished, settle the energy and prepare for the reflective dialogue.

Reflective Dialogue Questions

Our objective with this activity is to illuminate that with a servant leadership attitude and practice, we can be much more effective at accomplishing goals. When we have a singular self-oriented leadership practice, at least through this activity, we are slower and less effective. A selection of my go-to reflective dialogue questions includes the following

- How was leadership practiced during round 1, when people were seemingly fending for themselves?
- How was leadership practiced during round 2 (and 3) when a servant leadership approach was employed?
- What are the implications for servant leadership in your contexts?
- What can we learn from this exercise that can be applied to our own leadership practice?

The Leadership Challenge

During my 6-month English-language teaching volunteer stint in Nicaragua, the tagline of the center was *acepta el reto* ("accept the challenge"). Students who attended the center's classes were expected to dive into the curriculum, work through language-learning frustrations, squash their inhibitions, and imagine their future with English fluency. Now, every time Kouzes and Posner's *The Leadership Challenge* is referenced, I am reminded of the commitment that students made toward realizing their goals.

Since the late 1980s James Kouzes and Barry Posner have been sharing their model for transforming values into actions, visions into realities, obstacles into innovations, separateness into solidarity, and risks into rewards (Kouzes & Posner, 2017). The leadership challenge includes five practices—navigated by two commitments each. This leadership approach is designed for leaders to enhance their own practice while mobilizing others to accomplish extraordinary things.

The five practices of the leadership challenge are the core of this model. However, the authors articulate that if we are to be effective at leading, we need to understand that leadership is a relationship—a reciprocal process between those who aspire to lead and those who choose to follow (Kouzes & Posner, 2017). Based upon data from over 75,000 people from across the globe, as leaders, we need to prove to our followers—or would-be followers—that we are characteristically honest, competent, forward-looking, and inspiring.

Once people have granted us the opportunity to lead, we ought to infuse the leadership challenge commitments into our leadership practice. By doing so, we encourage meaningful relationships, establish credibility, and increase opportunities for others to engage in leadership. The five practices listed in the following build upon one another and are cyclical in nature. When engaging in the leadership challenge, we continuously encourage reflection, celebrate accomplishments, and strategically adjust for the future.

Model the way. Modeling the way is about demonstrating the behaviors we expect of others. This practice is essentially "walking the walk." Rather than simply dictating to followers, leaders do with followers. The commitments (leadership practices) include finding one's voice by clarifying personal values and setting the example by aligning actions with shared values.

Inspire a shared vision. Inspiring a shared vision is about setting a clear, dynamic path toward goal accomplishment. The vision creation and implementation processes are not a solitary act. The process should be a shared experience informed by the dreams, hopes, aspirations, and values of the followers. The commitments (leadership practices) involve envisioning the future by imagining exciting and empowering possibilities and enlisting others by appealing to shared aspirations and ambitions.

Challenge the process. Challenging the process involves thinking critically about the status quo and acting boldly to experiment with new ways forward. Here we tap into the spirit of what could be—not sitting back and reflecting on what could have been. The commitments (leadership practices) comprise searching for opportunities to innovate, learn, and improve as well as experimenting and taking risks by generating small wins along with learning from and capitalizing on mistakes.

Enable others to act. Enabling others to act is about cultivating collaborations so followers feel engaged and empowered. As leaders, we relinquish power and authority so that trusting and synergistic relationships can guide the group, organization, and community toward success. The commitments (leadership practices) encompass fostering collaboration by promoting cooperative goals and building trust and strengthening others by sharing power and decision-making.

Encourage the heart. Encouraging the heart is about applauding the shared experience, celebrating the contributions of followers, and showing sincere care for others' well-being. By "showing the love," we establish a culture of gratitude and thoughtfulness. The commitments (leadership practices) incorporate recognizing contributions of others by authentically showing appreciation and celebrating experiences to create a spirit of community.

Leadership Educator Praxis Activity

Leadership Theme: The Leadership Challenge
Exercise: Bridge Build (physically engaged activity)

Like servant leadership, the leadership challenge is quite popular—especially in a higher education context—because of the approachable language of the practices and the accessibility of Kouzes and Posner's (2017, 2018) texts. Their 2018 publication is a university student–specific book, *The Student Leadership Challenge*, that is famously utilized on our campuses, in both academic leadership courses as well as being a framework for cocurricular experiences.

Leadership educators need to be mindful, however, that in practice, it takes commitment—as the authors suggest—to operationalize the theory in tactical ways. For example, clarifying one's values, fostering collaboration, and authentically showing appreciation take a significant amount of time, energy, and attention. It is easy to facilitate a one-time leadership training that provides an overview of the leadership challenge. It is another thing entirely to craft and facilitate a leadership-developmental experience that truly engages participants to *acepta el reto* ("accept the challenge") and incorporate these practices into their leadership regimen. For leadership educators, an advantage of the leadership challenge is that the five practices (i.e., model the way, inspire a shared vision, challenge the process, enable others to act, and encourage the heart)

can be deployed in a variety of ways: An entire program can be facilitated in 2 hours or each of the five practices can be a 2-hour (or longer) training segment if you are designing a training series. Of course, these five practices can easily align with diverse experiential activities allowing each one to feel both connected to the whole and independent. If time is limited or the training is only intended to provide an overview of the leadership challenge, one strategically facilitated activity will need to be all-encompassing. I propose utilizing the Bridge Build activity.

Bridge Build

The Bridge Build activity necessitates participants utilizing selected materials to collaboratively construct a bridge. Of course, I want to emphasize the flexibility and freedom leadership educators have in designing an activity that resonates with their particular participants. If constructing a tower is more feasible, format the activity appropriately and instruct the participants to build that structure. The structure itself is not the critical feature of the activity. Rather it is the participants playing select roles and working collaboratively—that should be the focus of attention.

Materials

- build elements—anything you want to provide to participants that can be utilized to construct a bridge structure (e.g., toothpicks, marshmallows, spaghetti, duct tape)
- notecards or Post-Its with each of the five leadership challenge practices—enough for each participant to have one card

Instructions

- Begin by describing the participant objective. It could be to build the sturdiest bridge (or whatever structure has the most resonance for you and this particular group).
- Then determine teams for the competition. This could be a random selection, a numbered count, a predetermined grouping, or participant self-selection.
- Once participants are with their groups, make it known that there is one caveat: Every participant will be provided with a notecard (or Post-It) that details the explicit and *only* role they should play during the

activity. For example, if a participant receives a Challenge the Process notecard, their objective, through the entire activity, is to challenge the process with which the group is engaged. If another received Encourage the Heart, they should be exuberantly celebratory and complimentary of other participants.

- (*Note*: There do not need to be five participants per group, nor does there need to be one leadership challenge practice per group. There can be several Encourage the Heart holders in a single group or even a full group of Challenge the Process holders. That randomness may actually lead to a more robust reflective dialogue about the importance of leaders balancing all of the practices.)
- After sharing about the caveat, provide all of the materials and distribute the leadership challenge practices notecards.
- This is usually a timed activity so ensure that participants know the time allotment at the beginning and are provided countdown warnings throughout.
- Before engaging in the reflective dialogue, the participants should present their bridge and test for sturdiness.
- After this sharing has occurred, settle the energy and prepare for the reflective dialogue.

Reflective Dialogue Questions

Our objective with this activity is to illuminate that not one single practice is better or more essential than the others. Rather, leaders ought to practice all five. For example—as with this experiential activity—if a leader is only persistently challenging the process, followers may become disgruntled about the consistent and purposeful resistance. A selection of my go-to reflective dialogue questions includes the following:

- What role did you play (i.e., what practice did you have) and how did that make you feel?
- From your experience, how could the group experience have been more productive or fruitful?
- What does it mean when leaders only infuse one practice into their leadership repertoire?
- What is one leadership challenge practice you want to enhance or better incorporate into your healthy leadership habits?

- What can we learn from this exercise that can be applied to our own leadership practice?

Social Change Model of Leadership (7Cs Model)

The social change model of leadership development, affectionately known as the 7Cs model, was drafted by a collective of leadership scholars convened by the Higher Education Research Council in 1996. The objective of this *ensemble*, as the contributors were known, was to reconceptualize the ways in which university students experienced leadership learning and development (Higher Education Research Institute, 1996). Specifically, the scholars wanted to enhance leadership learning and competency building while focusing leadership on positive social change (Cilente, 2009).

Social change is about creating significant, long-term change by focusing on the root causes of social challenges or problems. In order to bring about this kind of worthy change, we need to understand that the work—leading—is not a solitary experience. It is a collaborative, relational one. It requires vision, hope, compassion, and many other leadership practices detailed in Part Three of this book. By cultivating the seven values of the social change model, the ensemble argues that leaders can realize their social change dreams.

The 7Cs are values—all beginning, not surprisingly, with the letter "C." When infused intentionally into our leadership practices, these values enable us to create the significant, systemic social change we desire. These 7Cs are positioned within three dimensions: individual, group, society. Figure 4.1 shows a rendering of the social change model of leadership.

Individual Dimension

The individual dimension provides a foundation for leaders to consider their intrinsic beliefs, attitudes, and motivations. This includes the C-values of consciousness of self, congruence, and commitment.

Although social change implies significant, systemic transformation at a grand scale, if we desire to create this kind of (r)evolution, we need to begin with ourselves—knowing deeply and intimately our personal beliefs and values. *Consciousness of self* focuses on leaders reflecting on their internal state—their identities, strengths, and ideals.

Figure 4.1. The social change model of leadership.

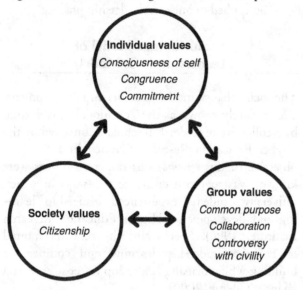

Note. Higher Education Research Council, 1996. Reprinted with permission.

Once we have come to know our beliefs and values, we need to act upon them. After developing a highly understood sense of self, we can act strategically—with consistency, authenticity, and power. With *congruence*, we purposefully direct our emotions and attitudes toward accomplishing the social change we desire.

Social change does not occur overnight in one fell swoop. This type of systemic, cultural change necessitates long-term engagement. The value of *commitment* implies investment. Leaders seeking social change are intensely devoted to their cause and prove their passion through their zealousness.

Group Dimension

The group dimension offers leaders strategies on how to effectively work with others to expand opportunities for generating social change. This includes the C-values of common purpose, collaboration, and controversy with civility.

Social change occurs when people rally together with shared responsibilities and collective action. The value of *common purpose* is essential as a way to bond and tether individuals together—especially in the long pursuit of social change. Leaders should ask, What are *we* endeavoring to change?

It is not enough to have a common purpose or the individual dimension values listed previously. Leaders need to purposefully invite others into the work.

By collaboratively partnering with others, the social change that is desired can be realized. *Collaborative* leadership practices increase effectiveness by capitalizing on diverse talents and perspectives.

Leading for social change is not easy. There will be conflicts. What matters is how to navigate and resolve these disagreements and diverging perspectives. The value of *controversy with civility* welcomes these encounters because of an approach laden with respect, honesty, open communication, and the pursuit of including all voices.

Society Dimension

The societal dimension encourages leaders to think beyond themselves and their immediate contexts as a way to ensure the social change they are working toward can have maximum impact. This includes the C-value of citizenship.

Social change is possible when we see ourselves connected to the communities and societies of which we are a part. *Citizenship* is an awareness of the interconnectedness and interdependence of others. When striving for social change, we recognize that the change we seek is not just for oneself; it is for all of us.

Leadership Educator Praxis Activity

Leadership Theme: Social Change Model of Leadership (7Cs)
Exercise: Intersections (physically engaged activity)

Similar to the leadership challenge, if facilitating a leadership training that utilizes the social change model of leadership, we can structure the training experience in a variety of ways. The entire model can be shared—with quickly facilitated experiential learning activities and reflective dialogue—in a 1-, 2- or 4-hour block. Or the training can be devised as a series or retreat experience where each of the three dimensions or seven values is explored on different days.

Although the social change model was originally designed for university students, if our leadership training contexts are with youth, nonprofit administrators, corporate executives, or university colleagues, there is no need to fret. The 7Cs have relevance for all of us—we just need to be mindful and strategic in how we offer examples and draw connections between the values and work experiences of our participants.

One way to experientially explore the 7Cs model is to employ the Intersections activity.

Intersections

The Intersections activity begins with participants connecting with others who share a commonality. Once all the participants have found a partner and identified their intersection, those pairs find another pair to create a group of four. This process unfolds until the whole of the participant body finds a common intersection with which they all connect and/or identify.

Materials

- N/A

Instructions

- Begin by sharing the first step of the process. That is, participants will find a partner and identify an intersection between them.
- Once in their pairs, they should discuss that intersection. One example could be having one brother sibling or being raised in New Jersey.
- After pairs have spent some time connecting, they should be invited to expand their intersections at a group level—to double their size by finding connections among another pair. All four of those participants should identify a commonality.
- Once the group of four have conversed, this process of intersection expansion should follow until the whole of the participant body is able to identify a single intersection point that has resonance with everyone.
- If there is time and interest, the whole process can start anew with individuals finding intersections with others. Of course, if that happens, the guideline is that any intersection that has been previously used by that participant is now exempt.
- After this sharing has occurred, settle the energy and prepare for the reflective dialogue.

Reflective Dialogue Questions

Our objective with this activity is to illuminate that leadership occurs in three dimensions—the local level (i.e., individual), the group level, and the communal or societal level. Of course, if a training opportunity is structured in a way that enables experiential learning activities for each of the 7 Cs, that is advantageous. This activity is best suited as an overview to encourage participants to notice the three levels of leadership engagement. A selection of my go-to reflective dialogue questions includes the following:

- What difference was there in finding intersections at the three levels: individual, group, and society?
- How did you see the 7Cs manifest in this experience (consciousness of self, congruence, commitment, collaboration, common purpose, controversy with civility, and citizenship)?
- Which of the 7Cs do you want to enhance or better infuse into your healthy leadership habits?
- What can we learn from this exercise that can be applied to our own leadership practice?

Relational Leadership Model

The relational leadership model, as the name implies, posits that leadership is relational. The authors—leadership scholars Susan Komives, Nance Lucas, and Timothy McMahon (2013)—suggest that the relational leadership model is not a theory. Rather, it is an aspirational framework that we can utilize to craft our own personal philosophies of leadership as well as engage in leadership practice, within our contexts.

Within the relational leadership model, the relationship between leaders and followers is the focal point of the leadership process (Komives et al., 2013). The other foundational bedrock of this model is that each of the five core components (leadership being purposeful, ethical, empowering, inclusive, and a process) necessitates the triad of *knowing-being-doing*. In other words, those engaged in the leadership process need to be knowledgeable (*knowing*—having an understanding), self-aware (*being*—having an attitudinal disposition), and able to make things happen—act (*doing*—implementing a skill).

> *Leadership is purposeful.* Being purposeful is aligned with having commitment to the goals we pursue. Relational leaders *know*

the systems, understand the contexts, and are dedicated to the vision for which they strive. These individuals are (*being*) hopeful, focused, determined, and persistent. When *doing*, these leaders identify goals, think creatively, involve others and incorporate their ideas, and stay committed when confronted with challenges and adversity.

Leadership is ethical. Ethical recognizes that leadership is for good—it is value-laden. If decisions and actions are unethical, it is not considered leadership. Relational leaders *know* how systems of justice and injustice work—and how their leadership decisions and actions influence those systems. These individuals are (*being*) committed to socially responsible behavior and social justice, trustworthy, and authentic. When *doing*, they do so with integrity, courage, reliability, and trustworthiness.

Leadership is empowering. Empowering characterizes leadership as something that reduces the obstacles and barriers that limit involvement while also encouraging the individuals involved to have ownership in the leadership experience. Relational leaders *know* about power and the power structures and dynamics present in the leadership situation. These individuals are (*being*) concerned for the learning and growth of others, value others' contributions, and are comfortable relinquishing their own power and authority. When *doing*, they share information, invite the voices of others, and celebrate and affirm others.

Leadership is inclusive. Inclusivity recognizes the importance of diverse others and perspectives. Relational leaders *know* that our identities play a role in what we know, how we are perceived, and the ways in which we show up in the world. These individuals are (*being*) open to differences, value equity, and are concerned for the marginalized. When *doing*, they build coalitions, ensure diverse perspectives—especially of the disenfranchised—are included and listened to, and strive to create more equitable and just outcomes as the result of their leading.

Leadership is a process. Process highlights the ways in which groups come together to create change. It should be intentional, synergic, and momentum raising. Relational leaders *know* group processes, the motivational needs of others, and how to navigate dissonance. These individuals (*being*) value processes as much as outcomes, appreciate systems perspectives, and are guided to motivate diverse others to persevere. When *doing*, they collaborate, balance purposeful pauses with action, challenge the group to perform better, and celebrate accomplishments.

Leadership Educator Praxis Activity

Leadership Theme: Relational Leadership Model
Exercise: House Drawing (physically engaged activity)

The relational leadership model was designed for university students who want to make a difference (Komives et al., 2013). I believe that many would argue the five principles are (or should be) universally recognized as important for effective leadership—across organizations and contexts and not limited to just the university. It is well received because the concepts are easy to understand and the model has name recognition within higher education, student affairs, and leadership fields. For leadership trainings, the relational leadership model is structured in such a way that leadership educators have many options for facilitation directions. One is to utilize the triad of knowing-being-doing. Another is to focus on the five core components of leadership: purposeful, ethical, empowering, inclusive, and process-oriented. A third option, which I highlight here with the House Drawing activity, is to harness the energy of the title—by focusing on relationship building and engagement.

House Drawing

The House Drawing activity empowers participants to express the strengths of their relationships by tapping into their inner artist and drawing a house. The catch is that participants, in triads, are sitting back-to-back-to-back, in a triangle. In front of each participant is a piece of paper in which they are expected to draw houses identical to their partners'. However, they are not permitted to look at their collaborator's drawing. They can only vocalize instructions.

Materials

- paper (one piece for every participant)
- writing utensils

Instructions

- Begin by inviting participants to find two other partners in order to make a triad. Once grouped, they should find a seat.
- Then instruct the participants to sit back-to-back-to-back (in a triangle fashion) so that they cannot peek at their collaborators' papers. Ensure they are all positioned before moving along to the next instruction.
- Now they should be instructed that they are to draw houses *identical* to their partners'. However, the catch is, they can only verbalize the house drawing—they may *not* peek at their partners' houses.
- This is a timed activity. Be sure to make everyone aware as to how much time they have at the beginning and then provide countdown reminders.
- Additionally, they should know that this is a competition to see which group will be hailed as the best collaborative, relational house drawers.
- Finally, it wise to keep the instructions vague so that each group can determine for themselves how they want to proceed through the House Drawing activity.
- When the activity has concluded (i.e., when the time has ended), the participants should be invited to compare their drawings with their partners'—and then with the whole group.
- After this sharing has occurred, settle the energy and prepare for the reflective dialogue.

Reflective Dialogue Questions

Our objective with this activity is to engage in a relational leadership experience. Through the reflective

dialogue, we can inquire about how the triad of knowing-being-doing as well as the five core components manifested in their house drawing. A selection of my go-to reflective dialogue questions includes the following:

- In this exercise, how were knowing-being-doing enacted?
- In this exercise, how were the five components of the relational leadership model (purposeful, ethical, empowering, inclusive, and process-oriented) expressed? (*Note*: These can be offered as a group—or asked individually.)
- What did we learn about strong, synergistic relationships through this exercise?
- What can we learn from this exercise that can be applied to our own leadership practice?

Connective Leadership Model

What if leadership was about balancing polarities? Leadership, then, would be about navigating the tensions that exist between time in reflection and energy exerted through action. It would balance our own internal development as a leader with follower engagement. It would also balance directing tasks with relinquishing our own control in order to delegate responsibilities. Lipman-Blumen (1996), writing in the mid-1990s, suggested that leadership effectively hinged upon balancing the polarities of *interdependence* and *diversity*. She saw these as two contradictory forces, pulling in opposite directions. A leader's task is to work within this tension.

Our interdependencies were increasing (and seemingly still are) at unprecedented rates. This has led to the increasing ineffectiveness of the authoritarian, competitive, and ruggedly individualistic styles of leadership (Lipman-Blumen, 1996). These interconnections among individuals—leaders and followers—necessitate a different type of leading.

At the same time, the importance and relevance of our diversities and distinctive identities have increased in greater frequencies—and still are. Decision-making from the sole perspective of the leader—one who wields power and privilege—is limiting, flawed, and destined for consequences. Understanding the values, seeing the vision, and hearing the voices of diverse others—especially the marginalized and disempowered—should be of paramount concern to leaders.

Interdependence and diversity are perceived paradoxically. In the throes of enormous—and often uncomfortable—change, to seek the shelter of our familiar distinctive identities is our modus operandi. We revert back to where we have comfort, familiarity, and a sense of home, rather than pursue that which causes uneasiness and angst. Engaging with others and their otherness is often unfamiliar and uncomfortable.

As leadership educators dedicated to the learning, growth, and development of our participants, our objective, as the late educator Peter Magolda used to teach those of us who studied with him at Miami University (Ohio), is to make what is perceived to be the strange familiar—and the familiar, strange. Doing so enables us, in our leadership trainings and other leadership contexts, to navigate this tension between interdependence and diversity, among other polarities.

Lipman-Blumen (1996) suggests that this connective era is both (a) bristling with unprecedented problems where solutions to earlier dilemmas are essentially irrelevant and, all the while, (b) marked by constant jostling and movement in the connections among people, organizations, and ideas. The challenges leaders face in this era include shorter and shorter time frames in which to make decisions, limited second chances, the need to diagnose and solve labyrinthine problems with innovative solutions, the ability to see systems so as to achieve goals beyond the initial problem, the difficulties caused by organizational boundaries and physical borders, and thinking and planning for the long term while succeeding in the short term.

The consistent leadership decision-making backdrop of these challenges are the tensions between interdependence and diversity. In this new connected era, there is a desire for leaders who can effectively navigate these tensions. These leaders focus on six domains:

- using ethical decision-making to navigate organizational currents, negotiate conflict, solve group problems, and expand supporters' abilities and loyalties by entrusting them with challenging tasks
- acting from a place of authenticity and accountability
- building community and connections so that a welcoming environment and sense of belonging can be cultivated

- adopting a long-term vision and making decisions that align with endurance
- entrusting, enabling, and ennobling the widest set of followers by encouraging and empowering them to join in the leadership process
- embarking on and committing to a personal odyssey designed to discover deeper understandings of themselves, their followers, and the contexts in which they lead

In addition to these overarching domains, the connective leadership model illuminates nine "achieving styles"—behaviors—that are drawn from the reservoir of our everyday actions (Lipman-Blumen, 1996). Lipman-Blumen (1996) describes it in this way:

> Beginning in childhood, we all learn how to get things done, how to accomplish our goals. Given that we are raised by different types of parents and caretakers with different expectations and values, we all don't learn to emphasize the exact same behaviors. Some of us learn to confront tasks single-handedly, others learn to seek help; some learn to delegate, while others master alternative strategies for achieving their goals. Through trial and error, success, and failure, we also discover combinations of strategies that tend to work for us. Achieving styles are simply behaviors for accomplishing goals, social technologies or personal methods for engaging in the work of living and leading. (p. 115)

These nine leadership styles are grouped into three domains: direct, relational, and instrumental. See the model shown in Figure 4.2.

Direct Domain

The focus here is on mastering one's own task—and includes the intrinsic, competitive, and power styles. The intrinsic achiever's excitement comes from the pleasure of the work itself, excelling in the task, and meeting a personally meaningful challenge. Leaders have an internalized standard of excellence. Competitive achievers delight in winning and being "the best." Leaders are driven to compete and win against others—they have an external standard of excellence. Leaders thirst for opportunities to exert their influence. Power achievers revel in taking charge, coordinating efforts, bringing order out of chaos, and directing both people and projects.

Figure 4.2. The connective leadership model.

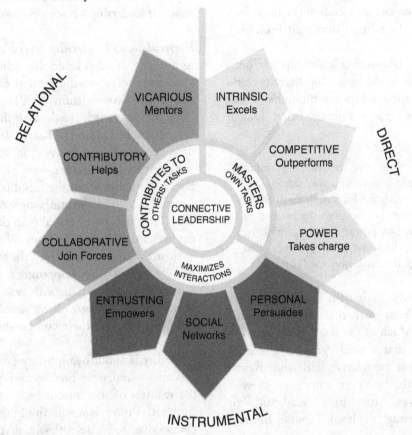

Note. From Lipman-Blumen and the Connective Leadership Institute, 1996. Reprinted with permission.

Relational Domain

Here the focus is on contributing to others' tasks—and includes the collaborative, contributory, and vicarious styles. Collaborative achievers are stimulated by interactions between group members—the synergy among these individuals is both the fuel and the reward. Leaders prefer to accomplish goals within the milieu of a group. Contributory achievers are gratified by assisting others in achieving their goals. Leaders recognize that identifying with others' goals and contributing to the requisite tasks will lead to accomplishment and satisfaction. Vicarious achievers deeply identify with and internalize the dreams and goals of others and celebrate accomplishments as if they were their own. Leaders enact supportive roles to encourage and guide others to success.

Instrumental Domain

Here the focus is on maximizing interactions—and includes the personal, social, and entrusting styles.

Personal achievers maximize their charisma, abilities, and past achievements as leverage for future success. Leaders use their traits and skills—intellect, wit, charm, physical attractiveness, and talents—to position themselves for success. Social achievers amplify relationships and networks so they can be leveraged toward goal achievement. Leaders use their relationships to position themselves for success. Entrusting achievers wholeheartedly believe that everyone, if given the opportunity, can contribute in personally meaningful and rewarding ways toward goals. Leaders assume that others want to be involved and assist.

The connective leadership model is an important contribution to the leadership landscape and can be a valuable resource for leadership educators. The premise of the model suggests that leaders engage ethically, authentically, relationally, reflectively, and in ways that focus on the long term with serious and significant investment from followers. The achieving styles can also be utilized strategically by leadership educators to help participants understand the rationale behind their leadership behaviors and craft ways to unlock other styles that can be infused into their leadership practice.

Notwithstanding, connective leadership has been excluded from much of the leadership literature and conversation—even though Lipman-Blumen's (1996) book was nominated for a Pulitzer Prize. Dugan (2017) reflects:

> For over 20 years, connective leadership has influenced how leadership is enacted across sectors. . . . The omission of connective leadership from many leadership texts is inexplicable given the breadth of its impact. . . . This says a great deal about how the dominant leadership literature privileges works that do little to challenge the status quo. (p. 228)

I agree with Dugan (2017) that the dominant leadership literature privileges work that resists confronting the status quo. Much of the leadership literature is pop culture stuff that is rarely grounded in anything substantial. The connective leadership model has remarkable depth. However, some may view it as inaccessible. It was written by an academic. For example, halfway through the book, Lipman-Blumen (1996) asserts,

> This chapter first describes the intellectual impetus behind the model. It then reviews the early work on achieving styles and the intellectual process that eventually linked achieving styles to connective leadership. We then delineate the model, its empirical base, and three instruments developed to test and apply the model. (p. 114)

Toward the end of the book, she writes, "In some inchoate way, we sense that despite our Odyssean search leadership remains an immanent, mysterious process" (p. 325). I wonder, if leadership is something that is available to everyone—not just the elite and academically privileged—if this is the language we utilize?

It should also not be shrugged off that Jean Lipman-Blumen is a woman. The extreme majority of leadership scholars in the mid-1990s were men (White men to be exact). I can only assume and imagine that she was not perceived as a trusted source or had the same level of recognition compared to male scholar-counterparts,

regardless of her remarkable credentials and significant depth of leadership knowledge.

Koestenbaum's Leadership Diamond

As an aside, another leadership scholar, writing at this same time, explores this notion of balancing polarities. Peter Koestenbaum (1991) proposes that the work of leaders is in navigating the tension between four forces. His notion is that, if we are able to balance these tensions effectively—the contradictory ideas and conflicting emotions—we will exhibit greatness. He suggests that when the mind is stretched, it never reverts back to its limiting, tightened dimensions— the greater the space created with this healthy tension, the better the leadership (Koestenbaum, 1991).

Structurally, his model is in the shape of a diamond. It is comprised of four opposing forces—*ethics* in tension with *courage* along with *reality* in tension with *vision*. Figure 4.3 provides a visual representation of the diamond with these components in tension with one another.

Reality is about being firmly grounded in the here and now—understanding, accepting, and coping with the realities of the current leadership situations and contexts. Vision is about thinking big, maintaining perspective, being relentlessly alert, and seeing with

Figure 4.3. The leadership diamond model.

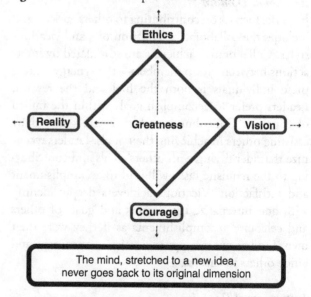

Note. Adapted from *Leadership: The Inner Side of Greatness* (p. 33) by P. Koestenbaum, 1991, Jossey-Bass. Reprinted with permission.

clarity—it is "having a sense of legacy and destiny and at all times keeping that sense in view" (Koestenbaum, 1991, p. 84). Here, we hold the tension between thinking and doing, reflecting upon and holding firmly to our vision, while recognizing the reality of our current contexts and situations.

The other tension within this diamond is between *courage* and *ethics*. Courage refers to the willingness for risk—to act with sustained initiative. This is balanced with ethics. Ethical leaders, in the midst of real challenges and obstacles, lead from their authentic selves and deeply engrained character. In the words of Koestenbaum (1991), ethics means "you know the power of love and that you act on that wisdom. . . .[Leaders] appreciate the personal enrichment that comes from being of service" (p. 89). With this tension, we have the courage to advance opportunities in ways that align with our integrity and authentic selves. If this model sparks your interest, I highly recommend *Leadership: The Inner Side of Greatness*, where he provides immense detail on the diamond model and each of these tensions.

Leadership Educator Praxis Activity

Leadership Theme: Connective Leadership Model
Exercise: Rope Pull (physically engaged activity)

Connective leadership is about navigating the tensions that exist between time in reflection and energy exerted through action. With this leadership framework, leaders balance their own internal priorities with that of their followers and groups. Although the formal leadership model expresses the two polarities of interdependence and diversity, for the sake of the Rope Pull activity, we expressly focus on notions of tension as well as self in connection to others.

Rope Pull

The Rope Pull activity is one of the more physically strenuous activities offered in this book. Participants begin by sitting on the floor with the soles of their feet flat against the ground. They will be arranged in a zigzag order so that their legs are crisscrossed with the participants sitting across from them—see Figure 4.4

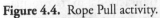
Figure 4.4. Rope Pull activity.

Note. Reprinted with permission.

for reference. A long heavy-duty rope is laid on top of their toes. Once everyone is situated appropriately, as a group, they will need to use the rope and, in one fell swoop, lift themselves from sitting to standing without falling over or falling back.

Materials

- long, heavy-duty rope (in the climbing, sailing, or exercise TRX style as appropriate)

Instructions

- Begin by laying the rope on the floor in a straight line. There should be plenty of space on either side of the rope—for the participants and to ensure that when someone loses balance, they do not back into furniture, a wall, or something else more dangerous.
- Participants are then instructed to find a partner and sit down across from one another—one on either side of the rope. (It is best if partners are roughly the same height, although not required.)
- Then they are to crisscross their legs, under the rope, in a zipper formation so that the feet are arranged in an every-other zigzag configuration.
- At this point, you should share the objective—to collectively, in one fell swoop, move from sitting to standing (in unison) without toppling forward or backward.
- After the instructions are provided, participants should have time to ask questions and discuss among themselves how they should proceed.
- Most likely, it will take three or four attempts before they are able to accomplish the task.
- *Note*: To do so, the rope will need to be pulled tight—with an appropriate amount of tension—and participants will need to trust one another. Additionally, it is wise to have participants of similar weight and height across from one another—although not a necessity.
- After the participants complete the task, they will be elated. This is great energy to capitalize on for the reflective dialogue.

Reflective Dialogue Questions

Our objective with this activity is to explore the tensions that exist between reflection and action as well as self and other. Both are significant components of this experiential learning activity. A selection of my go-to reflective dialogue questions includes the following:

- In this exercise, how did you balance the tension between reflection (the planning and dialogue with the group) and action (lifting yourselves up)?
- In this exercise, how did you balance the tension between yourself doing the work and working in concert with the others in the group?
- What did we learn about strong, synergistic relationships through this exercise?
- What can we learn from this exercise that can be applied to our own leadership practice?

Bad Leadership

Bad leadership is not actually a leadership theory, model, or framework. Notwithstanding, it is important to understand, especially in the context of this leadership transition from transactional to transformational approaches of leading. As leadership began to be understood as a developmental experience guided by positive outcomes for followers, leadership scholars began to study and explore what was meant by *bad* leadership.

Kellerman (2004) crafted a continuum of bad leadership. Generally, bad leadership is understood and characterized as either ineffective or unethical—with many subcategories within each.

Ineffective bad leadership is the failure to produce the desired change or accomplish stated goals. Ineffective leadership includes *incompetence*—leaders lacking the will or skill to be effective, *rigidity*—leaders' unwillingness to adapt to new ideas or information, and *intemperance*—leaders' lack of self-control, which is aided by others who are unable/unwilling to intervene.

Unethical bad leadership is the failure to distinguish right from wrong. Unethical leadership includes *callousness*—leaders who are unkind and uncaring for the needs and concerns of others; *corruption*—leaders who lie, cheat, and steal for personal gain; *insularity*—leaders who disregard the health, safety, and well-being of others; and those who are outright *evil*—leaders who purposefully inflict physical or psychological harm on others.

Ineffective leadership is easier to respond to. It is quickly identifiable and is often unintended. Once raised, leaders can make intentional improvements to be more effective. Unethical leadership is completely different. This has much to do with the intentionality of leaders to act, specifically in this manner, to achieve ends that align with their personal desires—regardless of the impact it has on others or their organizations. Unethical leadership is commonly referred to as *toxic* leadership.

Lipman-Blumen (2005) found that toxic leaders have certain distinguishable characteristics and actions. Toxic leaders characteristically lack integrity, act with arrogance, engage in corrupt behaviors, want for more with a focus on personal greed, consistently fail to act with competence and effectiveness—especially when attempting to solve critical problems and make significant decisions, and disregard how their actions impact their own wellness and the well-being of others. In practice toxic leadership includes violating basic standards of human rights through intimidation, marginalization, demoralization, and other acts of harm; dictating to followers that they, as the leaders, are the only people who command authority and decision-making capabilities; playing venomously into the fears and concerns of the followers; failing to nurture future leaders and an unwillingness to distribute or transition power to others; and treating followers well—while persuading them to hate and/or destroy others.

Kusy and Halloway (2009) add to this list by sharing that toxic leaders engage in three distinct actions: shaming through humiliation, sarcasm, and mistake-pointing; acting with hostility in a passive manner including passive aggression, distrusting of others' opinions, being territorial, and verbally attacking others when receiving negative feedback; and sabotaging their team by surveilling, meddling in team members' affairs, and abusing their power to punish others.

Where does this toxicity come from? One scholar suggests it is rooted in self-preservation (Carter, 2011). Leaders, in both the conscious and subconscious mind, ask, What actions will lead to my own protection and advancement? If leadership decisions are not for their own benefit, leaders won't act in accordance with them—or may defy those decisions.

Baron-Cohen (2011) has studied the science of evil. He recognizes that the first step is to see others as objects. Rather than see followers for their humanity, toxic and evil leaders see them as either an object

in the way of accomplishing goals or as something to be strategically utilized to achieve certain results. As leadership educators, the first step to curbing toxic leadership is to train our participants to see the humanity, value, and worth in others—even those we may deem as enemies.

Leadership Educator Praxis Activity

Leadership Theme: Bad Leadership
Exercise: Collage (reflective [artistic/creative] activity)

For leadership educators, understanding bad leadership is imperative. Many of our participants may be struggling with bad leaders in their organizations or communities—or very well may be bad leaders themselves. By understanding nuances of bad leadership, we can craft training experiences that aim to make restorative changes. We need to understand the spectrum of bad leadership as well as the root causes. With this knowledge, we can guide our participants toward healthier leadership practices—as both leaders and followers. A Collage activity encourages participants to think deeply about what they understand bad leadership to be and to act creatively to showcase—and then share—this understanding.

Collage

A Collage activity empowers participants to think creatively and then visually showcase their creativity. Essentially, participants are provided magazines, glue, and construction paper or cardboard to serve as a base. They then rummage through the magazines to select exemplars of that topic—in this case, bad leadership. Once compiled, participants are invited to share their collage with partners, small groups, or with the participant body as a whole.

Materials

- magazines, lots and lots of magazines for participants to review and cut up
- glue or another adhesive
- construction paper or cardboard to serve as a base of the collage

Instructions

- When it is time for the activity to begin, invite participants to clear off their space. It is best for this activity to be on a table or a hard surface.

- Provide the materials (magazines, glue, and construction paper) for the participants.
- Share with them that the idea is for them to create collages of intermixing pictures—cut from the magazines and glued to the construction paper—in a way that articulates bad leadership. If they see something in the magazines that they believe is an exemplar or model of bad leadership, they should cut it out and place it in a personal collection. Once the collection is sizeable and they feel ready to move on from the magazines, they can then begin to arrange and glue these pictures on the construction paper.
- Once the pictures are placed and glued, we can slide into the reflective dialogue.

Reflective Dialogue Questions

Our objective with this activity is to creatively explore our participants' notions of bad leadership. A selection of my go-to reflective dialogue questions includes the following:

- How did it feel to be searching for models and exemplars of bad leadership?
- How easy was it for you to find these models and exemplars of bad leadership?

- How do we see these models and exemplars of bad leadership in our day-to-day lives outside of this training bubble?
- What can we learn from this exercise that can be applied to our own leadership practice?
- *Note*: A bonus activity following the reflective dialogue—depending on the participants and how attached they might be to their collages—might be to cut up all of the collages or to safely burn them. We would do this as a symbolic gesture to relinquish bad leadership and to focus on our own good leadership practices and healthy habits as we leave the training bubble.

Conclusion

The postindustrial leadership theories brought about a significant shift in how leadership was thought of and engaged. Here leadership is no longer about surface-level traits, skills, and behaviors. With this shift, leadership is about cultivating substantial relationships with followers—connections that transform followers because of how leaders can be of service to them and their collective pursuits.

CHAPTER 5

Contemporary Leadership Theories

ASECOND SEISMIC LEADERSHIP CULTURAL shift occurred in the 1990s and into the 2000s. This shift capitalized on the transformative nature of leading by focusing on the developmental role and responsibility of leaders. These theories, as a collective, return to the leader. Rather than focus on the surface-level traits, skills, and behaviors of leaders—and the surface-level interactions between leaders and followers—found in the industrial theories, we now focus on the character, values, and principles of leaders—as well as the depth of relationships between leaders and followers.

Adaptive Leadership

Adaptive leadership, as the name implies, offers an approach to leading grounded in effectively navigating—*adapting to*—challenges. This leadership framework was introduced by Ronald Heifetz (1994) as a way for leaders to focus attention on the adaptations and processes necessary to effectively respond to changing environments. This approach emphasizes the activities of leaders—including mobilizing, organizing, empowering, focusing attention, supporting—and more. Gerunds (i.e., words ending in -*ing*) are utilized purposefully because of the implied action of these activities. With adaptive leadership, leading is not a passive experience—it is active, physical, and engaged.

Rather than view the leader as a hero coming to save the day, the adaptive leader is one who assists people in confronting and countering tough problems. Formally, *adaptive leadership* is defined as "the practice

of mobilizing people to tackle tough challenges and thrive" (Heifetz et al., 2009, p. 14). Leadership, in this context, is not limited to simply working through challenges—it is about enabling others to flourish in the face of struggles.

Adaptive leadership is informed by four viewpoints—with the notion that leadership is value-laden at the core. That is, leadership has value—it is something we assume is for good (Heifetz, 1994). Leadership is prized and something for which we aspire. Leadership is ultimately about thriving—not just working through challenges to get through them. As we adapt to the challenges, we become better because of the process. Adaptive leaders view their leadership practice through four lenses (Heifetz, 1994):

Systems perspective. Problems are complex and dynamic and interconnected through webs of relationships.

Biological perspective. People learn and grow (i.e., evolve) as a result of adapting to the challenges they face.

Service orientation. Adaptive leaders serve followers by diagnosing the challenges and activating followers to find solutions.

Psychotherapy perspective. A safe and supportive environment is conducive to effectively navigating internal and external challenges.

When these four viewpoints are combined, leadership, then, is about getting followers to engage in "deep learning that alters the assumptions of and values that drive individual and collective behaviors" (Dugan, 2017, p. 266). As part of this, leadership needs to be detangled from authority. Just because someone has authority does not necessarily mean they are actually practicing leadership—because at its core, adaptive leadership is about the actions of individuals, not the roles, ranks, or positions they hold.

As adaptive leaders, once we have infused these four perspectives into our leadership approach, our next objective is to identify the challenges before us. We know that, as leaders and leadership educators, we are constantly confronted with challenges. They are relentless. The first step to navigating them effectively is to recognize if they are adaptive or technical.

Technical challenges and their responses are clearly defined with easy-to-implement solutions. Adaptive challenges do not have clear solutions and necessitate collective engagement and decision-making. Often, challenges are a combination of technical and adaptive. It is the leader's responsibility, in part, to effectively determine which response will lead to an outcome where people can thrive.

Technical challenges imply a clear understanding of the specific action(s) that need to be undertaken (knowing the solutions)—and utilizing authority to make executive decisions and responses. For example, we are facilitating a training and the air conditioner is off. It is getting very warm. Here we know what to do and have the personal authority to confront the challenge ourselves.

Adaptive challenges have no clear or definitive actions to be undertaken. It is vital to work collaboratively—to mobilize followers—so that collective decisions leading to the greater good can be executed. To highlight this, we can envision that during the middle of a training we're facilitating, a minor earthquake rumbles. It has created a bit of chaos and lots of discomfort. In this scenario, there is no clear, definitive action to take and we do not have the sole authority to make the decision. The response should be collective—due to the nature of the challenge. Effective adaptive leadership necessitates six leader behaviors:

Get on the balcony. Adaptive leaders are able to purposefully pause, observe, assess, and understand the nuances of the challenge while in the midst of the chaos. "Getting on the balcony" enables the leader to see the big picture and interconnected systems.

Identify the adaptive challenges. Adaptive leaders are able to speedily analyze and accurately diagnose challenges. By clearly and quickly identifying the adaptive challenges, followers can be mobilized to respond with minimal exposure to limiting thoughts, attitudes, emotions, and actions.

Regulate distress. Adaptive leaders are able to manage the expectations and stress levels of followers. By regulating distress, leaders establish a holding environment that restricts destructive, destabilizing, counterproductive responses to the challenges.

Maintain disciplined attention. Adaptive leaders are singularly focused on navigating challenges and engaging followers to stay committed to the tough work before them. By maintaining disciplined action, the challenge can be resolved rather than ignored, forgotten, or worse.

Give the work back to the people. Adaptive leaders recognize that leadership is not a solitary act. By giving power and meaningful work to followers, dependency on the leader is reduced and levels of commitment and productivity are increased.

Protect leadership voices from below. Adaptive leaders are open to the ideas of others and purposefully listen to followers—especially those who have been marginalized or are on the fringe. Protecting leadership voices from below is a practice of inclusivity that enables leaders to gain the trust and confidence of others.

In addition to the leader behaviors, as leadership educators it is important to know and recognize the four common challenge archetypes. These four archetypes may often overlap, creating a complex constellation of adaptive challenges (Dugan, 2017):

Gap between espoused values and actual behaviors. Adaptive work is about clarifying the values that are promoted and ensuring the actions of individuals align with those values. As leadership educators, adaptive leading would be appropriately highlighting the disparity between a client's espoused values and their practices, for example, if their mission explicitly values diversity and their customer base is two-thirds women but they only have White male executives.

Competing commitments. Adaptive work is about determining the weight and impact of our competing commitments, sharing and educating followers about them, and ultimately coming to a decision to reduce competition. As leadership educators, adaptive leading is balancing the pursuit of continually adding more leadership training programs to the schedule while recognizing the need for high levels of preparation and high-quality performance.

Speaking the unspeakable. Adaptive work is about establishing a container where people are encouraged and feel safe to share their honest, authentic opinions—even if they may seem heretical. As leadership educators, adaptive leading is about creating courageous spaces so that participants are able to confidently share about their experiences and safely challenge the status quo.

Work avoidance. Adaptive work is about harnessing the energy of followers to keep them committed to the challenge with which they wrestle. As leadership educators, adaptive leading is posing questions strategically throughout a training—and especially when hosting a reflective dialogue—so as to keep people thinking critically about their challenges and working toward resolution.

Leadership Educator Praxis Activity

Leadership Theme: Adaptive Leadership
Exercise: ABCs Challenge (physically engaged activity)

Adaptive leadership has gained significant attention because it reframes how we think about and practice leadership. Adaptive leaders know how to confront challenges in ways that create significant change.

Adaptive leadership is an important framework and theory for leadership educators because of how accessible it is for our participants. The language is easy to grasp, and each of the six adaptive leadership behaviors (getting on the balcony, identifying adaptive

challenges, regulating distress, maintaining disciplined action, giving the work back to the people, and protecting leadership voices from below) lend themselves to experiential learning activities. We can also engage in activities that approach this leadership framework from an overarching perspective. For this book, I have selected the ABCs Challenge activity.

ABCs Challenge

The ABCs Challenge activity is a quick experiential activity that is packed with power. It seems so easy, yet, for the participants, it becomes clear it is most certainly not as easy to execute as first perceived. The group is expected to work their way through the alphabet—for an added bonus in reverse—to accomplish the task. The catch is, no one person can say two letters in a row, there can be no longer than 2 seconds between letters, no two people can say the same letter at the same time, and nothing can be written. This activity also works with a number count.

Materials

- N/A

Instructions

- Explain to the group that their task is to work their way through the alphabet or number sequence with the following rules:
  - No one person can say two letters in a row.
  - There can be no longer than 2 seconds between letters.
  - No two people can say the same letter at the same time.
  - No assistance from writing is permitted.
- Once the instructions have been provided, tell them, "Begin."
- (*Note*: It is important, especially at the beginning, to be militant about the rules. Make sure they start from the beginning each and every time a rule is broken. If you find that the group is performing well and making their way through the alphabet quickly, for a secondary round, you can enhance the challenge by requiring them to do it with eyes closed / blindfolded or so that they are facing away from the other participants. As a savvy leadership educator, you can stack these challenges to make the activity more complex,

which will further highlight the difference between technical and adaptive challenges.)

- After the participants complete the task, settle the energy and prepare for the reflective dialogue.

Reflective Dialogue Questions

Our objective with this activity is to explore the differences between technical and adaptive challenges. If this were a technical challenge it would be easy for a participant (who is deemed "the leader") to simply say the alphabet and be done with it. As an adaptive challenge, there is no clear leader, no clear process, and a need for the collective to work collaboratively to achieve the goal. A selection of my go-to reflective dialogue questions includes the following:

- Why do you believe this was an adaptive challenge—compared to a technical one?
- How does this experience equate with the adaptive challenges we face outside of this training bubble?
- Based on this experience, how can we be more adaptive in our leadership practice so we can better navigate these types of challenges?
- What can we learn from this exercise that can be applied to our own leadership practice?

Fundamental State of Leadership

What if leadership were not just about behaviors, tools, techniques, and practices that can be exported, replicated, and imitated—but as a *state* of being (Quinn, 2004)? And, what if there were two states of leadership? One was the normal state—how we regularly operate. In this state, we seek to reduce uncertainty and create the conditions for equilibrium. Here, we strive for comfort and control—we avoid anything and everything that shifts our balance. At the surface, this doesn't sound bad. However, when compared to the fundamental state, by practicing normally we limit our potential for greatness. Furthermore, we constrain ourselves from maximizing our strengths, authority, and opportunities to thrive.

When operating from the fundamental state of leadership, we increase our personal influence. This

optimum state is not about developing traits or skills—the focus is on cultivating a sense of one's own potency, influence, and being. Quinn (2005) describes significant differences between the normal state of leadership and the fundamental state of leadership (see also Quinn, 2004; Quinn & Quinn, 2015; Quinn & Spreitzer, 2006).

In the normal state we are comfort centered—we stick to what we know. We follow the path of least resistance. We reduce uncertainty, preserve our current mindset, limit our levels of (healthy) challenge, and avoid confrontation.

In the fundamental state we are purpose-centered—we venture beyond the familiar territory. We pursue worthy goals and ambitions even if they seem daunting. We move beyond problem-solving to purpose-finding. We strive for systemic, meaningful, and important change—and we bring along others in a collaborative way.

In the normal state we are externally driven—we comply with others. When we are externally driven, we try to appease and please those who we perceive to have power and authority. We make decisions based on others' values.

In the fundamental state we are internally driven—we behave according to our own values. When we are internally driven, we behave and operate from a place of personal empowerment and core values. We act with authenticity, confidence, and integrity. We know ourselves and are able to shine in our own light.

In the normal state we are self-focused—we place our own interests above others. When we are self-focused, we pursue strategies of self-interest. Others tend to be seen as objects of control or manipulation. We internalize and hold fast to a "What's in it for me?" attitude.

In the fundamental state we are others-focused—we place the collective good first. When we are others-focused, our relationships are strengthened due to higher levels of trust and respect. We have stronger resonance leading to increased synergy and cohesion resulting in our followers being more deeply engaged and committed to the work.

In the normal state we are internally closed—we block internal stimuli to avoid risk. When we are internally closed, we resist attempts to relinquish our own control and authority—thereby limiting the potential and opportunities for others. We avoid learning and development because they require change.

In the fundamental state we are externally open—we have a learning disposition and pursue opportunities for (healthy) challenge, growth, and development. When we are externally open, we become adaptable and excited about the potential for change. We are learning centered and take advantage of opportunities. We capitalize on our resiliency to shift obstacles into opportunities and problems into potentials.

With this model, shifting from the normal state to the fundamental state is predicated upon asking four different questions: What result do I want to create? Am I internally driven? Am I other focused? Am I externally driven?

What result do I want to create? When we are comfort centered, we seek the path of least resistance. We are constantly in a reactionary state—attempting to establish equilibrium by neutralizing problems—to stay in our "safe/comfort zone." By asking, "What result do I want to create?" we tap into the depth of our full potential and are challenged to think beyond our safe/comfort zone. It is this question that encourages the pursuit of making a contribution and difference in our community or organization. To ask and answer this question is to identify something positive that we want to bring into existence.

Am I internally driven? When we are externally driven (i.e., in the normal state of leadership), we attend to the expectations of others. Their desires, interests, and outcomes are the center of our attention—as is our desire to impress and control others. This may lead to both the disintegration of the connections between our own values and behavior as well as feelings of insecurity and fear. By asking, "Am I internally driven?" we focus our attention on our own desires, interests, outcomes, fears, and values. It is this question that encourages an integration between our values and behaviors. To ask and answer this question is the impetus for self-authorship in our leadership practice and life.

Am I other-focused? When we are self-focused, the result tends to be isolation and loneliness. Leadership is a relational experience, and a self-focused normal state practice does not allow us to maximize our potential. If we objectify others, we are likely to be objectified in return. By asking, "Am I other-focused?" we recognize our interdependence and the

social ecology with which we lead and live. It is this question that encourages synergistic connections, increased feelings of harmony, deeper levels of trust, stronger collective identity, and enhanced collaborative efforts.

Am I externally open? When we are internally closed we limit our potential by becoming attached to what we "know." Trying new things is irrelevant because "this is how we have always done it." Knowledge acquisition and learning are minimal. By asking, "Am I externally open?" we shift from an attitude of knowing to an attitude of exploring. We move from a fear-driven disposition to one that welcomes obstacles and challenges as a growth opportunity. This approach to leadership is likely to generate new strategic insights because we are not limited by past perspectives and leadership practices. See Figure 5.1 for an adapted visual of the questions asked to shift from the normal state to the fundamental state of leadership.

Leadership Educator Praxis Activity

Leadership Theme: Fundamental State of Leadership
Exercise: The Most Delicious Meal (physically engaged activity)

The fundamental state of leadership is one of the least well known of all the leadership theories, approaches, models, and frameworks included in this book. Yet it is, in my belief, one of the most powerful. Much of this is due to how the framework is positioned—through questions. Rather than dictate that one should move from the normal to fundamental, which is what we hope for as leadership educators, we ask our participants to critically examine four questions. What result do I want to create? Am I internally driven? Am I other focused? Am I externally driven?

Another beautiful thing about the fundamental state of leadership is that it is structured for us to craft a standalone workshop or series based on these four components. This theory is a favorite of mine because we can easily utilize experiential activities, reflective dialogue, and storytelling to illuminate each of these four focus areas. For example, all of us have real-world stories that highlight how shifting from being comfort centered to results centered manifests in practice and leads to positive change.

The fundamental state of leadership asks leaders to consider if they lead from a normal state or fundamental state. In the normal state we are comfort centered, externally driven, self-focused, and internally closed. We are exceedingly more powerful, self-authored, and effective when operating from the fundamental state. Here we are results centered, internally driven, others focused, and externally open. We know, inherently, that the normal state is limiting and the fundamental state is empowering. Yet these are not necessarily a dichotomy—one or the other. Leadership educators will want to honor the spectrum and utilize leadership training experiences to inch participants along from the normal state to the fundamental state in each of those four

Figure 5.1. Questions asked to shift from the normal state to the fundamental state of leadership.

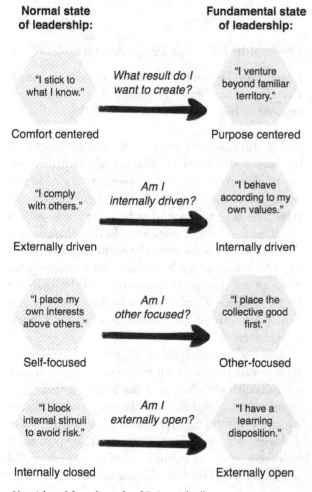

Normal state of leadership:		Fundamental state of leadership:
"I stick to what I know."	*What result do I want to create?*	"I venture beyond familiar territory."
Comfort centered		Purpose centered
"I comply with others."	*Am I internally driven?*	"I behave according to my own values."
Externally driven		Internally driven
"I place my own interests above others."	*Am I other focused?*	"I place the collective good first."
Self-focused		Other-focused
"I block internal stimuli to avoid risk."	*Am I externally open?*	"I have a learning disposition."
Internally closed		Externally open

Note. Adapted from the works of Quinn and colleagues.

domains. To highlight the difference and the developmental process, we can engage participants in the Most Delicious Meal exercise.

The Most Delicious Meal

The Most Delicious Meal activity is a small-group activity in which the participants are to craft what they believe is the most delicious meal. However, as you can expect, it is not as simple as just drafting a menu. Participants will receive a role, based upon the eight characteristics of normal and fundamental states of leadership, and need to act solely from that perspective. What is so appealing about this experiential learning activity is that it can be expanded or reduced in levels of time and energy investment depending on the nature of the training and resources available. What I describe in this book is a basic form— a simple written description of the meal. It can be enhanced, though, if participants needed to design an elegant menu, for example. At another level, which I have facilitated during intensive training experiences when we have the time and structure for an immersive activity, is to provide a budget so they can design the menu, go to the supermarket, and cook their most delicious meal for the group. This becomes a comprehensive experience that lends itself to team-building, communication, and many other leadership competencies that can be unpacked during the reflective dialogue.

Materials

- paper and writing utensils for each group
- worksheet with normal and fundamental state roles and characteristics

Instructions

- Begin by welcoming participants to your (make-believe) kitchen. (If you have a chef's hat or apron, that's incredible—this is the time to use it.)
- Explain that their objective is to draft their most delicious meal—in small groups.
- Each participant will receive a specific role— based upon the eight normal and fundamental state characteristics.
- *Note*: Groups can be of any size and do not need to have equal distribution of normal and fundamental state roles. What's important is

for the participants to experiment with these roles and notice the difference when acting or witnessing them in action.

- Once engaged in their roles, they are to cocreate a meal according to parameters you determine: three course, five course, seven course, specialty ingredient, and so on.
- Their meals will be presented to the whole group at the end of the allotted time.
- To add extra flavor (pun intended!) to the experiential learning activity, you can invite the whole group to vote on their favorite meal of all the options.
- After the participants complete the task slide into the reflective dialogue.

Reflective Dialogue Questions

Our objective with this activity is to experiment with these normal and fundamental state roles. In the reflective dialogue, we want to inquire about what the participants noticed as to the differences when acting them out or witnessing them in action. A selection of my go-to reflective dialogue questions includes the following:

- What did it feel like to act out your normal state role?
- What did it feel like to act out your fundamental state role?
- What did you notice about the differences between normal state and fundamental state role characteristics in action through this activity?
- How do you see these normal and fundamental state characteristics in practice outside of the training bubble?
- What can we learn from this exercise that can be applied to our own leadership practice?

Complexity Leadership

Although *complexity leadership* is the most popular name, this leadership framework has also been called *systems* or *systemic leadership* and *new science leadership*. Regardless of title, it is the confluence of at least nine different academic disciplines that contribute to a way of thinking about leadership. For example, it pulls from systems thinking to emphasize boundaries

and feedback loops, theoretical biology to highlight organic and evolving characteristics of organizations, and graph theory to accentuate connectivity and networks (Goldstein, 2008). With a complexity approach, scholars and practitioners believe we are better enabled to respond to the challenges of today and tomorrow than what had previously been at our disposal.

Complexity leadership asserts that we, humans, are brilliantly designed for leading, in an older, less connected, and more predictable version of the world—one that focused on efficiency and control (Garvey Berger, 2019). We tend to make decisions based on what we think is most probable—judging the future by what we have seen in the past. This then seemingly predisposes us (whether by cultural history or genetics) to suppress the swarm of changes we encounter (Uhl-Bien & Marion, 2008). Our traditional response is that of command and control. Our leadership predisposition is to respond by centralizing our command of the situation with top-down, hierarchical control.

Historic leadership assumptions and responses do not align with contemporary leadership challenges that are laden with unpredictability. For example, historically, leadership has been (and, I argue, still is) centered on the personalities of leaders and their power, position, and prestige. Leadership outcomes necessitated top-down coordination with formal and positional leaders exerting their force to shape and will these outcomes into realization. And leadership responses were (and are) framed and implemented in terms of direct linkages between the cause and the effect.

Cause and effect are like the sleight of hand in a magic show—they distract us from everything else that is contributing to the "magic" (Garvey Berger & Johnston, 2015). In our minds we create stories—especially when there is not a straightforward (cause-to-effect) narrative or when we have limited information. When these details are limited, we draw conclusions as to why that is and how to best respond. With a complexity leadership approach, we are better able to understand our patterns, habits, and judgments because we take steps back to see the whole system at play (Garvey Berger & Johnston, 2015). This then empowers us to be more intentional and explicit in our response to the challenge before us—without making up stories and responding to the fiction and fantasy.

Complexity leadership is an unsettling, complicated, and often troubling leadership model because it challenges our "givens" of leadership—specifically the individualistic Western mindset rooted in predictable outcomes, logical relationships, and linear cause and effect (Marion, 2008). Margaret Wheatley (1999) did not mince words when she offered that this individualistic mindset of leading is "totally inappropriate" (p. 6) for today's challenges. The leadership habits and solutions that used to work—top-down, transactional, power laden, using blame or accusations—are only going to, at best, *not* respond to the challenge before us. Or worse, it may result in the opposite of what we intend—harm, destruction, and even greater challenges.

Our contemporary leadership challenges necessitate a different way of leading. Complexity leadership proposes that effective leadership creates conditions where *localized* individuals are empowered to take initiative, make decisions, and build interdependencies. If we want to be effective at leading within these contemporary contexts, we need to (a) understand the situation from a whole-system perspective, (b) recognize that our interconnected networks create blurred boundaries, (c) honor the nonlinearity of cause and effect, (d) flow with the dynamism and fluidity of the challenge, and (e) remember that our systems can be only be influenced, not controlled (K. Allen & Cherrey, 2000).

Within complexity leadership, the natural catalyst of innovation and spark of change are the webs of relationships between the stakeholders. Leadership, then, is the process of influence that arises through these relationships and interactions. With this model, leadership is rooted in a highly engaged perspective of mutuality—*We are in this together*; interdependence—*We are intimately connected to one another*; and shared accountability—*We are all responsible for the outcome* (Goldstein et al., 2010).

To practice complexity leadership, we need to first change our habits. We can do this in several ways. For instance, we need to ask different questions. Currently, we tend to ask questions to confirm our hypotheses. We should shift to ask questions out of curiosity. When we change the impetus and way we ask questions, we can become more thoughtful, effective, and successful (Garvey Berger & Johnston, 2015). We also ought to intentionally seek out multiple and diverse perspectives so that we can see and interpret the system from multiple angles. We should invest in reflective space and meaning-making opportunities.

It's hard to look at modern life and see our capacities for reflection and meaning-making. We don't use our gifts to be more aware or thoughtful. We're driven in the opposite direction. . . . If we want to influence any change, anywhere, we need to work with this powerful process rather than deny its existence. We need to understand that all change results from a change in meaning. (Wheatley, 1999, p. 147)

Outwardly, we should construct generative networks of change and optimize relationships (K. Allen & Cherrey, 2000; Goldstein et al., 2010). In these networks, our objective is to enhance resonance among the stakeholders, expand the quality of information shared, and encourage noticing novelty. When leaders strive for equilibrium and stability by imposing control, we constrict people's freedom and inhibit change. Thus, we create the conditions that threaten survival (Wheatley, 1999). Rather, by celebrating connections, inviting information sharing, and empowering others to notice new things (or old things in new ways), significant, lasting, and positive change is possible.

We expect our leaders—especially those in positions of power and authority—to provide direction and create a sense of security that we know where we are going. Even if we, as the leaders, are unclear as to the destination, we can provide clarity around the direction (Garvey Berger & Johnston, 2015).

Doug Silsbee (2018), a thought leader and leadership coach focusing on mindfulness and presence, suggests that for all of us, regardless of our leadership roles, there are three processes for humanizing ourselves and expressing our humanity in complex times: sensing, being, and acting.

Sensing focuses on receiving energy and information. When we accurately sense, we significantly increase our clarity and access to important information. That, then, empowers us to wisely choose where we direct our attention.

Being concentrates on processing energy and information. It is our inner state. When we are attuned to our being, we are able to both observe our actions and reactions and intervene in cycles of mindless reactivity.

Acting harnesses the power of expressing energy and information. Silsbee (2018) articulates four practices for acting in complexity-appropriate ways. In acting, we experiment with healthy attitudes; develop fruitful connections; navigate challenges with fluidity, agility, and responsiveness; and ground ourselves in stability among the chaos.

Each of these three processes manifests in three domains: context, identity, and soma. Context relates to the environment. Identity is centered on our mental state. Soma refers to these processes in our

bodies. Figure 5.2 shows Silsbee's (2018) nine panes of presence-based leadership.

Leadership Educator Praxis Activity

Leadership Theme: Complexity Leadership
Exercise: Object Toss (physically engaged activity)

Complexity leadership stands as an affront to traditional hierarchical frameworks and models of leadership. This is one of the more challenging

Figure 5.2. The nine panes of presence-based leadership.

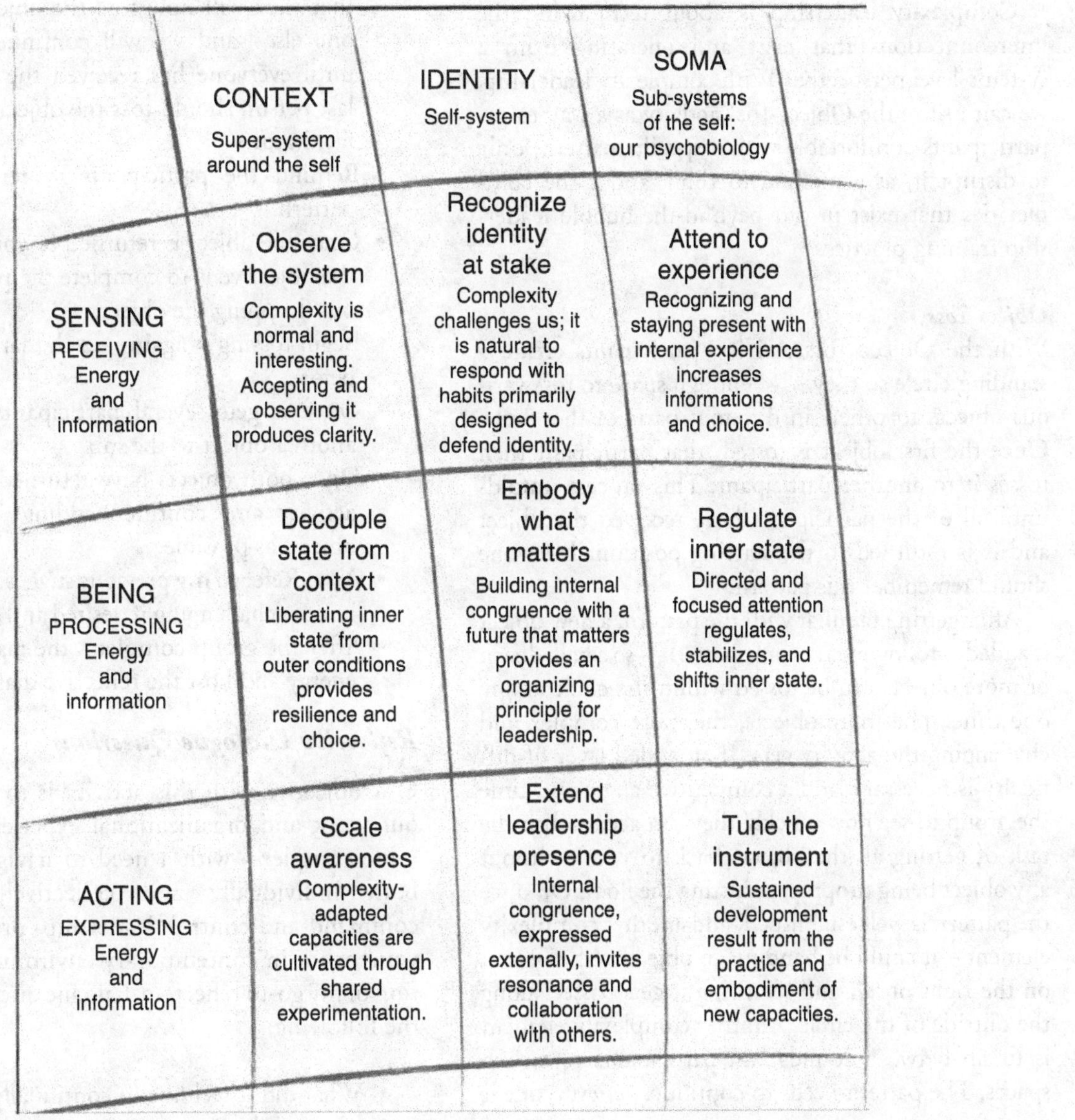

Note. Adapted from *Presence-Based Leadership: Complexity Practices for Clarity, Resilience, and Results That Matter* (p. 77) by D. Silsbee, 2018, Yes! Global. Reprinted with permission.

theories to incorporate into our trainings for two reasons. First, we need to dive into the literature and really know this stuff—not just the theory, but systems thinking in general. (More on this can be found in the Thinking Systemically section in chapter 7.) If we expect to facilitate on it, we need to be able to teach our participants about the fundamental principles and basic components of the theory. Second, complexity leadership is bewildering for many participants because it is disorienting. It is complex. It shakes to the core everything they've known about leadership. This is a wildly different construct of leadership than what people have been conditioned to understand. It also encourages wildly different practices of leading than those to which many—or most—of our participants are accustomed.

Complexity leadership is about recognizing the interconnections that exist and operating from a systems-level perspective. With complexity leadership, we can utilize the Object Toss activity as a way to get participants comfortable with a specific pattern, only to disrupt it, as a method to think about the complexities that exist in our beyond-the-bubble leadership training practices.

Object Toss

With the Object Toss activity, participants create a standing circle so they have enough space to toss various objects to others in different parts of the circle. Once the first object is tossed, that participant then tosses it to another participant. This process unfolds until all of the participants have received the object and it is returned to the starting position. Everyone should remember this pattern.

After getting familiar with the pattern, a new object is added—following the same pattern—so a half-dozen or more objects can be tossed within the circle at any one time. The more objects, the more complex and challenging the activity gets. If an added layer of difficulty is necessary, add a competitive angle and time the group to see how quickly they can accomplish the task of getting all the objects back to you—without any object being dropped or hitting the floor. Or, once the pattern is well established, add another complexity element—it could be handing an object to the person on the right or left and requiring it gets passed along the outside of the circle. Another complexity element is to, in between rounds, ask participants to switch spaces. The pattern needs to continue, yet everyone is an unfamiliar spot.

Materials

- objects for tossing (e.g., balls of various sizes, toilet paper, paper towel roll, rubber chicken)

Instructions

- Explain to the participants that they need to create a standing circle. (It is often easiest to do this by asking them to form the circle shoulder-to-shoulder and then back up 2 feet each.)
- Once positioned, explain that you will toss an object to someone around the circle.
- Toss that object to that person.
- Once that participant has the object, instruct that they will now toss the object to someone else—and we will continue doing this until everyone has received the object. The last person should toss the object back to the facilitator.
- Remind the participants to remember the pattern.
- Once the object is returned to you, share that the objective is to complete the pattern without dropping the object.
- Begin tossing it again—to the same person as before.
- Once it gets several participants deep, add another object to the mix.
- Once both objects have returned, restart the activity and continue adding in as many objects as possible.
- *Note*: Refer to my previous suggestion to make it more challenging if desired and appropriate.
- After the group completes the task, settle the energy and host the reflective dialogue.

Reflective Dialogue Questions

Our objective with this activity is to highlight that our work and organizational experiences are often quite complex—with a need to navigate challenges both individually and collectively. Traditional command-and-control leadership practices simply won't work in contemporary environments. A selection of my go-to reflective dialogue questions includes the following:

- What did it feel like to continually have more objects added to the mix?

- How does this activity compare with the complexities of our beyond-the-training bubble work and organizational experiences?
- What can we do to better navigate complexity—as individuals and as a group?
- What can we learn from this exercise that can be applied to our own leadership practice?

Theory U (Presencing)

Theory U—also known as *presencing*—introduces a leadership theory and methodology that empowers individuals to dive deep into their mental framework so as to create a synergistic integration of thinking and doing. Leading with theory U engages us in a process to step away from reenacting limiting habits and reducing our reactive (and often mindless) responses to challenges. When leading reactively, our thinking is rooted in downloading mental models from the past. Our acting, then, is a reenactment and reenforcement of limiting habits.

With presencing, our thinking is guided by purposefully pausing so as to increase our awareness and to see the interconnections that exist. Our acting is deeply connected to our authentic selves and serves the whole. This deeper level of leadership is coupled to the emerging future.

The "U" process was first articulated by a group of leadership scholars to engage individuals in enhancing their leadership practice (Senge et al., 2004). By engaging deeply in our thinking and acting, we confront limiting, reactionary voices. After becoming aware of our voice of judgment, our voice of cynicism, and our voice of fear, we are able to open our minds, hearts, and wills. Scharmer (2007, 2018; see also Scharmer & Kaufer, 2013) has dedicated his career to sharing this leadership framework. In addition to his books (highly recommended), he has created the Presencing Institute and designed a (free) EdX course—ULab—as a way to empower individuals from across the globe to move from reactive learning and leadership practices to deeper learning and leadership practices (www. presencing.org).

In its simplest construct, theory U encourages us to *observe observe observe*. In this phase, we spend time gathering the "data" through intentional inspection, investigation, and inquiry. Then, we *retreat and reflect*. We get away from our normal routines and spaces by purposefully pausing so as to contemplate the meaning behind the "data" we've acquired. Finally, we are positioned to *act in an instant*. We make things happen, with immediacy, because we engaged in the observation and reflective work—and can apply our learning to practice.

Advanced constructs of theory U include seven core components. Figure 5.3 is a visual depiction of the seven major components of theory U.

Suspending

When we lead reactively, we exercise limiting habits. We "download" past actions and repeat them in every new situation. This does not allow us to lead effectively. Rather, by suspending, we create the time, space, and energy to engage in fresh, powerful ways. From the scholar(s):

> Seeing freshly starts with stopping our habitual ways of thinking and perceiving . . . suspending does not require destroying our existing mental models of reality—which would be impossible even if we tried—or ignoring them. Rather it entails . . . hanging our assumptions in front of us. (Senge et al., 2004, p. 24)

Observing

After we suspend our judgment, we begin observing the people and situation. We "see" in new ways. We stand in a place of wonder and awe—not in a place

Figure 5.3. Theory U.

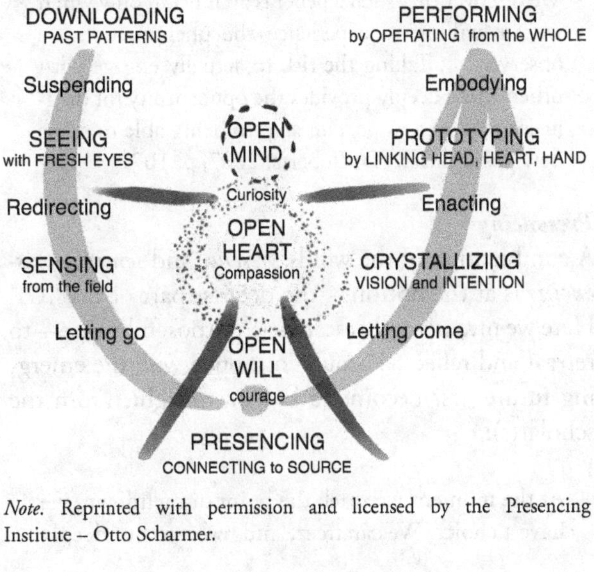

Note. Reprinted with permission and licensed by the Presencing Institute – Otto Scharmer.

of assumptions. In this phase of the U process, we open our minds to new possibilities for what could be. From the scholar(s):

> Become a blackbelt observer and listener . . . let the data talk to you—from the exterior realm (third-person view) to the more subtle levels of human experience (the second-person and first-person views). Thus the practice of letting data talk to you applies not only to objective, exterior data . . . but also to empathic, intersubjective data. . . . The impact of deeper levels of listening is profound: They function like a welding flame on the process of social reality creation. They can melt the walls of habitual interaction that keep us separate from the world, from one another, and from ourselves. (Scharmer & Kaufer, 2013, p. 169)

Sensing

Sensing allows us to break down the barriers and borders between the self (myself) and the system. With an open heart, we become one. Rather than placing blame, we recognize the roles we play in the system and the opportunities to contribute to healing and growth. From the scholar(s):

> Sensing is the beginning of the call to leadership. Seeing detail and context at the same time allows us to see from the whole, rather than from just our previously narrow view. . . . After we feel compelled to act, we need to find ways to break down false illusions so that we can see the true challenges that we need to address. Life experiences result in many illusions about the circumstances around us. For instance, we may see homeless people in the street asking for help; yet, the illusion we have is that this is their choice. . . . We discover that such a belief is an illusion only when we are willing to experience the phenomenon we observe. . . . Taking the risk to actually engage with others more deeply provides the opportunity for disillusionment, an important step to being able to sense new possibilities. (D. Roberts, 2007, p. 107)

Presencing

A combination of the words *presence* and *sensing*, *presencing* is at the bottom—the deepest part of the "U." Here we intentionally escape—a purposeful pause—to retreat and reflect. Through our open will, the emerging future first becomes a beacon of light. From the scholar(s):

> At the moment we reach the point of meltdown, we have a choice: We can freeze and revert to our deeply

engrained habits of the past, or we can stop and lean into the space of the unknown, lean into that which wants to emerge. (Scharmer & Kaufer, 2013, p. 29)

> In summary, each of us is not one but two. Each person and each community is not one but two. On the one hand, we are the person and community that we have become on our journey from the past to the present—the current self. On the other hand, there is the other, the dormant self, the one that is waiting within us to be born, to be brought into existence, to come into reality through our journey ahead. Presencing is the process of connecting these two selves. To connect our current with our authentic self. (Scharmer, 2007, p. 189)

Crystallizing

Following the presencing retreat (and reflection), we move forward with a clarified vision. There is a sense, while the ideas and direction crystallize, that "I can't not do it." In other words, there are no options—it has to be done. We harness the power of intention. From the scholar(s):

> In the U-Process, we enter the . . . phase with clarity about what we need to do next. We usually don't know exactly where this action is going to take us, but we know what the next steps are and in what direction to take them. We have a picture in our minds of what we want to create. We may not be able to see all of the tiny details of the picture, but nonetheless we have a real sense of its broad details, shapes, and colors. We call this capacity crystallizing. (Hassan, 2006, p. 5)

Prototyping

As we move from crystallizing to prototyping, we utilize our intentions to move formally into action. We confidently do the work that is necessary in this moment. These are not necessarily grand gestures, but small, purpose-driven acts . . . one step at a time. From the scholar(s):

> A prototype is a microcosm of the future that you want to create. Prototyping means to present your idea (or work in progress) before it is fully developed. The purpose of prototyping is to generate feedback from all stakeholders about how it looks, how it feels, how it matches (or does not match) people's needs and aspirations, and then to refine the assumptions about the guiding project. The focus is on exploring the future by doing rather than by analyzing. . . .

A prototype is not a plan. It is something you do that generates feedback. But a prototype is also not a pilot. A pilot has to be a success; by contrast, a prototype may fail, but it focuses on maximizing learning. (Scharmer, 2018, p. 118)

Performing

The final phase of the "U" process is performing. We have now experimented and made adjustments through prototyping. This phase is about realizing the potential that exists and embodying the opportunity before us. We are fully immersed, present, and purposeful in our actions. From the scholar(s):

> Just as the delivery of a newborn makes the real beginning of parenting, prototyping marks the real beginning of co-creating. What follows [performing] is the need to shape a context that allows the newly arrived being to take its next developmental steps. Once the living prototype is delivered and assessed, the question is how to take it to the next level of its journey— how to embed it in an institutional infrastructure that allows it to evolve. . . . This institutional infrastructure may be a set of supporting places, practices, peers, processes, and rhythms that allow the new to be developed and sustained. (Scharmer, 2007, p. 218)

Leadership Educator Praxis Activity

Leadership Theme: Theory U (Presencing)
Exercise: Haiku (reflective [artistic/creative] activity)

Theory U is a powerful theory for leadership educators. I love how it gives us the flexibility to meet our participants where they are by going as deep as appropriate. We can frame it as the three general practices (observe, retreat and reflect, and act in an instant), which I've executed for youth-focused leadership trainings as well as for limited-time (e.g., 1-hour workshops) programs. Or we can go significantly deeper with the full framework.

Scharmer's writing and web resources are extensive and commanding. They are replete with stories and examples that allow us to connect this material to the lives and work of any participant. This is the future of leadership. Leadership educators should invest time, energy, and resources into exploring theory U because of the profound impact it can have in our own lives and in the lives of our participants.

Theory U is a leadership model predicated upon deep levels of thinking matched with intentional action. The books and resources available illuminate the significance that this process can play in navigating challenges and accomplishing goals. Although it utilizes the letter "U" to visualize how one works their way through the model, it is best illustrated as a spiral; with every pass through each of the phases, we deepen our level of understanding, which leads to enhanced abilities to perform. When exploring theory U with my participants, I like to infuse creative expressions into the experience so it doesn't feel so heavy. One way to accomplish this is to invite participants to draft and share haiku poems about various features of the theory U leadership model.

Theory U Haiku

Utilizing a haiku is an opportunity for participants to flex their poetic muscles. The objective is to use the three-component Japanese formula. The first line has five syllables; the second, seven; and the third has five syllables. Leadership educators can utilize any type of framing question. For a theory U–themed training, we can invite participants to draft their haiku as an individual or in groups. We can also give them the freedom to select which aspect of the framework they want to draft a poem to highlight—or randomly assign them a section so as a collective all of the elements of the theory are covered. Based on the haiku poems, this type of activity also enables us to assess our participants' understanding of theory U and if we might need to revisit a particular component to reenforce learning. Here, I provide two examples—one for a simple construct of theory U and another for the advanced construct.

Simple construct: *Observe, observe, observe*

Line 1 = 5 syllables	Look at what I see.
Line 2 = 7 syllables	Taking a step back to view.
Line 3 = 5 syllables	Before reflecting

Advanced construct: *Crystallizing*

Line 1 = 5 syllables	I can't *not* do it.
Line 2 = 7 syllables	A vision is in my mind.
Line 3 = 5 syllables	Clarity to act.

Materials

- worksheet (for participants to draft their haiku poems)

Instructions

- Provide the worksheet, notecard, or large Post-It—and writing utensils—for participants to draft their haiku poems.
- Share the parameters for writing haiku poems:
  - Line 1 = 5 syllables
  - Line 2 = 7 syllables
  - Line 3 = 5 syllables
- Detail that the haiku needs to reference an aspect of theory U. You can determine whether participants should select their own section or if each section is preassigned.
- Once the poems have been drafted, it is advised to have participants share their poems in pairs or small groups.
- An added layer of theoretical engagement would be to model the reflective dialogue component of the experiential learning activity after theory U. Engage your participants in the following way after the haiku poems have been drafted and shared in partner or small groups:
  - First, take an *observational* stance about what they heard. How does this message resonate with their understanding of theory U?
  - Second, *retreat and reflect* on the meaning behind the haiku messages. What message was being conveyed through the haiku?
  - Third, *act* by celebrating the poetry and detailing how they will put this learning into their own leadership practice.
- After they have engaged with their partners or small groups in this process, you can bring the entire participant body together for a larger group sharing and reflecting exercise along with the formal reflective dialogue.

Reflective Dialogue Questions

Our objective with this activity is twofold. On a technical level, we want to reflect upon, explore, and encourage the use of the theory U phases. Additionally, we want to explore the haiku poem so our participants can reap the benefits of this creative learning opportunity. A selection of my go-to reflective dialogue questions includes the following:

- What was most intriguing about theory U? Frustrating?

- How might you utilize theory U outside of the training bubble?
- How was this process of drafting a haiku poem for you?
- How might you use poetry or other creative expressions as part of your leadership-developmental process?
- What can we learn from this exercise that can be applied to our own leadership practice?

Conviction in Action

Can leadership be defined in three words? Dennis Roberts (2007), a highly regarded and respected leadership educator, believes so. He suggests that the essence of leadership is *conviction in action*. After decades of reading about, reflecting upon, and training others in leadership, Roberts (2007) became frustrated with the ways in which research and theory complicated what he believes is at the core of leadership practice: aligning our personal passions with the needs of the organization or community with which we serve.

Like many other contemporary leadership theories, models, and frameworks, Roberts (2007) recognizes that leadership is not limited to position. Rather, it is something anyone—all of us—can (and should) do when circumstances are such that there is alignment between the community or organizational challenge and the readiness of the individual seeking to lead. The most trustworthy and powerful leadership emerges from a deep calling to act—when the question of "if I should act" dissolves into the questions of "How can my actions contribute to creating the change that is necessary now?" and "What do I *need* to do in this moment?"

Roberts (2007) details seven assumptions at the heart of conviction in action:

- *It is inclusive.* Leadership is not limited by position. Individuals who are called to make a difference—and act upon that calling—are exercising leadership.
- *It involves inner and outer work.* Leadership involves the inner exploration of the individual (the "in"vironment) as well as tangible, tactical work in the environment. "If I have not looked carefully at the things I value

most, then I have no source of power within that sustains my commitments and shapes my interactions with others" (D. Roberts, 2007, p. 97).

- *It results in action.* The precise reasons for the success of the world's most celebrated social movements are hotly debated in academic literature and activist circles, but their beginnings are incontestable: Somebody *did* something (Kielburger & Kielburger, 2004). This philosophical underpinning of leadership—somebody does something—results in action.
- *It is based on honesty and openness.* If we are to put our convictions into action—to engage in leadership—we need to have synergistic relationships that celebrate mutual work. Mutual work can only be guided by honesty and openness.
- *It fosters courage.* When we act from a place of deep conviction, we are pulling from a wellspring of courage. When leading with conviction, we are able to cultivate resiliency and overcome doubt—we believe wholeheartedly that the impossible becomes I'm-possible, that it can be achieved.
- *It sows seeds.* Conviction in action serves as a catalyst for others' aspirations. When convictions and actions are expressed, the seeds of possibility are planted in the minds of others.
- *It creates connections.* When we lead with this framework, others are attracted to us and encouraged to pursue their own convictions in action. This establishes a web of connections and synergies necessary for sustained work—both inner and outer.

The depth of conviction that calls us to action can come from many different places. Often, it emerges from pain and suffering, from the destructive acts of others, or recognizing a significant gap between reality and the ideal. Conviction may arrive like a lightning bolt—powerful and immediate. We are suddenly called—with vigor and attention—to lead from a place of passion (D. Roberts, 2007).

Often, though, our convictions emerge over time—tentative at first. An initial experience may stimulate our interest. This interest then can be nourished through self-reflection, asking questions of depth and

significance, and meaningful dialogue. We can dabble with action ideas. In the early stages, these convictions are not enough to demand undivided attention—it is simply a fascination. As other experiences occur, we are reminded of our convictions, deepening our sense of needing to act. Rather than a lightning bolt, conviction can be cultivated in the same manner as grains of sand in an oyster—ultimately transforming the initial grain into a praiseworthy pearl. Regardless of how the conviction arises, moving from conviction to action is essential for leadership practice.

Leadership Educator Praxis Activity

Leadership Theme: Conviction in Action
Exercise: Values Exploration (reflective [worksheet] activity)

Although not as widely regarded as it should be, conviction in action is best known in university administrator and student affairs circles. *Deeper Learning in Leadership* (D. Roberts, 2007) was written for this audience, yet it does not have the same level of popularity as the relational leadership or social change model. Notwithstanding, this model is an incredibly valuable resource for leadership educators. In part, this is because Roberts (2007) approaches this model from the lens of a scholar-*practitioner.* He knows what it means to practice leadership and approach leadership training and development from the perspective of someone who knows intimately what it means to work in the field.

The emphasis that leadership is conviction *in* action provides us the opportunity to articulate over and over again—and then some more—that leadership is *not* about power, position, prestige, or personal reward. Rather, leadership is about discovering what lights our fires, brings us to life, gives us wings, and then directly applying these passions and convictions to the needs of our communities and organizations. We all have convictions. And all our communities and organizations have serious and significant needs. This approach provides a theoretical foundation so that we can engage our leadership training participants in doing the discovery work and then putting those passions into practice in ways that are meaningful, productive, and resolving.

As previously mentioned with other theories, conviction in action allows for diverse training experiences. Because the model incorporates several other theoretical perspectives (i.e., adaptive leadership, theory U, and flow—see chapter 10), it offers opportunities for integration across theoretical frameworks. It can be facilitated as a one-time overview in a short session. It can also be devised as a leadership training programming series where each session deeply explores a different facet—replete with experiential learning activities—for participants to truly experiment with, internalize, and then apply their leadership learning.

Conviction in action, as a leadership approach, is grounded in individuals understanding themselves—their passion, purposes, and power—and then doing something about it—acting in ways that can bring about desired change. I am particularly fond of implementing a Values Exploration exercise as an experiential learning activity to assist participants in that first part of the theory—connecting deeply with self.

Values Exploration

The Values Exploration activity provides an extensive list of values on a single worksheet page. Participants are invited to review the entire list and select their most important leadership values. This should not be positioned as aspiration or hope—literally, what are their most important leadership values? Once they have selected, participants can narrow their initial list to their top two most essential—those values that guide their pursuits, day in and day out. Because all of our leadership trainings are designed for practical application, after the values have been selected and narrowed, we invite participants to craft an action plan regarding the ways in which those values can be even more explicit as part of their leadership practice. Alternatively, we can suggest they select another second-tier value of importance and action plan around how that value can have more of a presence in their leadership practice.

Materials

- worksheet with an extensive listing of values

Instructions

- Provide the values worksheet to the participants.
- Instruct the participants to carefully review *all* of the values listed—and select their most

important six, or eight, or 10 values (substantially more than three). Of course, if they want to add a value that is not listed, they are more than welcome to.

- Once the initial values of value are selected, invite the participants to engage in a pair-share or small-group dialogue about which ones were selected and why. Large-group sharing is also a possibility.
- Then participants should be instructed to narrow that list to their most important and valued values. These are the driving factors for leadership (and life) decision-making, pursuits, and guidance. Engaging in a pair-share or small-group dialogue—and then the large-group share—about which ones were selected should be repeated.
- I then suggest, prior to the formal reflective dialogue, for participants to engage in conversations about what's next. How might they further implement these values into their leadership practice or enhance their leadership practice by ensuring it is better informed by these values.
- Following these conversations, participants should have enough fodder for a robust reflective dialogue.

Reflective Dialogue Questions

Our objective with this activity is to begin by exploring our most deeply held values. We can only put our convictions in action if we know that by which we are convicted. Our convictions are mightily tethered to our values. Once the values are understood, we can explore how those can manifest in our practice so we can shift into action. A selection of my go-to reflective dialogue questions includes the following

- How do you see your values as guides for your leadership decision-making?
- How might you better utilize your values to make leadership decisions?
- What value needs a bit of a boost (i.e., needs more presence) in your leadership practice?
- What is your action plan to bring these values to life in your next leadership challenge?
- What can we learn from this exercise that can be applied to our own leadership practice?

Spiritual Leadership

Spiritual leadership is not a typical theory. It is difficult to quantify, let alone define. It is a bit elusive because it is an approach to leadership that focuses on connecting to the deepest part of our Selves (capital "S"). To be ultra and explicitly clear, spiritual leadership, in this context, is not a religious take on leading. (There is plenty of that material. A simple internet search yields a tremendous amount on how to excel at leading a religious community to leading in the light of historical faith figures—Buddha, Confucius, the Dalai Lama, Jesus, Krishna, Maimonides, Mary Baker Eddy, Muhammed, Zoroaster—and the list goes on and on.)

Spiritual leadership—formally and informally—is described in many ways: sacred, self-discovery, source, synchronicity. This is a sampling of how it is articulated and intersects with leadership:

The qualities of leadership are inner, spiritual qualities. They do not involve "doing" as much as "being." If you have the "being" worked out, the "doing" will come naturally. The reverse is not true. (Ritscher, 1986, p. 62)

I define spirituality . . . as a state of mind or consciousness that enables one to perceive deeper levels of experience, meaning and purpose than a strictly materialistic vantage point would offer. Spiritual leadership means leading from those deeper levels. The most powerful and sustainable progress . . . may not result from willful efforts to plan, control, determine, and push forward but from a profound openness of heart and mind that allows more-powerful possibilities to unfold. (Thompson, 2004, p. 62)

Spirituality is an unseen force that is both part of humankind and at the same time greater than humankind. It's the force through which all people are connected, the great force that no one can completely understand even though most people recognize it in some form. . . . It's a way of being human, a blueprint for fulfilling your human potential. . . . As you move further away from spirituality, you are at your worst; you are less human, less connected and less fulfilled. Conversely, as you move toward it, you are more human, more humane, more connected, and more fulfilled. (Houston & Sokolow, 2006, p. xxiv)

The conventional view of leadership emphasizes positional power and conspicuous accomplishment. But true leadership is about creating a domain in which we continually learn and become more capable of participating in our unfolding nature. A true leader thus sets the stage on which predictable miracles, synchronistic in nature, can—and do—occur. (Jaworski, 1998, p. 182)

Leadership is not simply something we do. It comes from a deeper reality within us; it comes from our values, principles, life experiences, and essence. Leadership is a process, an intimate expression of who we are. It is our whole person in action. (Cashman, 2008, p. 22)

What can we elucidate from these statements about spiritual leadership, more broadly? First, that leadership scholars and practitioners alike—all of us—have differing notions and language for spirituality. Notwithstanding, spiritual leadership is engrained in deep-level connections to our authenticity, sense of self, connections to others and the world around us, and whatever we deem to be life-source. Jaworksi (2012) suggests that "seeing the world as open and full of possibility is the fundamental shift of mind that opens the door to connecting to the Source" (p. 165). Although the sources of spiritual nourishment and renewal are highly individualistic, generally, this shift of mind occurs when we engage in intentional contemplative practices, energy practice, and spending time in nature—something available to all of us, regardless of spiritual grounding or meaning-making paradigms. Thompson (2004) warns us that consistency of practice is essential for developing our capacity to lead from a spiritual dimension. These habitual practices must not become numbing exercises and routines. Our spiritual leadership practice should be persistently renewing.

When we do cultivate these practices, the results are powerful. Rogers and Dantley (2001) express nine capacities and insights of those who possess spiritually intelligent leadership:

- They have a deep sense of the interconnectedness of life and know intimately what it means to be a part of and create community.
- They know themselves well and practice integrity, reflection, and collaboration.
- They can suspend their own assumptions in order to truly listen to and understand others.
- They know what they ultimately serve and are connected intimately with a higher power.

- They do not depend only on themselves for the vision of the organization or cause to which they are committed.
- They use power ethically and can give it away without feeling a loss of self.
- They do not project pain or addiction on others—they recognize and mediate their shadow side.
- They create conditions that release human possibility and creativity.
- They are life-giving.

Leadership can be understood as bringing out the best in others, which is quintessentially spiritual (Mullen et al., 2014; Vaill, 1989) Spiritual leadership is about our continuous, ongoing journey to discover and develop our inner capacities so we can positively impact our organizations and communities. It is about *being*, rather than *doing*. As Jaworski (1998) suggests, spiritual leadership is about creating "an opening to 'listen' to the implicate order unfolding, and then to create dreams, visions, and stories, that we sense at our center want to happen" (p. 182).

Leadership Educator Praxis Activity

Leadership Theme: Spiritual Leadership
Exercise: Personal Flags (reflective [artistic/creative] activity

Spiritual leadership is an intriguing approach for leadership educators. I find that many of us—and our participants—are hungry to connect to the deepest part of ourselves—our spiritual dimension. This leadership lens is one such way to encourage our participants to explore their inner state as a way to enhance their holistic well-being, connections with others, and effectiveness of their work. Nevertheless, this is a sensitive subject. It is deeply personal. It is sometimes (if not often) shunned in public spaces and work environments. And, regardless of how we all know that connecting to the deepest part of our selves will lead to healthy and important changes, it may not be taken seriously. It may be for these reasons that the next theory, authentic leadership, is much more approachable and acceptable as a training topic and theoretical grounding.

Spiritual leadership is less about connecting to a religious dogma than it is about deeply grounding ourselves in an ethical foundation and leading from our core purposes. When we connect to our own personal understandings of life-source, we are practicing spiritual leadership. When informing leadership trainings with this theoretical approach, I like to get creative with experiential learning activities. This enables participants to tap into different ways of expressing themselves than the traditional asking a question (from the facilitator) and then reflecting and speaking. The Personal Flags activity is one such opportunity.

Personal Flags

The Personal Flags activity is an opportunity for participants to activate their artistic spirit. The objective is to provide a forum for participants to design and craft a flag that represents their Selves (capital "S"). For spiritual leadership–oriented trainings, focusing on a prompt of significance and meaning is where we want to be. For instance, Who am I? What are my deepest held values? or What do I cherish most in the world?—all empower participants to think deeply and creatively as they translate responses to their artistic works.

Materials

- art supplies—construction paper, markers, paint, magazines for picture cutouts, yarn, and so on

Instructions

- Provide the art supplies.
- Instruct the participants to engage in a purposeful pause and think deeply about the prompt—rather than dive right into producing the poem or flag. (*Note*: You may even want to begin with a breathing exercise to get participants at an appropriate energy level.)
- Provide a prompt that serves to frame the activity.
- *Note*: After providing these instructions, give them plenty of time and space to get expressive. Welcome the silence.
- Once the flags are created, invite participants to share their works of art and creative expressions.
- Following these conversations, participants should have enough fodder for a robust reflective dialogue.

Reflective Dialogue Questions

Our objective with this activity is for participants to connect with the deepest part of themselves—and then to express it through creative measures. A selection of my go-to reflective dialogue questions includes the following:

- How was this (creative) process for you?
- (Ask the group) Do you see or sense that these flags truly represent the other participants? Why?
- How might this serve as a reminder for us as we practice leadership beyond the training bubble?
- What can we learn from this exercise that can be applied to our own leadership practice?

Authentic Leadership

Authentic leadership is arguably the most contemporary theoretical approach to effectively leading. Still in its formative stages, there are no clearly articulated and agreed-upon definitional parameters, core tenets, component parts, or methods of measurement (Dugan, 2017; Northouse, 2021). There are, however, three general perspectives of authentic leadership: intrapersonal, interpersonal, and developmental:

Intrapersonal perspective. In the intrapersonal perspective, the focus is on the internal condition of leaders—their self-knowledge and self-regulation. Authentic leaders lead from clearly defined personal convictions and are considered "originals" due to their intentional exploration, unpacking, and derived meaning from their life experiences. As we think about authentic leaders from the intrapersonal perspective, questions to consider include these: Do leaders have a strong, grounded concept of their values and vision? Are they leading from a place of deeply held convictions?

Interpersonal perspective. In the interpersonal perspective, the focus is on the relationships and depth of engagement between leaders and followers. Authentic leaders have "real" relationships with followers grounded in care and genuine support for the success and well-being of the others. As we think about authentic leaders from the perspective of the intrapersonal perspective, questions to consider include

these: Do leaders act naturally regardless of the contexts or differences in followers? Do leaders cultivate the authenticity of their followers?

Developmental perspective. In the developmental perspective, the focus of attention is on how authentic living and leading is nurtured over time in the leader—as a developmental process. Compared to the intrapersonal perspective, which is more of an objective perception (from an outsider's perspective, Do these leaders have the authentic internal conditioning?), the developmental perspective is a process-oriented approach—Are leaders cultivating developmental gains in four general domains (Avolio, 2011)?

> With *self awareness,* we wonder, Are leaders spending time understanding their strengths and weaknesses, values, emotions, goals, motives, and identity?
>
> With an *internalized moral perspective,* we ask, Are leaders utilizing their moral standards and values to guide behaviors?
>
> With *balanced processing,* we inquire, how are leaders instituting honesty and objectivity when making decisions—even when situations are emotionally charged?
>
> And with *relational transparency,* we question, Are leaders showing their true selves by sharing openly—including their emotions, motives, and difficult decision-making processes?

The true north model of authentic leadership incorporates data from interviews of over 100 corporate executives (George, 2003; George & Baker, 2011). These leaders identified five core characteristics of authentically leading:

- They have a strong sense of purpose—they know who they are and what they are pursuing.
- They have deeply held values about the right thing to do—that is, they employ a moral compass that guides their actions.
- The leaders establish trusting relationships with others—and recognize the power and importance of synergistic connections.

- They demonstrate self-discipline—by focusing on important goals and staying committed in the face of challenges and obstacles.
- And authentic leaders are sensitive and empathetic to the plight of others—they listen to their concerns, model healing behaviors, and show them compassion.

Leadership Educator Praxis Activity

Leadership Theme: Authentic Leadership
Exercise: How Do I Occur? (reflective [partner and dialogic] activity)

Authentic leadership often feels elusive. We and our leadership training participants know what authenticity is. We and our leadership training participants know that authentic leadership is a good thing. Yet many of us and our leadership training participants are reluctant to infuse authentic leadership into our practice because it means coming face-to-face with fears, limitations, and (potentially) failures—as well as relinquishing control and authority. The fact is, doing this type of developmental work—cultivating authenticity—is difficult.

Authentic leadership, the most contemporary of the all the theories, focuses on leaders acting from a place of integrity. With this leadership approach, understanding ourselves is essential. We can learn about ourselves when trusted others share critical feedback regarding how we are perceived. The How Do I Occur? activity does exactly that.

How Do I Occur?

The How Do I Occur? experiential learning activity is an opportunity for participants to partner with another trusted individual to ask, respond to, and dialogue about how one is perceived by others. In pairs, participants serve as either interviewer or interviewee. Both participants will play both roles before the exercise comes to a close. Interviewers are expected to ask their partners questions about how they are perceived. Interviewees respond with honest and authentic answers. These responses are intended to provide insight and growth areas for the interviewer so that change can be made to their leadership in practice. Sample questions include the following:

- What kind of first impression do I give?
- What kinds of things can I be counted on to do?

- What would you *not* count on me to do?
- In what kinds of circumstances/situations am I good to have around?
- In what kinds of circumstances/situations would it be best to have me working on other things?
- In what kinds of situations do I "come alive" and breathe life into others?
- In what kinds of situations do I disengage or shut down?
- How well do I demonstrate authentic appreciation for others?
- How well do I inspire others to pursue new initiatives?
- How willing am I to share authority and power with others?
- How well do I honor commitments even when presented with challenges?

Materials

- worksheet with selected questions

Instructions

- Begin by inviting participants to find a trusted partner. (*Note*: This activity only works for those participants who have trusting relationships and a certain level of professional intimacy.)
- In their pairs, instruct them to identify who will begin as the interviewer and interviewee. (You can also decide this in easy ways—for example, whoever has the darker color shirt or whose name begins closes to the letter "J.")
- Once the participants are paired and settled, provide the question worksheet.
- The interviewer shall ask the interviewee to answer honestly and authentically.
- Following those responses, the participants switch roles and begin the process again.
- Following these conversations, participants should have enough fodder for a robust reflective dialogue.

Reflective Dialogue Questions

Our objective with this activity is for participants to learn about themselves by listening to honest and authentic responses from a trusted peer about how they are perceived. A selection of my go-to reflective dialogue questions includes the following:

- How was this experience for you?
- Which role was more difficult—the interviewer or interviewee? Why?
- What did you learn about yourself from this experience?
- What can we learn from this exercise that can be applied to our own leadership practice?

Conclusion

It is essential that leadership educators study and appreciate the history and progression of leadership theory. From the industrial (i.e., trait approach) through to the contemporary (i.e., authentic leadership) theoretical lenses, we see each of these in our leadership practices (or hope to). Leadership educators utilize these theoretical frames to inform our training experiences. Doing so promotes effective leadership for our participants. When we inform our trainings with theory, they enhance the potential for leadership learning and development, skills enhancement, capacity building, and boosts to practical application.

In summation, we seem to have come full circle in our exploration of what makes good leaders and leadership. The study of leadership in the early 20th century began by focusing on surface-level traits and behaviors, how differing contexts and situations necessitate differing leaders and leadership approaches, and the leader-centric relationship between leaders and followers. After decades of exploring leadership through the lens of the leader, a transformation occurred. This caused a shift that focused on leadership as a developmental relationship and experience rather than a transactional one. Leaders had the responsibility to not only accomplish goals but engaged in that work while also holistically enriching the lives their followers. With this shift, leadership clearly became value laden—for good. Our most contemporary leadership theories build upon this transformation. *Leadership*, by most scholars today, is understood to be for positive means. Yet we have returned to the leader as the focal point—albeit at a significantly deeper level than our original theories. Leadership with this contemporary lens focuses on the internal state and holistic being of leaders—their authenticity and *realness*. Rather than see this as having come full circle—in a cyclical manner, it should be perceived as a spiral—a deepening with every pass.

CHAPTER 6

Leadership Themes and Topics

THE DOZENS AND DOZENS of theories, models, and frameworks from which leadership educators can inform our leadership trainings are impressive and necessary. Yet there are other themes and topics that add depth to our trainings, highlight growth opportunities in our participants' understanding of leadership, and enable us to expand our repertoire of training offerings. Within this book, I offer an exploration into a selection of themes, including followership; demographic considerations—including leadership and gender and culture; socially just and culturally responsive leadership; leading and other developmental relationships; and leadership ethics.

Followership

Leaders and followers are inextricably intertwined. Leaders need followers. Followers need leaders. For each of the roles to actually exist—leaders and followers—the other is indispensable. Leaders need followers or there is nobody to lead. Followers need leaders or there is nobody to provide the direction, guidance, and visioning necessary to achieve leadership objectives. Yet the leadership industry focuses almost exclusively on leaders. As Riggio (2020) offers, in Western society, we have had a fascination—almost an obsession—with leaders and leadership, to the exclusion of followers and followership. Blumen (2008) highlights that while considerable resources are spent on leadership training and development, virtually no resources are allocated to the development of constructive followership skills.

The term *follower*, to some (especially in the United States of America), is perceived as a derogatory term. To be labeled as a follower is an insult (Kellerman, 2008). Parents raise children to be leaders and avoid being followers. This is engrained in our psyche as young people well beyond the family.

Within pop culture, music, movies, and promotional advertisements, we often hear how important it is to be a leader—and to avoid being a follower at all costs. The Imagine Dragons song "Thunder" refers to escaping one's life—to break free from the limitations of the "box" and "mold," from "yes sir" and being a "follower." On the big screen, every superhero movie ever made positions leaders-as-superheroes as the saviors—coming to save the world, literally. Followers are always in a supporting role—marginalized and needing to be saved—designed to be "less than" the leader. Kellerman (2008), in her book *Followership*, highlights the example of a long-running Audi car advertisement that celebrated a "Never Follow" tagline and attitude. Such images, lyrics, and messages inform what we believe and understand about followership. That being—or being seen—as a follower should be avoided because it is clearly second best.

Leadership educators need to learn about and embrace followership to enhance the leadership and followership skills of our training participants. As Kellerman (2008) advocates, better followers beget better leaders. She promotes the notion that followers should not be second to leaders, nor leaders' appendages. Rather, followers are a force and a phenomenon to be reckoned with in their own right. Similarly, Chaleff (2009) suggests we need a model of followership that embraces, rather than rejects, the follower identity. His premise is that leaders rarely use their power wisely or effectively over long periods of time unless they are supported by followers. And Robert Kelley (1988, 2008), the original campaigner for heightened consideration of followership, indicates that followership is worthy of its own discrete research and training. Simply, conversations about leadership need to include followership because leaders neither exist nor act in a vacuum without followers. These scholars implore the leadership community to recognize the importance of followership education—in addition to and as a part of leadership education.

Followers can be defined by their rank as well as their behavior (Kellerman, 2008). By *rank*, followers are subordinates who have less formal or positional power, authority, and influence than their superiors—leaders. By *behavior*, followers go along with what someone else wants and intends. Multiple scholars (Adair, 2008; Kellerman, 2008; Kelley, 1998, 2008) have devised followership styles and models to differentiate various levels of followership. I invite you to explore the nuances of each of them. As a compilation, they describe, at one end of the spectrum, followers as bystanders (Kellerman, 2008), disgruntled or disengaged (Adair, 2008), or as sheep (Kelley, 1998, 2008). Generally, these followers are passive and rely on leaders to provide direction and guidance. If they have ill will toward leaders or organizations, they will provide little value, or worse, may be subversive.

At the other end of the spectrum are followers identified as diehards (Kellerman, 2008), disciples (Adair, 2008), and star followers (Kelley, 1998, 2008). These followers are highly engaged and productive. They have healthy and positive attitudes toward leaders and organizations and are so deeply committed to the leader, organization, or cause that they would be willing to put their lives on the line. In two words: supremely dedicated.

Kellerman (2008) offers general parameters for what differentiates good followers from bad followers. Engagement and motivation are the two primary factors:

- To do nothing—to be in no way involved—is to be a bad follower (follower with no engagement or motivations).
- To support a leader who is bad—ineffective and/or unethical—is to be a bad follower (engaged follower with questionable motivations).
- To oppose a leader who is good—effective and ethical—is to be a bad follower (engaged follower with questionable motivations).
- To support a leader who is good—effective and ethical—is to be a good follower (engaged follower with noble motivations).
- To oppose a leader who is bad—ineffective and unethical—is to be a good follower (engaged follower with noble motivations).

Chaleff (2009) expands upon what constitutes good followership by articulating five dimensions of courageous (good) followership. First, followers have the courage to assume responsibility. These individuals discover and create opportunities to fulfill their potential and maximize their value to their groups, organizations, and communities. Followers also have the courage to serve—the second dimension. With this dimension, they live into the hard work required to serve leaders.

The third dimension is having the courage to challenge. Courageous followers give voice to what they believe does not align with ethical practices or best pursuits for the group, organization, or community. Similarly, these people have the courage to participate in transformation. When change is needed, courageous followers champion the need for change. Finally, the fifth dimension for courageous leadership is having the courage to take moral action. These followers recognize and act upon those pivotal moments when they need to stand against a leader's orders and authority.

Recent scholarship on followership indicates that individuals ultimately play both roles—leader and follower—simultaneously. This is branded as *connecting leadership* (Jaser, 2021) or *everyday leadership* (Riggio et al., 2021). This leadership concept recognizes that leader behaviors are not only demonstrated by individuals in traditional leader roles. Followers often engage in leader behaviors. With this construct, the connecting leader coenacts and concurrently embodies the roles, identities, and positions of both leader and follower. Understanding leadership and followership from this perspective democratizes the way we think about the subject—and practice—and advances in the direction of reducing our temptation to romanticize it (Jaser, 2021). I expect that much more on connecting and everyday leadership will be published and promoted in the years and decades to come as we more fully explore leadership and followership—and the integration as well as blurred lines between the two.

Leadership Educator Praxis Activity

Leadership Theme: Followership
Exercise: Pirate's Booty (physically engaged activity)

Leadership educators need to be well versed in followership. Leadership and followership should be thought of in tandem—"as inseparable, indivisible, and inconceivable the one without the other" (Kellerman, 2008, p. 239). Unfortunately, many of our training participants think solely of leaders and leadership, without recognizing the duality of the relationship between leader and follower, leadership and followership. We know—though it's rarely if ever made explicit—that followership is inherent in leadership (Stech, 2008).

Part of our interest in exploring followership is to emphasize the distortion that often takes place with leadership. A quote from leadership scholar Ira Chaleff (2019) highlights this relationship between leadership and followership—leaders and followers. He frames this in the context of enslavers and the enslaved:

> One can hardly characterize the relationship of enslavers as leaders and those enslaved as followers, any more than one can characterize a rapist as a leader and rape victim as a follower. Nevertheless, if placed in the leadership-follower continuum, slaveholders would undoubtedly see themselves as the leaders, whom the enslaved better damn well follow, or else! This is a brutal distortion of what we consider the bounds of legitimate leadership and followership, yet a distortion found all too commonly in history and in contemporary autocratic and dictatorial regimes. (p. 13)

Even in less inhumane examples, we see notions of leadership guided by power, prestige, and personal reward. As leadership educators, we can utilize experiential learning activities to highlight the role and importance of followers—either as propagators of venomous leadership or to challenge and confront that toxicity. If there are enough participants (enough to form multiple groups of seven participants), I like to facilitate the Pirate's Booty activity. With this larger-size participant body, it gives everyone an opportunity to be involved and nurtures reflective dialogue where everyone can participate and share about their personal experiences in the activity.

Pirate's Booty

The Pirate's Booty activity is not physically demanding but does require participants to work together (or not) to accomplish a goal by deciding on which island to pursue hidden treasure. Each participant will be provided one of seven roles based on Kellerman's good and bad followers as well as an activity instruction sheet. Then, based on the role and instructions, they will need to determine which island to go to. You will need to creatively draft a selection of islands with differentiated features. For example, island 1 is the closest to the ship but is known for a den of venomous snakes. Island 2 is lush with tropical fruit but the farthest away, and there are not enough rations for everyone to survive. Island 3 has a safe harbor and small village—of cannibals. Depending on the physical environment of the training space, you could post signage in different parts of the room to highlight where the islands are. This way participants will need to physically move their group to their selected island—to add a bit more flavor to the experience rather than just sitting and dialoguing. Ultimately, each group will need to select an island before time runs out, or they all perish at sea.

Materials

- worksheets
  - Pirate's Booty overview and instructions
  - Pirate's Booty island options
- role cards that indicate
  - Captain Goode (a good leader)
  - Captain Bade (a bad leader)
  - Crew Member Knope (to be in no way involved in decision-making)
  - Crew Member Saber (supports the bad leader)
  - Crew Member Oger (opposes the good leader)
  - Crew Member Sugar (supports the good leader)
  - Crew Member Obel (opposes the bad leader)

Instructions

- Begin by providing the worksheets (instructions and island options) to all of the participants. Then read the overview out loud so that all participants understand the activity and how they will proceed once they receive their role.
- Provide each participant with a role card, secretly. (It will be important to have both captains in each group. However, the crew members should be randomized so that each group has a different arrangement of crew to vary the experiences of these groups—which will add fodder to the reflective dialogue.)
- Once the activity begins, time the experience. (Thirty minutes is more than enough time. Participants, especially if they are not fully living into the roles, may end in 10 or 20 minutes.)
- Once all of the groups have selected their islands, have them share why they selected that one, and slide into the reflective dialogue.

Reflective Dialogue Questions

Our objective with this activity is to offer an opportunity for participants to understand the nuances of leader–follower relationships and begin to think more critically about how important followers are to decision-making processes. The activity creates the context for followers (crew members) to support—or not—leaders (captains) as they decide which island to pillage. This then becomes fodder for the reflective dialogue. A selection of my go-to reflective dialogue questions includes the following:

- How did it feel to be in your role? Why do you feel that way about it?
- How do we see these roles manifest in "real life"?
- What can we learn about leadership from this activity?
- What can we learn about followership from this activity?
- What can we learn from this exercise that can be applied to our own leadership *and followership* practice?

Demographic Considerations

Why is it important to explore leadership from gender, culture, and diverse global perspectives? Simply, leadership has mostly been understood from the perspective of those who have wielded power— White men of privilege. Across history, from this viewpoint, "others" and "outsiders" weren't capable of leading. Still, because leadership studies and literature are mostly from this same paradigm, the insights and leadership contributions from women, people of color, and individuals from beyond the United States of America and Western Europe are potentially viewed with skepticism or a deficit perspective. For this reason, as leadership educators, we need to be fluent in the dynamics between gender, culture, and diverse global perspectives and leadership. Doing so will enable us to recognize the implicit and subconscious biases by which we—and our leadership training participants—ground our leadership understandings and inform our leadership practices.

Gender

Not long ago a serious question could be asked: "Can women lead?" Today, to most of us, this question sounds utterly ridiculous—absolutely preposterous, although, unfortunately, not to all. Through the vast majority of human history—including in the early 2020s—women have rarely been considered as leaders (Heifetz, 1994). Women are still sometimes seen as inferior leaders compared to men. Much of this is due to how we understand gender and gender roles (Northouse, 2021).

Gender is a social construct. When something is *socially constructed*, we assign meaning to it through social engagements—the things we do and say with other people (Owen et al., 2021). Societally and socially, we ascribe meaning to differing genders and gender roles. In Western society, traditionally, these gender roles are identified in two ways: male-bodied people who perform masculinity and female-bodied people who perform femininity. Leadership has historically been identified and reserved as a masculine practice—for men. Women leading traditionally meant that unwritten rules were being broken. These *gender rules* and *gender roles* continue to have significant implications regarding the ways gender influences leadership—in thought and practice.

Before going any further, it is absolutely critical to mention that the leadership scholarship focuses on binary constructs of gender—that is, male or female. Transgender and nonbinary expressions of leadership are only starting to be explored.

Gender inequality manifests in both tangible and intangible ways (Cosgrove, 2010). Tangibly, we can see the difference in wages. According to Payscale (2022)—a compensation platform—in 2020, women made only $0.81 for every dollar men made. This is only down by $0.07 since 2015. The intangible and hidden manifestations of inequality are fiercer and more ferocious. Women may need to work a "double day"—a focus on income generation as well as family responsibilities—or a "triple day"—a focus on income generation, family responsibilities, as well as community activism—resulting in around-the-clock work to guarantee family survival (Cosgrove, 2010).

Both consciously and unconsciously, men have limited the opportunities for women to lead—this is particularly true for executive-level positions. Iannello (1992) describes the notion of hierarchy as originating in the 5th century to denote the top-down delegation of power and determination of functions. Contemporary organization theory suggests that hierarchy relates to a system where the distribution of power, privilege, and authority is both systematic and unequal (Iannello, 1992). To be clear, our contemporary hierarchical organizations, which tend to be male dominated, are systematically structured to ensure that power, privilege, and authority continue to be wielded by those who currently have the power, privilege, and authority—men. Here are two examples.

A study of mentoring opportunities for corporate board–level women found that limited mentoring experiences of these women led to negative effects on appointments to additional corporate boards (McDonald & Westphal, 2013). The scholars chose to explore first-time women board members to public companies in the United States of America. The 1,305 male and female participants received and submitted responses to a survey detailing their mentorship experiences as neophyte participants on corporate boards. The study found that women received less mentoring support than their counterpart first-time male board members. This ultimately resulted in fewer additional board appointments due to the reduced contact with potential connections as well as training on ways to engage successfully in their role. I wonder how many of your organizational or institutional board members are women? Further, how many of them received adequate training and support for their role?

Women are also underrepresented in the leadership structures of the Ivory Tower in academia. Barriers continue to exist for women interested in entry to and advancement within the male-dominated leadership system of colleges and universities. Historically, women have experienced a deficit of networking opportunities, in addition to lower levels of advancement—particularly in research careers—all of which continues today (Gardiner et al., 2007).

Overt and subtle behaviors have included assignments to time-intensive but less powerful committees, resource inequities, stereotyping, and unclear professional etiquette. All of these behaviors exacerbate social isolation and combine to discount, discourage, and disadvantage women at all levels of the Ivory Tower (Association of American Colleges, 1986).

We have constructed glass ceilings and labyrinths that impede opportunities for women to achieve positional leadership roles and hinder their leadership performance. (For a more robust and detailed listing of metaphors for women in leadership see Julie Owen's [2020] *We Are The Leaders We've Been Waiting For: Women And Leadership Development In College*.) The glass ceiling is an invisible barrier that prevents women from ascending to the upper echelons of organizations. The leadership labyrinth (Eagly & Carli, 2007) describes the abundance of challenges and obstacles all along women's leadership and professional journeys. Three key factors inform the labyrinth metaphor.

Human capital refers to fewer resources afforded for the education, training, and development of women. *Gender differences* suggest the perception that women are less effective at leading than men. And *prejudice* recognizes the bias toward women rooted in traditional understandings of gender rules and gender roles.

Although the perceptions and actions of men are the driving force—due to how power has historically and contemporarily been wielded—women have also contributed to the leadership labyrinth.

How gender is perceived, constructed, created, and enacted in the context of work has as much to do with women's perceptions and women's interactions . . . as it has with the obstacles of masculine culture that prevent more women from achieving leadership. (Vongalis-Macrow, 2016, p. 100)

As leadership educators, we can incorporate strategies for dismantling the glass ceilings and labyrinths that women face at three levels of change: personal, organizational, and societal (Iannello, 1992; Northouse, 2021; Vasquez, 2016).

Personal strategies include providing support and mentorship for women and opportunities for leadership skills development and capacity building, decreasing gender stereotypes, and utilizing personal power, privileges, and authority to raise the visibility of women's contributions while advocating for enhanced opportunities for women. Organizational strategies include diversifying leadership opportunities; increasing equity in pay, promotion, and traditionally gendered experiences (maternity/paternity leave); and dismantling hierarchical structures for consensual organizational structures. Societal strategies include ensuring gender equity in both work and domestic responsibilities, significantly increasing funding and resources for women's education and entrepreneurship, and government, corporate, and institutional policymaking—with reward and punishment structures—to enhance opportunities for women in formal leadership roles.

Leadership Educator Praxis Activity

Leadership Theme: Gender and Leadership
Exercise: Labyrinth (physically engaged activity)

It is imperative that leadership educators understand the disparities in thought, tradition, and contemporary practices between men and women in leadership. Our societal perspectives—both conscious and subconscious—have created the conditions for women to be seen as inferior. This is even more pronounced with regard to formal leadership positions, roles, and capabilities.

As leadership educators, we can utilize our awareness of the disparity to provide intentional leadership training and development experiences to better engage our participants so they can be more aware and awake to these disparities while also preparing them to make changes at personal, organizational, and societal levels. The Labyrinth activity can be facilitated to highlight these differences.

The Labyrinth

The Labyrinth activity physically engages participants to make their way through a maze. Participants will see either a 5 × 5 or 6 × 6 grid of items (possibly bigger if there are many participants)—I like to use sport cones, rubber bases, or paper plates. (See Figure 6.1 for a visual of the "labyrinth" as well as the facilitator map used to determine correct or incorrect steps.) Their objective is to locate the appropriate path from the entry point to the exit. Leadership educators design it in advance and draft a personal notecard for record-keeping. Then, as participants make their way, they will step from one cone (or plate) to the next. If that is the correct step, they will continue. If it is incorrect, they will be instructed to leave the labyrinth, and the next participant will have an attempt. In this exercise, although only one participant is in the labyrinth at a time, each team member needs to be aware of the right steps taken so that the group can accomplish the task of making their way through the maze.

This activity works well as a competition with up to four groups trying to be the first to finish. In this case, each group begins on a different side of the maze. Note that if multiple groups are participating, a "facilitator" for the other groups will be necessary to determine if those participants are making the right moves. It is too difficult for a single facilitator to be monitoring more than one group.

Specifically, this activity illuminates gender disparities when multiple groups are participating. Although participants can be in mixed-gender groups, one of the groups can have a secretly elongated path with many more steps to goal accomplishment—that is, getting out of the labyrinth. This can be utilized during the reflective dialogue to highlight how women face significantly more obstacles compared to men.

Materials

- sport cones, rubber bases, or paper plates or paper towel sheets—something to indicate the appropriate place to step as participants make their way through the labyrinth
- notecard with the labyrinth map for each facilitator

Instructions

- In advance of the training, facilitators should draft a map path of 15–20 steps that participants will need to make from start to finish. Identical maps should be drafted for each group facilitator participating in the labyrinth.

Figure 6.1. A visual display of the "labyrinth" with the facilitator map.

Note. Reprinted with permission.

- When on-site, prepare the labyrinth with evenly placed cones, plates, or whatever else is utilized to differentiate stepping locations.
- When it is time for the activity, begin by getting the participants in their groups and positioned on their own labyrinth starting side.
- Then provide instructions for how to move within the maze: Participants can step forward, backward, right left, diagonal right forward, diagonal right backward, diagonal left forward, or diagonal left behind. (It is important to physically show these movements.)
- If participants make the correct move (per the hidden map that the facilitators have), they can continue. If incorrect, they will need to exit the labyrinth, and the next team member begins from that group's starting place.
- This process continues until each person of each group exits the labyrinth.

- Once all of the participants have completed their movement through the labyrinth, settle the energy, and slide into the reflective dialogue.

Reflective Dialogue Questions

Our objective with this activity is offer an opportunity for participants to work collaboratively to accomplish a task. We can highlight gender disparities in leadership by (secretly) tasking one group with a longer path to the maze's exit. This then becomes fodder for the reflective dialogue. A selection of my go-to reflective dialogue questions includes the following:

- How did it feel to be in the group who had a longer labyrinth?
- What connections can we draw between this activity and opportunities for women in leadership?

- What can we each do about this in our leadership practices?
- What else can we learn about leadership from this activity that is important for our leadership practice?
- What can we learn from this exercise that can be applied to our own leadership practice?

Culture

We know that there is not one magical, correct way to lead. Leadership is personal, situational, and contextual. What is considered "good" or "effective" leadership is socially constructed and varies depending upon the particular identities and culture(s) of the group, organization, neighborhood, country, or society (D. Roberts, 2007). _Culture_ is generally defined as the shared set of learned beliefs, values, norms, symbols, and traditions that are common to specific groups of people (Northouse, 2021). Although palpable and recognizable in any given time and space, it is a dynamic, moving phenomenon (Cabral, 1974). In the context of university communities, differing residence halls tend to have distinct cultures—as do varied student organizations and professional departments. What makes each entity unique is how the involved individuals have infused their learned beliefs, values, norms, symbols, and traditions into the fabric of its living space, organizational dynamics, and professional operation.

Leaders can cultivate healthy cultures by generating a shared sense of meaning, values, beliefs, and bonds between themselves and their followers. Crafting stories and rituals that energize and inspire followers can be utilized to drive this culture building. That notwithstanding, culture is not a top-down prerogative. When hierarchical leaders demand and dictate a specific culture, it tends to result in negative and limiting consequences. The culture is the collective sentiment and impression among all the stakeholders—often cocreated naturally through time and consistent actions.

Beyond our organizational cultures, we must also be sensitive to others of diverse cultural backgrounds. This is understood as intercultural sensitivity. As leaders and leadership educators, it is important for us to analyze our own identities (e.g., gender, nationality, race, religion, social class, etc.) as well as those with whom we engage and train. This has many positive

implications. By deepening our levels of intercultural sensitivity, we increase our self-efficacy, strengthen our understandings of our identity, and enhance our cultural competency (Beatty & Manning-Ouellette, 2022).

The developmental model of intercultural sensitivity (Bennett, 1986, 2013) is designed to identify the various stages of intercultural sensitivity. This can be utilized for our own development as well as when training others in leadership—specifically in moving from ethnocentric to ethnorelative perspectives. It is important to note that integration of cultures in one context does not automatically translate to others. For example, a leadership educator may have integration with university students compared to a defensive stance with executives of a corporation—or vice versa. Or a leadership educator may have greater ethnorelativity with Latin American training contexts than African or Asian or European contexts where there may be stronger ethnocentrism. Simply stated, intercultural sensitivity in one domain does not automatically translate to others.

Those who are ethnocentric are in the denial, defense, or minimization phases. With denial, people believe their cultural experience is the only one that is real and valid. There is little to no thought of the "other." With a defensive stance, one's belief system is guided by a notion that "we" are superior and "they" are inferior. One feels threatened and is highly critical of the "other," often labeling them as strange, less than, or deficient. With a minimization perspective, other cultures are trivialized or viewed romantically. One tends to deny differences and only seek to see similarities.

With enthnorelativity, individuals have the potential to move through the phases of acceptance, adaptation, and integration. With acceptance, there is a sense that one can welcome others, reservedly. Although there may not be agreement with other cultures, generally, there is a curiosity and respect. With adaptation, individuals see the world through more inclusive eyes. Intentional behavioral changes occur so one becomes more inclusive and openhearted toward others. Finally, those who have integrated are easily able to move in and out of different cultural worldviews. There is an intrinsic disposition to celebrate the contributions and voices of diverse others.

Interestingly, researchers from across 140 countries are gathering data to compare differing leadership cultural practices, leadership characteristics, and trust factors. The Global Leadership and Organizational Behavior Effectiveness (GLOBE) research project continues to expand in scope, which allows us to expand our notions of leadership cultural practices, characteristics, and trust factors from across the planet. Check out the website for more details on the study and data (https://globeproject.com/).

The GLOBE study is particularly important because an incredibly vast amount of leadership literature is firmly rooted in a Global North or Western paradigm. For example, most leadership books are written in English and rarely translated into other languages. Even the pop culture material is seldom offered beyond English. To highlight this point, in order to effectively train nonprofit leaders in Nicaragua, I needed to write a training manual—and then have it translated into Spanish. There were simply no substantial resources available in the native language of our participants that provided a theoretical knowledge base to inform their learning or their leadership trainings. This was a first-of-its-kind text that detailed diverse leadership theories from the past century made accessible to Spanish-language readers.

That the vast majority of leadership literature is exclusive to the privileged around the globe is a travesty. This propagates the hegemonic perspective that those considered to be leaders or worthy of leadership are solely of the dominant global cultures. To everyone else, attitudinally, we're saying, "Not you! No way!"

Leadership Educator Praxis Activity

Leadership Theme: Culture and Leadership
Exercise: Thoughts in a Minute (reflective [personal engagement] activity)

Leadership educators need to be conscious of and committed to raising the voices of those who are marginalized—as a way to support vibrant and inclusive cultures within our participant organizations. This tends to happen by calling out ethnocentric perspectives and behaviors while celebrating enthnorelative ones. It is also essential that we spend time with the GLOBE data and other leadership material from diverse authors, perspectives, and locales to enhance our breadth and depth of leadership wisdom. This will also assist us in broadening our abilities to connect with diverse participants and recognize

the ways in which they conceptualize and practice leadership—not as better or worse, but as grounded in differing cultural understandings and practices.

Often, those whom we identify as *other* are perceived as "less than." Therefore, their leadership skill is less than ours as well. In this very quick Thoughts in a Minute activity—only a minute—we illuminate for ourselves thoughts on others. By illuminating these thoughts, we unearth our hidden biases and can work toward rectifying them.

Thoughts in a Minute

The Thoughts in a Minute exercise is a minute-long drill. Leadership educators ask participants to think about an "other" group. This can be at a grand level—a different global cultural group—or a local-level "other" group—student leaders from a differing entity (club, organization, athletic team, fraternity, sorority, residence hall, etc.). The process is simple—we ask participants to write down every thought that crosses their mind during that minute. Then we engage in some sharing through the reflective dialogue. We should be mindful, though, that this activity should be approached with sensitivity, as we are asking participants to be incredibly vulnerable in thinking and sharing about individuals and communities who are different and perceived as "less than."

Materials

* paper and writing utensils—enough for every participant

Instructions

* Begin by calming the energy of the group. We want participants to be at ease with calm minds.
* Once the energy is settled, share with the participants that they are to write, for one exact minute, every thought that crosses their mind about the "other" group.
* Once it is clear what the activity is, begin the clock.
* At the conclusion of the minute, participants will be ready to discuss their thoughts from the minute. This is the time to initiate the reflective dialogue.

Reflective Dialogue Questions

Our objective with this activity is to offer a glimpse into our subconscious biases. What is that we think of when just watching our mind wander in the context of "others"? This then becomes fodder for the reflective dialogue. A selection of my go-to reflective dialogue questions includes the following:

- What were some of the thoughts that crossed your mind when thinking about the "other"?
- What do these thoughts highlight about our subconscious biases?
- What can/should we do about it now?
- What can we learn from this exercise that can be applied to our own leadership practice?

Socially Just and Culturally Relevant Leadership

Leadership theories, principles, and practices are rooted, unsurprisingly, in the dominant hegemony. This is synonymous with other disciplines. For example, in traditional social science disciplines (e.g., history and political science), these fields' original researchers studied what was familiar—their own history and politics (i.e., that of five countries—Great Britain, France, Germany, Italy, and the United States). As these researchers began expanding their reach to other locales—primarily to places under their nations' colonial rule—they worked under the premise that the so-called "primitive" people and tribes had no history—except from the time of imposition from modern outsiders (Wallerstein, 2004).

Like social science researchers, leadership theorists research, write, and promote their understanding of leadership in ways that are engrained in their personal perspectives. Unsurprisingly, leadership has historically—and continues to be—stained with a very White, male, and Christian coating. Our global understanding of leadership is heavily imbued with this lens. Unless we purposefully pause and analyze this, especially for those of us—like me—who are part of this dominant hegemony, the influence is invisible.

Now, as we enter the third decade of the 2000s, we need leadership theories, principles, and practices that respond to our ever-expanding and changing cultural mosaic (Bordas, 2012). Rather than avoiding or outright excluding contributions from diverse communities, we need to celebrate and center them. Beatty and Guthrie's (2021) *Operationalizing Culturally Relevant Leadership Learning* takes a deep dive into how we might do this. They pose critical questions for us to reflect upon: What does centering the lived experiences, knowledge, and skills of people of color look like in leadership learning? How do leadership educators understand their own biases and socialization in leadership learning in order to design more equitable and just leadership learning spaces for the purposes of transforming participants engaged in leadership? before exploring the answers.

Leadership has a long history of exclusion and disenfranchisement. When it comes to marginalized populations and people of color being identified as "leaders" or "doing leadership," examples within the leadership literature are limited (Bertrand Jones et al., 2016). We within the leadership industry regularly fail to incorporate leadership texts by diverse authors or promote studies of leadership beyond those who have historically wielded power and exerted their authority. This has had—and continues to have—generational implications.

Young people of marginalized populations, for too long, have rarely seen themselves or representatives as leaders (Bertrand Jones et al., 2016). This exacerbates exclusionary beliefs that "I am *not* a leader," "We don't lead, we follow," or "Leading is not something I/we can do." Worse, people with marginalized identities may equate *leader* or *leadership* with abuses of power, oppression, or control (Rezaei, 2018).

In the leadership field, and certainly by what is being promoted in this book, leadership is a developmental phenomenon available to all of us. Theoretically, we can each develop leadership skills and enhance our leadership capacities so we can serve as exceptional and extraordinarily effective leaders.

We, the broad leadership educator community, believe and like to promote that *anyone can be a leader*. Yet, for many of our leadership training participants—namely Black, Indigenous, and other participants of color—there are systemic challenges that make this notion of "being a leader" quite different and possibly nonexistent (Suarez, 2015) than for people who look and live like me—a White man.

For example, those with marginalized identities are often silenced and unwelcomed by the very act of questioning why one's identity is relevant to leadership learning or why a commitment to justice is essential to transforming antiquated perspectives of leadership (Suarez, 2015). It is for this reason that socially just and culturally relevant leadership has emerged as an important facet of leadership learning.

In a study that explored issues of justice, equity, and oppression, Klau (2017) noted two themes, in particular, that are relevant here. First, the dynamics of obedience and conformity play a powerful role in preserving the status quo of unjust systems. When those with power and authority fail to question injustice and intervene in the face of oppression, the status quo—injustice and oppression—prevails. Second, individuals at the top of systems of privilege and oppression may have very limited insight into the nature of those systems. Although one's system blindness may not be directly or overtly racist, the effect is palpable. Those with power and privilege, when not recognizing the institutionalized and systemic oppression at play, have significant difficulty understanding the lived experiences of others at differing locales within the system.

How might we, as leadership educators, guide significant and systemic change? We need to infuse socially just and culturally relevant leadership into our leadership training philosophy and practice.

Socially just leadership education is strategically at the intersection between leadership education and social justice work (Guthrie & Chunoo, 2018)—it exists at the convergence of two adaptive imperatives: preparing people to lead and creating a fairer world for everyone (Chunoo & Guthrie, 2021). Social justice is premised on a society where all people have access and opportunity in an equitable manner (Teig, 2018b). Often this work is compartmentalized. Leadership training—focused on skills building and capacity development—is facilitated over here, while identity and social justice work is conducted separately over there. By integrating leadership training and education with a serious and intentional social justice lens, we will be strategically positioned to disrupt structural and systemic inequities.

As socially just leadership educators, our objective is twofold: (a) encourage students to cultivate their voice and agency while (b) empowering them to become social critics and active agents of positive and sustainable change (Chunoo & Guthrie, 2021). This integration of leadership training and development with social justice will limit the perpetuation of leadership fallacies and foibles connected to our cultural,

social, and scholarly history. Two contemporary and free resources include a downloadable PDF written by Jordan Harper and Adrianna Kezar (2021) entitled *Leadership for Liberation: A Framework and Guide for Student Affairs Professionals* as well as *The Social Action, Leadership, and Transformation (SALT) Model* (Museus et al., 2017)—a leadership framework that accounts for systemic oppression, power and privilege, and culture and identity.

Culturally relevant leadership learning (CRLL) infuses leadership development processes with an understanding of how systemic oppression influences educational and organizational contexts (Guthrie et al., 2016). CRLL is a framework for transforming leadership development opportunities to address the advantages and disadvantages of difference. Specifically, it encourages leadership educators to attend to the learning experiences of marginalized populations and their experiences of oppression (Bertrand Jones et al., 2016).

Foremost in culturally relevant leadership learning is an acknowledgment of how power and oppression—both as historical legacies and contemporary realities—shape our understanding of leadership—specifically, how the powers of language, socialized understandings of culture, and institutional climate influence individuals' leadership identity, capacity, and efficacy to create sustainable and systemic social change (Bertrand Jones et al., 2016). *Identity* relates to notions of *who* I am. For each of us, our identities are an ever-evolving, socially constructed self-portrait—they are deeply embedded in historical, political, and cultural norms. *Capacity* conveys impressions of *what* I am able to accomplish based on my knowledge and skills. It is our overall ability to effectively engage in the practices and processes of leadership. *Efficacy* expresses *how* I believe in myself. For leadership, our efficacy indicates our belief in being able to lead effectively.

Leadership educators who are serious about developing the leadership capacities of their participants—so they are knowledgeable, skilled, and empowered to create lasting structural and systemic change—need to do important and difficult work. This includes both our own work and facilitating experiences that safely welcome intensive examination of social identities, exploration of structural inequalities, and the erasure of slanted systems that propagate dominant hegemony and groups (Teig, 2018b). Tactically, exceptional leadership educators embrace conflict, value authenticity, acknowledge the humanity in all, and prioritize creative and critical perspective-taking (Watt, 2016). Cameron Beatty (2020), a remarkable and noteworthy leadership scholar, presented a webinar through LeaderShape in December of 2020 where he shared important considerations for leadership educators. Some of these, in a leadership training context, include

- engaging in extensive and intentional self-reflection with self and others—for both leadership educators and our participants;
- embracing vulnerability and mistakes;
- challenging participants who are performing hegemonic and oppressive forms of leadership (which often takes the form of "calling in"—rather than "calling out"—so as to create learning moments and encourage the opening to new ways of leading rather than being shut down and close-minded);
- creating a culture where participants can support and celebrate other participants and their capacity for leadership;
- shifting from theory to praxis, meaning we, and our participants, move from just having the knowledge to doing something about it—in practice (e.g., once we understand our privilege and can identify toxic hegemonic leadership ideologies, we must do the work to reduce that toxicity);
- acknowledging the role and impact oppression—consciously and subconsciously—plays in our leadership practice and unpacking and unlearning our embedded racist, sexist, homophobic, transphobic, and other isms and cultural phobias; and
- critiquing leadership models and theories—as well as programs—that are entrenched in hegemonic ideologies and oppressive to some groups.

These socially just and culturally relevant leadership approaches can be liberating—especially for historically marginalized and contemporary excluded populations. In our leadership trainings, we empower participants to interrogate their own lives and exercise agency, rather than being passive spectators (Beatty & Manning-Ouellette, 2018).

If we intend for our training experiences to be liberating, it is not sufficient to simply provide access and invitations to diverse participants. We need to challenge and change the systems that hold us captive—particularly marginalized and oppressed participants of color. We can do this in multiple dimensions: psychological, behavioral, and organizational (Bertrand Jones et al., 2016)

In the psychological dimension, we focus on cognitive and personal growth. Here, we emphasize individual views of group relations, perceptions and actualizations of discrimination, attitudes about difference and "others," and observations of institutional responses to diversity and inclusion.

In the behavioral dimension, we concentrate on the interactions between individuals and the quality of the interactions between individuals and culturally diverse groups. We can utilize reflective dialogue to assist participants in introspectively critiquing and offering contemplations on their behavior.

In the organizational dimension, we emphasize the structures and processes that guide the "business" of our institutions. This might include the formal or informal curriculum, budget allocations, hiring practices, and other ways our organizations reinforce their values.

It is also essential for us to ask important questions—of ourselves and our leadership training participants: What is leadership? Whose perspective is reflected and/or advanced in this idea of leadership? What are the cultural, historical, political, and social investments in fostering this notion of leadership? Is this leadership training approach or experiential learning activity inclusive of diverse participants? Do I have a process of understanding and checking my own unconscious biases? Whose scholarly voices are being utilized and promoted and whose are being neglected and erased? (Beatty & Manning-Ouellette, 2018; Mahoney, 2016). These types of questions empower us to facilitate important critiques of leadership theories, models, and frameworks—as well as practices that manifest as our leadership habits.

For people like me—White leadership educators—if we are to be engaged in socially just and culturally relevant leadership work, we should be cognizant of our approach. White followership is one particularly important method of celebrating the voices and centering the visions of those who have been marginalized and oppressed. More explicitly, if we, White folk, are to be engaged in racial and social justice work as leadership educators, we must actively center the experiences, sensibilities, interests, methods, critiques, and vision offered by people and communities of color (Villalobos, 2015). Our leadership practice in this space, as White people, is to practice followership.

Often what we do is approach social justice work from an internalized White superiority and savior construct, an "I'm going to save *them*" attitude and approach. To shift into White followership, we can practice six principles: invest in followership; do the homework of learning about White privilege and supremacy—at the personal, interpersonal, institutional, and structural levels; be authentic about who we are, what we know, and our blind spots; be participatory and visible—actually show up when it matters most; practice followership by asking about what is needed first—then doing it; and be strategic to challenge and change the oppressive systems and structures that keep people of color marginalized and silenced (Villalobos, 2015).

Intersectionality

It is also important to reference intersectionality here. *Intersectionality* is understood as the interconnections between social categorizations (e.g., race, class, gender, sexual orientation) with regard to overlapping and heightened systems of discrimination and disadvantage. At the foundation of intersectionality is that at any given time in any given society, the power relations of race, class, and gender (as examples) are not discrete or mutually exclusive entities. Rather, they build upon one another—and work together—to affect all aspects of our social world (Collins & Bilge, 2020). The emphasis here is that different dimensions of social life (e.g., economic, political, cultural, psychic, subjective, and experiential) cannot be separated out into definite and pure strands (Brah & Phoenix, 2004).

Kimberlé Crenshaw (1989) first introduced intersectionality as a paradigm that encourages multiple levels of examination to distinguish the role that these layers of identities play as influences on our individual experiences. For leadership educators, intersectionality requires we examine our practices through lenses of marginalization, inequalities, and power structures (Jones & Bitton, 2021)—not as standalone entities, but as layered lenses that either elevate or relegate one's power and authority.

Intersectionality has three core characterizations. The primary emphasis is on centering the lived experiences of individuals. Second is an exploration of how identity is influenced by systems of power and privilege and the interacting nature of these systems. Third, intersectionality's larger, grander objective is to contribute to a more socially just society (Guthrie et al., 2013).

Intersectionality challenges the notion that any one of these social categories can be utilized in isolation as an explanatory mechanism of a particular group's or individual's experience. Rather an investigation into the intersections of these social identities—in diverse contexts—is essential (Ropers-Huilman, 2013). For example, throughout the United States of America, a woman who identifies as Latina is—either consciously or subconsciously—disadvantaged not solely because of one of her identities (being a woman *or* being Latina), but doubly—because she is both a woman and Latina. And if she identifies as Afro-Latina (Latina with African ancestry), the societal discrimination and associated limitations are tripled.

Leadership Educator Praxis Activity

Leadership Theme: Socially Just and Culturally Relevant Leadership
Exercise: Tower Build (physically engaged activity)

Within the leadership literature, the depth of the discussion on issues of justice and equity has been surface-level, at best. The deeper-level concepts of privilege, discrimination, and oppression are almost nonexistent. Leadership educators have a responsibility to infuse socially just and culturally relevant scholarship and practices into our knowledge base—and then trainings. If we want to build a future rooted in justice and equity, we need to acknowledge and illuminate the discriminatory history of leadership's theoretical foundations and our current cultural assumptions and practices.

Before doing this work with our participants, as leadership educators, we need to engage in it internally. It is an imperative that we have a strong awareness of our own identities and privileges—if we are going to be effective social justice and culturally responsive leadership educators. Finally, we need to better understand the intersections of our own and our participants' identities and how discrimination and disadvantage limit opportunities for our participants to excel and thrive. Exceptional leadership educators firmly recognize that those who wield power hold the privilege of writing history. We are squarely positioned to raise the voices of those who historically experienced—and often continue to experience—having their voices shunted aside and silenced.

Over the last century, our leadership literature was written by and about those who wielded significant power and prestige. It was engrained in their personal perspectives—the White male Christian narrative. Because of this, leadership has been practiced as a mechanism for exclusion and disenfranchisement. Socially just and culturally relevant leadership challenges this as we move deeper into the 21st century by leveraging leadership practice for justice and equity. When thinking about our leadership theories, understandings, and practices—the stories we've been told that express leadership truths—it is important for us to ask three questions: Who writes these stories? Who benefits from these stories? Who is exempt from these stories?

Ladson-Billings (1995) drafted a foundational statement on culturally relevant pedagogy for teachers. We can translate her wisdom for leadership educators. Culturally relevant leadership educators have a particular conception of self and others, social relations, and conceptions of knowledge.

Regarding conceptions of self and others, culturally relevant and socially just leadership educators believe that all of our participants are capable of leadership development; believe that we are on a journey—perpetually in the process of *becoming*—and can enhance our pedagogical approach to facilitating training experiences; see ourselves as members of the training community (rather than from outside or above); and inherently believe that training is about empowering our participants to learn and make meaning from the training experience rather than be lectured to.

From a social relations perspective, culturally relevant and socially just leadership educators maintain fluid participant–trainer relationships; demonstrate connectedness with all participants; develop a community of learners, and encourage our participants to engage and learn collaboratively while being responsible for one another's learning.

Culturally relevant and socially just leadership educators, from a conceptions of knowledge lens, recognize that knowledge is not static—it is shared, recycled, and coconstructed; knowledge must be viewed critically; and trainers must be passionate about leadership development and learning.

The Tower Build activity in and of itself can be utilized for multiple training themes. Leadership educators position it for socially just and culturally relevant leadership by limiting resources for different participant groups and then engaging in purposeful reflective dialogue to unpack the experience and translate the learning into socially just and culturally relevant leadership practice.

Tower Build

The Tower Build empowers participants to build their tallest and sturdiest tower—in competition with other participant groups. I prefer to use children's cardboard boxes of various sizes, shapes, and colors because they enable the participants to actually construct a tower that needs chairs to reach the highest point. That adds a different flavor to the activity than just a tower that can be constructed on a tabletop.

To connect this leadership theme to the activity, it is important to provide the various groups different amounts of resources (i.e., building blocks), planning time, execution time, construction space, and other variables. All of this is utilized in the reflective dialogue to process, unpack and translate which sociocultural groups have benefited—both historically and in contemporary contexts—from privilege and which have not.

Because this is an essential topic, I want to draw our attention to other experiential learning activities that can be facilitated in connection to socially just and culturally relevant leadership. An internet search on each of these will provide remarkable resources for leadership educators. Cross the Line—and its variations—is one of the most popular. In this activity, participants respond to statements and questions by crossing a line or moving into a circle depending on the format and structure of the experiential learning activity. Sample statements and questions might include the way people routinely mispronounce your name, how you've been teased because of your accent, or your experience of being stopped by authorities because of the color of your skin.

Another activity, which necessitates serious planning and collaboration with others, is the Hunger Banquet. This is a meal-based experiential learning activity that explicitly focuses on poverty and its implications. When participants enter the banquet, they are assigned an identity—typically to be part of a group—poor, middle class, wealthy. Wealthy participants—the fewest participants—are offered a lavish meal; middle-class participants, a decent meal; and the poor—also the vast majority of participants—are only given a bowl of rice or beans.

In chapter 11 of Landreman's *The Art of Effective Facilitation: Reflections From Social Justice Educators*—a book and chapter I cannot recommend enough for leadership educators!—an activity, the House of Privilege, is described (Ropers-Huilman, 2013). This is a variation of the Tunnel of Oppression experiential learning activity. As can be elucidated, this program is designed, in a hands-on fashion, to explore oppression and its effects.

As another resource, in his book, *Race and Social Change: A Quest, A Study, A Call To Action*, Max Klau (2017) details what is called The Separation Exercise that is hosted as part of a week-long immersion experience through the National Conference for Community and Justice. I do want to emphasize that I do not advocate this be replicated in our contexts. The facilitators of The Separation Exercise are trained to navigate the complexities of the experience—having engaged with and cultivated relationships with the participants over the course of a week. Notwithstanding, the description of the experiential activity—and Klau's research—illuminates the potential power and importance of these types of experiences.

Material

- children's building blocks

Instructions

- Prior to the experiential learning activity, possibly the training itself, organize the building blocks into the appropriate amount of groups. Remember, the different participant groups should be allotted different amounts of these resources. It should also be noted that although other materials are not provided, their use (so long as it is safe) should be welcomed by facilitators.
- When it is time for the Tower Build activity, arrange the participants into groups; typically four to five per group works well.

- Provide the instructions that they are to build the tallest and sturdiest tower they can by the end of the allotted time.
- Before actually beginning the timer, make it clear which groups have certain restrictions—for example, one group might only be allowed to build in a tiny corner of the training space.
- *Note*: You can also add restrictions and/or remove restrictions as the time elapses.
- Once the alarm has sounded, bring the group back together and test the height, strength, and durability of the towers. Award a winner.
- At the conclusion of the awards ceremony, the participants will be high energy and clearly articulating their frustrations at the lack of fairness. These are important emotions and should be leveraged in the reflective dialogue.

Reflective Dialogue Questions

Our objective with this activity is create the conditions to tangibly explore power and privilege. Our reflective dialogue should focus on what was experienced, how it translates to beyond-the-bubble oppression and inequity, and what our participants can do moving forward to be more socially just leaders. A selection of my go-to reflective dialogue questions includes the following:

- What did you experience in this activity? (This question should be asked repeatedly to participants who were part of the variously resourced and privileged groups.)
- What did you notice about the other groups?
- What did you do to support or dismantle the other groups? Why?
- How does this experience translate to what we know about privilege, inequality, oppression, and justice?
- What can/should we do about it now?
- What can we learn from this exercise that can be applied to our own leadership practice?

Leading and Other Developmental Relationships

We've come to understand that leading is a developmental experience. Leaders—especially in the context of contemporary theories, models, and frameworks—are responsible for the learning, growth, and development of others. This is a core tenet of leading. Through these developmental relationships, the participants (a) explore who they are, (b) cultivate skills to shape their lives, (c) learn how to engage with and contribute to the world around them, and (d) develop the capacities to thrive.

Leading is not the only developmental relationship at our disposal. Often, *leading*, as a term, is used interchangeably with *advising, coaching, guiding, mentoring, modeling, sponsoring*, and *supervising*. When leadership educators serve in these other developmental roles, we can accelerate our participants' leadership development.

It is important for leadership educators, though, to have clarity regarding both the importance as well as differences between these developmental relationships. All of these developmental relationships hold weight and significance—yet are ultimately effective in certain contexts and relationships. Understanding the nuances between them—so they can be appropriately and effectively applied—is a serious task.

Role modeling, for example, is an opportunity to display skills and worthy attributes. It does not, however, require a significant or mutual personal relationship. Leading, in comparison, is an opportunity to display those same modeling skills and attributes. It does, though, necessitate a significant and mutual relational investment.

Advising, as another developmental relationship, does require a connected relationship between the two individuals—the advisor and the advisee. It does not necessarily need to be an emotionally connected relationship for an effective advising experience. The focus of advising, rather, is on technical guidance (W.B. Johnson et al., 2010). In comparison, the development of technical skills is one component of the relationship between leader and follower. For effective leading, much more is expected, including the depth of the relational connection as well as the pursuit of a common, worthy goal.

Sponsoring is a work-related developmental relationship. The sponsor's focus is on their protégés professional development and advancement. Sponsors advocate for promotion and provide professional relational connections. Leading is not solely focused on the occupational skills development and advancement of their followers—although many leaders incorporate that into their practice. Leading focuses on navigating challenges and working toward goal accomplishment. Furthermore, sponsoring necessitates that sponsors hold senior-level roles and tend to wield significant formal power and influence within their organization or professional field. Leading does not necessitate formal authority within any organization or professional field.

Similarly, *supervising* and leading are closely related because of leading and managing often being confused and conflated. Managers are often supervisors. The key difference is that supervising is role-bound. Leading is not determined by role, but by the actions of leaders. Supervisors have very specific roles and responsibilities related to the execution of supervisee work responsibilities (Hawkins & Shohet, 2020).

With the expansion of the *coaching* industry—specifically with the proliferation of leadership coaches—the similarities and differences between leading and coaching have been scrutinized. Coaching tends to focus on performance enhancements, having a specific agenda when in coaching dialogue sessions, a fee associated with the services, and a shorter time of relational engagement (Clutterbuck, 2008). In contrast, leading is not typically fee-based nor does it necessarily utilize a preset agenda for dialogue and leadership engagements. Leading also tends to have a longer time of engagement than most coaching commitments (Garvey et al., 2018) and is not limited by individual performance enhancements—but by engaging in work and expending energy connected to navigating challenges and working toward goal accomplishment.

Mentoring and leading are also closely related. Although both strive for the holistic development of others (mentees or followers), the difference is situated within the objective of the developmental relationships. Mentoring is a distinctive relational learning experience whereby participants, through intentional challenge and support, enhance the personal growth and professional/skills development of their collaborator(s) (Kroll, 2016). Leading includes this challenge and support for the growth of others, but not as the sole focus. This developmental work is part and parcel of delivering the change that is needed.

Table 6.1—originally drafted by Murphy and Kram (2014) and expanded upon to include leadership—differentiates leading from some other developmental relationships by a focus on roles and goals of the relationship. Table 6.2 details when each of these developmental relationships should best be deployed.

TABLE 6.1: A Description of Developmental Relationships to Highlight Roles and Purposes of the Relationships

	Roles	Purpose
Leading	Leaders Followers	Developing the skills and capacities of others while navigating challenges and pursuing goal accomplishment
Coaching	Coaches Coachees/ Clients	Performance development
Mentoring	Mentors Mentees	Holistic development
Sponsoring	Sponsors Protégés	Visibility and opportunities
Supervising	Supervisors Supervisees	Guiding work responsibilities

Note. Adapted from *Strategic Relationships at Work: Creating Your Circle of Mentors, Sponsors, and Peers for Success in Business and Life* by W. Murphy & K. Kram, 2014, McGraw-Hill; and expanded upon.

TABLE 6.2: A Description of When Each of These Developmental Relationships Is Best Deployed

Leading	Best executed when followers need inspiration and guidance to confront obstacles and pursue worthy goals
Coaching	Best executed when coachees/clients are in need of and desiring intentional opportunities to enhance their performance
Mentoring	Best executed when mentees are in need of and desiring intentional opportunities to wrestle with big questions
Sponsoring	Best executed when protégés are in need of making connections and advancing in their professional contexts
Supervising	Best executed when supervisees are in need of structure and direction to accomplish the objectives of their position, role, and work responsibilities

Another way to visualize the differences between leading and other developmental relationships is to consider developmental relationships based upon the level of intent and the level of involvement necessary by the participants. Originally designed by Mertz (2004) and expanded upon, the pyramid in Figure 6.2 is utilized to differentiate the level of intent as well as level of involvement needed for each developmental relationship.

Intent is concerned with the rationale (the why) behind the relationship. For what purposes (the ends) are those individuals engaging in the experience? *Involvement* is concerned with the depth of engagement associated with the relationship. Physical and emotional costs, intensity of interaction, and the nature and level of investment for the participants are factors contributing to the involvement side of the scale.

Role modeling necessitates a low level of intent and a low level of involvement. Advising, coaching, and sponsoring demand a reasonable amount of intention and involvement. And as evidenced in Figure 6.2, mentoring and leading are predicated upon a high

level of intent and a high level of involvement. It is for this reason that leading and mentoring are most commonly interchanged—that exemplar leaders are often hailed as exceptional mentors.

Within the leadership and developmental relationship literature, there are two threads that, in part, differentiate these growth-oriented relationships from one another: challenge and support (Sanford, 1967).

Support is the distinctive experience of being and feeling valued. If we are supported, we have a deep sense and belief that we can bear the weight of challenging situations (Day et al., 2009). Support manifests through recognition, validation, and providing others with a sense of belonging (Earnshaw, 1995). In practice, leaders provide support when they serve as a guide to resources and a source of comfort and healing (Daloz Parks, 2000). Support is provided in tandem with challenge. Without challenge, support is simply affirmation.

Challenge has been identified as an appropriate strategy and a key ingredient to learning, growth, and development (Burgess & Butcher, 1999; Butcher,

Figure 6.2. Pyramid of developmental relationships.

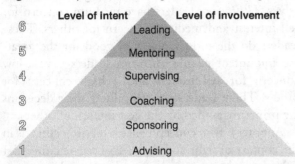

Note. Adapted from "What's a Mentor Anyway?" by N. Mertz, 2004, *Educational Administration Quarterly, 40*(4), 551, and expanded upon.

2002; McNally & Martin, 1998). Challenge is utilized to create cognitive dissonance through the questioning of thinking and the critiquing of preconceptions and tacit assumptions (Burgess & Butcher, 1999). When challenged, in healthy and productive ways, we are stretched beyond our comfort levels in ways that provide motivation and opportunities to learn, grow, and develop (Day et al., 2009).

Daloz (1986) illustrates the connection between challenge and support and the outcomes when either low or high levels of each are engaged. Low levels of both challenge and support result in stasis. High levels of challenge with low levels of support lead to retreat. High levels of support and low levels of challenge produce confirmation. High levels of both challenge and support generate growth. This is important for leadership educators to think about in both the context of our own leadership practice as well as how we regulate challenge and support in our leadership training facilitation.

Leadership Educator Praxis Activity

Leadership Theme: Leading and Other Developmental Relationships
Exercise: Shoe Swap (physically engaged activity)

So often, our leadership training participants mix and match and conflate these developmental relationships. This results in the poor execution and performance of the developmental experience. Learning and growth are stunted if supervision is desired but advising is implemented or if leading is needed at a particular moment but what is provided is role modeling or mentoring. It is for this reason leadership educators need to know the foundational

differences, roles, and goals of these developmental relationships so we can properly train our participants to recognize the power that they each wield when acted upon appropriately. The Shoe Swap activity provides participants an opportunity to experiment with different developmental relationships as they work through a challenge toward goal accomplishment.

Shoe Swap

It is best for participants to have clean socks for this activity. Participants are instructed to remove their shoes and place them either in the center of the training space or a different room entirely. The shoes are then shuffled and mixed. Participants find a partner and are provided a notecard with a specific developmental relationship. In this role, they are to direct their partner to retrieve their shoes. That is, participants retrieve their partners' shoes.

Materials

- notecards, each with a different developmental relationship (i.e., coach, mentor, supervise, and lead)—one for every participant

Instructions

- Begin by inviting participants to remove their shoes and place them in the appropriate place—either the center of the training space or a different room entirely, to make the activity a bit more challenging.
- Once the shoes have been appropriately placed, you should shuffle them so they are all mixed.
- Only then should participants be invited to find a partner.
- Once pairs are settled, provide a developmental relationship notecard to each participant.
- Instruct the participants that they are to utilize that developmental relationship as a way to get their partner to retrieve their shoes. No other assistance shall be provided (e.g., pointing to them)
- If time is available after everyone's shoes are retrieved, participants can unshoe, find a new partner, switch developmental relationships, and repeat the activity.
- Once all of the participants have their own shoes, enter into the reflective dialogue.

Reflective Dialogue Questions

Our objective with this activity is to offer a hands-on experiential activity for participants to experiment with the diversity of developmental relationships. By knowing how to best coach, mentor, supervise, and lead, participants will be well positioned to maximize these roles. A selection of my go-to reflective dialogue questions includes the following:

- What developmental relationship role did you have—and how did it feel to be in that role?
- What role would have been better for you to accomplish this task? Why?
- What did you learn about yourself from this experience?
- Which developmental relationship do you want to enhance for your own practice?
- What can we learn from this exercise that can be applied to our own leadership practice?

Leadership Ethics

Ethics was an important theme in the writings of Plato and Aristotle millenia ago. *Ethos*, the word they utilized, translates to "customs," "conduct," or "character." Today, we understand ethics to be about the values and morals that individuals, cultures, and societies deem as desirable or appropriate (Northouse, 2021). Ethics is a socially constructed and subjective concept and fluctuates based upon the particular values and morals of individuals, cultures, and societies in varying contexts at various times. What may be deemed as desirable or appropriate in one context or culture or time may be perceived as blatantly unethical in another. Similarly, ethical conduct in one context or culture may be strictly enforced. In another, it may just receive a shrug of the shoulders. Rather than think of leadership ethics as a set of inflexible rules, we may want to consider them as "operating guidelines" or principles with which we should operate. Ethical behavior should be considered based upon a spectrum.

Within this spectrum, there are three general ways that ethics are classified. Based upon the conduct and character of leaders, they either have a high level of concern for their own self-interest, high level of concern for others, or are situated somewhere in between (C. Johnson, 2018; Northouse, 2021).

Leaders with *ethical egoism* have a high concern for self-interest and low concern for others. These leaders act based upon the greatest good for themselves. *Utilitarian* leaders have medium concern for self-interest and medium concern for others. These leaders do the most amount of good for the greatest amount of people. *Altruistic* leaders have a low concern for self-interest and a high concern for others. These leaders act ethically if their decisions are primarily guided by the best interest of others.

Another way to conceptualize leadership ethics is in the context of light and darkness. Leaders either cast light or shadows upon those with whom they engage (C. Johnson, 2018; Palmer, 2000). *Light* is a reference to leading in ways that are nourishing, humanizing, and celebratory—acting in accordance with the healthy cultural norms and ethos of that particular context and community—so that people can flourish and thrive. When the opposite occurs, leaders act in ways that cast shadows.

Shadow-casting leaders subject their community to damaging and destructive behaviors that reduce and limit well-being. Their exploits contradict the healthy cultural norms and ethos of that particular context and community. There are various leadership shadows that can be cast. Two particularly poignant ones include the *shadow of power*—when leaders become "drunk" on power, they utilize it for harmful or strictly self-serving means—and the *shadow of privilege*—when leaders take advantage of their position or influence to limit others or solely advance their position or enhance their resources.

These shadows are primarily cast due to the uninformed, ill-examined inner darkness of leaders. If we desire to cast more light than shadows, we need to engage in the discovery work to understand our shadow "monsters" (Palmer, 2000), identify how they create and make manifest shadows, and work diligently to bring forth the light to overwhelm these shadows cast by different types of monsters:

The insecurity monster. Leaders do not have confidence in their abilities and feel threatened by their followers.

The battleground mentality monster. Leaders focus on winning at all costs and are always positioning themselves and their organizations for competition.

The functional atheism monster. Leaders blindly believe that everything that happens—good or bad—is tethered to themselves.

The fear monster. Leaders are constantly limiting themselves and their organizations due to distrust of others.

The denying death monster. Leaders are not able to face the reality that projects or programs may need to come to a close for the health of the organization.

The evil monster. Some leaders take joy in causing pain and terror.

If we are to shine light on these shadows and confront these monsters, models and frameworks are important. In order to engage in ethical decision-making and behaviors, implementing four psychological processes can serve as a foundation (Rest, 1986, 1993).

Leaders begin by cultivating *moral sensitivity.* Leaders can't make ethical decisions if there is a lack of clarity that a moral problem exists. This is all about recognition. It is followed by *moral judgment.* Once identified, leaders make judgments and determinations for future action based on what they believe is right or wrong. Next is *moral focus*: Once judgments are made, confidence and motivation are necessary for leaders to follow through on moving from thinking to acting. Finally is the development of *moral character.* Leaders courageously execute the plan by tapping into their deeply held values. Additionally, C. Johnson (2019) promotes various practices that can improve leaders' ethical performance:

Discovering vocation. Vocation is synonymous with "calling." What am I here to do? Where am I going? What are my special gifts and superpowers? How can I do the most good?—these are calling questions. By determining our purpose, we can become grounded in ethical and moral decision-making.

Identifying personal values. Our personal values serve as a source of navigation—they drive our decision-making and behaviors. By identifying, exploring, and self-authoring our personal values, we position ourselves to act in moral and ethical ways.

Drawing upon spiritual or meaning-making resources. Often, faith (in the broadest conception of the term) is a foundation for ethical decision-making and behaviors. By pursuing a spiritual grounding or engaging in purposeful meaning-making activities, we can enhance our ethical performance.

Developing character. When we develop our moral and ethical identity, we are cultivating our character—the values that consistently guide our thinking, behaviors, and actions.

Character has been referenced in both models noted previously. So, what is character? *Character* can be understood as the collection of traits, values, and virtues that define a person (Newman, 2019). It is a holistic perspective that takes into account the thoughts, attitudes, and actions of individuals—both in public and in private, externally and internally. Trust, in leadership—specifically for individuals in positions of power and authority—is based on presumed character, rather than skills (Urry, 2003). For this reason, character needs to be developed so leaders are seen as trustworthy, capable, and reliable. To develop character, there are select dimensions that can be practiced and enhanced (C. Johnson, 2019; Newman, 2019).

Character development begins by cultivating healthy habits—by continuously and relentlessly practicing the behaviors we want to come naturally and to be known for. We also express our vulnerability. We build character by boldly risking exposure by sharing honestly, including our faults and limitations. Character is cultivated by living with integrity and authenticity. We do this by being consistent and true to ourselves. When leading, we act with accountability. That is, taking ownership—and following through—with the projects and obligations to which we commit. Finally we practice the triad of courage, compassion, and humility. By acting courageously, showing love and care, and honoring the value and voice of others, we nurture our character.

Leadership Educator Praxis Activity

Leadership Theme: Leadership Ethics
Exercise: Up, Down, and All Around (physically engaged activity)

Just as nuanced as leadership theories, ethics (in the context of leadership), due to its social construction and subjectivity, is more fluid than solid. Although this is the case, leadership educators should not shy away from trainings that explore ethics. In fact, this is the reason it is so important for us to offer this topic as part of our training repertoires. Only by engaging our participants in reflective inquiry and dialogue on this topic can we assist our participants and the groups, organizations, communities, and associations of which they are a part wrestle with and determine where on the spectrum they want to be, what shadows have emerged, and ways to develop character. We can utilize the Up, Down, and All Around activity to explore how participants' beliefs affect various scenarios.

Up, Down, and All Around

The Up, Down, and All Around activity encourages participants to respond to different scenarios—typically in picture form—by moving their bodies up (from a chair), down (to a seated position), or to spin around in a circle. This can also be structured as a completely seated activity. Participants can raise their arms and show their spirit fingers or drop them toward the ground or to make arm circles to indicate feeling good (the displayed picture or scenario is ethical), feeling bad or uncomfortable (it is not ethical) about that scenario (sitting down), or feeling unsure or with mixed emotions about that scenario (spinning around), respectively.

Materials

- pictures (typically as a slide deck) of ethics images or scenarios (e.g., an image of a stereotypical bank robber or back-to-back pictures of a happy family with a puppy—in comparison to a photo of a puppy mill in poor condition)

Instructions

- Begin by sharing the instructions that participants will be asked to move up (to stand), down (to sit), or all around (to spin around) based upon if they believe what is being shown is ethical (up), not ethical (down), or unclear (spin all around).
- Once the instructions are provided, begin showing images or scenarios from the slide deck.

- It may be worthwhile to engage in some dialogue in between pictures or between every few pictures to get a sense from participants why they are standing, sitting, or spinning. This can be utilized in the forthcoming reflective dialogue.

Reflective Dialogue Questions

Our objective with this activity is to intentionally explore how we understand ethical behavior. Only by understanding it first can we practice ethical leadership with strong character and integrity. A selection of my go-to reflective dialogue questions includes the following:

- How did you feel about standing, sitting, or spinning—thinking back, would you change any of your movements now?
- What did you notice about how other participants responded in different ways? Are they wrong?
- How do we navigate nuance within ethical situations?
- What can we learn from this exercise that can be applied to our own leadership practice?

Conclusion

Above and beyond the dozens of theories explored in the previous chapters, these themes and topics enhance our leadership knowledge base and expand the opportunities for our participants to explore leadership. When we facilitate training experiences on followership; demographic considerations—including leadership and gender and culture; socially just and culturally responsive leadership; leading and other developmental relationships; and leadership ethics, we create leadership learning experiences that can have far-reaching implications. Namely, we create shifts in our participants' understanding and practice of leadership so it becomes centered in notions of belonging, equity, justice, and purposefully raising the voices of those who have historically been excluded.

Leadership Theories, Models, Frameworks, and Themes—Part Two Conclusion

With the immensity of leadership theories, models, frameworks, and themes at our disposal, there is no shortage of options or opportunities with which we can frame and inform our leadership trainings. We now have a solid understanding of what leadership is—at least the many ways that leadership scholars have articulated it. Or maybe we are more confused and concerned than before because of the breadth of ways that we can conceptualize and ground our notions of leadership with this knowledge.

It is my hope that, as leadership educators, we can confidently articulate the trajectory of how notions of leadership expanded from the foundational theories (industrial and postindustrial), through the transformation phase, to contemporary perspectives—as well as various leadership themes. I encourage the utilization of this book as a starting place. These theories, models, frameworks, and themes are just a high-level overview. There is much more to be learned—and much weightier ways to inform our trainings by going directly to the sources and exploring the diversities of leadership literature. This material is unquestionably essential to our effectiveness as leadership educators—it is the foundation for our work.

PART THREE

LEADERSHIP PRACTICES, SKILLS, AND COMPETENCIES

LEADERSHIP THEORIES INFORM WHAT we *know* about leadership. Leadership practices inform what we *do* when leading. Our leadership practice is ultimately derived from the compilation of our daily leadership routines and decisions—our *habits*. With intentional attention, these can become healthy leadership habits.

Habits are essentially our brain's effort to save energy. An efficient brain enables us to stop thinking constantly about basic behaviors and entertain more complex thoughts. Habits can be ignored, changed, or replaced. Unless we deliberately create new routines, our limiting habitual practices will prevail (Duhigg, 2014). This illuminates and reinforces the notion that leadership is a lifelong developmental journey that requires constant attention, energy, and investment. For most, we need to first unlearn the habits that result in our limiting leadership behaviors. Then we can learn and infuse healthy habits into our leadership practice.

Healthy leadership habits are synonymous with leadership skills and competencies. When implemented into our leadership regimen, we consider them a leadership practice. Charles Duhigg (2014), author of *The Power of Habit*, suggests that we create healthy habits by first establishing a cue—a trigger for our brain that indicates it is time to go into automatic mode. Then we engage in a routine to make it rememberable (a habit). Finally, we establish rewards so our brain recognizes this cue and routine as valuable—worth remembering.

Duhigg (2014) indicates there are two essential elements to ensuring habits become . . . *habits*. We need to capitalize on and celebrate small wins. Small wins have

enormous power. Their influence is disproportionate to the accomplishments of the victories themselves. Second, opportunities for success increase dramatically when others are involved. The personal belief in establishing a healthy leadership habit is crucial—and grows out of communal experience—even if the community is only as large as two people.

To take our healthy leadership habits to advanced levels—world-class, mastery levels—there are certain features to consider. In *The Talent Code*, Daniel Coyle (2009) indicates that to become world-class with any of our habits, we should engage in deep practice. Deep practice includes motivational fuel, masterful guidance, and repetition. We need to understand and tap into the *why*, at the deepest level of our selves. This sustains us through the obstacles, challenges, struggles, and significant energy investment to become talented at optimal levels. We also need guidance from trusted and consummate coaches and educators to indicate where we can improve—and how to make those improvements. Finally, we need to repeat the healthy habit over and over again so it becomes a natural practice. Repetition is invaluable and irreplaceable.

For leadership educators, these points are fundamental to our work. During our leadership trainings, we craft opportunities for our participants to engage in experiential activities. These experiential activities are designed as small win experiences. We then follow the experiential learning activities with reflective dialogue so they can capitalize on communal engagement. Here, we strategically pose questions to engage participants in thinking critically about their *whys* and

105

assist them in uncovering and tapping into their motivational fuel. We serve as masterful guides.

Offering trainings aimlessly is not going to accomplish the goal of developing effective leaders. We need to be strategic and purposeful in offering trainings that focus on participants' competencies that are either in need of strategic adjustments or enhancing their capacities to so that they perform exceptionally, regularly. This means that we have work to do to cultivate a deep leadership training practice and healthy leadership training habits—which is what this book is intended to support. And we initiate opportunities for our participants to begin repetitive processes that will ultimately occur beyond the training bubble as a way to nurture their own healthy leadership habits.

Leadership educators need to be fluent and well-versed in varied leadership practices—not just to know *about* them. The reason is simple and straightforward. Our leadership practices are the actions taken to ensure we smoothly navigate challenges, optimally pursue desired changes, and efficiently progress toward goal accomplishment.

The following four chapters are included for multiple reasons. We cannot masterfully train participants in a leadership skill if we have not cultivated it as part of our own practice. These competencies need to be our own healthy leadership habits. Albeit not a definitive list, this is a comprehensive list of a dozen-and-a-half leadership practices that can inform our leadership trainings—with tailored experiential learning activities and instructions for each of these practices.

In addition to what I offer in this book, I invite you to explore other resources. Student Leadership Competencies (https://studentleadershipcompetencies .com/) along with the Charlie Life and Leadership Academy (https://charlieacademy.org/) offer resources for leadership educators and our participants—namely university students. They are both wide-ranging and informative.

The four chapters in Part Three are arranged by general types of leadership practices: cognitive, emotive, cooperative, and generative. At the end of each practice, I offer instructions for facilitating an experiential learning activity that focuses on cultivating that practice as well as go-to questions for hosting reflective dialogue. These praxis components directly connect the healthy leadership habits to potential facilitative experiences for *your* trainings.

CHAPTER 7

Cognitive Leadership Practices

THE FIRST GROUPING OF leadership practices focuses on intentional thinking. They are cognitive in nature. This includes visioning, thinking systemically, practicing mindfulness, and integrating reflection with action. When we focus our attention on these four skills, we get into the right mindset and headspace to intensify our leadership practices.

Visioning

Visioning is the leadership starting point. If we don't know where we are heading, we most certainly won't be able to decipher the best way forward. Nor will we be able to distinguish when we have arrived at our goal or objective. Visioning enables us to dig deeply into our quest—to dive into the layers of *why*. We're not interested in the surface-level factors. No. We decode the essence of our belief. Why is *this* so compelling? Why can I not do anything but *this*? Visioning is absolutely essential for leaders—especially as we pursue depth of clarity.

Followers need leaders with clear and compelling visions. We know that followers are more profoundly invested in supporting leaders who are connected to a deep sense of purpose. The vision is the crux with which we can mobilize energy, resources, and others in pursuit of this worthy objective. As a leadership practice, leaders need to begin with a vision.

A vision, in the broadest sense, is our ultimate guiding philosophy of the future. It provides direction, meaning, and purpose. A vision offers a sketch of what could be. We accept the challenge of *this* vision because it is overwhelmingly empowering. This is our calling. This is our most worthy goal. This is what we are in service to. This is life-giving.

A vision and mission are quite different. The vision serves as the road map. It is a clear and concise articulation of the ultimate goals and objectives toward which we strive. The vision expresses the ideal state—the *almost* unachievable future. It is the one True (capital "T") pursuit that harnesses our attention and energy. It is a constant force in our lives.

A mission describes the tangible, tactical actions that enable the vision to be realized. These are specific activities, programs, and policies—the actions in the most literal sense—that facilitate vision realization.

Let's explore a few examples to make this real—from an individual, programmatic, and organizational level. For me professionally, *I envision a world where leadership educators have the knowledge, skills, and dynamism to facilitate exceptional leadership trainings*. This is a vision that speaks to *my* deepest work-related desires. The work that I do as an educator at the University of Rhode Island, with my nonprofit, in my social relationships, in my digital media presence—in all aspects of my life—are about ultimately realizing this vision. One of my mission actions is teaching an academic course, Facilitating Leadership Development, at the University of Rhode Island. Another would be crafting Leadership Trainer's breadth of programming and resources for those charged with and responsible for the leadership training and development of others. Writing this book is a third example of how I am living into my vision as a mission practice.

At a programmatic level, the Leadership Trainer Certification Program *aspires to be the undisputed authority in certifying leadership trainers.* This is almost unattainable, right? What are the metrics for being the "undisputed authority" of anything? This is a model vision statement because it provides direction and a guiding force for all of the mission entities (actions) with which the team members and stakeholders should engage. If our team members' actions do not align with and enable the Leadership Trainer Certification Program (LTCP) to become the undisputed authority in certifying leadership trainers, they either should not be part of the organization or their contributions should be altered to better align with this vision. Regarding mission actions, outwardly (i.e., externally facing to the world), they include the actual retreat programs, scholarships, grants, and other incentives to make it easier for diverse prospective participants to say "yes" in becoming certified master trainers. We also have a YouTube Channel with our *What The F@*# Is Leadership!?* video-interview series where we interview expert leadership scholars, exceptional leadership educators, and other extraordinary individuals—many of whom serve as master trainers for the LTCP. Inwardly (i.e., internally facing for those who are involved and invested in this vison realization), the LTCP master trainer application asks candidates why they believe intentional leadership training is essential. If our master trainers do not believe that intentional leadership training is vital, it is safe to assume they will poorly ensure the LTCP becomes the undisputed authority in training leadership trainers. Additionally, organizational team members immerse themselves in leadership literature and attend leadership-oriented professional gatherings to keep abreast with the latest leadership research as well as build relationships within the leadership scholarly and practice community.

Organizationally, visions empower and encourage all of the stakeholders to be involved, committed, and aligned with their ultimate pursuits. This is true for small-scale family-owned businesses, global corporate entities, and everything in between. My favorite local coffee shop, Recreo, in West Roxbury (Boston), Massachusetts, believes *it is our vision to bring high quality Nicaraguan coffee to you, while practicing social and environmental stewardship.* For the owners, baristas, and other staff, they are driven by ensuring social programs in Nicaragua serve the harvesters—these include a school for the children who live on the plantation, an infirmary, community programs, recreational opportunities, and more. They are committed to environmental policies that support the continued generation of robust coffee beans that are safe to pick, process, and consume. Finally, they create a café culture that is engaging and informative—teaching customers and community members about Nicaragua, the plantation, coffee, and other relevant information that supports opportunities for people to feel comfortable receiving their high-quality Nicaraguan coffee.

Institutions of higher learning are also devoted to envisioning better worlds. My doctoral alma mater, Fielding Graduate University, has the vision of *educating leaders, scholars, and practitioners for a more just and sustainable world.* At the University of Rhode Island, the college with which I am affiliated, details that we will *prepare individuals who are locally engaged, nationally respected, and globally involved in the work of educational, organizational, and economic justice.* With both of these examples, there is clarity as to what they pursue—a just and sustainable world and local engagement, national respect, and global involvement in the contexts of educational, organizational, and economic justice, respectively. At both of these institutions, their academic programs, certifications, cocurricular programming, and other endeavors focus on bringing these visions to life.

A leadership vision consists of seven essential elements (Ndalamba et al., 2018):

- *Knowledge of oneself.* A compelling leadership vision begins with profound self-knowledge. It is imperative that leaders are intimately connected to their self-authored authentic selves as a starting point for bringing forth a captivating vision.
- *Commitment to others' growth.* For vision realization to occur, we need to understand and act upon the development of others—and create opportunities for others to contribute in meaningful ways.
- *Recognizing the need to change.* Understanding that change is constant and healthy for growth is an important leadership asset. Leaders who recognize this will be better able to navigate challenges and obstacles as they pursue their vision.

- *Understanding the context.* Recognizing the contexts that surround the vision is a prime task for leaders. This enables leaders to pursue appropriate action to work toward vision realization.
- *Defining the right problem.* Each leadership vision is dedicated to solving a significant problem. By realizing this vision, the problem is solved. This is why it is imperative to define the problem accurately.
- *Communicating the problem.* In addition to defining the problem the vision intends to solve, leaders need to articulate its significance and how the action plan will bring about positive change.
- *Executing the action plan.* Once a vision has been crafted and communicated—and the plans have been designed—leaders need to mobilize followers to strategically execute that plan.

Developing a vision begins with a purposeful pause—an opportunity to be quiet, still, and silent—to reflect on what is at the heart of our individual or organizational pursuits. One's vision

is the thing that continually renews your spirit . . . the indomitable force that moves you to action when nothing else can, yet grounds you with a single whisper in your quietest moment; it is at once the bedrock of your soul . . . the wind beneath your wings. It spells out the most overarching goals you want and need to achieve. (Loehr, 2007, p. 44)

When drafting a personal vision statement, generally, leaders want to be forward-thinking and spend time ruminating about questions of meaning and depth—the driving forces, layers deep—that serve as a foundation for their pursuits. The reverse approach is also a possibility—to envision a gravestone or draft a hypothetical obituary. After a long life of many accomplishments, what do you want your legacy to be? What is that one sentence or statement that encapsulates your life? What were you striving for? How do you want to be known or remembered?

When crafting vision statements as part of a program or organization, we want to be mindful of not utilizing hifalutin, pretentious language that is disconnected from reality—disconnected from the people

with whom we are supposed to be working to realize that vision. Organizational values should be drafted in a way that expresses the values and pursuits of those who serve the organization and those who want to be served by the organization. They should be crafted *with*, not just for, employees, members, constituents, and other stakeholders.

Once it has been developed, we need to artfully and articulately communicate it. The vision will be difficult to realize if nobody knows about it. The vision needs to be adapted to the desires and visions of the followers. An effective vision has resonance. It is for this reason that top-down approaches to vision where the executive (or executive team), behind closed doors, writes a vision and demands others follow it typically have a tepid response. People do not feel particularly connected to it, and this form of communication—a demand—is not responded to well.

The values and mission practices need to be shared in a way that people understand, agree with, and believe is possible. By sharing the values of the vision—along with the mission practices—followers will be better able to connect their work to the greater goal. This provides all those involved (leaders and followers) with a deeper sense of commitment and authentic belief that the work (even menial tasks) have worth.

Goldstein et al. (2010) articulate what happens when a vision creation and dissemination process is closed-door and top-down:

Consider for instance, this typical story told about organization change. First, the top executives develop and describe a "vision" for the organization; they set about enrolling those further down the hierarchy into this vision. In turn, that "guiding coalition" is supposed to go around coaxing key players to also buy into that vision, with the assumption that the more coherence across individuals and departments, the more successful the change will be. An all-consuming change effort now ensues, resulting in only occasional success at best, and sometimes even pure disaster. (p. 77)

Vision attainment is not something that we check off—like on a to-do list. Rarely is a vision ever complete. Implementing a vision requires stamina. It necessitates significant, focused effort over a substantial amount of time. Leaders continuously and consciously make decisions—and guide followers in efforts—that are always pursuing the vision realization. Leaders should always be asking, "Does this task, program, project, or expenditure align with our vision?" If so, great! Get it! If not, leaders should seriously reconsider if it should be pursued. What is its value if it does not align with mission objectives and lead toward vision realization?

Leadership Educator Praxis Activity

Leadership Theme: Visioning
Exercise: Tombstone and Obituary (reflective [worksheet] activity)

Visioning is often a sound training topic—especially at the start of the year or the launching of a new group or organization. It is an important way for individuals, groups, and organizations to think strategically and comprehensively about what's to come. Visioning-focused trainings serve as opportunities for participants to garner commitment from diverse stakeholders, set the tone for the year or task ahead, cultivate relationships, and then provide fodder for the reflective processes that promote healthy goal setting.

Leadership educators have a repertoire of examples to utilize as models for their participants. These illustrations provide tangible guidance as our participants craft their own. Additionally, when facilitating vision-themed trainings, we need to carve out significant time for participants to reflect upon their visions. This is important time and space for simmering to occur—especially as visions require connections to the deepest part of ourselves and our pursuits.

Providing a clear and compelling vision is the first act of leadership. How else will others be prepared, inspired, and empowered to follow if there is not a captivating vision? To assist leaders in developing this kind of vision, we can utilize either the Tombstone or Obituary activity. I'll share both in the context of a personal leadership vision. This can also be translated for a group, organization, or community context.

Tombstone

The Tombstone activity guides participants in drafting a succinct message that embodies the core characteristics of the leader—what you would find on a tombstone. These are short—even fewer characters than a tweet—and highlight the grandest-level

personification of the leader. Participants will consider, when the time comes, for what were they most proud?

Materials

- worksheet—I suggest using a worksheet with a full-page tombstone picture or graphic rather than just a blank sheet.
- writing utensil

Obituary

The Obituary activity guides participants in drafting a dispatch that highlights their accomplishments. To complete this activity, participants should future-think about, at the end of their life, what they want their legacy to be. For what do they want to be remembered? What were their major accomplishments? These are then drafted in a way to self-motivate and inspire the pursuit of this worthy aspiration.

Materials

- paper
- writing utensil

Instructions

- For both activities, begin by settling the energy and prepare participants to think seriously about the legacy they want to pursue.
- Once participants are settled, provide the worksheet and invite them to meditate on, at their end of life, what will be written—in stone or on paper.
- Provide participants time and space to allow ideas to simmer. This activity is not one that should feel rushed.
- As time gets close to expiring (another pun intended), signal them so they can begin to wrap up their musing and writing.
- Participants can then be invited to share in pairs, small groups, or the group-as-a-whole prior to the reflective dialogue.

Reflective Dialogue Questions

Our objective with this activity is to offer participants a glimpse of their possible future. By thinking about what they hope to accomplish, they can begin to craft a vision. This vision serves as a guiding path forward toward the development of a legacy about which they have pride and pleasure. A selection of my go-to reflective dialogue questions includes the following:

- How was this process of drafting a tombstone message or obituary?
- Why is *this* the vision or legacy you hold for the life you will lead?
- What did you learn about yourself from this experience?
- How can others support you as you bring this vision and legacy to life?
- What can we learn from this exercise that can be applied to our own leadership practice?

Thinking Systemically

Thinking systemically and thinking conventionally are two wildly different ways to perceive and respond to the world around us. Conventional thinking is not suited to address the complex and chronic problems leaders often face (Stroh, 2015). With conventional thinking, we can easily trace a connection between problems and solutions. Others tend to be the problem—*they* deserve the blame and *they* need to change; And with conventional thinking we tend to focus solely on short-term wins to the exclusion of long-term return on investment.

Systems thinking is entirely different. In this way, we recognize that the connections between problems and causes may be both indirect and deceiving. We unsuspectingly create our own problems—and our quick fixes tend to have significant unintended consequences. Yet, when we implement a few critical and coordinated changes, we can drive large-scale systemic change (Stroh, 2015). Peter Senge (1990), a foremost thinker on leadership and systems thinking, offers that "systems thinking is a discipline for seeing wholes. It is a framework for seeing interrelationships rather than things, for seeing patterns of change rather than static snapshots" (p. 68). Before exploring systems thinking any further, it is important to understand what a system is.

Donella Meadows (2008), a pioneering systems thinker, defines a *system* as an interconnected set of elements coherently organized to achieve something.

There are three overarching features to a system: the elements, interconnections, and the function or purpose of the system.

The elements are the stuff of the system (both tangible and intangible)—the things and entities that make up the system. The interconnections indicate the ways these elements interact with one another. The function and purpose is the goal of the system. Often, the function of a system is its own perpetuation (Meadows, 2008).

In a leadership training system, the elements might be the participants, training materials, and the vibe or felt level of energy in the space. The interconnections might reflect the relationships between participants—which impact the type of energy in the space. Similarly, the training materials interconnect with the participants, which impacts the use of the materials, as well as the energy of the participants—materials might get participants excited or anxious. Each element interconnects and influences the system. The intended purpose of this leadership training system is to create a space for leadership learning.

Systems are influenced by inflows and outflows. When an element increases or decreases in value, we consider it a stock. *Stocks* are the elements of a system that we can see, feel, count, or measure at any given time. The inflow impacts and influences *into* the stock. The outflow impacts and influences *out of* the stock.

Within our leadership training system, participants will serve as a stock example. The inflow factors include traffic on the highway—the more traffic, the less stock (participants). The inflow might also be prior-training synergistic relationships. The stronger the inflow (strong relationships) the more stock (participants) we have in the training. Outflows work similarly. In the context of training materials—worksheets for this example—there is less stock (worksheets) when we have more participants. If each participant needs a worksheet, we'll have less at the end of the training if there are 36 participants compared to 18 participants. Stocks fluctuate. Yet they do not rise and fall immediately. There is a lag between the flow and the impact. Our stock of worksheets does not just magically drop to the number of participants when they arrive. It takes time for the worksheets to leave the leadership educator's hands and make their way to each and every participant. The impact occurs. Yet it takes time for the significance of the impact to be felt.

What I've just presented are systems basics. Let's dig a bit deeper.

Systems are self-perpetuating. They change minimally, if at all, so long as the interconnections and purpose remains the same. Elements can experience massive change and, yet, the system persists. The number of participants in a training or the type of training materials can change—the system, though, stays, generally, intact. The system is still a space for leadership learning. If the interconnections or the purpose changes, that is when the system is altered. If the interconnections among our leadership training participants become so strained and scrambled due to ill will and resentful relationships the system shifts—it can no longer be a safe space for leadership learning. The energy in the space and the attention of our participants is not focused on leadership learning, but on the relationships (interconnections) between participants.

Systems operate as loops—often referred to as *feedback loops*. Senge (1990) explains these loops as circles of influence. There are two types of loops: balancing feedback loops and reinforcing feedback loops. A balancing feedback loop reinforces the patterns of behavior within the system. If during a 5-day retreat-style leadership training, each morning begins with a 1-minute breathing exercise, participants within that system will become accustomed to that experience and, as a feedback loop, by day 3 begin to enter the training space in quiet preparation for the breathing practice.

A reinforcing feedback loop, also known as a runaway loop, enhances the change that is imposed on it. Essentially there is an exponential increase or decrease within the system. For example, at this same 5-day retreat-style leadership training, if the morning session goes longer than expected, the next sessions would also go longer than expected—at a magnified rate. To get tangible, if the first session is 10 minutes over the expected time allotment, the second session would compound to be 20 minutes longer than the original end time. By the end of the day, if there are no interventions we would be starting the nightly check-in nearly an hour over the schedule's originally stated time.

David Peter Stroh (2015), an international expert and consultant on systems thinking, details why systems thinking is an essential leadership practice. With systems thinking, we can motivate others to change because we can illuminate their role in exacerbating the problems they seek to fix. With systems thinking, we can catalyze collaboration because we can illuminate how we collectively create unsatisfying results. When thinking systemically, we can harness others' focus to attend to a few coordinated changes that lead to significant impact. Also, systems thinking stimulates continuous and prolonged learning—a vital characteristic for meaningful and robust change within our systems.

It is excruciatingly difficult for us to change a system. All the other practices in this book are in our control to develop and enhance. A system, though, not so much. Yet as leaders we can think systemically and enhance our capabilities to live and work effectively within systems. These practices will enable us to more smoothly operate within the systems we can identify—as well as the ones we barely recognize.

First, we need to understand the system at play. We do this by observing. Before making changes in the system, we step back and watch it work. What are the elements, interconnections, and purpose of the system? What inflows are impacting the stock? What outflows are impacting the stock? Are feedback loops or reinforcing loops at play—or both?

Second, we do an internal assessment and ask ourselves what mental models are influencing our perspective of the system? Our mental models are our deeply held images and assumptions about how the world operates (Senge, 1990). Here, we tune into our beliefs about the system and unearth our misconceptions. We become more self-aware. "Increasing self-awareness is an intervention in and of itself, and the precursor to making any other changes" (Stroh, 2015, p. 46).

Third, once we understand the system and have recognized what and why we believe what we do about the system, we share about it widely. The more people who know about the system, the better we can all operate within it. While sharing about the system, it is important to utilize systems terms.

Meadows (2008) offers that our language matters. For example, if we, at a societal level, are discussing productivity and profitability in our organizations but not resiliency, the system will behave in favor of productivity and profitability—not resiliency. If in our leadership training system, the language is rooted in notions of leadership that emphasize power, prestige, and position, our participants are going to internalize that and create posttraining systems of leadership in practice dictated by power, prestige, and position. More tangibly, if our end-of-year celebrations only applaud positional leaders, we are reinforcing a system—in language and in practice—in which leadership is only recognized as a positional feat.

Finally, systems are often more complex than we imagine. It is crucial that leaders leverage their learning dispositions and seek to explore new ways of understanding and influencing the systems at play. The moment we believe we've mastered a system, we've begun to fail at navigating it.

Leadership Educator Praxis Activity

Leadership Theme: Thinking Systemically
Exercise: Keep Me in the Middle (physically engaged activity)

Systems thinking enables leaders to recognize and understand the interconnections that exist within the systems of our lives. By noticing and appreciating how they operate, we are better positioned to respond in dynamic and useful ways. This is probably the most difficult leadership practice for leadership educators. It is a complex topic that deserves multiple training touch-points—not to mention participants who have the discipline to keep at the learning when it seems particularly complicated. This is not in any way a suggestion to limit your interest in training others in systems thinking. Rather it is an invitation to pursue this topic with intentionality and depth.

When facilitating a systems-thinking training, it is wise to build it into a multipart experience where the concepts are layered on top of one another with plenty of examples, visuals, experiential learning activities, and reflective dialogue. Processing is needed for participants to understand the concept—and to recognize how they might apply it above and beyond the training. By delivering this topic in a scaffolded way—over several training interventions—you enable participants to sit with the concepts in between the time together and empower them to deeply connect with the material in ways that matter—rather than a surface-level and topical exposé of systems thinking. The Keep Me in the Middle activity is a wonderful experience that captures how these interconnections impact and influence others—in the moment.

Keep Me in the Middle

The Keep Me in the Middle activity invites participants to casually move around the training space with one specific mission—to keep their bodies equidistant from two other participants in the training. These two other people are self-selected by each participant and are expected, at least in the beginning, to be secret. In essence, every participant is attempting to stay in the middle of their two participant reference points. As one participant moves, others will certainly move to stay in the middle. This activity illuminates, though an experiential learning opportunity, many features about systems—including their complexity, interdependencies of elements, inherent delays, and so on.

Often, participants select their secret points of reference based on their relationships—friends. One way for leadership educators to avoid this, if desired, is to request that these secret selections be someone with whom the participant is familiar and another a participant with whom there is unfamiliarity.

Materials

- N/A

Instructions

- Begin by ensuring the training space has sufficient space for participants to move around smoothly and safely. All chairs, tables, and other obstacles should be removed.
- Once the training space is clear, tell the participants they are to each select two people, *secretly*, to serve as their points of reference. Give them enough time to scan the room and decide, in *secret* (this point can't be stressed enough) who these two points of reference will be.
- Then describe that each individual participant has one objective—to stay equidistant from their two points of reference. That is, to keep themselves in the middle of their selections.
- Once the participants understand the rules and expectations, say "begin" and let the activity flow.

Reflective Dialogue Questions

Our objective with this activity is to bring attention to how systems operate—with complexities, interdependencies, inherent delays, and more. By trying to keep themselves in the middle of their secret points of reference, participants can get an initial sense. The reflective dialogue is when we highlight what happened by asking strategic questions about their experience. A selection of my go-to reflective dialogue questions includes the following:

- Could you identify who you were a point of reference for? How did that become clear? What did you do (how did your behavior change) once you had that awareness?
- What did it feel like to have to continually move to stay in the middle?
- This was a system—what can we learn about the complex nature of it?
- This was a system—what can we learn about the interconnections within it?
- This was a system—what can we learn about the delays that are a part of it?
- What else did you learn or witness from this activity about systems and thinking systemically?
- What can we learn from this exercise that can be applied to our own leadership practice?

Practicing Mindfulness

Mindfulness is being aware of what is happening internally—our thoughts, sensations, emotions, and attitudes—as well as what is happening externally—our physical body, other people, events, and the natural environment—all in *this* precise moment—the present. It is about being awake and attending to our internal state and external environment. Mindfulness is about purposefully paying attention and seeing things as they are, nonjudgmentally, rather than what we prefer to see—it is not taking sides in the pushing and pulling of the mind (Nelson et al., 2020). It is about training the mind. In Tibetan, "training the mind" is known as *lojong. Lo* means "intelligence," "mind," "that which can perceive things." *Jong* means "training" or "processing" (Trungpa, 2005).

With mindfulness, we are able to see the situations before us with clarity, accept these situations without attaching to them, and respond in healthy, productive ways. Training the mind is likened to cultivating a garden. It can be intelligently cultivated or allowed to run wild—regardless, it will bring forth vegetation. If we do not plant and nurture beneficial seeds, then an abundance of useless weeds—or potentially damaging invasive species—will grow. In this "mind is a garden"

metaphor, which do you prefer? A garden of weeds and invasive species that can wreak havoc or an intentionally designed and nurtured oasis that supports a thriving ecosystem?

Naturally, we make leadership decisions based on past conditioning—often referred to as *downloading* (see theory U in chapter 5). We utilize previous experiences to inform how we respond to the current situation. This is not optimal. Our mind when not exercised is fallible and limits our ability to make wise decisions. Mindfulness is a mind-training experience. Just as if we wanted to train for an athletic competition or learn a new academic subject or develop a skill (e.g., cooking), we need to intentionally train, study, and prepare. Mindfulness is the same. Mindfulness trains us to become present—rather than reactionary.

Michael Bunting (2016), author of *The Mindful Leader*, articulates that

developing as a leader is about cultivating our inner strength to stay true under fire, to ask questions we don't know the answer to, to stay balanced when our world is turning upside down, to stay kind and respectful when the heat of anger and frustration is coursing through our veins, to courageously hold ourselves and others accountable when we want to slip into avoidance and self-justification. It is about enabling ourselves to connect with others with authentic compassion. . . . Perhaps above all, it is to stay real, to keep coming back to honesty and humility. (p. xx)

To be clear, this is not a technical competency. It is a behavior. Leadership failures are rarely due to technical incompetence or botched tactical responses—the *x* factor in leadership is behavior (Bunting, 2016).

Mindfulness is the behavioral process of actively noticing new things. When we notice new things—with intention—we position ourselves in the present. This is energy begetting, not energy consuming. Often people mistakenly perceive that mindfulness is stressful and exhausting. Rather, the alternative is what is stressful—for example, the mindless negative evaluations, constant chatter in our mind, and worrying about "what ifs."

When we lead mindfully, even in the toughest of circumstances and situations, we are able to purposefully cultivate a state of internal wellness and serve as a beacon of goodness, responsiveness, and clarity for others. Mindfulness is not about playing a trick on our mind, nor is it about pretending that stress does not exist. It is neither about hiding from reality nor recognizing that terrible, painful experiences are a part of our daily lives. Rather, mindfulness is a practice that enables us to become fully present to circumstances however they may be, without creating attachment or unnecessary drama. Mindfulness is about releasing our attachments. When we do this, we can initially limit and then end the suffering that results from not being present. "When we are not blinded by the intensity of our emotions, when we allow a bit of space, a chance for a gap, when we pause, we naturally know what to do . . . we gradually stop strengthening habits that only bring about more pain to the world" (Chodron, 2009, p. 29).

Mindfulness is not about overcoming insecurities or worries. Rather, mindfulness equips us with the strength and resilience to move toward them, embrace them, feel them, and live with them—but without allowing them to dominate our lives. Mindfulness practices are the doorway to providing the insight and compassion through which we uncover our insecurities—and then heal them—so we can engage with ourselves and others with unselfish intentions (Bunting, 2016).

Leadership scholars Richard Boyatzis and Annie McKee (2005) suggest,

> Living mindfully means that we are constantly and consciously in tune with ourselves—listening carefully to our bodies, minds, hearts, and spirits. The best among us consciously develop the capacity for deep self-awareness . . . understanding our inner experiences. Attending to ourselves like this enables us to be very clear about what is most important to us; it allows us to engage our passion and build on positive emotional states. Attending carefully enables us to recognize early on when we are heading down the wrong path—toward allowing a slight compromise in our values, making a wrong decision, or ignoring our health. People who live mindfully catch problems before they become serious, because they pay attention to their inner voice: a voice that includes intuition, wisdom, and a subtle but very sophisticated analysis of what is going on in the world. (p. 113)

Just like caring for a garden, one needs patience, time, nourishment, and healthy energy to develop a mindfulness practice. There are four stages of mindfulness development (Bunting, 2016):

Stage 1: No mindfulness. There is no awareness and no accountability for actions. In this stage, in the context of leadership training, we can think about a common educator error—overstepping our bounds and trying to force a "learning opportunity"—usually related to the false assumption that it is *our* training rather than it being *theirs*—our participants. Without mindfulness, we may interrupt participants, fail to appropriately read the room, or move too quickly to the next aspect of our training before participants are able to process the learning from the current experience. In this example, educators are unaware of their actions, the frustration they cause, and the negative impact it is having on the performance of the training program.

Stage 2: Mindfulness too late. There is awareness—but only after an incident. In this stage, leadership educators, only after the training has come to a close, recognize their faults and lack of awareness in the moment. It may be by reading training evaluations, deeper reflections on the experience, or a follow-up conversation with a participant that they recognize how their mindlessness impacted the learning opportunity and intended outcomes of the training.

Stage 3: Mindfulness of the impulse. There is further awareness—and the recognition of the need to pause before acting. Leadership educators in this phase often catch themselves mid-training by recognizing their mindless impulses to interrupt, recognizing the facial expressions of disengaged or dissatisfied participants, or how they are forcibly guiding conversations. This impulse awareness allows us to make critical decisions regarding our actions. By practicing mindfulness, over time, our awareness and presence during trainings—and in all of our leadership practices—increases.

Stage 4: Dissolution of the impulse and habit. With mindfulness, limiting and mindless habits cease. Mindful leadership educators are fully present, fully engaged, and fully connected to participants. Although there are times where interrupting occurs, reading the room is overlooked, and we may move too quickly through our trainings, they are far fewer and less severe. It is our mindfulness that allows leadership educators to tap into the spirit of our trainings, the explicit developmental desires and implicit needs of our participants, and ways to craft dynamic and engaging leadership learning experiences that go beyond fulfilling our intended learning outcomes.

Leadership Educator Praxis Activity

Leadership Theme: Practicing Mindfulness
Exercise: Grape Meditation (reflective [personal engagement] activity)

Mindfulness is about being here now. Being. Here. Now. When we are mindful, we are able to stay present in this particular moment with energy and attention on the task at hand. We're not beholden to the past or dreaming of what's to come. We are here. Mindfulness is one of the most difficult leadership training topics for leadership educators because many of our participants—especially developmentally younger folks—are constantly trying to fill their minds and time with stuff. Mindfulness is the practice of reducing that mental clutter and engaging fully on the here and now. It goes against what we are seemingly conditioned to do.

As you already know, every leadership training should include experiential learning and reflective dialogue. This is especially true for a mindfulness-focused training. When we intentionally, continually, and in a guided fashion practice mindfulness, our participants' opportunity for acquisition and internalization increase exponentially.

In these sessions I believe it is important to first highlight how our minds operate in normal conditions—with innumerable thoughts guiding our attention in each minute. From there, during our trainings, we can practice—through experiential learning activities and reflective dialogue—ways to become more aware and in tune with our thoughts, sensations, emotions, and attitudes. The objective of this work—for ourselves and our participants—is to respond to the events of our days in ways that are more mindfully aligned with our values and our vision for who we want to be and

how we want to show up in relationship with ourselves and others. The Grape Meditation activity allows us to see what for most of us is very familiar—a grape. Yet, through this exercise, we are able to engage with it in newer and deeper ways. We practice mindfulness by connecting our senses to the grape.

Grape Meditation

The Grape Meditation activity invites participants to utilize all of their senses, in a purposeful, strategic, and guided way, to cultivate a new relationship and experience with grapes. In this experiential learning activity, leadership educators facilitate a step-by-step process that encourages participants to focus their energy and attention on a grape.

Materials

- grapes—one for each participant with some extras

Instructions

- Begin by providing each participant with a grape—express that they do *not* eat it, yet.
- Once delivered, they should be informed that this same grape will be utilized for the entire activity and to please be gentle with it.
- The activity centers around each sense and becoming more aware (mindful) of that grape—something we tend to be fairly mindless about. It is intended to be a silent activity—aside from your instructions. (*Note:* This may make participants uncomfortable.)
- For the meditation, begin by asking the participants to utilize their sense of *sight*. They are to spend the next minute or two simply looking at the grape. Your questions to consider asking while in their meditation might include the following: What do you see? What color is it? Are there veins? What is something new you see in this familiar object?
- Then move on to the sense of *sound*. Ask the participants to bring the grape to their ear. What does it sound like? What do you hear? When you shake it, does it make a noise? What about when you put pressure on it?
- Then move on to the sense of *smell*. Ask the participants to bring the grape to their nose.

Sniff. What do you smell? What memories arise from the smell?

- Then move on to the sense of *touch*. Ask the participants to roll the grape between two fingers. What does it feel like? Is it squishy or firm? When you scratch it, what happens? What does it feel like rolling on your arm or cheek?
- Then, finally, move on to the sense of *taste*. Invite participants to place the grape in their mouths—but not to eat it. Don't bite it . . . just let it sit on your tongue. What do you taste? What sensation do you feel from that taste? Now, gently bite into it—how does the flavor change?
- After some time, ask them to slowly chew until the grape no longer exists. When chewing, remind them that there is no rush and that the center of attention is on mindfully chewing—paying deep attention to every up and down motion of the jaw and the sound of the grape, the smell of the grape, the feel of the grape, and the flavors of the grape.
- Once all of the participants have finished their grape, slide into the reflective dialogue.

Reflective Dialogue Questions

Our objective with this activity is to make the familiar strange through a mindfulness activity. Grapes are an easy-to-eat fruit that we often don't think about or pay much attention to. With this experiential learning exercise, we are able to engage with it in a new way by focusing our energy and attention on it. A selection of my go-to reflective dialogue questions includes the following:

- How many of us have ever engaged with a grape like this before? What did we learn about the grape that was surprising?
- How was this experience from a mindfulness perspective? Was it comfortable? Uncomfortable?
- How might we be more mindful about such mundane, regular things in our lives?
- How might we infuse mindfulness into our leadership practice?
- What can we learn from this exercise that can be applied to our own leadership practice?

Integrating Reflection and Action

Exceptional leaders oscillate between reflection and action. They spend time both in deep thought and fully immersed in practice. The vacillation between reflection and action encourages intensity in action and depth of reflection. During the reflective interlude, we create opportunities to learn from prior experiences (prior actions) while gathering new energy to pursue our work (and *Work*) with more vigor and fervor (D. Roberts, 2007).

On the surface, we seem to recognize the importance of both. Yet rarely do we engage purposefully at the depth of reflection needed to take our leadership practice to the apex level. The same can be said with regard to our leadership practice—rarely do we have the presence, when in action, to perform optimally. Frederick Buechner (1993), the American author of over 30 published essays, poems, novels, and an autobiography offers that "vocation is the place where your deep gladness meets the world's deep need" (p. 119). If we are to do great and meaningful work in the world, we need to truly understand our deep gladness—and then do the things that connect our gladness to the world's deep needs. We first engage in reflective processes to uncover our profound joy and then apply that in contexts that are healing and reparative for our community's pressing needs.

David Viscott (1993), the late psychiatrist and media personality, offered that "the purpose of life is to discover your gift. The meaning of life is to give your gift away" (p. 83). A purposeful life includes both reflection and action. We need to initialize this by engaging in the internal work of discovering our gifts. Then, we do something about it—we act—to give those gifts away.

I invite you to take a purposeful pause moment and consider: What is your deep gladness? What are your significant gifts? What are your superhero powers? What lights your fire? What makes your heart sing? What brings you profound joy? What are you feeling called to do?

Yet just sitting with these questions and your reflections needs to be matched with action. To act purposefully, though, we ought to strategize around how to give away our gifts that meet great needs: Where is my organization's or community's greatest need? Who is the chorus to sing my song? Where can more light shine? What weeds need to be uprooted? Why do we do it this way when other ways may be better? Altogether, these are the type of reflective questions that are foundational for maximizing the healthy leadership habit of integrating reflection with action.

Reflection

"Those of us seeking to be inspirited by the call to make a difference in the world have no choice but to take the journey of self-discovery" (D. Roberts, 2007, p. 129). Roberts (2007) perfectly captures that essence of reflective practice. If we desire the opportunity to create significant and systemic change—to make a positive difference—we need to do the inner work of self-discovery. This inner work begins with reflection.

Reflection is the process by which people make meaning of their experiences (Volpe White et al., 2019). Reflection, especially in the context of leadership learning and development, is not just sitting back and thinking. Reflection requires cognitive and affective complexity to consider past experiences, understand current contexts, draw conclusions, infer meaning, and consider applications for the future (Volpe White et al., 2019).

Reflecting is not about tuning out. We don't spend this time in a defocused or relaxed state. We tune in. The most pragmatic and powerful practice for working through complexity, navigating crises, and crafting innovations is to purposefully pause and engage in reflective inquiry. When we pause in this way, we engage in intense and focused inquiry—questioning, experimenting, observing, listening, and evaluating (Cashman, 2012).

Purposefully pausing enables us to be powerful and strategic in our work. It is the calculated capability to step back so that we can move forward with greater clarity, momentum, and impact. Pausing holds the creative power to reframe and refresh how we see ourselves, our relationships, and our work. We utilize purposeful pauses to identify our capabilities, isolate our challenges, infuse strategy into our postpause tactics, and innovate in meaningful ways. It is this pragmatic practice of deep, reflective inquiry that leads to purposeful change (Cashman, 2012). The greater the complexity, the deeper the reflective pause required to convert the complex and ambiguous to the clear and meaningful. Pausing helps us move from transactive engagements to transformative change, from hyperactive energy to highly intentional actions.

As easy as it may sound, purposefully pausing—intentionally engaging in reflective processes—is not intuitive. Without proper guidance and frameworks

this time may be confusing, frustrating, or mismanaged (Volpe White et al., 2019). Reflection methods are diverse and should be employed in ways that are personally meaningful and constructive. These may include contemplative practices such as meditation, mindfulness, walking labyrinths, yoga; creative and artistic pursuits including coloring, drawing, playing music, sculpting, visiting the theater, watching film; intentional dialogue; written expressions and journaling; and traveling to explore new places.

Purposeful pauses are strategic interruptions infused into our daily routines to enhance our presence and mindfulness. Doing so empowers us and others to create opportunities to see things in new ways, voice concerns, question the experts and those who wield power, interrogate the rationale for why things happen the way they do, ensure solidarity, scheme ideas for enhancements, and challenge the status quo.

All of these activities are intended to encourage the strange becoming familiar and the familiar becoming strange—while also instilling a bit of uncomfortability. New awareness opens the door to new possibilities. New possibilities unlock opportunities for new ways forward to create the systemic and transformational change that we desire.

Often, leadership is understood or recognized by what is accomplished (or not); the outcomes of our actions dictate effective leadership. This is habitually measured by time investment. We tend to create honor badges by how many hours we worked on a project or in a week. We take pride in staying up through the night to complete an assignment. Yet, as Jim Loehr, a performance psychologist and founder of the Human Performance Institute, offers, *energy*, not time, is our most precious resource—it is the fundamental currency of high performance (Loehr & Schwartz, 2003).

Purposefully pausing and intentionally reflecting enables us to maximize our energy so that we can pursue the change that's desired and needed in our communities. Reflection is the strategic space—a time to be quiet, still, and calm—where we can capitalize on noticing what we have failed to previously notice. The reflective space is intrinsic to creativity and intimate connection.

Sounds become music in the spaces between notes, just as words are created in the spaces between letters. It is the spaces between work that love, friendship, depth, and dimension are nurtured. Without time for recovery, our lives become a blur of *doing* unbalanced by much opportunity for *being*. (Loehr & Schwartz, 2004, p. 34)

Unfortunately, none of us can maintain high levels of performance indefinitely. "Intense work, focus, expenditure of physical and psychological energy—all of these require renewal. The down period of oscillation [reflection] allows us to regroup, rest, feed, and replenish the reservoirs that we have depleted through hard and diligent work" (D. Roberts, 2007, p. 127). When reflecting, we intentionally take ourselves out of the action space and dedicate energy to the internal pursuit of asking questions of meaning and depth. Although answers may arise, the value of our purposeful pauses—of reflecting—is to wrestle with the questions and to see what emerges.

Before moving on to action, I illuminate the power and potential of reflection through creative expressions. I begin with a story—the story of the Oak and Willow tree:

In the tale of the Oak and Willow tree, the Oak boasted of its strength. With arrogance and pride, the Oak teased the Willow for bending and swaying with the slightest of breezes. The Oak delighted in its strength and chastised the Willow for its delicacy. Before long, a great wind blew! The wind splintered the Oak's branches and trunk, completely damaging the tree. The Willow, though, was flexible, resilient, and responsive—and received little damage from the swirling power of the great wind.

With reflection, we become like the Willow—flexible, resilient, and responsive to the world around us. Without reflection, we can become so patterned and resistant to opposing thoughts or evidence that we err and gaff—or worse, break and splinter under pressure.

Reflection, when engaged purposefully, results in the pondering questions that we've not considered before. This may feel like retreating and can seem as if it is pulling us away from our pursuits. Rather, the opposite occurs. Taking time for the reflective interlude helps to assure we stay on track and that we pursue our goals for the right reasons (D. Roberts, 2007).

In her poem "Fire," Judy Brown (2016) captures the essence of how powerful reflective pauses can be—in the form of the space between our actions:

What makes a fire burn is space between the logs, a breathing space. Too much of a good thing, too

many logs packed in too tight can douse the flames almost as surely as a pail of water could. So building fires requires attention to the spaces in between, as much as to the wood. When we are able to build open spaces in the same way we have learned to pile on the logs, then we can come to see how it is fuel, and absence of the fuel together, that make fire possible. We only need to lay a log lightly from time to time. A fire grows simply because the space is there, with openings in which the flame knows just how it wants to burn . . . can find its way. (p. 34)

As leaders, if we want to be as powerful and effective as we dream of being, we ought to pay attention to the space between. Rather than shift from task to task or project to project, we need to purposefully carve time for breathing spaces—reflective spaces. By doing so, we can better find our way and productively perform.

Finally, a quip often attributed to R. D. Laing (n.d.), the Scottish psychiatrist: "The range of what we think and do is limited by what we fail to notice and because we fail to notice that we fail to notice there is little we can do to change until we notice how failing to notice shapes our thoughts and deeds."

When we inhibit opportunities to engage in purposeful pauses and reflective inquiry, we limit ourselves. Essentially, we become complicit in failing to notice how our actions and leadership practices are limited.

Reflection, though, is just one phase of the reflection–action oscillation practice. How we—as leaders and leadership educators—engage in action matters significantly too.

Action

We all know that a journey of a thousand miles—really of any distance—begins with a single step. Leadership action is about taking that step. Kielburger and Kielburger (2004) offer that the precise reasons for the success of the world's most celebrated social movements are hotly debated in academic literature and activist circles, but their beginnings are incontestable: Somebody *did* something. Leadership action is about doing things. Yet we don't just randomly take steps or do our things haphazardly. We need to act in ways that align with our values and in the direction of our pursuits—with great intention, awareness, and focus. Our actions should be rooted in the insight garnered from our reflective pauses and applied in strategic and precise ways.

This section on action is less about what tactical decisions should be made in different leadership situations. Every situation is different and necessitates a distinctive response. Yet we can prepare for each and every leadership action with purpose if we effectively manage our *energy*. "Fundamentally, leadership is mobilizing, focusing, and renewing energy in the service of the agreed upon mission. Energy is highly contagious, both positive and negative" (Loehr & Groppel, 2008, p. 36).

For leaders, we ought to be aware of the four domains of energy (Loehr & Groppel, 2008; Loehr & Schwartz, 2003). Doing so will enable us to capitalize on our physical and emotional energy—allowing us to perform optimally. These domains are organized by high energy and low energy as well as positive and negative energy.

Low and negative energy results in feelings of depression, defeat, burnout, hopelessness, and exhaustion. High negative energy produces fear, anger, anxiousness, resentfulness, and defensiveness. Low energy mixed with positive energy yields relaxation serenity, tranquility, and peacefulness. Finally, the combination of high and positive energy encourages confidence, connection, joy, and invigoration.

Energy cultivation and management is a strategic leadership practice. Loehr and Groppel (2008) discuss it in the form of a four-tiered pyramid—with physical at the base level, then emotional energy, followed by mental energy. Spiritual energy is at the apex of the energy pyramid. If we are to optimally perform as leaders, our energy-management approach needs to be comprehensive and multidimensional. We need to incorporate energy-cultivating strategies and practices at each level of the pyramid.

Within the *physical energy* foundation tier, we focus on our eating, sleeping, and moving. The foods we eat are a critical source of energy. Literally, food is digested and transformed into energy. We need to consistently find a balance between feeling stuffed and hungry. We need to strategically fuel our bodies with nutrients that lead to healthy emotional, mental, and spiritual energy.

Sleep—rest, more broadly—is the essential mechanism for renewal. We need a healthy dose and depth of sleep for us to feel renewed, refreshed, and energized. Sleep is also a moment for our bodies to grow and repair. We need to stop thinking about sleeping as a

weakness—particularly in the context of naps—which can be a powerful source of midday energy.

Physical activity and movement is the third component of physical energy. Exercise, including strength and cardiovascular training, can lead to marked improvement in our energy reserves as well as our well-being. Yet leaders also balance their time by periodically taking a stroll, stretching, and shaking our bodies out of our sitting stupors. This type of movement and physical activity can have a profound impact on our work, engagement, and productivity—especially if we find ourselves sitting at a computer or desk for long episodes.

Emotional energy is enriched when we have healthy relationships and satisfy our own healing needs. Leadership is a relational experience. If we are to excel at leading, we need to cultivate dynamic and healthy relationships. This is not just so we can garner trust. It is because these types of relationships are renewing and energizing. We have a greater and deeper sense of fulfillment when our relationships are nourishing. Sometimes, our relationships support our emotional healing. Other times, we need space away from an individual, group, or humans altogether. Actively engaging in healing processes is difficult, yet important work. When emotional tolls limit our energy, we need to recover by engaging in practices that empower us to heal and then thrive. Healing may look and feel different from person to person. We each need to discover and implement the appropriate mechanism for us to engage in this work so that in our own ways we can flourish. Often, emotional healing is best supported by seeking professional counseling.

The third tier of the energy pyramid is our *mental energy*. We cultivate our mental vigor and vitality by harnessing the power of visualizations, positive self-talk, and effective time management. By spending intentional time thinking about the future, we are more likely to lean and live into that future. Visualization is an important way to cultivate mental energy because it sets a preparatory tone and instills confidence in an attainable future. Positive self-talk shifts from healthy thought and projections to vocalizing our strengths and skills. Yes, talking to ourselves is an important mechanism for increasing mental energy and well-being. This empowers ourselves to greatness. Positive self-talk should become a morning habit and nightly ritual as a way to enhance our sense of self and increase our mental energy reserves. In addition to visualizing and expressing positive reinforcements, leaders are able to maximize their energy by managing their time. This includes letting go of the multitasking myth. By focusing on one task at a time, we will be able to capitalize on and accomplish much more than by diverting our energy to multiple priorities.

At the apex of the energy pyramid is our *spiritual energy*. Here, spiritual energy is not associated with religious observance; rather, it concerns intentionally cultivating a deeply held set of values along with a purpose for our work and engagements beyond our own self-interest (Loehr & Schwartz, 2003). The apex of the energy pyramid consists of those personally meaningful elements that ignite our spirit, drive full engagement, and maximize performance.

I purposefully use the term *integrating* for this section header. Typically, we discuss reflection and action as a balance. When we engage in the balancing act, we tend to pursue the exact right neutral space between the two elements. With reflection and action, we don't necessarily want to balance the two; we want to integrate the two so that we can maximize our energy to be as effective and powerful as we dream of being. D. Roberts (2007) describes it as an oscillation between two. This then becomes a process of swinging back and forth between reflection and action much like a pendulum swings.

Our reflective and action practices are all about energy. By integrating the two, we craft our daily schedule and experiences that encourage us to maximize our energy during action and purposefully renew our energy during reflection. This process of integration should be thought of as a perpetual loop of purposeful reflection and action followed by a continuation of more disciplined loops of reflection and action. This repetitive and everlasting process supports our ability to be fully energized and engaged in our leadership responsibilities and practice.

Leadership Educator Praxis Activity

Leadership Theme: Integrating Reflection and Action
Exercise: Monument Build (physically engaged activity)

Leadership educators maximize our energy in order for our trainings to be as dynamic, learning-oriented, and engaging as our participants need and expect them to be. When we are exhausted and drained, we are going to be significantly less effective than when we are fulfilled and maximizing the four hierarchies of the energy pyramid. Furthermore, those leadership educators who have healthy reflective practices are going to more easily respond to participants through their engagements and inquiries. Reflection and action, though, are not independent entities. For leadership educators, they need to be integrated into one leadership practice.

In the context of facilitating leadership trainings focused on integrating reflection and action, using stories, poetry, and models assists participants in grounding their understanding in something a bit more tangible than just speaking vaguely about reflection and action. Most of our participants are going to know, in the broadest sense, what *reflection* and *action* are. Yet, if we truly want them to enhance their leadership practice in the context of integrating these two elements, we need to get as tangible and practical as possible. It is for this reason that this training topic is typically infused with many hands-on experiential activities and reflective dialogue to explore the topics—with less talking about reflection and action.

The integration of reflective practices with action is the cornerstone of effective leadership practice. Simply reflecting (without acting) does not result in any meaningful change. Simply acting (without reflecting) leads to mindless behavior. Both are essential. To highlight this, leadership educators can utilize the Monument Build activity. I prefer to use magnetic building blocks (also referred to as Picasso tiles) because they are colorful, easy to assemble (and disassemble), offered in varying shapes, and easily transported.

Monument Build

Imagine building a monument to yourself or your group or organization. In this activity, participants will do exactly that. The build activity is just the vehicle for important leadership learning, though. In this activity, participants will construct a monument that celebrates themselves (or their team/organization) in a very specific process—one that integrates time in reflection with time in action.

During the activity, participants, either individually or in small groups, will construct a monument that speaks to their successes and legacy. However, they will either be in a reflective phase (when they are *not* permitted to touch the blocks) or in an action phase (when they are required to be constantly adding pieces). These phases could be 2 minutes in reflection and then 2 minutes in action, 5 minutes in one and then 5 minutes in the other, or random time allotments for each, random distribution for differing participants and groups. The idea is to mix it up so that during the reflective dialogue participants can highlight how both are necessary—that to be effective leaders, they need to oscillate between reflective practices and action.

Materials

- magnetic building blocks (Picasso tiles)

Instructions

- Begin by inviting the participants to find their place or create a group.
- Once settled, distribute or centrally place the magnetic building blocks.
- Describe to the participants that they are to build the most magnificent monument to either themselves, their group, their organization, or whatever has relevance and resonance.
- Explain, though, they have a very specific process for how to accomplish their monument build. They will only be permitted to construct during the action time. During that phase, they are required to always be placing a block. During the reflection phase, they are *not* permitted to touch the blocks—only plan for the action phase.
- You can keep all of the participants on the same schedule or provide a slip of paper that details their particular process. I like to facilitate this with the latter. This enables different participants and groups to be working on their monument in different ways during each of the timed segments. I find that this leads to more dynamic reflective dialogues.

- After the time has ended and the monuments are completed, participants should describe their monuments to the whole of the participant body.
- Finally, invite participants to share about their experience in the reflective dialogue.

Reflective Dialogue Questions

Our objective with this activity is to highlight how essential the integration of reflection and action is in our leadership practices. By forcing participants into one or the other during each of the timed segments—and depriving them of authoring their own integration, they come to know how important each are. We utilize that as fodder for the reflective dialogue. A selection of my go-to reflective dialogue questions includes the following:

- How did it feel to be in the reflection phase?
- How did it feel to be in the action phase?
- What was the toughest struggle in the activity?
- What did we learn about integrating reflection and action into our leadership practice?
- How might we better integrate reflection and action into a healthy leadership habit?
- What can we learn from this exercise that can be applied to our own leadership practice?

Conclusion

These leadership practices focused on skills and capacities that enhance our cognitive aptitude. When we develop healthy leadership habits in these domains, we are able to focus our own and our followers' attention on the things that matter most (visioning); see the challenges and obstacles we face in a new light—so that we can overcome them (thinking systemically); center ourselves to be more present in our day-to-day leadership and decision-making activities (practicing mindfulness); and exert energy effectively to be our best selves (integrating reflection with action).

CHAPTER 8

Emotive Leadership Practices

THIS GROUPING OF LEADERSHIP practices focuses on emotional development and relational connections. Although there is substantial personal and internally focused work, the purpose of cultivating these healthy leadership habits is to enhance synergies with others. When we focus our attention on these four skills—cultivating emotional intelligence, offering compassion, being hopeful and optimistic, and displaying gratitude—we nurture resonance with others, which magnifies our leadership practice.

Cultivating Emotional Intelligence

Our social and cultural understandings of leadership assume that the brightest among us are the best suited to lead. And by brightest, these individuals have the highest IQs. They are, by all intents and purposes, book smart in the traditional ways. This is how we typically understand and associate intelligence with leadership.

There is a better away to assess and understand intelligence in relationship to leadership capabilities, though: emotional intelligence (EQ). In Aristotle's *Nicomachean Ethics*, the famed Greek philosopher shared that "anyone can become angry—that is easy. But to be angry with the right person, to the right degree, at the right time, for the right purpose, and in the right way—this is not easy" (Goleman, 1997, p. ix).

It should come as no surprise that Daniel Goleman (1997)—a forefather of EQ—begins in the preface of his perennial book *Emotional Intelligence* with that quote. Traditional notions of intelligence would indicate that we have a conceptual, cognitive, scientific, and philosophical understanding of the anger emotion. EQ, though, is knowing how to skillfully direct our anger, with the right amount of our anger, at the right time for our anger, with the right purpose for our anger, and in the right way to express our anger. For effective leadership, there is really no need to ask the rhetorical question—which is the preferred intelligence? EQ is the far superior intelligence for leaders. Think about it like this—no matter how smart we are (i.e., regardless of the height of our IQ scores), when we are emotionally unraveled, we cannot recall information, stay focused, learn, or make sharp decisions. Our intellect cannot work at its best without our EQ (Goleman, 1997).

EQ is concerned with our abilities to (a) motivate ourselves and persist in the face of obstacles, setbacks, and challenges; (b) control our impulses for immediate enjoyment and welcome delayed gratification; (c) appropriately regulate our moods; (d) limit distresses from overtaking our abilities to think; (e) empathize and show compassion for ourselves and others; and (f) stay optimistic with hope (Goleman, 1997).

All of this begins by first knowing our and others' emotions. Only by noticing and recognizing them can we be positioned to control and regulate them, persist through impediments, and effectively manage our relational engagements with others.

In his follow-up book, *Working With Emotional Intelligence*, Goleman (1998) underscores that EQ, just like leadership, can be learned. For this reason it *should* be learned and infused into our leadership regimen.

Joshua Freedman (2019), a pioneer in the practical application of EQ, indicates that leaders who have higher EQ have stronger people relations and decisions along with fiercer self-management capabilities. This then leads to more feelings of being valued among team members. The result is both more and better work outcomes. Both Freedman (2019) and Goleman (1997, 1998) emphasize the importance of EQ because of the significant gains indicated in the data. For example, EQ enhances personnel productivity and financial performance, employee retention and consumer loyalty, and personal metrics of well-being for both emotionally intelligent leaders and those with whom they engage.

How do we cultivate EQ for our own practice, while training others to capitalize on enhancing their EQ? There are plenty of frameworks and literature that can inform and instruct. Here, I share a compilation of Goleman's (1997, 1998) insight, Freedman's (2019) six seconds model, and Bariso's (2018) application method.

It begins with an internal approach. We need to know ourselves and tune in to our emotions. This emotional awareness is the starting point. From there, we need to take ownership over, manage, and intentionally respond to our emotions. This is self-mastery. Tactically, we want to acknowledge and label our emotions. Doing so enables us to identify our emotional triggers, enhance our self-awareness, and avoid making decisions that are emotionally charged. As we practice this work and witness the positive outcomes, we become motivated to engage in emotionally intelligent practice toward others.

As we become more masterful at knowing ourselves, we can shift to emotionally intelligent social awareness, engagement, and management. Here we become more in tune with and can accurately perceive the feelings of others—specifically how those emotions manifest into behaviors. Emotionally intelligent leaders are able to strategically capitalize on the behaviors that can drive desired outcomes. Much of this is posited on empathy and connecting deeply with others.

As a helpful reference, Bariso (2018) offers a 10-commandment list of practices to enhance our EQ. These include (a) pondering feelings, (b) learning to pause, (c) controlling our own thoughts, (d) learning from other perspectives, (e) practicing empathy, (f) praising others, (g) apologizing, (h) forgiving, (i) being authentic, and (j) never stopping learning.

Leadership Educator Praxis Activity

Leadership Theme: Cultivating Emotional Intelligence
Exercise: Feeling Words (reflective [personal engagement] activity)

Emotional Intelligence is a core feature of our ability to perform during leadership trainings. This is the crucible of leadership practices. When leadership educators are void of EQ, we will inevitably fail to effectively prepare our participants to be the changemakers they desire to be.

EQ allows us to be fully present and engaged in our trainings. With EQ, we can become aware of our triggers in the face of challenges and confrontations while also becoming aware of participant reactions to our messages, experiential learning activities, and expressions shared during reflective dialogue. Emotionally intelligent leadership educators are able to model this essential and healthy leadership habit and tactically prepare participants to be emotionally intelligent leaders. We do this by enhancing emotional literacy and assisting participants in recognizing their emotional patterns. From there, we can practice navigating emotions, imbuing hope and optimism into our regimen, and pursuing noble goals. Cultivating EQ begins by gaining awareness of our emotions. That happens when we can name them, literally. This is what the Feeling Words activity is designed to do.

Feeling Words
The Feeling Words activity establishes a timed forum for participants to list as many of their "feeling" words as possible. This activity is intended to test and expand emotional literacy. Following the timed individual reflection, participants are paired and grouped to share about their list.

Materials
- paper
- writing utensils

Instructions
- Begin by hyping up the competitive spirit of the activity. It will be a contest to see who can list as many "feeling" words and emotions as possible. Several examples include *energized*, *joy*, and *optimistic*.

- Once these instructions are given, ensure all of the participants have paper and a writing utensil—and prepare the timer.
- Sixty seconds is a sufficient amount of time.
- Following the timed portion, pair or group participants so they can compare their lists.
- When those conversations have come to a close, slide into the reflective dialogue.

Reflective Dialogue Questions

Our objective with this activity is to enhance participants' emotional literacy. This begins by becoming aware of our "feeling" words and emotions—literally listing them—and then dialoguing about what they are, the differences and nuances between them, how they show up in our lives, how we can quell the limiting ones, and best practices for enhancing the empowering ones. A selection of my go-to reflective dialogue questions includes the following:

- How many "feeling" words did you list?
- What are some slight differences between those words?
- How do these "feeling" words show up in your life?
- How can you quell limiting emotions?
- How can you infuse the empowering emotions more regularly into your leadership practice?
- What can we learn from this exercise that can be applied to our own leadership practice?

Offering Compassion

If relationships are the currency of power (which they are), and if energy is the currency of effectiveness (which it is), then compassion is the currency of leadership. Compassion-centric practices and policies are critical to powerful, effective leadership. Compassion enhances relationships and fuels energy. It is a radically inclusive, universal leadership practice with unlimited potential for creating the change we desire.

Compassion, like leadership, is defined and understood in multitudes of different ways. Faith leaders, leadership scholars, and others offer these understandings and definitions:

- Compassion is an attitude of principled, consistent altruism. (Armstrong, 2010, p. 9)
- Compassion isn't simply opening a spigot and coating everything in a treacly, all-purpose goo. It requires a gut hunch that whatever I do unto others, I do unto myself (p. viii). It is kindness without condition (p. 9). (Barasch, 2009)
- Compassion is empathy and caring in action. (Boyatzis & McKee, 2005, p. 178)
- It is not simply a sense of sympathy or caring for the person suffering, not simply a warmth of heart toward the person before you, or a sharp clarity of recognition of their needs and pain, it is also a sustained and practical determination to do whatever is possible and necessary to help alleviate their suffering. (Rinpoche, 1993, p. 191)
- Compassion is a courageous stance against nihilism. (Shapiro, 2006, p. 19)

Although there are various ways to conceptualize compassion, two overarching themes have emerged that make this a distinct form of care—and a third that is incredibly important to leading:

Compassion is an intrinsic feeling. It is deeply held feeling of concern and empathy. This is not surprising based on the derivation of the word *compassion.* Armstrong (2010) notes the meaning of the word from Semitic languages—*rahamanut* in postbiblical Hebrew and *rahman* in Arabic, both related etymologically to *rehem,* meaning "womb." Cannato (2010) expresses that the literal word *compassion* means "to suffer from the bowels." Both of these descriptions visually portray compassion coming from within our bodies—at the center and core of our selves.

Compassion is frequently understood as a sharing of suffering or sharing in suffering. This word is taken from its Latin etymology—*com* ("shared") and *pati* ("suffering"). Although compassion is commonly understood and perceived in this way, the individual witnessing the pain and suffering does not take on the pain and suffering. Shapiro (2006) eloquently describes what it means to *suffer with*:

If I come to you in pain and you end up with the same pain, all we have done is added to the world's suffering. We have done nothing to alleviate it. I want you to understand my pain, to respond to it deeply, but not to take it on yourself. I want you to help me see what you see and what I cannot see . . . Mirror my experience, but do not take it on as your own. (p. 22)

Compassion drives action. This is what separates compassion from its sibling concepts: sympathy and empathy. Sympathy is simply feeling sorry for another person. With sympathy, there is an emotional response (feeling sha_____n to the other and ce_____ard alleviating thei_____ostantial than sympa_____he pain and sufferin_____e. There is an emotional_____l feeling moved by th_____r, compassion is n_____*suffering with* the other—it involves action. Compassion is more than just noticing and feeling the suffering of others; it is responding to their pain. Leadership practices that incorporate compassion are those in which pain and suffering are reduced. Leadership can be enhanced when leaders develop their capacity to witness pain and then respond to alleviate it.

University faculty members who research compassion and leadership—through a consortium they founded called CompassionLab—found that pain and suffering have serious implications for the wellness, effectiveness, and productivity of individuals and organizations (Kanov et al., 2004). Three particularly intriguing insights highlight the implications when our leaders and organizations are void of compass_____people have diminished _____une systems. Dep_____ter likelihood of _____yee grief impacts wo_____ximately $75 billion_____eglected, colleagues _____resulting in persona_____al organizational impact.

As leaders employ compassion practices as part of their leadership regimen, the positive implications have lasting effects. People are healthier, live longer, and are more productive (Ferrucci, 2006); emotional connections are strengthened and performance is enhanced (Lilius et al., 2008); and there are increases in customer satisfaction and profitability (Osland et al., 2007).

Compassion, as a leadership practice, ought to be directed inwardly and outwardly. Significant,

transformational change is rarely ever top-down, but more often inside-out. We've all heard the phrase, "Think globally, act locally." There is no more local than you can get than by connecting deeply in love and care and compassion with yourself. Pema Chodron (2009_____at wh_____l acceptance of _____: of ourselves in _____t home with ou_____home in the wo_____ows, so does ou_____

Self-compassion is understood as extending care and kindness to your self. Research in self-compassion indicates that leaders who are compassionate toward themselves experience greater psychological health and resilience than those who lack self-compassion. This inward showing of care is positively associated with life satisfaction, positive relations with others, wisdom, personal growth, happiness, and adaptive coping with failure (Neff, 2011).

Metta practice is essentially the act of sharing loving-kindness. This most common metta meditation is in five parts—beginning with oneself as a habit to cultivate self-compassion. We begin by reflecting on four statements:

- May I be free from fear.
- May I be free from compulsion.
- May I be blessed with love.
- May I be blessed with peace.

In this first stage, we begin to feel metta for ourselves by focusing on feelings of inner peace, calm, and tranquility. Often, practitioners will utilize the image of a golden beam or shower of light flooding our bodies as we focus on freedom from fear and compulsion as well as blessings of love and peace, calm, and tranquility.

In the second part, we extend these well wishes to loved ones. We might imagine a beam of golden light shining on them while sending thoughts of protection, gratitude, and celebration. The third part is when we begin to include acquaintances into our metta reflections. These are people we have neutral feelings for—those we do not know very well, but are often on the periphery of our lives. For these individuals we focus on their humanity by sending thoughtful well wishes. For the fourth part of the metta practice, we include those w[...] ties with— potential [...] er enemies. Our obj[...] or hurtful thoughts [...] em. In the final stag[...] nd beyond our netw[...] everyone freedom f[...] s blessings of love an[...] calm, and tranquility.

Naikan is a Japanese term translated to mean "inner seeing"—it is not about changing anything, but to pause and reflect. It is a structured compassion-cultivating practice that helps us to understand ourselves and our relationships. To practice Naikan, leaders ask themselves three questions: What have I received today? What have I given today? What troubles and difficulties have I caused today? Although these questions may seem simple and straightforward, our insights and realizations may prove to be powerful as we seek to become more compassionate toward ourselves and others.

Both metta and Naikan begin with a focus on oneself. Yet they are not limited to oneself. These compassion practices are ultimately about cultivating healthy relationships with others by emphasizing self-compassion. Daloz Parks (2000) comments,

> In a constructive encounter with otherness an empathic bond arises from recognizing that the other suffers in the same way as we, having the same capacity for hope, longing, love, joy, and pain. . . . This kind of perspective taking gives rise to compassion. (p. 140)

By extending compassion outwardly, we enable individuals to immerse themselves in *being human*. No matter how small the gesture, so long as it entails a compassionate attitude and approach, the impact can be magnanimous. For example, authentically inquiring about the well-being of others, providing a warm hug to a person in need, or bestowing verbal gestures of support are small gestures with a potentially profound impact. Other behaviors include making yourself physically and psychologically available to others, listening without judgment, and creating an environment—a holding space—for pain to be expressed.

> Compassion asks us to go where it hurts, to enter into places of pain to share in brokenness, fear, confusion, and anguish. Compassion challenges us to cry out with those in misery, to mourn with those who

are lon[...] [...]mpassion require[...] [...]ble with the vul[...] [...]owerless. Compa[...] [...]ondition of bein[...]

Tonglen is a Tibetan Buddhist meditative practice of giving and receiving. When practicing Tonglen, we give others our happiness, well-being, and peace of mind while imagining the taking of their pain (Rinpoche, 1993). It is in this process that we become liberated from selfishness because we reverse our usual logic of avoiding suffering and seeking pleasure.

Our common response to suffering is to look away. Others' pain may raise our fear, anger, confusion, or other limiting emotions. Instead of avoiding these feelings, we can practice Tonglen to be more compassionate. To begin, sit quietly and breathe deeply. Then imagine the pain and suffering of another. As you breathe, inhale the pain and suffering of the other. And exhale compassionately with love, support, and goodwill.

These next two practices can be utilized in tandem. *Right speech* is based on asking ourselves three questions prior to [...] to be shared does no[...] [...] from saying it is the [...]

- Is it true?
- Is it kind[...]
- Is it nece[...]

Intentional listening—often referred to as *active listening*—is a foundational practice for a compassion-centric healthy leadership habit. This is how we prove, as leaders, that we care about others. Intentional listening is approached without an agenda. The goal is to create the conditions to simply understand others.

Leadership Educator Praxis Activity

Leadership Theme: Offering Compassion
Exercise: Metta, Naikan, Tonglen, Right Speech and Intentional Listening (reflective [personal engagement] activities)

Compassion is often viewed as a very soft leadership practice—if it is viewed as a leadership practice at all. We hold the assumption that leaders are supposed to be tough, firm, and stoic. Compassion is perceived as an affront to this notion of leadership. Yet the research and data support that when leaders infuse compassion-based practices into their repertoire, the impact is profound.

Leadership educators should welcome opportunities to develop the compassion capacities and practices of participants by first illuminating the data to set the tone and indicate the overwhelming rationale for compassion. Then we should illuminate through experiential activities and reflective dialogue how our current practices, void of compassion, are simply not encouraging others to perform at their peak. Finally, these trainings should introduce and provide space for participants to experiment with tangible compassion-raising practices.

I offer four compassion-enhancement experiential learning activities that are all reflection oriented. Their flavor is slightly different from one another, but their instructions are essentially the same.

Metta (Self-Compassion)

Metta practice is essentially the act of wishing yourself and others well. Metta practice can be used as a habit to cultivate compassion that begins by reflecting on four statements:

- May I be free from fear.
- May I be free from compulsion.
- May I be blessed with love.
- May I be blessed with peace.

Following this initial reflection for a set amount of time, invite participants to imagine a beam or shower of golden light onto a loved one—while sending them thoughts of protection, gratitude, and celebration. We then advance in the activity to repeat this process for an acquaintance. The fourth phase of the activity is to send loving kindness, as difficult as it may be, toward an individual we dislike and are having difficulties with. Before sliding into the reflective dialogue, we complete the metta practice by wishing everyone— all of humanity—freedom from fear and compulsion as well as blessings of love and peace, calm, and tranquility.

Materials

- N/A

Naikan

Naikan is a Japanese term translated to mean "inner seeing"; it is not about changing anything, but to pause and reflect. To practice Naikan, leaders ask themselves three questions:

- What have I received today?
- What have I given today?
- What troubles and difficulties have I caused today?

When facilitating this activity, be sure to leave ample time for participants to deeply reflect on each of the three questions. Although no materials are necessary, this activity can be enhanced if participants have writing materials and can detail their responses.

Materials

- N/A

Tonglen

Tonglen is a Tibetan Buddhist meditative practice of giving and receiving. When practicing Tonglen, we begin by sitting quietly and breathing deeply. Then we imagine the pain and suffering of another. As we breathe, we inhale and imagine releasing the pain and suffering from the other. When we exhale, we send compassionate love, support, and goodwill. Like the others, this is *not* intended to be a 60-second activity. It is a purposeful breathing exercise that should provide an ample amount of time for participants to experience—even if it may be uncomfortable for them.

Materials

- N/A

Right Speech and Intentional Listening

Right speech is based on asking ourselves three questions prior to speaking—if the comment about to be shared does not meet all of the criteria, refraining from saying it is the compassionate decision.

- Is it true?
- Is it kind?
- Is it necessary?

Right speech is paired with intentional listening— often referred to as *active listening*. When we listen with intention, we seek to understand others—rather than trying to refute, rebut, or reply. With this activity, participants can be paired and asked to share a story about a meaningful life experience or defining moment in their lives. While in pairs, the participants each practice right speech and intentional listening.

Materials

- N/A

Instructions

- Begin by setting the mood and settling the energy of the participants.
- Once participants are in a mindful mental space, suggest they sit up straight with hands on their laps and feet firmly pressed on the floor.
- For each of these exercises, I suggest beginning with deep breathing—instructing participants to inhale and exhale with deep, long breaths.
- Once a good rhythm has been found, guide them step-by-step, question-by question from the previous brief descriptions. Although there are three or four questions referenced for these practices, participants should sit with each question for several moments—an ample amount of time to reap the benefits of these compassion-cultivating exercises—as they inhale and exhale.
- When the compassion-based breathing exercises come to a close, gently invite participants to share about their experience in the reflective dialogue.

Reflective Dialogue Questions

Our objective with this activity is to introduce or reinforce compassion-based breathing exercises to our participants. This may feel very uncomfortable at first—or through the entire engagement—for them based upon their experiences with these types of breathing exercises and focused attention. Good. Only through these types of practices can we develop a healthy compassionate leadership practice. A selection of my go-to reflective dialogue questions includes the following:

- How did it feel engaging in this compassion-based breathing exercise?
- What emotions arose for you?

- How do you feel now, after we've engaged in this practice—compared to before?
- What can we learn from this exercise that can be applied to our own leadership practice?

Being Hopeful and Optimistic

Hope is an attitudinal disposition. When we have a healthy sense of self and a healthy sense of our goals, our chance for success increases exponentially. Often, though, we attach to limiting thoughts, attitudes, and actions—rooted in fear, doubt, anger, frustration, and other draining emotions. By attaching to these thoughts, attitudes, and actions, we apply energy to restrictions, restraints, and regulations. Hope, as a healthy leadership practice, is energizing. Hope is an attitude of opportunities rather than obstacles. Hope is an attitude of potentials rather than problems. Hope is an attitude of futures rather than failures.

Hope enables us to believe that the future we envision is attainable, and to progressively move toward our goals and visions (Boyatzis & McKee, 2005). Hope is not a Pollyanna, blinded-by-optimism, rose-colored notion of the future—a foolish perspective of the future that is disconnected from truth and reality. Rather, hope is a deep connection to what we know is possible. With hope, we realistically understand the challenges ahead, yet, in the face of those obstacles, we authentically believe in our pursuits. Hope, as a leadership practice, is rooted in a solid, realistic plan to achieve our goals. When we experience hope, we feel elated, exhilarated, and energized about a future that is possible—even in the face of serious obstacles and opposition.

Hope is a science—it has been researched—and can be measured. When we apply the science of hope to our lives, it can change us. The formal definition of *hope* is the "belief that your future can be brighter and better than your past and that you actually have a role to play in making it better" (Gwinn & Hellman, 2019, p. 9). At our core, as hopeful people, we have clearly articulated goals, the motivation to pursue these goals, the determination to overcome obstacles and obstructions, and the pathways to achieve our goals. When we embrace the language of hope, we talk differently, act more intentionally, and live our lives with greater purpose than before.

Hope has three core elements—goals, pathways, and agency. Hope is initially activated when we know and recognize what we are pursuing—our goals. Hope is not impulsiveness. It is guided by intention—a deep understanding and knowing that our goals can be achieved.

Hope increases when pathways to goal accomplishment are identified. Designing pathways to success enhances our sense of self and heightens our appreciation for what is possible. Pathways is plural. By discovering alternative routes, we become more flexible, nimble, and adaptive in achieving our goals. In this way, we do not become overly deflated when preventative measures impede our initial pathway.

Hope is fueled by willpower. By having agency (see Nurturing Self-Efficacy and Confidence in chapter 10) we are able to see ourselves as capable of goal accomplishment. This is what motivates us to continue on in the face of challenge and struggle. Agency is about shifting the impossible into the I'mPossible . . . *I Am Possible.*

Hope has been referenced as a science due to the research and inquiry into its impact. As Gwinn and Hellman (2019) state, every published study of hope indicates that hope is the single best predictor of well-being. Within the workplace—where leadership often manifests—hope has positive implications for enhanced performance, reduced turnover, and increased job satisfaction. Hopeful individuals set more goals, are better at critical thinking, and have superior problem-solving abilities. They record higher levels of commitment to the organization, helpfulness toward others, are significantly more likely to be engaged in their projects, and approach new tasks vigorously—reducing burnout and turnover. Hope serves as a magnet—an attractor—that strengthens synergies and connections among people. Think about it; we often want to be surrounded by hopeful people rather than those with rage, despair, or apathy, right?

So how might leaders cultivate hope as a leadership practice? First, we need to understand the core tenets of hope. We need to explore the literature and research on hope to understand exactly what it is. Then we need to spend time in a reflective space identifying and integrating goals, pathways, and agency into our leadership practice.

Next, we want to measure our hope. We do this by becoming aware of the hope status within ourselves and those with whom we lead. Are we hopeful? Are our followers hopeful? If so, amazing, let's continue to get after it! If not, let's identify the limiting factors.

If after assessing our hope status, we find that increased levels of hope are necessary, we need to cultivate personally meaningful dreams and aspirations. Where there are hope deficiencies, we want to create relevant and realistic goals and pathways—for ourselves and our followers. Questions to consider include the following: Are the goals realistic and clear? Are there multiple pathways to success? Do I and my followers have a healthy sense of agency and empowerment?

As we continue toward goal accomplishment, we want to continually evaluate our progress. We enhance hope by assessing this progress toward goal accomplishment. If the assessment is less than ideal, we can create new pathways forward as well as recalibrate our sense of agency.

Finally, we always want to be in a position of moving toward goal accomplishment. Small steps in the right direction matter. Inching forward is better than no movement at all. The quickest way to lose momentum and attach to limiting emotions, attitudes, and actions is to be working toward unrealistic goals. It is necessary to take time to ensure small steps can be taken to work toward the ultimate vision. It is not enough to just ensure that the goals are realistic and attainable; we actually need to do something. By accomplishing small tasks, we can work our way toward what we truly believe is possible. What should I do right now, if I were the one person needed to achieve this goal? What is the one thing I can do—no matter how small—that I can do right now to make a small difference in the direction of progress? Do something. Do something. Do something.

Hope and optimism are aligned, yet slightly different. Hope is a positive belief in the future and what is possible. Optimism is a disposition. It is a habit of thinking and outlook that leans toward positivity. Like hope, optimism can be learned and cultivated.

Pessimists exhibit learned helplessness. It is a state of mind in which one cannot control or change negative circumstances (Delucca & Goldstein, 2020). In his book *Learned Optimism: How to Change Your Mind and Your Life*, Martin Seligman (1991) describes how we can shift this learned helplessness—what he considers our explanatory style—to alter our disposition to be more optimistic.

Our explanatory style is how we explain limiting events and experiences in our lives. We can explain an event as either permanent or temporary. When we believe a limiting event—or what it implies—is permanent, we become pessimistic and train our brain to believe that the situation won't change. A temporary limiting event has the potential to get better. This is an optimistic outlook.

We can explain a limiting situation as either pervasive or specific. If it is pervasive, it becomes all-consuming and encompasses every aspect of our life. This is a pessimistic outlook. An optimistic outlook recognizes these situations are specific to this time, place, and situation.

Last, we can utilize an explanatory style to differentiate the cause of a negative event. A pessimistic disposition is one in which individuals internalize negative events as caused by themselves. There's an *It's all my fault* attitude. To shift to optimism, we recognize that these negative events were caused by external forces and that we are in control of how to respond.

To enhance our optimistic disposition and practice optimism, we need to train ourselves to see the good. We can do this by keeping records of things that went well, noticing the fluidity and impermanence of our situations, taking a purposeful pause when we notice our minds wandering to pessimism, and breathing deeply into a better future.

Years ago, I cofounded an organization called iBELIEVE. It was an enterprise launched with my best friends that was designed to share the power of belief—that we can create significant and lasting change when we believe in ourselves and believe in our goals. We hosted workshops and other trainings that, looking back, synergize with this process of cultivating hope and optimism. Kevin Bickart MD/PhD, a neurologist and neuroscientist at UCLA's Steve Tisch BrainSPORT and Neurobehavior programs, crafted a methodology that we called the "Progress Process." It was a five-step clarity-raising process that was utilized as a foundation and methodology for these trainings and workshops.

The Progress Process was born out of what he considers the Intention-Action Dilemma. The predicament many of us find ourselves in is that what we intend does not always come to fruition. This is commonly due to one of these four reasons: We either (a) don't have clear intentions; (b) don't have a clear plan to actualize our intentions; (c) don't follow through with our intentions; and/or (d) don't overcome obstacles (Bickart, personal communication, June 8th 2022). As a way to generate clear intentions, craft clear plans, enhance follow-through efforts, and effectively overcome obstacles, we would facilitate trainings with experiential activities and reflective dialogue that utilized the Progress Process methodology and worksheet.

The Progress Process starts with participants identifying a meaningful GOAL. "We start by setting a progressive goal. This is a big goal, a life goal, a goal that you believe in, a goal that will help you and others. To progress, you must think big first and get realistic after. Next, write out actionable steps that will lead you to your goal. Put deadlines on your goals and steps. Finally, set up a reminder system to keep you on track" (Bickart, personal communication, June 8th 2022).

Once we know what we are pursuing, we can move to the STOP phase. Here, we become aware of beliefs—specifically the limiting ones. Literally, we would ask, What are the factors—thoughts, attitudes, beliefs, and/or actions—that are preventing you from achieving your goal?

When we gain some clarity on our limiting beliefs, we can move to the BEGIN phase. In this phase we shift our mental frame from the limiting factors to the empowering ones—we begin to be positive. Here we want to clarify for ourselves why this goal is important or beneficial to ourselves or our organizations.

Next, we shift into action, the GO phase. We act on what we believe. In our trainings, it was difficult to have participants engage in their actions because they often necessitated time and space beyond the training bubble. As a way to facilitate this portion of the Progress Process during our training experiences, we invited our participants to write down, as explicitly as possible, the three actions they were going to engage in following the training that would enable them to work toward goal accomplishment. We would structure these GO-actions around activities that could occur in the next hour, next day, and next week. At other times, we invited them to draft the three most important things that need to do in the coming month.

Finally, the last step in the process is to BELIEVE. We invited our participants, if they authentically believed it was possible to accomplish their self-identified goal, to sign the bottom of their worksheet. We recognized that having this hopeful stance, optimistic disposition, and authentic belief in these goals was going to magnify opportunities for success. And like most processes, we expressed that this process was cyclical and should be replicated over and over and over again with all of the goals we strive to accomplish.

Leadership Educator Praxis Activity

Leadership Theme: Being Hopeful and Optimistic
Exercise: Ideal Me/Real Me (reflective [worksheet] activity)

Peter Magolda, an inspirational educator and personal mentor of mine, to whom this book is dedicated, would often become flustered by what he considered my "chronic optimism." I believe, so deeply, in the power and importance of hope and optimism as a personal and leadership practice. By understanding what these concepts are and then intentionally cultivating them, we maximize our potential to accomplish all that we set our minds to.

Exceptional leadership educators hold fast to hopeful dispositions. It is our hope that enables us to create the conditions for our participants to recognize that their wildest dreams are possible and to be empowered to manifest those dreams. In our trainings, we should continually repeat the possibility of success to our participants. For example, if we are engaged in a timed activity, with each round of the activity, we can reduce the time allotment, making it more challenging—while continuing to prod the participants into believing that goal accomplishment is possible.

When we are hopeful, our chance for success increases exponentially. With the Ideal Me/Real Me activity, we engage participants in thinking about their vision (ideal), current reality (real), and the pathways to get from here to there (action items to build a bridge between the two).

Ideal Me/Real Me

The Ideal Me/Real Me activity is structured so that participants begin by thinking about the ideal. The question might change—it could be what they perceive the ideal leader to be, in a broad sense—or a particular role at a localized level (e.g., leadership educator). Regardless of the question, they draw characteristics on their worksheet that epitomize that. For example, if an ideal leader is a great communicator,

participants might draw a megaphone to typify it. After drawing elements for the ideal, they flip the paper over and engage in the same process for how they see themselves, currently, as a leader or leadership educator. This is not the end of the exercise. The most important part is to clarify the path for these participants to move from how they see themselves now to their ideal. This is the hope-raising part of the experiential learning activity.

Materials

- worksheet (double-sided) with a stick figure or other image of a person on one side labeled "Ideal Me"; on the other, "Real Me"
- writing utensil

Instructions

- Begin by distributing the Ideal Me/Real Me worksheet.
- Then instruct participants to stay on the Ideal Me side.
- Participants will be guided to draw pictorial representations of their ideal self in relationship to a specific identity (i.e., leader or leadership educator).
- Time should be allotted for them to draw these pictures, so set reminders.
- When the time concludes, participants should be invited to share a selection of their pictures either in pairs, small groups, or as a large group.
- *Note*: An option for this activity is to have a large Post-It note in the front of the room and have a selection of participants draw one of their examples for the public—and then describe what it is and why.
- Once the Ideal Me section has concluded, participants should engage in the same process for the way they really see themselves as leaders or peer advisors.
- The Real Me portion is not intended to be a values statement—these real elements can be what they do great as well as what needs improvement.
- Following their drawing, they should engage in the same pattern of conversation—in pairs or small groups or in public with the large group.

- Finally, as we enter into the reflective dialogue, you will highlight the difference between the real and the ideal—with the plan of creating action steps to bridge the reality with what is hoped for in the ideal. These action steps are the pathways to shifting the real into the ideal.

Reflective Dialogue Questions

Our objective with this activity to provide a space for participants to cultivate hope by illuminating pathways to move from how they identify themselves, really, to their ideal. A selection of my go-to reflective dialogue questions includes the following:

- How was this process for you in comparing your ideal to where you see yourself now?
- What is your pathway to get from the real to ideal? Who can leverage support and encouragement as you build that bridge between the two?
- How else can we cultivate hope as we work toward living our best, ideal selves?
- What can we learn from this exercise that can be applied to our own leadership practice?

Displaying Gratitude

Gratitude is tricky. It is a rare leadership competency that, even if practiced genuinely, may be perceived as shallow, inauthentic, or displayed for unsavory means. It defies easy classification. It is conceptualized as an emotion, an attitude, a moral virtue, a habit, a personality trait, as well as a coping response (Emmons & McCullough, 2003).

Formally, *gratitude* is defined as (a) a recognized gain (b) coupled with the judgment that someone or something else is responsible for that gain (Solomon, 1977). Essentially, there is a willingness, on the part of the receiver, to recognize seemingly unearned recognition and value. With this understanding, gratitude has three critical components: a benefactor (giver), benefice (the gain), and a beneficiary (receiver).

Gratitude gains (benefices) may come in the form of praise, benefits, and gifts. That is, they are physical items and material things as well as spiritual feelings or emotional rewards. These gains are the consequence and effect of something beyond ourselves. They could be from other persons, animals, nature, or supernatural beings (L. Chen & Kee, 2008).

My brother, Seth, is a remarkably caring father, husband, sibling, son, and friend. During the COVID-19 pandemic, I was taken aback in gratitude for a small gesture that I believe highlights the ways this definition of *gratitude* manifests in action. It is important to mention that during this time frame, I received both a promotion from the University of Rhode Island and spent at least one afternoon a week caring for my nephew, Louis—some weeks with a bonus Friday-night sleepover. I don't play an active uncle-ing role because I'm forced to or because I expect any accolades. I love it! I cherish these opportunities to cultivate a relationship with Louis (and now Rose—who was born during the pandemic, on my birthday!) and look forward to our weekly engagements.

I already know that Seth is grateful for my presence in his son's life. I also know he is grateful for the few hours a week he (and my sister-in-law) can have with unadulterated time to focus on work as well as their relationship. He verbally shares his thankfulness every week when I leave their home.

As a way to express his gratitude, above and beyond what I expected, as well as to honor this promotion, he purchased a beautiful handcrafted bowtie-facemask combo pack. I wear bowties as part of my faculty attire—and a facemask because I care for others in my community. I was so incredibly grateful. This gift was a recognized gain—it was an unexpected and touching gesture and emotional wellspring.

If we were to take a closer look at Seth's gratefulness for my time with Louis, the gain is a few hours to not worry about providing parenting responsibilities. Prepandemic, a tangible gain manifested as not worrying about picking up Louis from school. I could be counted on for the pickup and a few hours of play before dinnertime. Seth also recognizes that as the receiver of this gain, someone else is responsible—me, Uncle Jon.

It is important for leaders to cultivate gratitude as a leadership practice. There seems to be a consensus among those who are researching and writing about gratitude—there is a strong connection between multiple and varied positive implications and gratitude. This includes increases to one's future expectations, happiness, life satisfaction, physical health—including more exercise and sounder sleep—prosocial behaviors (e.g., more empathic, forgiving, helpful, and supportive than are their less grateful counterparts), relational connections, and overall well-being (Butler Bass, 2018; Emmons & McCullough, 2003; McCullough et al., 2002).

In one example, a study of athletes found that gratitude promoted both psychological and physical well-being (L. Chen & Kee, 2008). In this study, those who infused gratitude into their practice had increases in both life and team satisfaction as well as a reduction in burnout.

Similar results are found in workplace studies. Gratitude reduced toxic workplace attitudes and negative emotions such as envy, anger, and greed (Müceldili et al., 2015) while also generating feelings of belonging (Gostick & Elton, 2020). Adrian Gostick and Chester Elton (2020) describe in *Leading With Gratitude* that, with gratitude, performance is boosted, morale is increased, and relationships are strengthened. They go on to share that organizations where gratitude is infused into the culture are more profitable, with higher satisfaction rates and increases in employee engagement. "A lack of gratitude is a form of stupidity. It leaves on the table an enormously powerful tool not only to inspire people to reach their potential, but to better understand the true nature of their contributions" (p. 6).

Gratitude is not an either-or phenomenon. It is not that one has gratitude or does not have gratitude. Gratitude, in practice, rests upon a spectrum. We can enhance our gratitude practice by increasing our disposition toward gratitude—also known as our grateful disposition.

A grateful disposition is a generalized tendency to recognize and respond with grateful emotion to benevolence and the positive experiences and outcomes that we obtain (McCullough et al., 2002). There are four facets to a grateful disposition: intensity, frequency, span, and density.

Intensity refers to the magnitude of gratitude feelings. A dispositionally grateful person who experiences a positive event feels more intensely grateful than would someone less disposed toward gratitude.

Frequency denotes the number of feelings of gratitude in a certain time span. A dispositionally grateful person reports feelings of gratitude more often than someone at the other end of the gratitude disposition spectrum. For grateful people, what are perceived as simple favors or acts of politeness elicit feelings of gratitude.

Span refers to the number of circumstances and factors for which people feel grateful at a given time. Dispositionally grateful people might feel grateful for their families, work opportunities, health, community engagements, and life itself—in addition to enumerable acts of gratitude. People less disposed to gratitude recognize fewer factors of gratitude in their lives.

Density indicates the number of sources (e.g., people, animals, nature, or supernatural beings) to whom one feels grateful in relationship to a single positive outcome. When sharing about to whom one feels grateful for a certain gain, a dispositionally grateful person might list many sources. Fewer sources tend to be offered by someone less disposed toward gratitude (McCullough et al., 2002).

To dive a bit deeper, Diana Butler Bass (2018) has crafted a four-domain model. In this model, personal (me) and public (we) expressions of gratitude are on opposite polarities, as are feelings (emotions) and actions (ethics). The result is quadrants that emphasize (a) me and emotions, (b) me and ethics, (c) we and emotions, and (d) we and ethics.

Me and emotions focuses on personal feelings of gratitude. Butler Bass (2018) offers that part of the reason gratitude is complicated is because of the internalized and mixed feelings of dependence and interdependence. "Dependence may enslave the soul, but interdependence frees us" (p. 22). When we feel the soul-crushing feelings of obligation and debt (i.e., payback) of offering gratitude, we feel dependent. Rather, we ought to shift this mindset and move into a perspective of gratitude as mutual reliance upon gifts or gains. Furthermore, particularly for the masculine readers, these personal feelings of gratitude are neither sentimental nor soft. Unfortunately, gratitude has been feminized and relegated to a "less-than" status. Instead of shying away from these deeply emotional feelings of gratitude, we should celebrate—and act upon—basking in our own feelings of gratefulness and showering others with thankfulness when opportunities arise.

Me and ethics is a focus on personal awareness and the practice of gratitude—actions. It is a disposition that can be chosen, cultivated, and infused into our practices as healthy habits. When this does happen, we change. The positive implications shared previously are the result. Gratitude gives us new perspectives on our own lives—in part because of how it fosters resilience.

We and emotions is a social, celebratory dynamic of gratitude. In this quadrant, the emphasis is on the social—breaking down walls. "Reaching beyond ourselves comes naturally when we are grateful" (Butler Bass, 2018, p. 100). This is particularly important in individualistic societies and postpandemic life. We need to make intentional efforts to express gratitude toward others in specific, authentic, and consistent ways if we are to cultivate our gratitude disposition.

We and ethics, the final quadrant, emphasizes gratitude as a measure of community and social justice. Gratitude, although felt individually, is inherently social. It is placed at the intersection of myself and the other—other persons, animals, nature, or supernatural beings. "True gratitude, real gratefulness, the kind of transformative thanksgiving that makes all things new, cannot be quiet in the face of injustice" (Butler Bass, 2018, p. 139).

Gratitude is not practiced as a perfunctory act or something to check off a list. Gratitude needs to be authentic and specific. For example, we can intentionally solicit and act upon the advice and suggestions of trusted colleagues and highlight small wins as an intentional way to celebrate the contributions of others. There should be both repetition in our gratitude as well as gifts and gains that are personally tailored. For example, if after a leadership training, we decide to send thank-you notes to our participants, drafting them as generic "I appreciated your comments" is not an act of gratitude. For these notes to be authentic expressions of gratitude, they should indicate specific comments that had personal relevance and resonance or initiated a transformative moment in the training.

If we truly want to cultivate our disposition of gratitude, we need to infuse gratitude into a daily practice. *Me* options include reveling in the ordinary, sitting in wonderment and awe, journaling our gratefulness, observing the blessings and benefits in our lives, and witnessing the magic and superpowers of others. *We* practices include writing notes, authentically offering forgiveness, explicitly and in personally meaningful ways for the recipient recognizing their contributions, restoring trust and confidence, honoring others—and doing all of this often and repeatedly.

Leadership Educator Praxis Activity

Leadership Theme: Displaying Gratitude

Exercise: Gratitude ABC List (reflective [group engagement] activity)

Imagine that you receive a thank-you note from a leadership educator whose workshop you attended last week. There's an initial rush of excitement as you open the envelope. All that's there, though, is a rote note—a generic "thank you for participating." How deflating! In any context, receiving this kind of gratitude gift devalues our investment.

On our campuses and in our organizations, leaders often neglect thanks-giving. If they do offer gratitude, it is often in a mass-production format that is nonspecific and unintentionally unkind. We need to do better. Leadership educators should model authentic and specific gratitude-giving as well as infuse a culture of gratitude into our trainings. We need to cultivate a disposition of gratitude into our own healthy leadership habits and regimen. Doing so increases our value and connectedness to our participants and enhances the occasion for their internalization of their leadership learning and its implementation into their practices.

One tangible way we can do this during our trainings is to verbally and sincerely thank our participants for offering their wisdom and experiences by sharing words of affirmation and repeating their vocalized contributions. Another, especially for longer-term trainings—like a retreat or a programmatic series—is to provide or engage participants in creating "mailboxes." With these mailboxes, participants and facilitators can draft notes of gratitude and celebration and share with one another.

Gratitude is one of the most difficult training topics because experiential activities rarely focus on this explicitly. One such activity, though—the Gratitude ABC List—is a great example. Please note, this is a competitive activity where partners or small groups will be competing against others to craft a list of things they are authentically grateful for. As a competitive activity, it may be important as the facilitator to remind participants that the root of the activity is about reflecting upon what we are grateful for, not the competition. We can use this as fodder for the reflective dialogue following the activity.

Gratitude ABC List

When facilitating the Gratitude ABC List, participants are organized into small groups. This activity works well when there is a large participant body because of the competitive nature of the experience. Once arranged, they will be given a worksheet or a plain piece of paper. The objective is for the small groups to draft a list of things for which they are authentically grateful—one item per letter. For example, for the letter "F," participants might draft "Facilitator," or for the letter "M," they might share "Master Trainer."

As a competitive experience, once all the pairs and groups have their list, for every item that is original and not repeated by another, those groups receive a point. The group at the end of the alphabet who has the most points wins. As the facilitator, you can infuse one "challenge" to make it a spicier activity. That is, each group has one challenge that they can use strategically to ask another group why that item is something for them to be authentically grateful for. Based on the response, the whole of the participant body can vote to determine if they get the point or not.

Materials

- worksheet with A–Z listed on the left column (or just a piece of paper per group)
- writing utensils

Instructions

- Begin by inviting the participants to gather in small groups of their choosing or your choice.
- Share the instructions that they as a group, in competition with the other groups, are to identify and list one item per each letter that they are authentically grateful for.
- You will then share how points are calculated: There will be one point awarded for each unique item (one that has not identified by any other group). The group at the end of the alphabet that has the most points wins.
- Optional: Choose if you want to include the "Challenge" component. If so, offer each group one challenge they can use strategically to ask another group why that item is something to be authentically grateful for. Based on the response, the whole of the participant body can vote to determine if they get the point or not.

- Once you have made your way through the entire alphabet by tabulating points on a projected screen or whiteboard, announce the winner and slide into the reflective dialogue.

Reflective Dialogue Questions

Our objective with this activity to think deeply about all of the things for which we are grateful. The Gratitude ABC List experiential learning activity, because of its competitive nature, is an energy-raising way to show our gratefulness. A selection of my go-to reflective dialogue questions includes the following:

- How did it feel to be thinking of all the things for which we are grateful?
- How did you tangibly express your gratitude through this exercise?
- How did you center gratitude even in the face of competition?
- What did you learn about gratitude that is worth remembering beyond the training bubble?
- What can we learn from this exercise that can be applied to our own leadership practice?

Conclusion

The leadership practices in this chapter focused on our emotional engagement and presence. When we develop healthy leadership habits in these domains, we are able to nurture resonance and synergistic relationships with others. Specifically, we can regulate our own emotions and recognize ways to appropriately respond to our followers' emotions (EQ), show loving-kindness to ourselves and others (offering compassion), focus our energy and attention on the positive future (being hopeful and optimistic), and celebrate our own and others through the life-giving force of being authentically grateful (displaying gratitude).

CHAPTER **9**

Cooperative Leadership Practices

HE THIRD COMPILATION OF leadership practices focuses on skills to enhance cooperative and collaborative engagements with others. Communicating, engaging with groups and teams, motivating others toward goal accomplishment, and navigating dissonance and toxicity will assist leaders in crafting leadership experiences that bring out the best in themselves and their followers. These healthy leadership habits are about getting our hands dirty to traverse leadership challenges and pursue worthy goals.

Communicating

We know that leadership is a relational experience. Effectively leading hinges upon nourishing, robust, and dynamic engagements between leaders and followers. That engagement is propelled by communication. In a broad sense, healthy communication follows a four-part cycle (see Figure 9.1).

Leaders tend to begin with relaying—especially those with formal positions, power, and authority. That is, they engage in sharing information. This sharing should be offered with compassion and clarity. Once information has been communicated, leaders embrace the receiving of information. Here, they listen and accept responses verbal and otherwise with openness. Next in the communication cycle is the opportunity to engage in reflecting. Leaders encourage the reflective processes for both themselves and their followers. This is the phase when the information is processed so it can be deeply understood and internalized. Not until the information is internalized can

it be acted upon in appropriate ways that create the desired outcomes. Repeating is the follow-up step in the cycle. Leaders and followers repeat what was heard (and internalized) to ensure all stakeholders are synergized and can move forward as a united front. Of course, as a cycle, the four steps are reiterated. Once information is repeated to ensure collective understanding, it is typically relayed to others in order that change can occur—particularly in the form of ideas being implemented into action.

Figure 9.1. Four-part communication cycle.

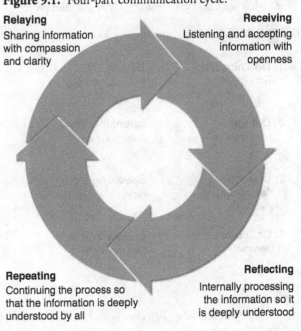

Relaying
Sharing information with compassion and clarity

Receiving
Listening and accepting information with openness

Repeating
Continuing the process so that the information is deeply understood by all

Reflecting
Internally processing the information so it is deeply understood

Kahane (2004) suggests that solving tough problems (i.e., leading) occurs when we shift the ways in which we talk and listen. Often, we are closed in our approach. We rehearse and reload our rebuttals—before even attending to what others have to say. We tend only to listen to ourselves and the recordings we make in our minds. We stick to what we know—dictating or talking politely. By dictating, we utilize an authoritarian, unilateral approach. This has unintended consequences for our visions and work because the messaging is not received well. Talking politely, although it sounds nice, is not a healthy leadership practice either. Here we say the things we think the other person wants to hear—not what they need to hear or the things that will move us closer to goal accomplishment. With politeness, we tend to be timid rather than tap into the courage necessary for leadership.

When we invest in open talking and listening as leaders, we invest in the pursuit of our worthy goals. "If talking openly means being willing to expose to others what is inside of us, then listening openly means being willing to expose ourselves to something new" (Kahane, 2004, p. 73). Kahane goes on to share that

> to create new realities, we have to listen reflectively. It is not enough to be able to hear clearly the chorus of other voices; we must also hear the contribution of our own voice. It is not enough to be able to see others in the picture of what is going on; we must also see what we ourselves are doing. It is not enough to

be observers of the problem situation; we must also recognize ourselves as actors who influence the outcome. (p. 83)

Listening reflectively is synonymous with deep listening (if we are the receiver) or being listened to fully (if we are the speaker).

> Something quite wonderful occurs when we are listened to fully. We expand, ideas comes to life and grow, we remember who we are. Some speak of this force as a creative fountain within us that springs forth; others call it the inner spirit, intelligence, true self. Whatever this force is called, it shrivels up when we are not listened to and thrives when we are. (Lindahl, 2008, p. 11)

Leadership is relational. We can't effectively lead unless we are engaged with and in communication with others. Synergy is what we seek. Communication is the vehicle for synergistic relationships. Conversation creates the world—and if we want to live in a better world—we need to shift and deepen the structure of our attention (Scharmer, 2007, 2018).

Otto Scharmer (2007, 2018; Scharmer & Kaufer, 2013)—the leadership scholar and designer of theory U (see chapter 5)—describes the fields of conversation and listening. These fields are about the four levels of quality of our conversations and listening. If we want to communicate effectively, we need to progress from the surface to deeper levels. Figure 9.2 details Scharmer's fields of communication.

Figure 9.2. The fields of communication.

Note. Reprinted with permission and licensed by the Presencing Institute—Otto Scharmer.

In the first field, we talk nice. This is a downloading approach of utilizing ritualistic language. We speak from a place of expectation—saying things that we believe the other(s) want to hear. It is generally polite and laden with empty phrases. Leaders conform by holding back from speaking freely. What is offered are those things that fit into the dominant framework and conversational patterns of the group. Here we operate from within our own bubble.

In the second field, we talk tough. This is commonly understood as debate. We speak from a place of one-way sharing of information, opinion, and objective. It is confrontational. Leaders make their perspective known and limit their listening. Although diverse viewpoints are offered, there is limited openness to them. Here, we operate from our reactions.

In the third field, a shift occurs from separation to connectedness. Reflective inquiry and dialogue are the hallmark practices of conversation. At this level of conversation, there is a sincere back-and-forth where those involved relinquish their defensive stance to reflect on what is being offered by the other(s). There is a deep listening that allows leaders to see themselves as part of the solution. Here, we operate from a reflective stance—rooted in reflection and inquiry.

Finally, in the fourth field of conversation, there is a spirit of collective creativity and generative flow. Here, new ideas, imaginings, identities, and inspired energy are the norm (Scharmer, 2018). More, the dialogue evolves to be a collective, synergistic experience where leaders speak from what is moving through them—without reservation. Here, we operate from a generative space—with an emphasis in cocreation.

Just as conversing is a healthy leadership habit, listening is. Listening, at these deeper levels, is essential. Our ability to listen deeply can transform conversations and our leadership practice. As shown in Figure 9.3, the fields of listening begin with downloading. We listen from habit. Leaders at this level only listen to reconfirm what they already know. We are completely closed.

Within the second field we engage in factual listening. We listen from an objective perspective. Leaders utilize what they hear to disconfirm information. They seek information to prove themselves right and disparage other perspectives. At this level, there is a slight opening of the mind.

The third field of listening is empathic. With this approach, leaders relinquish their need to be right and listen from a place of learning. They approach discourse from the perspective of the other(s)—to understand diverse viewpoints and advance forward in ways that result in the best outcome, regardless of whose idea it was. There is an opening of the heart at this level.

The fourth field of listening is generative. Through our listening and engagement, we create a space for something new to be born. We open our will.

Figure 9.3. Scharmer's fields of listening.

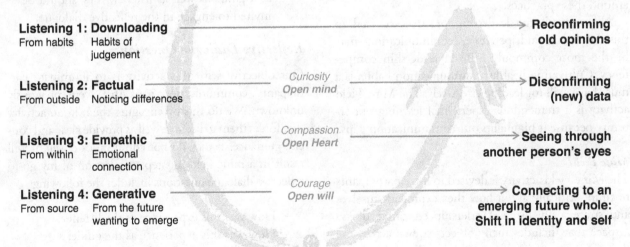

Note. Reprinted with permission and licensed by the Presencing Institute—Otto Scharmer.

Scharmer (2007) details that at this level the texture and outcomes of the experience significantly differ from the others:

> You know that you have been operating on the fourth level when, at the end of the conversation, you realize that you are no longer the same person you were when you started the conversation. You have gone through a subtle but profound change. You have connected to a deeper source—to the source of who you really are and to a sense of why you are here. (p. 13)

Leadership Educator Praxis Activity

Leadership Theme: Communicating
Exercise: Mine Field (physically engaged activity)

Communication is often a hot topic in leadership trainings because there is a seemingly endless opportunity for improvement. It seems to be particularly pressing with younger generations whose communication habits are informed by texting, social media, and other structures that distance individuals from face-to-face interaction. Our technologies have created barriers, borders, and distances that encourage level I (downloading) or level II (debate and factual) styles of communication and listening. These are closed approaches (Kahane, 2004).

As leadership educators, when facilitating communication-oriented trainings, experiential approaches can have a profound impact. In this way, our trainings serve as a channel for our participants to become witnesses of their communication and listening behaviors and then create intentional change around these practices.

Although all the leadership practices covered in this book are indispensable, communication may be the most commonly utilized leadership competency. Cultivating healthy communication habits is a must-have skill for leading effectively. The Mine Field activity is a tremendous experiential learning opportunity because it highlights our communication gaps.

Mine Field

The Mine Field activity is devised to force participants to think critically about how they express themselves and strategically listen. Leadership educators devise a space that includes many objects strewn across the floor. Participants, in partnerships, will need to work together to get one partner, blindfolded, from one end of the space to the other—without bumping into any of the "mines." The other partner will serve as the guide to instruct them on how to move and meander through the mine field.

Materials

- blindfolds
- lots of items that can be safely used as "mines" (balls, extra blindfolds, paper, writing utensils, etc.)

Instructions

- Prior to the exercise—potentially before the training begins—design the mine field with all of the elements strewn across the floor.
- To begin the experiential learning activity, arrange the participants into partnerships.
- Once in pairs, detail to the whole group that one partner will be blindfolded and needs to be guided through the mine field while the other partner serves as the guide. Although the guiding partner can walk beside the blindfolded one, it is best to ensure they stay on the outside of the mine field to make the activity a bit more challenging. This puts greater pressure on both partners to communicate more strategically and listen more carefully.
- "After the first partner navigates through the mine field," invite them to switch roles so everyone serves in both capacities.
- Once all of the participants have participated as a guide as well as listener, they should be invited to engage in the reflective dialogue.

Reflective Dialogue Questions

Our objective with this activity is to illuminate participants' communication gaps that were previously unknown. We do this by engaging them in an activity that forces them to listen as well as provide clear and concise guidance. If they do not communicate well, it will result in a mine field misstep. A selection of my go-to reflective dialogue questions includes the following:

- How was this experience as the listener?
- How was this experience as the guide?
- What did you notice about your communication style and skills?

- What is a communication growth area that you will commit to improving?
- What can we learn from this exercise that can be applied to our own leadership practice?

Engaging With Groups and Teams

There is certainly a diversity of perspectives on what leadership is or how one can best be of service as a leader. There is no disagreement on leadership as a relational experience. Leadership happens when people working together aim to create change and accomplish goals. It happens when intentionally engaging with others. This is especially true in group and team contexts. (For the purposes of this section, the terms *groups* and *teams* are utilized interchangeably.)

Groups can be defined quite broadly—as simply as two or more people (Williams, 2010). For our purposes, as leadership educators, it is important to define *groups* specific to our context. Groups, then, can be understood as three or more individuals, connected by their social relationship, distinctly gathered for a specific and shared purpose (Kroll, 2016). With this definition, it is important to note that groups are more than one or two people. Three people, at a minimum, comprise a group. These people are also connected in some way. They have relationships. They may not know one another personally, but they have a connection—for example, working in the same organization. And they have a specific and shared purpose—working on an important project or trying to accomplish a mutual goal.

Although people have engaged in groups for . . . ever, the studying of groups began in 1895—following street mobs in Paris, France—by two French sociologists. Emil Durkheim (1895/1982) wrote about social facts—those values, structures, and phenomena that transcend the individual and establish norms for the social community. In the context of groups, *social facts* are those rules and norms that are present without needing to be vocalized—the guiding principles for how group members engage and operate when together. A tremendous illustration of a social fact would be to think of a staff or team meeting. For me, as an example, when serving as a residence director, we would meet on every Thursday morning in the same central office conference room for our weekly staff meeting. I'm a creature of habit, and I am perennially

early, so I would show up, claim my (same) seat every week, and mentally prepare for the conversation. One week, after a long night of responding to emergency and not-so-emergency on-duty calls, I showed up on time for the meeting—rather than early. It just so happened that a campus colleague was invited to this staff meeting to discuss collaboration opportunities between our two offices. She sat in my seat. *My seat.* In our office, everyone had their informally "assigned" seats. This is where everyone sat every week. Our seating arrangement was a social fact for the group. It was a norm that we all acknowledged within our office community. Our colleague interrupted this social fact—at least for me.

The other sociologist, Gustav Le Bon (1895/2009), explored what he called the *collective mind*. This collective mind influences individuals to act in unusual (typically unconscious) ways when engaged in groups. He attributed Paris's mob behavior to this collective mind. When students rush the football field or basketball court after a high-profile win or championship victory, this is the collective mind. They know, consciously, that rushing the court or field may be dangerous for themselves, the athletes, and others, yet the collective mind takes over and students get wrapped up in the atmosphere. Similarly, many hazing incidents are rooted in collective mind. The group mentality takes over, causing decision-making by the collective that would not have otherwise happened. The collective mind, in action, makes it very difficult for an individual oppositional voice—usually the voice of reason—to be heard.

Research indicates that creativity, performance, and goal accomplishment are enhanced when leaders effectively engage groups through collaboration and welcoming the diverse and divergent voices of others. This is a much more difficult task in practice than on paper because powerful and positional leaders often exert significant influences on groups and teams. These influences may be intentional and for nefarious reasons. They may also be due to the developmental locale of the followers. For example, as we know from college student development theory, younger students (developmentally) tend to view the world dichotomously—as in either-or, yes-no, right-wrong perspectives. They also view those with power and authority as the sole decision-makers. When individuals with this developmental perspective participate in group work, they may self-silence their voice in deference to the leader. Unwittingly, the leader in this scenario limits opportunities for goal accomplishment because voices are excluded from the planning and decision-making processes—affecting the performance of those involved (West, 2003).

Leaders are encouraged to welcome dissenting and divergent perspectives—without retaliating against or delivering repercussions for those who believe differently. Otherwise, the work of the team can be disabled rather than enhanced. Nemeth and Nemeth-Brown (2003) suggest that dissent can be liberating—it can release people from pressures of conformity while stimulating critical thinking—resulting in enriched decision-making and productivity. When leaders refuse to welcome dissent and divergent perspectives, the result is often groupthink—which can be debilitating. Groupthink is when the collective foolishly believe the same thing or just "go along" out of fear or frustration. This can be dangerous. As leaders, we need to create the conditions that welcome diverse and divergent perspectives. In practice, leaders should act in certain ways to encourage dissent and celebrate divergent perspectives (West, 2003). This includes delaying offering opinions as these tend to be weighted due to the power and/or position of the leader; protecting the voices of marginalized or minority perspectives; delaying criticism of contributions by neutrally asking for alternative ideas; and serving as a facilitator for the group by inviting information, hosting conversation, relaying messages, asking questions, and integrating responses—before a formal decision is made.

It is important for leaders to understand the ways in which groups develop over time so as to appropriately guide (and possibly intervene) and provide the necessary guidance. Since the mid-1960s, Bruce Tuckman (1965) has been exploring how groups engage and perform. We, as leaders and leadership educators, can utilize his model to gauge where groups are functioning and to help them move along to the next stage.

1. *Forming.* In this first stage, forming, the group members are just getting connected. There is a tone of positivity and politeness. Generally, group members are careful not to offend anyone or be too vulnerable.
2. *Storming.* In this second stage, storming, the group members are now acquainted with one another and tension begins to arise. This is when boundaries are established—and crossed. Unless the tension and conflict is handled appropriately, the group may implode. As leadership educators, we can assist groups in moving through the storming phase to norming.
3. *Norming.* In the third phase, norming, group members resolve their differences, capitalize on strengths, and get into a good groove of collaboration and support. In this phase, group members develop stronger commitments to the goal—leading to progress and initial accomplishment.
4. *Performing.* The final working phase, performing, is highlighted by the group members' high level of commitment, engagement, and success in accomplishing their goals. It feels great to be a part of this group! This is where the group members are in flow.
5. *Adjourning.* In the last phase, adjourning, group members purposefully put closure to their group experience. If group members have worked through to the performing phase, this is a celebratory occasion. If not, adjourning may be a relief.

Talented leaders and leadership educators recognize the group's developmental locale as they work their ways through the stages of group development. Our role is to ensure team members are feeling valued and valuable, empowered and engaged, inspired and invested. Synergistic work rooted in the creation and sharing of knowledge is where we want to be; this is when groups are their most effective and powerful.

Not all groups operate from a place of synergy and performance. This if often due to dysfunctional behavior. Lencioni (2002, 2005) describes five dysfunctions of teams that limit their abilities to accomplish goals:

- *Absence of trust.* Great team members trust one another on a deep, connected, and, emotional level. They are comfortable being vulnerable with each other about their weaknesses, mistakes, and fears. They are completely open with one another, without filters.
- *Fear of conflict.* Team members who trust one another are not afraid to engage in passionate dialogue around important issues and decisions. They do not hesitate to disagree,

challenge, or question others—because they collectively operate in the spirit of finding the best way forward.

- *Lack of commitment.* Team members who are able to engage through healthy conflict are able to achieve genuine buy-in because every team member is seen as valued and valuable to the work of the team. When team members are valued, they willingly share ideas and perspectives that otherwise would have been kept silent.

- *Avoidance of accountability.* Team members who are committed to their peers and the work do not hesitate to hold one another accountable. They engage honestly and authentically with one another, regardless of positional role or status.

- *Inattention to results.* Team members who trust one another, engage in healthy resolution of conflict, commit to the project, and hold themselves and others accountable are likely to set aside individual agendas to focus on the needs of the team.

When the five dysfunctions are attended to, what emerges may be considered a *hot group* (Lipman-Blumen & Leavitt, 1999). A hot group is a lively, high-achieving, dedicated group, whose members are turned on to an exciting and challenging task. While engaged in their hot groups, the members are completely captivated—in heart and mind—to the exclusion of almost everything else. They do great things fast (Leavitt & Lipman-Blumen, 1995).

When the conditions align, hot groups are able to effectively solve impossible problems or beat unbeatable foes. And when hot groups are allowed to flourish unfettered by the usual organizational constraints, their energy and inventiveness can benefit organizations enormously.

Hot groups have several major characteristics. First, members have a total preoccupation with the task. Members of hot groups feel their work is immensely significant and that it demands their complete and undivided attention. Leaders create the conditions for team members to be laser-focused on their tasks. Second, members are fueled by high performance standards. These hot group members are stretched and inspired to move beyond their prior performance

limits. Leaders determine these performance standards while motivating group members to pursue these worthy goals. Finally, members have a sense of ennoblement. Hot groups members have a sense that their work is for a higher purpose—they are on a journey that is supremely worthwhile. Leaders ensure that the group members believe they are on a righteous path and are breaking new ground, establishing significant change.

Leadership Educator Praxis Activity

Leadership Theme: Engaging With Groups and Teams
Exercise: Lava Lake (physically engaged activity)

Developing the effective functioning of teams is a prime task of leaders. Never in the history of the world has one person single-handedly accomplished significant change solely by his-or-her-self. Never. We are only able to accomplish greatness in collaboration with others. We are only able to create the change we dream of when mobilizing others in pursuit of that vision. Yet this practice does not come naturally. We need to work at it.

Leadership educators are often called upon to facilitate team-building and group development training sessions. We're called to serve in this capacity because of our outsider perspective and because our facilitative prowess is exceedingly important. Often, team, group, and organizational leaders are immersed too deeply in their teams, groups, and organizations and lack the knowledge or ability to harness the energy necessary to take their members where they collectively want to go. In this role, we shine a light on these groups' performance and opportunities to enhance their teamwork skills. We do it by intentionally engaging our participants in diverse experiential learning opportunities—purposefully followed by reflective dialogue—as a way to highlight their current performance locale and ways to structurally and systemically improve.

Many of the activities listed throughout this book can be shifted to focus on group development and team building. I have selected the Lava Lake activity to model one such opportunity.

Lava Lake

Watch out! A volcano has just erupted and now the floor is lava! The Lava Lake activity transports participants to a fictional place where they need to move from one area of the training space to another without touching the floor, grass, or pavement. They are given a minimal amount of lava-retardant supplies to assist them in making their way. They'll use these supplies to figure a way across the lava while working as a cohesive team. During the activity, it is important for leadership educators to be cognizant of when participants touch the lava with their foot or hand—because when they do, they lose the ability to use that limb.

Materials

- lava-retardant supplies might include rubber bases, paper plates, or paper towel sheets (anything that participants can stand on, shuffle across the ground, or easily move for others to utilize)

Instructions

- Prior to the exercise—potentially before the training begins, design the lava field as a separate place from the rest of the training. (The design does not take much. However, to make it more difficult, chairs and desks and other objects should be utilized to block easy paths from one side to the other.)
- To begin the experiential learning activity, share a story about a volcano exploding. This is a phenomenal experiential learning activity to explore your theatrical chops.
- Explain to the participants that they are not to touch the lava (floor) for there will be consequences. They will need to strategize and work cooperatively to make their way, utilizing the lava-retardant supplies, to the safe zone.
- *Note*: If a training has 10 participants, I suggest only providing three or four of the supplies. If the training has 30 participants, they could be broken into three groups who each need to make their way across the lava lake.
- These instructions are simple and limited on purpose. We want the participants to devise a plan and collaborate as they work toward goal accomplishment.
- Once all of the participants have made their way across the lava lake, they will be fired up and energized. Relish that while engaging them in a reflective dialogue.

Reflective Dialogue Questions

Our objective with this activity is to support the development of group and team building. This is a superior activity because of the forced collaboration. A selection of my go-to reflective dialogue questions includes the following:

- How was this experience for you?
- What did you do well as a group?
- What can be improved as a group?
- Based upon this experience, what are the key features of effective groups and teams?
- What can we learn from this exercise that can be applied to our own leadership practice?

Motivating Others Toward Goal Accomplishment

What should I do right now—and the for the rest of today—if I am the person needed to heal the world? The magic of this question, laden with depth and meaning, is that each and every one of us has a different response. We're all guided by different motivating factors as we seek to be a restorative force in our communities and the world, more broadly. These distinctions between us are based upon what we believe needs healing; our current commitments; the schedule we've crafted for the rest of the day; and our own needs, resources, skills, and abilities. Everyone is motivated— the leadership task is to understand the forces of each follower's motivation in order to activate them toward goal accomplishment.

There has been a long-standing assumption that for leaders, motivating others should be rooted in fear or greed. If leaders utilize threats and pain or strictly financial rewards, followers will be motivated to work hard at accomplishing goals. For some, these *extrinsic* motivating factors work well. Extrinsic motivations are based in external rewards such as not being berated or receiving a lucrative bonus for accomplishments.

Contemporary scholarship indicates that *intrinsic* motivations may be more empowering for followers. Intrinsic motivations are rooted in the personal joy and inherent meaning one derives from the task or activity itself. A survey of intrinsic motivations includes a sense of belonging; opportunities for achievement; developmental relationships and experiences; and learning opportunities, autonomy, and alignment with personal values (Middlebrooks et al., 2020). The leader's objective, then, is to identify and induce followers' deeply meaningful emotional connections to the tasks. When we emotionally experience the compelling reasons to do something (as well as the painful reasons to avoid those things), we are guided by remarkably powerful forces.

Abraham Maslow (1943), a forefather of motivation research, is revered for detailing a hierarchy of needs. In the mid-20th century he detailed what we now know as a pyramidic structure to specify various levels of motivational forces. What began as five distinct levels has been expanded to eight motivational needs. Their hierarchical nature signifies that without the foundational needs being met, we will not be able to address our higher-level growth needs (Lipman-Blumen, 2005).

The hierarchy of needs is arranged into three general categories—deficiency needs, growth (often referred to as psychological) needs, and self-fulfillment needs. *Deficiency needs* focus on our physiological needs at the base of the pyramid. The foundation of the hierarchy emphasizes our need to function—food, water, shelter, sleep, and other necessities that enable us to survive. Just above that are our safety needs. This includes our motivations for personal security, health, and opportunities to acquire resources.

When we have a reasonable level of satisfaction with meeting our physiological and safety needs, we have greater comfort in pursuing *psychological needs*. These growth needs begin with belongingness and love, which include intimate relationships, friendships, and connections of depth and meaning. Above that in the hierarchy is esteem. In pursuing this need, we strive for feelings of accomplishment, respect, recognition, and productivity.

At the apex of the original pyramid is *self-actualization*. This is a desire to become the most that one can be and includes pursuing creative expression, achieving potential, and appreciating life.

Beginning in the 1970s, Maslow amended his hierarchy to include three additional levels to the pyramid. Our *knowledge and understanding need* highlights our desires to acquire new skills and learning experiences. *Aesthetics* emphasizes our need for beauty and pleasing surroundings in our lives. And, the new apex became *transcendence*. Here, we pursue opportunities to assist others in reaching their potential.

The hierarchy of needs becomes much more tangible and real when we put it in context. If training participants are homeless or hungry, what is the chance they are going to put in maximum effort toward their learning? Nil. For these participants, the priority is to find shelter and food—not engage or participate in our leadership learning experiences—and certainly not be emotionally present even if they are physically present. Similarly, if an incident occurs in one of our trainings and a participant feels physically or emotionally threatened, that particular participant (if not many others) will be a long way from meeting their self-actualization needs. In this scenario, there is a more pressing need to be met.

Other research in motivation highlights that the reward attractiveness is dependent on two critical factors—how much of the reward is being offered and how much the individual values the particular type of reward being offered (Lawler, 2006). Let's explore this in the context of resident directors—leadership educators who are responsible for the well-being, safety, and developmental experiences of students living in residence halls. I was one—at three different institutions—during graduate school and at the start of my career. Most resident directors participate in on-call responsibilities in which they are available to respond to student needs at all hours of the day—from the irritating (e.g., a student locked out of his room) to the precarious (a suicide, fire, or hostage situation). As a young professional, the notion of a salary, meal plan, lodging, direct connections and developmental opportunities with students, among other benefits (rewards), all outweighed the frustration and stressors of 3:00 a.m. wake-ups. Over time, though, the amount and value of the reward, at least for me, reduced. I then went on to establish a nonprofit leadership institute because the intrinsic reward of establishing the organization and facilitating leadership development—as my primary work responsibility—was more powerful and rewarding than the extrinsic reward of "free housing."

Gareth Morgan (1997), the noted organizational theorist and scholar, indicates that our motivations and interests are not only fluid; they reside in three different domains: task, career, and extramural. Task motivations are the tactical elements of our work—the things we do on a day-to-day basis that get us excited or zap our energy. Career motivations pertain to our desires for a fulfilling professional trajectory and life. The extramural motivations are the driving forces beyond our work tasks and career development. These three domains are not independent entities; they may compete or synergize with one another depending on the contexts and situations in one's life. For example, travel is an important value of mine. In my role as a leadership educator, I get to travel the globe facilitating trainings. With this travel example, the tasks, career, and extramural motivating forces synergize into something healthy and powerful for me. They may also be competitive. With my previous resident director example, the task of responding to late-night phone calls became problematic to my extramural activities of completing my doctorate. It's not easy doing much, let alone writing a dissertation, when navigating a crises situations in the middle of the night.

Follower motivation, like all of our leadership practices, should and ought to be connected to leadership literature and scholarship. The path-goal leadership theory (see chapter 3) suggests that followers will be more motivated when their efforts lead to an intended outcome that they value. This is best enabled when followers feel competent, when their expectations are met, and when they value what they do (Northouse, 2021).

Transformational leadership (see chapter 4) also highlights follower motivation. In that theory section of this book, I offered Bass's (1985) four transformational leadership factors. One of them is inspirational motivation. Transformational leaders behave in ways that motivate followers by providing meaning, support, and (healthy) challenge to followers. Leaders do this by exhibiting enthusiasm and optimism, inviting followers to dream about and work toward a personally meaningful future, and participating in decision-making processes, especially when confronted with daunting challenges.

Practically, to tap into the intrinsic motivations of followers, leaders need perspicacity and perseverance (Beerel, 2009). Leaders should be creative, perceptive, and discerning in learning about follower motivations. It takes diligence for leaders to provoke and stimulate followers' self-motivation based on their own insights and realizations that action is required and they can harness their energy to contribute. This persistence, though, will amplify the opportunities to create the change that is desired.

Other ways to motivate followers include engaging them in personally meaningful work, keeping the meaningful elements at the forefront of thought and action, facilitating strong relationships and connections among collaborators, celebrating short-term wins, and actually facilitating change (Hickman & Sorenson, 2014; Wheatley, 2007).

Leadership Educator Praxis Activity

Leadership Theme: Motivating Others Toward Goal Accomplishment
Exercise: Library Design (reflective [group engagement] activity)

As we know, antiquated perspectives of leadership—those that celebrate leadership as power, prestige, position, and personal reward—are still woven through the fabric of our leadership practices. These archaic perspectives of leadership reinforce the notion that leadership is about motivating others through fear or greed—or both. Leadership educators recognize that follower motivation is varied based upon differences in intrinsic desires and positioning within the hierarchy of needs.

Our role is to facilitate dynamic leadership learning opportunities that illuminate the motivational options for leaders to engage with their followers—resulting in meaningful investments on behalf of the followers. Since we rarely spend time on the motivational forces behind our work and leadership decision-making, I offer that our motivation-focused trainings should capitalize on reflective experiences to assist our participants in digging layers-deep into their "why"—and engage in robust dialogue so they can articulate these inspiring forces. When followers are intrinsically motivated because of brilliant leadership grounded in responses to the depths of "why," the possibilities are endless. To get there, though, leaders need to understand the motivating factors of followers. The Library Design activity is an opportunity for our leadership training participants to think critically, in a fantastical way, about motivations. (I like to use a library as our structure because it is a universal building across cultural contexts and is also in a time of transition. Many libraries are shifting their physical structures and operational strategies due to the changing times, surge of electronic books, shifting needs or our communities, and other factors. Of course, feel free to utilize any structure that may be more appropriate for your audiences. These might include a corporate HQ, residence hall, student center, etc.)

Library Design and Construction
"Today is a great day! You're on the leadership team of a new community library task force and an anonymous

benefactor has given all of the requested and required funds to design a new state-of-the-art library." In the benefactor's letter, a story is shared. It says:

> Back in ancient times, when they were building the first libraries, a visitor was walking through the square and saw three builders. The visitor approached each one and asked what they were doing. The first one replied in a gruff manner, simply "laying bricks." The visitor continued along and asked the second builder. The reply, with a matter-of-fact attitude, was "laying bricks so that I can support my family with a roof over their heads and food on their plates." The visitor continued to the third builder. "What are you doing?" The reply, with a deep sense of pride and joy was, "I am building a library so that future generations have a place to study, learn, explore, rest, build community, and connect with others." You have some options before you, task force. Will you build this library because you have to, because it is good, or because you are connected to the power of this place at a deeper level?

This is a great way to start an experiential activity. It captures participants' attention and engages them in a story that links the theme to the experiential learning activity. In the Library Design activity, participants will need to design a library with explicit details describing the incentives for different populations to use it. For example, what would be a motivating factor for youth? What about a geriatric population? Working adults?

Materials

- library design worksheet—blueprint style worksheet with an outline of a physical building with various rooms that the participants can utilize to describe functions and uses, with space on the back—or another piece of paper—for participants to draft the motivating factors for different populations to utilize the library and a statement of their rationale for why these spaces will be utilized as such

Instructions

- Begin by organizing participants into groups of three or four.
- Once arranged, distribute the library design worksheet.

- Participants should then be guided to dialogue about and draft written descriptions of the motivating factors (incentive features) that will draw various populations to the library.
- Once these motivating factors have been determined, they should label the various rooms within the library that align with those motivational factors.
- After the time has expired, all of the groups should share their blueprints and incentives.
- Following this sharing, facilitate a reflective dialogue.

Reflective Dialogue Questions

Our objective with this activity is to reinforce the notion that different followers have varying motivational factors—just like the numerous library patrons. By getting in a mindset of meeting followers where they are at and connecting with their motivations, leaders can be more effective in working toward goal accomplishment. A selection of my go-to reflective dialogue questions includes the following:

- Which was more difficult—the library design or the motivational factors? Why?
- What did we learn about motivations through this exercise?
- What were you motivated by in this activity?
- What can we learn from this exercise that can be applied to our own leadership practice?

Navigating Dissonance and Toxicity

Dissonance is the default. Leadership scholars Richard Boyatzis and Annie McKee (2005) indicate that *dissonance* is when our behaviors do not align with our beliefs. With dissonance, there is a disconnect between the values we espouse and the leadership we practice. This disconnect, for many leaders, is not an unfamiliar phenomenon. Rather, this is our modus operandi.

Dissonance is essentially the inability to manage our emotions, attitudes, and behaviors due to a failure of connecting deeply with ourselves. Dissonance is driven by perpetually sacrificing ourselves without pursuing opportunities for reflection and renewal (resonance). Dissonance manifests both internally and externally. Within ourselves we have disquiet, distress, and disappointment. Externally, our work and personal relationships suffer—we drive people too hard—resulting in frustration, fear, and failure. Worst of all, dissonance is contagious. *Our* dissonance causes others to internalize these limiting emotions, attitudes, and behaviors increasing the havoc and impact.

Boyatzis and McKee (2005) describe the root of dissonance—when too much time and energy is sacrificed with too little nourishment, meaning, and joy received in return. Worst of all, dissonance is contagious. When we lead from dissonance, others contract it—resulting in poor performance, disruptive attitudes, and destructive decisions. Our dissonance causes others to internalize these limiting emotions, attitudes, and behaviors, increasing the havoc and impact. There are two causes of dissonance: power stress and the sacrifice syndrome.

Power stress is a particular type of pressure resulting from the need to execute complex and rapid decisions without clear choice. This leads to unhealthy thoughts, attitudes, and actions. Power stress is relentless because these types of decisions are seemingly ceaseless. Without engaging in renewal practices, prolonged power stress can be debilitating to our bodies and emotional well-being. Since it is contagious, it can be damaging to our relationships and devastating to the physical and emotional health and well-being of others. When unattended to, power stress leads to the sacrifice syndrome.

The *sacrifice syndrome* is a cyclical process of too much personal exertion—due to the stressors of power and authority—leading to ineffectiveness. Over time, the toll (both physical and emotional draining of our energy) results in limiting performance. This is then internalized—leading to dissonance. The sacrifice syndrome does not feel like a "syndrome" because this has become our normal way of working and being. We have normalized this behavior. Rather than create the change that is needed, we cope by establishing habits and behaviors that further entrench us in dissonance.

Dissonance is one form of destructive and damaging leadership; toxicity is another. Lipman-Blumen (2005) has studied toxic leaders and found that they have certain distinguishable characteristics and actions. Characteristics of toxic leaders include lack of integrity, acting with arrogance, engaging in corrupt behaviors, wanting more with a focus on personal greed, consistently failing to act with competence and effectiveness—especially when attempting to solve critical problems and make significant decisions, and disregarding how their actions impact their own wellness and the well-being of others.

In practice, the actions of toxic leaders manifest by violating basic standards of human rights through intimidation, marginalization, demoralization, and other acts of harm; dictating to followers that they, as the leaders, are the only people who command authority and decision-making capabilities; playing, venomously, into the fears and concerns of the followers; failing to nurture future leaders and an unwillingness to distribute or transition power to others; and treating followers well—while persuading them to hate and/or destroy others.

Fortunately, dissonance and toxicity (and bad leadership, generally) are not permanent. By engaging in renewal practices—creating resonance—we can become more profoundly in tune with ourselves, those around us, and our work. Most powerfully, with resonance, people synergize with others, leading to flow (more on flow in the next chapter). Resonant leaders are easily identifiable. They elicit in themselves and others compassion, courage, empathy, emotional intelligence, hope and optimism, joy, motivation, and—for the outcomes-oriented folks—results.

Many scholars suggest that there are specific leadership practices—focused both internally and externally—that can reduce dissonance and toxicity. For leaders themselves, inward-focusing practices include acknowledging personal weaknesses; connecting synergistically to personal and organizational visions; constructing a healthy work–life integration; cultivating leadership practices like compassion, hope, and mindfulness in ourselves; developing a strong and vibrant support system; establishing realistic (and ethical) visions and action plans; and humanizing others (Baron-Cohen, 2011; Boyatzis & McKee, 2005; Goldman, 2009; Kellerman, 2004; Kets de Vries, 2004; Kusy & Halloway, 2009; Lipman-Blumen, 2005).

Outwardly, leaders should be cultivating leadership practices like encouraging compassion, hope, and mindfulness in others; delegating responsibilities and initiating democratic or distributed decision-making practices; establishing a culture where sharing of dissenting and diverse opinions is encouraged; seeking and obtaining reliable information—and then disseminating it; nurturing healthy leadership ambitions of others; providing specific and targeted feedback for improvement; and reducing I/you and we/they dichotomies.

Leadership Educator Praxis Activity

Leadership Theme: Navigating Dissonance and Toxicity
Exercise: Number Cross (physically engaged activity)

Leadership training on dissonance and toxicity is important because rarely do our participants recognize they are modeling disruptive and troubling leadership practices. As stated in the first line of this section—dissonance is our default setting. It is difficult to recognize the impact we are having on ourselves and others because we are in it. In our organizations and workplaces, we attempt to slog through it because we've never had opportunities in which we could learn ways to confront those who create so much dissonance.

Leadership educators have an important responsibility to study the causes and manifestations of dissonance and toxicity so that we can easily identify them. Once identified, we should create training interventions to make our participants aware of the personally and otherly harmful practices that they impose. Needless to say, these developmental training opportunities should not just focus on awareness. Rather, they should become a holding environment and learning laboratory for our participants to become aware and then infuse healthier leadership practices into their regimen.

When focusing on dissonance and toxicity, we utilize experiential learning and reflective dialogue to assist participants in seeing these harmful leadership practices objectively. From an outsider lens, our participants will better be able to infuse healthy leadership habits into their practice rather than feeling targeted, shamed, or embarrassed.

The Number Cross activity is difficult. Because of how challenging it is, participants become quite frustrated and begin to place blame and exert unhealthy leadership practices. This is for two reasons: These are their default leadership settings and/or they assume this is the appropriate leadership behavior to accomplish the task. This activity provides a remarkable opportunity to shine a light on our leadership practice when challenges arise.

Number Cross

With the Number Cross activity, participants, in groups of four, need to utilize their assigned number (10, 5, 2, and 1) to add up to a sum total of 17. Yet, with quick math, those four numbers equate to 18. Leadership educators need to be cautious of how the dissonance manifests once the activity begins, not necessarily to intervene, but to utilize the emotional flare-ups as fodder for the reflective dialogue.

During the activity, participants will physically move from the start zone to the end zone. Each group will begin with all participants in the start zone. The objective is to have everyone move to the end zone, based on their numbers, to end with a count of 17.

To accomplish this task, participants will move from one zone to the other in pairs. Once crossed to the other zone, the participant with the higher number scores those points for the group. This person remains in that zone. Then, one participant in the end zone returns to the start zone—and scores those points there. This process continues until all group members are standing in the end zone with a count of 17. The solution is as follows:

- 1 and 2 cross (2);
- 1 returns to start (3);
- 10 and 5 cross (13);
- 2 returns to start (15);
- 1 and 2 cross (17) and all remain.

Materials

- numbered note cards—a 10, 5, 2, and 1—for every group

Instructions

- Begin by organizing participants into groups of four. (If this is not possible, a group of three can suffice—one of the participants will have two number cards.)
- Provide each participant a number card.
- Explain to the group their objective is to cross to the end zone by physically moving from the start zone to the end zone. Each group has cards numbered with either a 10, 5, 2, or 1. The objective is to have everyone move to the end zone, based on their numbers, to end with a count of 17. To accomplish this task, participants will move from one zone to the other in pairs. Once crossed to the other zone, the participant with the higher number scores those points for the group. This person remains in that zone. Then, one participant

in the end zone returns to the start zone—and scores those points there. This process continues until all group members are standing in the end zone with a count of 17.

- At the start, to heighten their limiting emotions, I usually state that no electronic devices can be utilized. To make it extra difficult, depending on the group, I'll sometimes add that no writing utensils can be utilized as well.
- Once the directions are shared, let them get after it.
- When the program eventually comes to a close, either through goal accomplishment by a group or time having elapsed, facilitate a reflective dialogue.

Reflective Dialogue Questions

Our objective with this activity to highlight how our limiting emotions—anger, frustration, disappointment—manifest into toxicity and dissonance. We end up acting in ways that limit productivity and effectiveness. A selection of my go-to reflective dialogue questions includes the following:

- I witnessed some limiting emotions—what happened during the activity?
- What impact did these limiting emotions have on our performance?

- How did we become aware that these limiting emotions were causing dissonance and toxicity in our group?
- What did participants do to reduce those limiting emotions?
- What can we learn from this exercise that can be applied to our own leadership practice?

Conclusion

The leadership practices in this chapter focused on leadership engagements with others—cooperative experiences that enable us to navigate obstacles and accomplish goals. When we develop healthy leadership habits in these domains, we are able to nurture healthy collaborations, partnerships, and activities that can enable us, our followers and colleagues, and our organizations to thrive. Specifically, we can share information and listen in ways that encourage others to be seen as valued and valuable to our leadership objectives (communicating); effectively traverse the rough terrain of group work while cultivating synergistic connections among team members (engaging with groups and teams); influence, inspire, and stimulate others toward greatness (motivating others toward goal accomplishment); and circumvent and resist poisonous leadership habits in our own and others' practice (navigating dissonance and toxicity).

CHAPTER 10

Generative Leadership Practices

THIS FINAL COMPENDIUM OF leadership practices are chunked together because of their generative nature. When we infuse these as healthy leadership habits into our practice, we create the conditions to personally flourish and for our organizations to thrive. These include nurturing self-efficacy and confidence, demonstrating grit and resilience, applying strengths and positive psychology principles, tapping into flow states, and embracing and extending cultural humility. These are not easy skills to develop. These are complex leadership practices, but when mastered, enable us to function at optimal levels—individually and organizationally.

Nurturing Self-Efficacy and Confidence

Effective leadership is often determined by the belief we have in ourselves. If we believe it is possible, it *is*. If we believe it is not possible, it *isn't*. That belief is the determining factor. This is the premise of self-efficacy.

The famed psychologist Albert Bandura (1977) detailed self-efficacy as the strength of our convictions in our own effectiveness. There are two core constructs to self-efficacy: outcome expectancy and efficacy expectation. The outcome expectancy is a recognition that certain behaviors will lead to a certain result. If we do *these* things, *that* will happen. An efficacy expectation is the belief that *I* can actually execute the behaviors that are necessary for success. If we believe that specific behaviors will lead to a specific result—and we trust that we have the knowledge and skills to accomplish the goal, we have self-efficacy.

Self-efficacy can be cultivated. We can enhance our levels of self-efficacy in four ways. Foremost among these is performance accomplishments. The more we do things, the more our confidence grows. As leadership educators, the more leadership trainings we facilitate, the stronger our self-efficacy so that we can create meaningful leadership learning experiences for our participants. By performing—and especially performing well—we deepen the reservoir of our confidence. This thereby enhances how we see ourselves as talented, savvy, and dynamic leadership educators capable of facilitating amazing and impactful leadership trainings.

We also enhance our self-efficacy through vicarious experiences. Simply by watching others, we can gain confidence in our own abilities. When we watch and study a seasoned leadership educator facilitate reflective dialogue, our confidence in performing as a facilitator increases. The more we observe and process what other leadership educators do, the more our sense of self-efficacy expands.

Verbal persuasion is another factor that enhances self-efficacy. The reason we entice participants in leadership trainings to vocalize their support for the other participants is because we know that one's confidence rises when verbally encouraged and persuaded. What we hear other people saying—either in the affirmative or negative—matters. Vocal reassurance about our abilities and possibilities significantly alters our sense of self and self-efficacy.

The final determining factor of self-efficacy is emotional arousal. When we are emotionally engaged and the challenge with which we are struggling mirrors our skills, we have higher levels of self-efficacy. When we are overcome with anxiety, fear, frustration, and anger due to the challenges being perceived as extreme, our self-efficacy weakens.

The bonus determining factor of self-efficacy is context. Situations matter and influence our belief in ourselves. As expert leadership educators, we may have high levels of self-efficacy when it comes to a certain communication-themed training. For this training, we've facilitated it innumerable times and know the ins and outs of how it can flow. We worked through the kinks and challenges and have a solid understanding of how our participants will react and respond to the experiential learning activities. We've got the timing down. Here, our self-efficacy is high. If, though, we're expected to facilitate a virtual training on leadership and ethics, we may have lower levels of self-efficacy because we are less familiar with facilitating this particular topic, the virtual platform, the participants, the timing, and the experiential activities. We believe in ourselves, just not as much as we do with the other training.

We're always our own worst enemy. We become our antagonist when we tune in and accept our self-doubt. Self-doubt is the questioning of our abilities (Jewell, 2017). When we see ourselves as imposters, phonies, frauds, and pretenders, we attach to limiting beliefs about ourselves. This attachment becomes a tight grasp on the notion that *I* actually can't execute the behaviors necessary to accomplish the task or worse, there are no behaviors that can lead to the results we desire. When this occurs, doing anything seems futile. Self-doubt results in the undermining of our performance, increasing the likelihood of failure, debilitating procrastination, comparing against others and seeing them as better, and defensive pessimism (Jewell, 2017).

Although our thoughts can't be seen, heard, or measured, they are remarkably powerful. As Seth Gillihan (2018), a psychologist and faculty member at the University of Pennsylvania, expresses, our minds don't just produce thoughts—they can notice and evaluate them. When we become witness to thoughts moving in a limiting direction, we need to purposefully pause. We use this intentional break to shift to undertakings that challenge and then change our mindset by looking for evidence that supports the limiting thought, look for evidence that does not support the limiting thought, look for errors in our thinking

about the limiting thought, and develop a more accurate and helpful way of seeing and understanding the situation. Once we've made this shift in thinking, we can cultivate our self-efficacy and confidence in the following ways.

We act. Specifically, we act *now*. Once we are aware of our self-doubt, we make an intentional and rapid shift. We raise our self-efficacy when we accept small yesses and make small gains. We build our confidence every time we create success. The premier way to secure these yesses and gains is to be self-empowered. We need to self-author our decision-making and be the ones to make these choices. And when we do have successes, we then need to honor and own them in compelling and healthy ways.

Preparing our physical state is also important. Utilizing power poses (think of your favorite superhero standing with confidence) to set our tone and intention is one such way. Being physically active enhances how we feel about ourselves.

We also ought to surround ourselves with the right people and in environments that will nurture our self-efficacy. The confidence we receive from witnessing others accomplish tasks is powerful. This is also true from the healthy challenge and support we receive from peers, colleagues, and other advocates. By authentically listening to their encouragement, we increase our reservoir of confidence and self-efficacy.

Leadership Educator Praxis Activity

Leadership Theme: Nurturing Self-Efficacy and Confidence
Exercise: Pillars of Power (reflective [worksheet] activity)

I think I can. I think I can. I think I can. I think I can. These thoughts matter. This type of confidence-raising thinking matters. Leadership educators utilize experiential activities and reflective dialogue because the hands-on nature of the learning experience cultivates self-efficacy and confidence. By immersing our participants in the engaging material, they are able to see themselves as capable of changing their behaviors by infusing their new leadership knowledge and skills into their practice. When we establish supportive holding environments, participants can witness and observe the successes of others while receiving encouragement and support as they navigate, individually and collectively, the challenges we devise.

As leadership educators, our training experiences empower participants to complete our trainings with deeper senses of self and stronger notions of *I can*. Tactically, we craft training experiences and holding environments that enable participants to win, succeed, and see themselves as powerful agents of change. We continually monitor their progress through experiential learning activities to ensure they shift to the reflective dialogue feeling empowered. With these trainings, our objective is to instill in our participants a deep sense of possibility and potential.

Self-efficacy and confidence are nurtured when we shift the way we think about ourselves and abilities. The Pillars of Power activity does exactly this.

Pillars of Power

For this experiential learning activity, we provide a worksheet or clean piece of paper that enables participants to think through and purposefully shift their thinking from limiting self-talk/thought to empowering self-talk/thought. The first step will be for participants to think deeply about situations that trigger negative self-talk. Then participants will draft what these negative or limiting self-talk statements are. Finally, participants will utilize the third column to detail how they might shift that self-talk to be empowering. Please note that this activity is best when participants feel comfortable and valued by the other participants since they will be exploring sensitive topics and triggering events.

Materials

- worksheet (for a precreated worksheet, you may want to utilize various colors to differentiate the three columns—red on the left for limiting self-talk and green on the right for empowering self-talk usually works well; alternatively, you could provide a worksheet with pillar imagery so participants draft their reflections inside three different pillars on the worksheet)
- writing utensil

Instructions

- Begin by distributing the worksheet.
- Once all of the participants have the worksheet and are settled, ask them to draft situations that trigger negative or limiting self-talk.

(These should be placed in the far-left pillar or column.)
- As the facilitator, you can decide if you want to infuse small- or large-group sharing before moving on to the second pillar.
- With the second pillar, participants will reflect upon and detail what their negative or limiting self-talk statements are.
- Again you can decide if you want to have dialogue among the participants or keep it as a personal experience.
- Finally, for the third pillar, participants will state how they might shift those limiting self-talk statements to be empowering ones—based on the particular triggering events in the far-left column.
- After the empowering statements are listed, you can invite sharing in partners or small groups before the formal reflective dialogue.

Reflective Dialogue Questions

Our objective with this activity is to highlight how confidence raising it is when we become aware of limiting self-talk (and the triggering events) and purposefully shift them to be empowering statements. A selection of my go-to reflective dialogue questions includes the following:

- How did it feel to think about and put to paper these triggering events?
- How did it feel to think about and put to paper this negative or limiting self-talk?
- How did it feel to think about and put to paper these empowering statements?
- How was this activity confidence raising for you?
- What can we learn about confidence and self-efficacy from this experience?
- What can we learn from this exercise that can be applied to our own leadership practice?

Demonstrating Grit and Resilience

Failure is fertilizer. This is the attitudinal disposition of grit and resilience. Leaders are perpetually navigating challenges, confrontations, and obstacles. How we utilize these trials and tribulations matters to our leadership capabilities. If we succumb to them, our well-being falters, and we feel demoralized. This can have grave ramifications for our leadership practice. The alternative is to see them as developmental, learning, and growth opportunities. In this way, our personal well-being is enhanced and our leadership practice is enriched. Cultivating grit and resilience is essential leadership practice.

Grit and *resilience* are slightly different from one another, yet often utilized interchangeably. Grit references how we work through challenges in the moment. The way we develop a healthy resistance to a potentially debilitating impact is resilience.

Angela Duckworth (2016) made grit famous. Her book, TED Talk, research as a professor at the University of Pennsylvania, and work through her organization (CharacterLab) have illuminated for us the power of grit. Grit has two components: passion and perseverance. We can each develop grit because we can identify our convictions and utilize them to propel us to persist and eventually persevere.

As Duckworth (2016) advises, there are four psychological assets that we can develop. First is interest. Passions matter. Grit manifests the most when we have a significant interest in what we are doing and attempting to accomplish. If we don't like what we're doing, we're not going to want to persist when confronting obstacles.

Next, we need to practice. If we want to be gritty, we need to carve out intentional time to be immersed in that interest. This time is focused and fullhearted. We resist complacency and stay engaged over and over and over again as a way to strengthen weaknesses and perseveringly navigate challenges.

Third is purpose. When we believe in our work and when we believe that we are the ones to create the change that is needed, our passion is ripened. It is crucial we identify our work as personally interesting while also integrally connected to the well-being of others. This mindset replenishes our motivation when difficulties arise.

Finally, we need to stay hopeful and optimistic. Being hopeful should not be considered as the last stage. Our wholehearted belief in a positive outcome is infused every step along the way (for more, see the section on Being Hopeful and Optimistic in chapter 8.).

An essential factor in these assets is agency. If we want to be gritty, we need to have agency. We need to feel self-empowered. We need to be in control. These passions, the time and energy for practice, and our purpose need to be ours. If they are heirlooms handed down to us as an expectation or forced upon us from external forces, we are going to be less gritty than if we become the decision-maker and internalize the decision-making processes. And we need healthy minds and healthy bodies to endure these challenges—vitality (Hanson & Hanson, 2018).

Nobody is immune from trauma or the reality of the human condition (Graham, 2018). The odds are we will each experience a debilitating disease, loss of a loved one, natural disaster, mass shooting, domestic violence, rape, racism and other "isms," homophobia and other "phobias," terrorism, war, or another horrific experience that inflicts significant physical or emotional pain. These events throw our lives into turmoil in unpredictable ways. Being resilient is not to be impervious to these adversities. Rather, resilience is the ability, while being deeply affected, to carry on with the important facets of our lives in spite of the trauma. The most resilient among us often recognize these events as growth experiences laden with meaning-making opportunities (Southwick & Charney, 2018). With resilience, it is less about what happens to us and more about how we respond.

Scholars who have studied the development of leaders have identified resilience as a core feature for potential leadership growth (Goodwin, 2018; Guthrie et al., 2021). The mark of leadership was how these leaders sustained ambition in the face of frustration and managed to put themselves back together after trauma. According to Goodwin (2018), these watershed experiences ultimately challenged, deepened, and then decisively molded their leadership.

The two most important factors that determine and predict our abilities to be resilient are our capacities for perception and response (Graham, 2018). The key to coping with any challenge—especially the traumatic events in our lives—is to shift our perception of it and response to it. Those of us who are notably resilient have successfully shifted from a *poor me* and/or *it's all my fault* attitude to an empowered *I* mindset. To build our capacities for resilience, we need to recognize our conditioning and then recondition our brains to be more resilient.

Our brains learn from experience, and if we have been programmed to respond to difficult situations by giving up or giving in, we can deliberately and intentionally choose to engage in new ways that encourage us to practice new response habits. These habits lead to new conditioning and resiliency. Some practices that support this reconditioning and resilience-raising include facing our fears; drawing on our religion, spirituality, and ethical or meaning-making foundation; tapping into the power of positive emotions; cultivating resonant relationships; being physically engaged and well; enhancing our self-awareness; engaging in reflective practice; centering our locus of control within ourselves; accessing objective perspectives of the situation; and practicing these resiliency-nurturing behaviors often (Graham, 2018; Guthrie et al., 2021; Southwick & Charney, 2018).

Tony DiCicco is the famed United States Women's National Team soccer coach who led the team to a gold medal in the inaugural 1996 Olympic Games (for women's soccer) and World Cup championship in 1999. I had the remarkable privilege of working with him and the Boston Breakers (a now defunct women's professional soccer team)—including Kristine Lily, Lauren Holiday (Cheney), Alyssa Naeher, and other premier soccer athletes—over two seasons as a facilitator of their team's leadership development. He epitomized grit and resilience and wove these leadership practices into the fabric of his coaching paradigm. Coach DiCicco framed it in the context of *failure as fertilizer*. He knew his teams were going to lose. He knew that relationships could falter based on his coaching approach and decisions. He knew that outside factors in his life and the lives of his athletes were going to impact what happened in practice and competition. Rather than succumbing to any of this, he utilized these opportunities for learning, growth, and development.

Coach DiCicco and former U.S. National Team sports psychologist Colleen Hacker write about this philosophy in *Catch Them Being Good*, a book that unearths the ways he was able to elicit success from his athletes and teams in high-pressure situations. Their practices included taking responsibility (i.e., not placing blame or finger-pointing), digging deep within to find growth opportunities, and then taking action to make those necessary improvements.

When engaging in this way, the key is to focus energies on the factors and variables that are under our direct control (DiCicco & Hacker, 2002). We begin by asking ourselves, How did I make it easy for this to happen this way? Then we need to release our connection to societal explications and implications of failure

as a supremely negative thing. We do this by extracting meaningful lessons from the experience and utilizing it to our long-term benefit. The authors suggest that until we learn how to deal with failure, we cannot fully succeed. Failures, obstacles, and challenges are necessary ingredients and experiences on our journey toward success. Failure is a part of living, a part of learning, a part of stretching beyond our comfort zone—it is a part of us striving or closing down (Mullen et al. 2014). With grit and resilience, we utilize failure as a fertilizer for action and capitalizing on our worthy pursuits.

Leadership Educator Praxis Activity

Leadership Theme: Demonstrating Grit and Resilience
Exercise: Four-Minute Scan (reflective [personal engagement] activity)

Failure as fertilizer is an essential paradigm for leadership educators. Our experiential activities are all laden with obstacles and challenges. They may create anxiety, frustration, and confrontation among participants. We can encourage the development of grit and resilience by ensuring to participants that our trainings are courageous spaces for failure—that there is wisdom in failing and much to be garnered and learned from inadequacy.

We can also intentionally frame our trainings as experiences for our participants to grapple with grit and enhance resiliency. Doing so empowers our participants to think critically about when they didn't achieve success or how they navigated through trauma. By safely exploring those personal stories and histories, along with cultivation strategies for grit and resilience, we take part in developing the next generation of leaders who can manage and navigate the challenges and obstacles we are sure to face in the coming years and decades.

Compared to self-efficacy and confidence-focused trainings, grit and resilience–themed trainings are entirely appropriate spaces for challenging experiential learning activities that may ultimately result in failure. The inability for participants to accomplish the goal, if framed artfully in the reflective dialogue, can serve to illuminate opportunities to develop grit and resilience. When facilitated well, this can be remarkably empowering for our participants.

What I chose to highlight here is more reflective in nature. The Four-Minute Scan activity is a quick (only 4 minutes!) exercise that can be replicated over and over and over again for leaders—especially when feeling overwhelmed, emotionally drained, and limited. It is through this scanning process that we can cultivate grit and resilience.

Four-Minute Scan

The Four-Minute Scan focuses on four different things over a 4-minute period—each for exactly 1 minute. Leadership educators guide participants to think about (a) how they are doing right now, (b) their breath, (c) their physical body, and (d) what needs to be released in order to move forward. Because of the nature of this activity, the Four-Minute Scan can be facilitated as a secondary experiential activity before proceeding to a reflective dialogue. For example, if facilitating an experience that draws out lots of emotions in the participants, the Four-Minute Scan is a great way for participants to focus their attention, center themselves, calm their nerves, and smoothly transition to the reflective dialogue.

Materials

- N/A

Instructions

- Begin by settling the energy. Participants will want to be in a relaxed state to focus on themselves over these next 4 minutes.
- This is a breathing exercise, so begin by instructing participants to breath in and out with deep, long breaths—repeatedly.
- After a half-dozen deep breaths, express that we will spend the next 4 minutes engaged in deep breathing and reflection.
- In the first minute, we explore how we are doing right now.
- In the second minute, we focus on our breath.
- In the third minute, we analyze how our physical body feels.
- In the fourth minute, we reflect on what needs to be released—emotionally—so that we can move forward toward our goals and visions.
- Once the fourth minute comes to a close, we can continue the deep breathing before entering the reflective dialogue.

Reflective Dialogue Questions

Our objective with this activity is twofold. We want to settle participants' energy so that they can focus on cultivating grit and resilience in the face of fears and obstacles as well as provide them with a tangible practice they can quickly and easily implement when feeling overwhelmed, distracted, and emotionally drained. A selection of my go-to reflective dialogue questions includes the following:

- How was this breathing exercise and scan for you?
- What did you notice or observe about your resistance or welcomeness to each minute?
- How might you include this exercise in your leadership regimen to cultivate healthy grit and resilience practices?
- What can we learn from this exercise that can be applied to our own leadership practice?

Applying Strengths and Principles of Positive Psychology

Even the most effective leaders have significant limitations. The difference between these individuals and mediocre leaders is that they know their limitations, focus on honing their strengths, and include others in their pursuits who fill limitation voids (Lewis, 2011). These leaders recognize the power of positive psychology and strengths-based leadership.

Positive psychology is not simply positive thinking. There is a significant distinction between the two. Although potentially beneficial, thinking positively is not rooted in rigors of scientific experimentation and endorsement (Lewis, 2011). Prior to the launch of this psychology subfield, the near-exclusive approach to psychological treatment was focused on pathology, helping people achieve symptom relief and return to a "normal" state (Csikszentmihalyi, 2006; Delucca & Goldstein, 2020). Positive psychology promotes the positive aspects of human life as a way to empower individuals to flourish and communities to thrive. Specifically, it harnesses the power of living a meaningful life guided by happiness, well-being, unleashing our potential, and maximizing our strengths. Those working at the intersection of positive psychology and leadership believe the essence of leadership is human flourishing (Ben-Shahar & Ridgway, 2017). If we are going to prosper and succeed, it is going to be through a strengths approach.

Martin Seligman, as president of the American Psychological Association, launched this subfield of psychology as a way to explore and promote a strengths approach—rather than a disease response—about human potential and what it means to live a life worth living. Since then, positive psychology has gained significant traction due to the intentional scientific approach, depth of data, and accessibility for the masses. With positive psychology and a focus on our strengths, we can all lead meaningful lives of depth and joy while manifesting our highest potentials.

Gallup is the global leader in assessing individuals' strengths. At the time of this writing, over 23 million people have taken the CliftonStrengths assessment as a way to identify their strengths. Based upon their research, they found that the most effective leaders are perpetually (a) investing in their strengths, (b) surrounding themselves with the right people to maximize their teams, and (c) recognizing their followers' needs so as to create a healthy culture and environment and maximize their strengths (Rath & Conchie, 2008).

Ben-Shahar and Ridgway (2017) suggest that most people are not reaching their full potential or achieving lasting fulfillment. These individuals do not know what it means to lead or succeed in leadership roles. All of this is based in an incorrect, antiquated formula rooted in hierarchy and the command-and-control power and authority style of leading. They propose a new way forward with strengths at the forefront.

The way forward begins by acquiring a positive mindset. The first thing leaders need to do is recognize that we all have strengths. By simply distinguishing that we do, in fact, have strengths, we place ourselves in an empowered state. The alternative is an unhealthy approach to leadership in which we believe we're no good and only received our opportunities by sheer luck. Once we shift to the strengths mindset, we need to identify our particular strengths. Once identified, we need to exploit them so they can be maximized to our own and our organization's benefit. Of course, we need to facilitate this process for our followers. By ensuring they have a positive mindset and have identified their strengths, we can implement their pursuit of our goals.

This positive mindset is also known as a growth mindset. Carol Dweck (2006), the psychologist and

Stanford University professor, suggests there are two ways with which we approach our lives. With a *fixed* mindset, we belief is that we're born with what we've got. This fixed mindset assumes that our character, intelligence, talents, and creativities are static. They can't be changed or developed. With this mindset, our successes are affirmations of inherent intelligence. Failure can have deleterious effects because it indicates we're not smart enough, talented enough, or good enough to succeed.

A *growth* mindset is a strengths-based and positive approach to living. With this mindset, we can inherently develop our skills and capabilities. Our character, intelligence, talents, and creativities are fluid and dynamic. With this mindset, our successes are affirmations of hard work, determination, grit, resilience, and a strengths-based learning disposition. Failure is not seen as toxic or detrimental to one's sense of self. Although it is recognized as a setback toward goal accomplishment, failure becomes a learning opportunity, healthy challenge, and fertilizer to nourish the next occasion to pursue success.

Fully accessing our positive mindset occurs by building positive moments and replenishing positive emotions (Ben-Shahar & Ridgway, 2017; Delucca & Goldstein, 2020). Negative emotions tend to narrow our thinking and limit our behaviors as a way to detect and eliminate threats. Positive thinking, spurred by building positive moments, broadens our perspectives and enhances our creativity. With this positive lens, we are able to see more possibilities, live in better alignment with our values, maximize our strengths, and increase our response resources (e.g., intellectual capacities, social capital, and physical health) when future challenges arise. Building positive moments is about shifting to a growth mindset and seeing the benefit and positivity in daily experiences—even the seemingly mundane.

Rath and Clifton (2004) offer that strengths-based and positive leadership occurs when we engage in five practices. These include (a) acting from a fulfilling relational approach; (b) highlighting the good; (c) cultivating meaningful relationships; (d) giving unexpectedly; and (e) being intentional and individualized when providing support, encouragement, and praise.

When we are a draining force—by making fun of others, exposing an insecurity, or highlighting errors and faults in a demeaning way—we limit our abilities to assist others in thriving. Rather, our approach should be that of filling others' emotional reserves and highlighting the good people are doing. We should also cultivate significant and meaningful relationships. By giving purposefully and unexpectedly while also providing intentional and individualized support, encouragement, and praise, we enhance opportunities for others to thrive and our organizations to flourish.

A strengths-based and positive approach to leadership is one in which followers feel trusted, compassion, stability, and hope (Rath & Conchie, 2008) By deliberately acting in authentic and kind ways, followers feel heard and seen while we feel good by truly honoring their personhood and presence.

Leadership Educator Praxis Activity

Leadership Theme: Applying Strengths and Principles of Positive Psychology

Exercise: Me at My Strongest (reflection [partner and dialogic] activity)

Positive psychology practices and strengths-based leadership can have a profound impact on the personal lives of our participants. As leadership educators, we want to create the conditions for our participants to flourish within our training experiences—and beyond. When our participants feel honored, valued, and seen because our trainings hone in and assist them in identifying, cultivating, and applying their strengths, they are positioned to thrive.

The most important feature of positive and strengths-based trainings is to capitalize on the application of their strengths. Often with these types of trainings, facilitators just utilize their time to identify the strengths of each participant. This is important to do. Yet, unless we move to the application of those strengths, it is just information. This is ever more important when facilitating trainings for work groups and collaborators. What do each of these individual strengths mean in conjunction with the others? This is where the focus of our attention should be; otherwise, there is no coordination between these strengths. To capitalize on this, leadership educators can engage participants in identifying their strengths. The Me at My Strongest experiential learning activity is designed for this purpose.

Me at My Strongest

For this reflective exercise, participants will think about and then dialogue with a partner or small group when they have been at their best—their strongest—that

is, when they have felt successful, empowered, and celebrated. What were the conditions that led to these strength feelings?

Materials

- N/A

Instructions

- Begin by asking participants to settle their energy and to think critically about when they were at their best—their strongest. What was the experience? What was it about the experience that was so empowering and encouraging?
- Once they have had ample time to reflect, they should find a partner or a group to share. (This can also be structured as a written reflection or a creative expression where they draw pictures or figures to symbolize this experience.)
- In this dialogue, participants should express what the experience was and the influencing features. This sharing will be utilized in the reflective dialogue.

Reflective Dialogue Questions

Our objective with this activity is to highlight how we each have strengths that can be capitalized upon. When we have a growth mindset and infuse positive psychology principles into our leadership practice, we can more easily navigate challenges, learn from failures, and prepare for future endeavors. A selection of my go-to reflective dialogue questions includes the following:

- What were the similarities between the strength stories that were shared?
- How might you capitalize on your strengths moving forward?
- What can you utilize as a reminder to tap the growth mindset when you are feeling fixed?
- What can we learn from this exercise that can be applied to our own leadership practice?

Tapping Into Flow States

We've all been in flow—commonly referred to as *being in the zone*. In technical terms, *flow* is the psychology of optimal experience (Csikszentmihalyi, 1990).

Practically, flow is the heightened awareness and focus that blocks out everything except for the goal (D. Roberts, 2007). People in flow often comment about losing track of time as well as a sense of place or space. They are so in the moment that those details become irrelevant.

As leaders, we perform optimally—at our peak—when we are in flow states. Flow tends to be the driving force behind athletic competitions, scientific breakthrough, innovations, enhanced work productivity, and business/organizational performance—not to mention happiness, joy, and deeply meaningful experiences.

Flow is the opposite of entropy. If entropy is inefficiency or a lack of energy, flow is when we capitalize on our energy and perform with outstanding efficiency. Flow is an ultimate state of consciousness—a peak state where we both feel our best and perform our best (Kotler, 2014). It is available to anyone, anywhere, so long as two conditions are met: Our challenges need to align and be appropriately matched with our skills. When the challenges or tasks do not align with our skill level, suboptimal or nonflow states arise. These include:

- anxiety (high challenge and low skill)
- worry (medium challenge and low skill)
- apathy (low challenge and low skill)
- arousal (medium challenge and medium skill)
- boredom (medium challenge and medium skill
- control (medium challenge and low skill)
- relaxation (low challenge and high skill)

Mihaly Csikszentmihalyi (1990), a founding father of flow, suggests that flow is available to all of us, at any time, because we have the power to create the conditions for it. Flow states generally occur when there is some structure to our activities, when there is a skill-building and learning opportunity, when explicit goals are clearly understood, when feedback is provided, and when the actors have opportunities to control their destiny.

Once these conditions are met, to cultivate flow, which should intentionally be nurtured, we first need to become aware of our nonflow states. With this recognition, we can then assess and understand why. Are the challenges too much? Are they not challenging enough? Are skills needing to be developed? Am I too skilled for the challenge?

Once the reason for the mismatch is identified, it is then a matter of deciding what part of the equation can now be modified. This is the task of the leader. Dennis Roberts (2007) articulates that leadership rooted with a flow practice means

living one's convictions, not as an act of will or competition, but as a compulsion to live at the edge of peak performance. We achieve flow by allowing ourselves to care deeply about the goal, striving for it with all of our ability, maintaining focus, seeing that we are making progress, and enjoying every minute as we contribute our best effort. (p. 125)

Just as individuals can achieve flow states, groups can too. Group flow is when each member of that particular group or team is in flow—which raises the connectivity and the performance level of the unit. Keith Sawyer (2007), author of *Group Genius* and an expert on innovation and creativity, suggests certain conditions that encourage group flow. Similarly Bill George and Doug Baker (2011), authors of *True North Groups*, detail the conditions that allow for groups to enter this high-performance state. I've detailed a composite of these conditions.

The group is organized around a clear and motivating goal. Each group member needs to connect deeply with the goal, believe it is attainable, and have a clear understanding of what success is.

Group members intentionally cultivate familiarity and synergistic relationships. These relationships are built around trust and accountability. Group members cocreate, adhere to, and challenge their own norms and expectations. When engaging with one another, group members enact constant and open communication and maximize their time together while utilizing meetings efficiently.

The group members practice close listening whereby each member is fully present and engaged in dialogue and accesses information by both what is spoken as well as from the silence. Group members practice complete concentration. They each have a focused attention on the work of the group and other group members. This also enables accountability.

The group members share control and authority, which allows for autonomy and personal authorship through the group engagement. The group members efficiently blend egos. There is an intentional melding of ideas and relinquishing of *me*-ness and *my* ideating. Group members support equal participation. This enables each member to be valued and seen as valuable to the success of the group.

Group members build upon small wins and are perpetually moving forward toward goal accomplishment. Yet group members also recognize reality. They accept that there is potential for failure, disaster, and disappointment.

Leadership Educator Praxis Activity

Leadership Theme: Tapping Into Flow States
Exercise: Peaks and Valleys (reflective [worksheet] activity)

Being in a flow state during a leadership training is magical. We feel like we are one with ourselves, one with our participants, and one with the world. When we are *in it*, there is no denying it. We can feel the healthy tension drive the group toward an unparalleled learning and engagement experience. It is obvious to those around us. It is palpable. In these flow moments, we often become most authentic to ourselves and others. In personal communication with leadership scholar-practitioner Dennis Roberts on this topic, he shared,

> My experience is that, when I enter flow, I connect with others in very different ways. When facilitating a group, however, not everyone will go there with us so the facilitator's challenge is to engage with those who are entering a shared flow experience while not ignoring others who are not. (personal communication, December 6, 2020)

A challenge indeed. As leadership educators, we aim to establish the conditions for participants to enter flow states and journey along with us in flow during trainings by infusing Csikszentmihalyi's (1990) wisdom into our work. We create structured experiences that differ from the normal circumstances and events in our participants' lives. The training space becomes an escape from the mundane. We ensure learning opportunities are stacked and scalable. Our experiential activities and reflective dialogue are the vehicles for this learning, growth, and development.

As leadership educators, we also provide explicit goals for the training time—and cocreate expectations around what healthy engagement should be. Through the training experience feedback is provided to continue inching participants closer toward goal accomplishment and deep levels of their flow state. Yet all the

while, we recognize that our participants need to be in control and manifest their training experience destiny on their own terms.

Notwithstanding, in terms of experiential learning activities, it is quite difficult to ensure flow occurs because each participant has different levers. I find it is best to inform these trainings with a reflective worksheet activity for participants to think about those experiences when they were in flow—and not. The experiences within those stories can be unpacked during the reflective dialogue for participants to think about, at a personal level, what it was about those particular experiences that enabled them to get into a flow state.

Peaks and Valleys

Participants are provided a worksheet with a squiggly arrow that creates peaks and valleys. The activity can be facilitated in two ways. Either the peaks are utilized to symbolize four flow moments; the valleys to represent four entropy or other limiting emotional states. Or you can utilize each peak and valley to indicate each of the eight states. Regardless of which option is selected, leadership educators utilize the worksheet to guide participants through thinking about their flow experiences so they can articulate the features of those experiences. With this understanding, participants are better enabled to replicate those experiences and provoke flow as a healthy leadership habit.

Materials

- worksheet (Peaks and Valleys worksheet)
  - Precreate or provide a worksheet where the participants draw a diagonal squiggly line with four points at the top and four at the bottom. See the example in Figure 10.1.
- writing utensils

Instructions

- Begin by distributing the worksheet or a blank piece of paper.
- Through this activity you will invite participants to either think about multiple flow (peaks) or limiting (valleys) states, or about experiences in which they had anxiety, apathy, worry, boredom, arousal, relaxation, control, and flow. There are eight positions on the worksheet, and each one is designed for these specific elements—in this order.

- At each step, participants will think about stories and situations in which they felt that way. They can draft notes highlighting elements of the experience and what it was about the experience that caused them to feel that way.
- At each step, it is wise to invite participants to find a partner (it can be the same partner throughout the entirety of the activity) to share their reflections.
- Once participants have worked their way through the entire worksheet, it is time for the reflective dialogue.

Reflective Dialogue Questions

Our objective with this activity is to provide a deeply reflective opportunity for participants to remember what provoked different emotional responses—particularly what encouraged them to achieve a flow state. We utilize this information during the reflective dialogue to help them translate how they can purposefully get into flow as a leadership practice. A selection of my go-to reflective dialogue questions includes the following:

- What did you notice about your flow stories that was different from the other stories?
- What can be pulled from that so that we can achieve flow states more regularly in our leadership practices?
- What did you hear—and what did you witness/experience—when your partner was telling their flow stories?
- What can we learn from this exercise that can be applied to our own leadership practice?

Figure 10.1. Image of flow peaks and valleys.

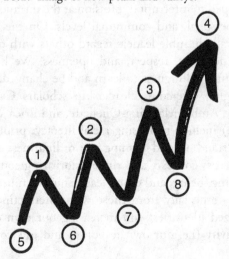

Embracing and Extending Cultural Humility

Leadership is a relational phenomenon. It is imperative that those who engage in the practice of leading examine their mental models (those deeply held images and assumptions about how the world operates) and preconceived notions of others—specifically in the context of diverse and differing cultures. Chan and Reece (2021) eloquently frame the rationale and importance for this leadership skill:

> Learning and retaining knowledge about cultures and different identities, particularly in the context of the workplace environment, tends to lodge individuals in their own mental models. Our worldviews are constructed by our own learned predispositions regarding how things should occur, which we develop from childhood, and put into practice in adulthood. These psychological underpinnings about the ways in which the world operates inform our abilities to think, communicate, and perceive occurrences throughout our daily lives. Moreover, these mental models . . . are constantly reinforced by our own assumptions, given that the way we experience life is largely informed by the existing beliefs. When our own assumptions are reinforced, we are often unable to discern objective truths from subjective interpretations. . . . Engrained assumptions regarding our perceptions of cultural differences tend to restrict us from learning, as our familiarity provides a safety net from knowledge that may challenge our presumptions about the way things are. In the context of diversity and inclusion within organizations, this poses an innate problem as the workforce becomes increasingly diverse and complex. (p. 125)

Tervalon and Murray-García (1998) coined the term *cultural humility* as a way to challenge the limitations of cultural competence. Although cultural competence is important, just understanding others' cultures is not enough. For many, *competency* indicates successful mastery of a skill set. This may further inequities rather than advancing equality and justice across cultures. Abe (2020) details a series of limitations of cultural competence. For instance, the term *culture* becomes a proxy for individuals of the dominant cultural group to *other* others, thereby exacerbating stereotyping. Cultural competence places an emphasis on *knowing* and *being competent* in understanding others' cultures. This emphasizes *mastery* and suggests that one's cultural incompetence stems from incomplete or incorrect knowledge. Cultural competence has also been critiqued for its lack of a transformative social justice agenda with assumptions that ignore power relations and structural inequities. And cultural competence does not take into account complex issues of intersectionality in identities. On the whole cultural competence has focused on skills and ways of doing. Cultural humility is an attitude and way of being (Mosher et al., 2017).

Cultural humility has three core components and operates at three levels: individual, interpersonal, and collective. First, extending cultural humility begins with leaders by embracing lifelong commitments to self-evaluation and critique. At the individual level, leaders engage in understanding their identities and cultural influences while locating themselves within their particular social frameworks. This practice of situating includes a recognition of their cultural and historical locale, along with an understanding of self in relation to power and privilege, oppression, and marginalization (Abe, 2020; Hammel, 2013). This intrapersonal focus also involves an awareness of one's limitations in their own cultural worldview as well as the limitations of their ability to fully understand the cultural background and comprehend the cultural experiences of others (Mosher et al., 2017).

Second, cultural humility is centered on redressing power imbalances. This operates at the interpersonal level. Here, leaders recognize the differences in others while not *othering* them. Leaders purposefully practice opening themselves and welcoming diverse cultural backgrounds and worldviews. Here leaders purposefully prioritize the development of mutual respect for others (Mosher et al., 2017).

Third, cultural humility emphasizes the development of mutually beneficial and nonpaternalistic partnerships with communities. This is cultural humility at the collective level. At this level, communities are viewed as possessing intrinsic value equal to that of the leaders' communities. With this lens, the perspectives, experiences, and contributions of community members are regarded as sources of valuable information, insight, and expertise. Consequently, a collective-level practice of cultural humility emphasizes respect for the dignity and value of community experiences, cultures, and perspectives—while being aware of and attuned to the structural forces, power imbalances, and social inequities that shape lived experiences for whole communities of people (Abe, 2020).

Social justice and cultural humility are intersecting constructs (Fisher, 2020). Cultural humility is the awareness of how culture shapes all individuals' experiences and perspectives, with specific attention to the impact of power, privilege, and oppression. Being culturally humble enables leaders to become more fully aware of social injustices and actively engage in socially just practice. Specifically, cultural humility is about a lifelong long-term sustained commitment to dismantle racist policies and practices, redistribute power, and ensure equal access to resources—at the individual, interpersonal, and communal levels (see Kendi, 2019; Wilkerson, 2020). Although each of us has a serious and significant part to play, the individual work to address social change will look different depending on one's positionality (Kutten, 2020).

Often, those from privileged identities have not taken advantage of opportunities to unlearn oppressive cultural norms that perpetuate barriers for marginalized individuals and communities (Wells, 2020). Whiteness, as an identity, is connected to power. This is because of learned blindness; apathy in unlearning the oppressive cultural norms that maintain structural exclusion and normalize brutality against Black, Indigenous, and other people of color; and purposeful defiance against antiracism efforts (Brookfield & Hess, 2021).

It is for this reason that White readers of this text, those of us who are part of an identity group who have historically (individually and/or culturally) wielded power and leveraged authority for racist means, need to engage in personal reflection to recognize how our Whiteness provides us with privileges while at the same time structurally and systematically oppresses others. Culturally humble White leaders are better equipped to interrupt oppression at the intrapersonal, interpersonal, and communal levels. On the whole, culturally humble leaders regard others with dignity, intrinsic value, respect, and openness. We have an authentic willingness to learn and be changed. Some strategies, offered by leadership scholars Cameron Beatty, Amber Manning-Ouellette, and Erica Wiborg (2021) include increasing racial literacy; prioritizing understanding and naming the ordinariness of racism across contexts and time; prioritizing sources of knowing, being, and doing leadership from people of color—especially from those with intersecting marginalized identities; and increasing our own critical reflexivity (i.e. our own responses and [dis]comfort) with themes related to access, justice, equity, diversity, and inclusion.

At the core of cultural humility is the concept of *humility*—the notion that a person has an accurate self-view, appreciation of others, and is generally teachable (Owens et al., 2013). A move from cultural competence to cultural humility is ultimately a transition from mastery of information regarding diverse cultures toward individual accountability, acknowledgment, and mitigation of power imbalances (Cox & Simpson, 2020).

Cultural humility requires that we take responsibility for our interactions with others by listening to diverse others while at the same time being attuned to what we are thinking and feeling about their diverse cultures (Isaacson, 2014). Other practices to embrace and extend cultural humility include purposeful self-reflection and the exploration of our own biases and stereotypes, becoming more flexible in our mindset, focusing on others and self (not just self), and believing that all humans hold equal value (Foronda, 2020).

Some contemporary scholars have drawn connections between mindfulness and cultural humility (DeMarsay, 2020; Fisher, 2020; Velott & Forté, 2019). A friend and incredible contemplative leadership scholar-practitioner, Thulani DeMarsay, completed her dissertation by exploring the lived experiences of organizational leaders with a contemplative practice. When discussing her research, she found that mindfulness decreases bias. For example, mindfulness assists leaders in developing an awareness of blind spots, interrupting cycles of automatic and habitual response, making the unconscious conscious, and improving the quality of presence. Facilitating a workshop for my nonprofit's board, she highlighted the following practices for leaders to embrace and extend cultural humility:

- cultivate greater self-awareness and self-inquiry
- improve quality of presence to be fully available and attentive to team members
- sit with uncomfortable feelings
- create space for reflection
- reduce polarized thinking
- develop habits of noticing
- engage in uncomfortable conversations with compassion
- foster a culture of empathy

Velott and Forté (2019) suggest certain mindfulness practices to reduce unconscious bias and embrace cultural humility. This includes beginning with defining our own culture. Then we focus our attention on expanding our self-awareness by considering our privileges and power. Finally, we must honestly explore our own biases, assumptions, and stereotypes instead of assuming that we don't have any. These practices ultimately have the potential to create greater openness, self-awareness, and self-reflection among leaders (Fisher, 2020).

Beyond the individual, when leaders express humility, it fosters a supportive climate with followers and within organizations and communities. This climate includes the enhanced sharing of information, generation of psychological safety, welcoming critical feedback, and noticing others' strengths (Chan & Reece, 2021). Under the direction of a culturally humble leader, followers become more inclined to express themselves authentically, increase the quantity and quality of creative outputs, and utilize their strengths (Tangney, 2000). When we practice cultural humility, we have the capacity to transform our organizations and communities by the fortune of being more attentive to the diverse cultural realities of others. Extending cultural humility is an essential leadership practice and healthy leadership educator habit.

Leadership Educator Praxis Activity

Leadership Theme: Embracing and Extending Cultural Humility
Exercise: Identity Mapping (physically engaged activity)

Embracing and extending cultural humility is essential for leaders. It is just as important for leadership educators. This is especially significant for the next generation of leadership educators. In the coming decades, the population in the United States of America, for example, of those who identify as White will decrease to 47%, compared to 67% in 2008 (Isaacson, 2014). This has serious implications for our training content, participant body, and participant experience.

In order for leadership educators to be fully equipped to train our participants, we must engage in explicit antibias and antiracism work as part of our preparation. This is how we embrace and extend cultural humility. "This can be crucial to the development of an appreciation for the manifold nature of identity and awareness of one's own biases so that they are able to effectively serve their populations" (Farrelly et al., 2021, p. 1).

As we facilitate trainings, we need to be able to navigate cross-cultural conflicts. These disagreements might include assessments of race relations and social movements; attitudes toward immigration; differences in religious, spiritual, or meaning-making worldviews; perspectives on abortion; welcomeness to gender identity and sexual orientation; participation in certain clubs and organizations; and more. Our cultural humility will enable us to navigate those conflicts as well as challenging commentary from our training participants.

Not only is it imperative for leadership educators to embrace and extend cultural humility, it is also important for us to utilize our trainings as a forum for our participants to cultivate cultural humility. To do so, we want to craft experiences that enable our participants to engage in critical self-reflection (which is the purpose of our Identity Mapping activity). We should also weave cultural topics and highlight examples from beyond the dominant hegemony throughout our trainings—not just those explicitly focused on cultural humility or a "diversity" topic, utilize community agreements to create a welcoming space for the learning community to call out microaggressions, and purposefully assign participants to groups with others who are culturally diverse. I want to highlight the Cultural Humility Learning Module (see Farrelly et al., 2021) that offers a weekly breakdown of themes and activities utilized in university classroom contexts that can be restructured or reenvisioned for trainings.

Laura Rendón's (2014) *sentipensante* approach to teaching has relevancy for leadership trainings, too. *Sentipensante* is derived from two words in Spanish. *Sentir* means "to sense or feel" while *pensar* means "to think." This approach to training participant engagement is intended to celebrate wholeness. It focuses on integrating the delicate balance between our inner life of intuition, emotion, and sense of meaning and purpose with the outer world of action and service. Further, it speaks to our humanity, compassion, and care for our self-worth along with the external world we inhabit.

Leadership educators utilize the *sentipensante* framework because of its emphasis on aiding participants in releasing limiting perspectives of themselves, fostering

high expectations, and assisting them in becoming agents of social change. Foundational to this pedagogy is (a) having a critical consciousness, (b) taking action to transform entrenched institutional systems and structures, (c) acting with love and compassion, and (d) working to heal as an agent of change (Rendón, 2014).

Having a critical consciousness (Freire, 2002) enables leadership educators to recognize systemic and structural inequities that often result from marginalization, powerlessness, and exploitation. Our trainings serve as holding environments and safe spaces to explore how these inequalities manifest and how our participants can take action to eradicate them through their own leadership practices.

Our trainings also serve as leadership learning laboratories so our participants can acquire the tactical leadership skills, proficiencies, and dispositions to tangibly work toward justice and equity. We encourage not just learning about justice and equity but working toward equal access to resources and opportunities for all.

As leadership educators, with a *sentipensante* framework, our approach to this work is with love and compassion. We center our training experiences in care while providing opportunities and purposefully raising the voices of our participants who have systematically had fewer privileges and resources.

Finally, our objective is to heal the divides that exist. We are bridge-builders. As thinking-feeling leadership educators, we utilize our power and platform to instill hope that our participants can serve as the agents of change necessary to confront the most pressing of challenges—specifically in the context of inequality.

Part of the reason *sentipensante* aligns with cultural humility is because it is grounded in contemplative practices. Leadership educators utilize deeply reflective experiences and prompts to assist participants in quieting their minds so as to enhance their personal capacity for deep concentration and insight. It is from this concentration and insight that we and our participants can, at a personal level, become more deeply aware of our own limiting thoughts, attitudes, and actions and craft action plans for change. At a societal level, this reflective space encourages awareness around inequities as well as opportunities to implement measures of social justice. Tactically, we can do the following things to infuse cultural humility and *sentipensante* into our leadership training practice:

- emphasize relationships, connectivity, and the betterment of the collective whole while reducing the overprivileging of competition, individual achievement, self-interests, and leadership rooted in power, position, prestige, and personal reward
- promote self-reflexivity and critical perspective taking so leadership training participants can become socially aware individuals
- utilize democratic approaches that are inclusive and reflective of our participants' backgrounds and needs
- infuse diverse and dynamic approaches into our experiential learning and reflective dialogue to create a welcoming, engaging, and developmental environment for all leadership training participants
- foster the transformation of our participants into the agents of change they dream of being and our community conditions necessitate
- model social activism and an ethic of care, compassion, validation, and the leadership practices we hope to impart to our participants

Sanchez et al. (2019) have found that experiential learning and reflective writing are particularly powerful in cultivating cultural humility in college students. The Identity Mapping activity is a stellar example. This is a tremendous exercise for us, as leadership educators, to better understand and embrace our own cultural humility. It can also be utilized in our trainings to extend and foster cultural humility among our participants. As we know, this self-reflection is the first step in embracing and extending cultural humility.

Identity Mapping

When facilitating the Identity Mapping activity, I begin by placing large Post-Its or printed sheets with identity features around the training space. These could be hanging on the walls or on the center of selected tabletops. There should be at least a half dozen or more identity features (e.g., educational status, gender, nationality, race, relationship status, sexual orientation, etc.) depending on the size of the group. (In chapter 1, I provide a sampling of personal identity features within my positionality statement. Any of those might be utilized for this activity.)

Once the activity begins, a question is posed to which participants respond by moving to the prelabeled table or place in the training space. They will select the location where their identity has the greatest saliency, for example, "When at my gym or exercise class, my identity feature that has the most saliency is . . . " Once participants have moved to the appropriate location, they should be invited to dialogue with the others in that particular space about why that aspect of their identity has the most saliency.

Materials

- identity features on a printout or large Post-It

Instructions

- Begin by placing the identity features on tabletops or against the walls. (There should be enough space between the identity features so that groups can gather and dialogue.)
- Ask a question regarding where their identity has the most saliency. Some examples include the following:
  - at the gym or exercise class
  - at my favorite restaurant
  - on a road trip
  - with my family
  - with my friends
  - in this training
- Once the question has been asked, give participants time to move to the appropriate location.
- The participants should then engage in dialogue with others who are at that location as to why that particular identity feature has the most saliency.
- Then engage the participants in a large-group dialogue about what was raised from the small-group dialogue.
- Once you have found a great pausing moment, share the next question.
- Repeat this process for at least four rounds—possibly more—if time allows and participants are enjoying the experience and then slide into the reflective dialogue.

Reflective Dialogue Questions

Our objective with this activity to provide a self-awareness-raising space so our participants can become more familiar with their dominant and nondominant identities and cultures. We utilize this information during the reflective dialogue to help them become more embracing of cultural humility. A selection of my go-to reflective dialogue questions includes the following:

- What did you notice about your more salient (dominant) identities?
- How does that understanding manifest in your understanding of yourself and your worldviews? (You can then ask the same questions with regard to nondominant identities.)
- How do you think your identities impact your role as a leader?
- What was illuminated through this activity that may have created barriers for engaging with people of difference?
- What will you do differently now that this has been illuminated?
- What can we learn from this exercise that can be applied to our own leadership practice?

Conclusion

The leadership practices in this chapter hone in on ways for us, as leaders and leadership educators, to thrive and our organizations to flourish. When we develop healthy leadership habits in these domains we cultivate a deep sense of worthiness and authentic pride in our capabilities (nurturing self-efficacy and

confidence); stand firm in our resolve to overcome obstacles (demonstrating grit and resilience); leverage affirmative and appreciative approaches to our leadership challenges (applying strengths and positive psychology principles); maximize opportunities to get into the zone (tapping into flow states); and serve as justice- and equity-oriented leaders who strive for systemic change with regard to the marginalizing of minoritized individuals and communities (embracing and extending cultural humility).

Leadership Practices, Skills, and Competencies—Part Three Conclusion

It should be no surprise that between all of these leadership practices, skills, and competencies, there is significant overlap and intersection. Cultivating our leadership capacities is a developmental process. As we grow and develop healthy leadership habits in one domain, others will be positively and progressively impacted.

In chapter 2 I describe the "what" and "who" of leadership and, I detail that we all know it when we see it. These practices comprise the *it* of leadership. We know who exceptional and extraordinary leaders are because they infuse these healthy leadership habits into their practice. These are the skills and competencies that we strive for when we attempt to emulate our leadership models, mentors, heroes, and exemplars.

PART FOUR

FACILITATING LEADERSHIP TRAININGS

WHOSE TRAINING IS IT? It's a simple question. You, the reader, are either formally or informally charged with and responsible for the leadership learning, development, and training of others. This is, after all, the intended audience of this book. So, back to the original question—*Whose training is it?*

Often, those leadership educators who are ill-informed or have limited experience mistakenly believe it is *our* training—the educator's training. It's not. It never was. It is our *participant's* training. It always was.

We are the facilitators of their leadership learning. We design and implement intentional, engaging, and dynamic leadership trainings so that our participants can *access* the training message and material, *internalize* the leadership learning, and then *apply* that learning to their leadership practice beyond the training experience. We create the holding environments and conditions for their leadership learning because it's their training.

Our focus of attention, as leadership educators, should always, singularly, be focused on crafting experiences that will meet their leadership training and development needs—whether that be cultivating their leadership capacity, strengthening their leadership skills and practices, or enhancing their leadership knowledge base. It is their training.

The most amazing and impactful leadership training experiences are developmental not because of luck or randomness. It is because exceptional leadership educators utilize a grounded approach to craft and facilitate leadership-developmental training experiences.

Yes, extraordinary leadership educators are knowledgeable about leadership theories and practices. Without that foundation, we are limited in our abilities to train others in leadership. Yet that knowledge is not enough. We also need to know how to craft facilitated experiences and then how to facilitate these trainings with dynamism so that participants' leadership learning can be maximized. Part Four explores how to how to craft facilitated experiences utilizing Leadership Trainer's Narrative Approach. We create a *training story*. A leadership training story has five elements, explored in chapter 12: the exposition, rising action, apex, falling action, and resolution. Chapter 13 highlights facilitation best practices when conducting a training. We begin, though, with chapter 11 to illuminate the crux of what enables our leadership trainings to be effective. If we want our participants to *access* the training material and message, *internalize* their learning, and then *apply* their learning to practice, it is imperative that our trainings incorporate experiential learning activities and reflective dialogue.

Experiential Learning and Reflective Dialogue

SITTING UNDER THE BODHI tree, the Buddha reflected upon the variety of ways that one can acquire wisdom. He noted three distinct variations. The first is received wisdom (*suta-maya panna*). Received wisdom is wisdom learned from others. It could be in the form of reading literature, listening to lectures and podcasts, or simply by being immersed in community life. "*Received* wisdom is not one's own wisdom, not something experienced for oneself. It is borrowed wisdom" (Hart, 1987, p. 89). Regardless of the source of received wisdom, we have not authored this wisdom for ourselves—we take it as Truth at face value.

The second variation is intellectual wisdom (*cinta-maya panna*). After reading or hearing a certain teaching, we consider it and examine whether it is rational, beneficial, and practical information. If it is satisfying, intellectually, we ultimately accept it as true. Still, this is not our own wisdom—only the intellectualization of the insight we have heard and acquired from others (Hart, 1987). In this form of wisdom acquisition, compared to received wisdom, we exert more energy into the process of attainment—we analyze the information and ultimately decide that it is compatible with our currently held beliefs, values, and worldview.

The third variation, experiential wisdom (*bhavana-maya panna*), arises out of our own experience—out of personal realization. This is wisdom that will bring about a change in our lives (Hart, 1987). Although received and intellectual wisdom are important for individuals to live safely (e.g., receiving wisdom about the dangers of touching a pot just off the burning stove) and to expand our awareness (e.g., reading about the lived experiences of people in foreign cultures), experiential wisdom is essential for our growth and development—especially in the context of leadership learning.

Leadership educators craft training experiences to facilitate the leadership learning and development of our participants. We do this by ensuring our participants can *access* the training message and material, *internalize* their leadership learning, and then *apply* that learning to their leadership practice. Yet so often we use training techniques that are not effective at promoting that type of learning and development—focusing on received and intellectual knowledge transactions. Historically, the go-to training method has been a lecture.

Lecturing has limited effectiveness (Fink, 2013). Lecturing is responded to with passive listening. Exceptional leadership educators create lived experiences, not just listening experiences for our participants. These experiences are necessary for the development of skills, competencies, and expertise (Day et al., 2009). As leadership educators who facilitate trainings, at the heart of our work is the strategic use of hands-on experiential learning activities and reflective dialogue.

This aligns with a recent report from the International Leadership Association (2021), in which they articulate general principles for leadership programs. Among the five principles is learning. They describe how the most effective leadership programs incorporate highly active and engaging instructional strategies and recognize the appropriate developmental level and maturity of the learner. They create a "trusted space" that integrates theory, practice, and experiential learning to build core competencies such as critical thinking, problem-solving, and teamwork. They promote engagement, dialogue, reflection, and active questioning of learners' experiences as both leaders and followers. (p. 4)

To ensure this type of leadership learning occurs, leadership educators purposefully integrate experiential learning and reflective dialogue into every training. In every training. In. Every. Training. Experiential learning and reflective dialogue are employed in tandem. If we utilize an experiential learning activity, we follow it with a reflective dialogue. If we utilize two experiential learning activities, we host two reflective dialogue opportunities. If our yearlong leadership program incorporates 18 experiential learning activities into the comprehensive experience, we host 18 reflective dialogues. With this model, participants are immersed in personalized hands-on learning-by-doing experiences and then internalize the learning from those experiences as they infuse healthier leadership habits into their leadership regimen.

Experiential Learning

Experiential learning is an educational experience whereby the outcomes (e.g., leadership learning and development) are achieved through personal immersion and involvement in the learning experience itself. Our lived experiences inform our learning and the acquisition of new knowledge and skills. Simply, learning happens by doing. This is not a traditional transfer of knowledge from the educator to participant. The emphasis of the learning experience—for the participant—is not on listening, observing, or studying. Rather, participants are fully engaged in hands-on learning. Participants engage in learning experiences via their own participation. With this perspective of experiential learning, the primary source of learning occurs through direct sensory experiences and in-context actions (D. Kolb, 2015). Experiential learning in our leadership training contexts is about crafting real-world, real-time, problem-based leadership challenges for our participants (Soria & Johnson, 2020).

Here I offer a tweaked definition of experiential learning originally utilized in the context of university student business education (Foster et al., 2021). This definition, now, is reshaped for the context of leadership educators who facilitate training experiences. *Experiential learning is a process where participants actively engage in learning through meaningful experiences and reflection upon those experiences to construct new knowledge, skills, and/or attitudes.* With this definition, the objective is participant learning—constructing new knowledge, skills, or attitudes. This learning occurs through both active participation in meaningful experiences as well as reflecting upon those experiences.

Experiential learning is often used interchangeably with like terms ending in either *learning* or *education*: experiential education, adventure education, challenge learning, environmental education, experience-based learning, gamification, or outdoor education (Beard & Wilson, 2018; J. Roberts, 2012). In our leadership training contexts, we strategically utilize experiential learning activities as a method and technique to provoke the leadership learning and development of our participants.

These activities can take on many forms. We can utilize case studies, games, reflective exercises, role playing, and simulations (Berkley & Kaplan, 2020; Silberman & Biech, 2015). Case studies are provided to participants so that they can actively read about and analyze a particular situation (i.e., a case). These can be real or fictitious, but with enough details to provide fodder for participants to reflect upon and dialogue about how they might proceed if they were entangled in that challenge. In this type of training experience, I explore the topic as a quick and broad overview and then share a written scenario that highlights a challenge upon which the participants will need to reflect and provide reflections on how they would proceed if leading through that experience. Then I host a reflective dialogue to integrate the conversations from the groups and individual participants before guiding a discourse on how they might implement their learning from this case study into their leadership practice.

Games are designed to provide an engaging—often competitive—atmosphere for participants as they pursue leadership learning. These games are not just inserted into our trainings for enjoyment factors. They are strategically structured to demonstrate particular concepts and to provide a forum for participant practice and ways to gain insight on their decision-making processes. The Great Card Race (see the Situational Approach section in chapter 3) is one game that can illuminate leadership skills in teamwork and communication, among others.

Reflective exercises usually take the form of worksheet-based activities or other introspective endeavors (e.g., journaling). Although participants are less physically engaged in reflective exercises compared to games, role playing, and simulations, these are structured as experiential opportunities because they invite our participants into a different headspace and mindset than their regular day-to-day leadership engagements. These moments to pause, be still, silent, and introspective are an important outlet for participants in our leadership trainings. Values Exploration (see the Conviction in Action section in chapter 5) is a reflective activity that enables participants to explore which values are of utmost importance. During the activity, participants identify, from a long list, their priority values. They are then asked to reflect upon and dialogue about how those values manifest in their lives and leadership practices.

Role playing summons participants to engage in scenarios to better understand leadership concepts and how to navigate leadership challenges. These are not intended to be dramatic, over-the-top, or outlandish exemplars. The more we can facilitate real-life role-playing experiences for our participants, the better they will be able to internalize that leadership learning and then apply it to their leadership practice. The Pirate's Booty exercise (see the Followership section in chapter 6) encourages participants to play various roles based on an assigned character. Once the activity comes to a close, we host reflective dialogue conversations to assist participants in ascertaining ideas for how they want to shift or adapt their own leadership practices based upon their role-playing experience.

Experiential activities can also be simulations. Simulations are intended to replicate real-world situations while maximizing real-time interactions. These are often difficult to include in training contexts because of the need for time and significant preparations. I like to highlight the "behind-closed-doors" activity utilized in orientation leader trainings, resident assistant trainings, and other campus-based organizational leader trainings. These are also quite popular for onboarding scenarios with new managers within corporate and other industries. Essentially, seasoned student leaders or professionals serve in various roles and act out behaviors to provide the newer student leaders or managers with opportunities to navigate probable challenges. These are conducted in a safe and closed environment so that the learners can create moments to pause, reflect, ask questions, and enhance their responses to these simulated real-world situations.

To better understand experiential learning, we can position it against conventional learning in leadership training contexts. In conventional learning, the focus is on the trainer and leadership training material. Conventional trainers have a message to share, and the entire experience is guided by ensuring that message is delivered from trainer to participant. With conventional learning, the structure of the training experience is attached to prescribed possibilities. There is a clear, explicit, and certain direction for the learning. The trainer—and often participants—know exactly what the outcome is going to be. It is predetermined by the conventional trainer. With this approach, the trainer is seen as the sole expert, and the learning is limited to the trainer's knowledge. In conventional learning, there is a traditional transfer of knowledge from the trainer to the participant. This is understood as the Freireian (1970/2002) banking model whereby a trainer makes a deposit of information into the minds of the participants. Here learning is assessed and monitored through memorization and the regurgitation of information.

Not only is this conventional learning problematic from a knowledge acquisition and skills development lens, this approach to learning is troublesome from a leadership lens. When we design and deploy conventional learning into our training experiences, it encourages passive engagement. This positions the trainer-as-leader as the power-broker and authority. When beyond the training bubble, this passivity translates to zapping the agency the initiative out of followers. More, conventional learning is anti-equity. This approach assumes all of our participants are ready and able to receive the same message from our lecture.

Experiential learning is entirely different. With experiential learning, the focus is on the participants. Our goal is to craft a developmental experience that resonates with our participants. We celebrate their wisdom by facilitating an experience that is explicitly focused on what is going to best be of service to them at that moment—which means we intentionally include their vision and voice in the training experience. With experiential learning, we are open and flexible to varying possibilities and directions for the training experience. In addition to investing significant time and energy in our preparations, we welcome spur-of-the-moment changes from our original plans—potentially significant ones—based on the desired developmental outcomes and learning opportunities needed in the moment. Within experiential learning, participants are seen as valued and valuable to the learning of others and share in the responsibility of the learning experience.

From a leadership lens, experiential learning celebrates our participants' authentic personhood as actively engaged leaders as well as their individual pursuits of meaningful goals—compared to leadership emphasized by power, position, or prestige held by the traditional presenter in conventional learning engagements. With experiential learning, this translates to our participants' comfortability with engaging in and enacting leadership beyond the training bubble rather than waiting to be told to do so.

More, experiential learning is rooted in equity. This approach assumes all of our participants are valued and valuable to the learning of others. We all have something to contribute and learn. It also assumes that all of our participants learn what is most meaningful to them rooted in who they are and where they are at in their leadership journey.

To highlight the difference between conventional and experiential learning, I share an example from a Leadership Trainer Certification Program Immersion Retreat I facilitated. If I approached this situation from a conventional lens, I would have missed an incredible opportunity for learning, potentially impaired the relationships that had been cultivated, and damaged the integrity of the space we had cocreated. At the time, I was facilitating a session on *Trainer Presence*. My plan was to utilize a 10-minute video clip to highlight the remarkable abilities of the actor to capture the audience's attention and immerse them in his story. The clip I wanted to highlight was about the death of his childhood pet. It was a powerful portrayal that, to me, captured the essence of how leadership educators can utilize presence, props, and story to transport participants to a mind space that leads to learning and development.

That clip, though, was an entry point for what would become an exploration into the impact of suicide on a young boy's life. The entire hour-long production highlighted the actors' struggles with suicide—particularly with his mother's attempt at ending her life when he was a child. Although what I intended to play did not mention or reference suicide, it followed a disclaimer about the sensitive nature of the film's subject. As we watched this clip, it became an emotional experience for our group. One of our participants had personally struggled with suicidal ideation and attempt. Another's brother had committed suicide. It became very clear that continuing with the original plan and forcing a training session on Trainer Presence would be detrimental to what our participants and training community needed and desired at that moment.

As a collective, informed by our participants, we crafted a holding environment to process and unpack this experience. We discussed issues of mental health as well as wellness and well-being. Later, participants commented about how meaningful it was to pause, shift, and craft this space rather than ignorantly barrel ahead with the original topic.

It is the experience itself that enables the learning. The more the experience has resonance with our participants, the stronger the opportunity for learning. As the facilitator of experiential learning, we are the conduit between the experience and our leadership training participants. Table 11.1 highlights the significant differences between conventional and experiential learning.

Foster et al. (2021) compiled research data from numerous studies that all suggest participants learn best through direct experience and that experiential learning is more effective in generating cognitive, behavioral, and attitudinal outcomes. In one meta-analysis in particular (Burch et al., 2019), the findings illuminated the participants experienced superior learning outcomes with experiential approaches—specifically with understanding a social issue, developing personal insight, and cognitive development. All three of these areas are critical for leadership learning and development.

When facilitating experientially informed leadership trainings, leadership educators should perform less as "teachers" and more as facilitators or coaches or guides. Specifically, leadership educators design leadership learning laboratories where participants are encouraged to courageously experiment with leadership practices as they are guided through exploration, reflection, and authentic dialogue.

Western conceptual notions of experiential learning extend back to the early Greek classical period

TABLE 11.1: A Description of the Major Differences Between Conventional and Experiential Learning

Conventional Learning	Experiential Learning
Trainer/training is material focused.	Trainer/training is participant focused.
Learning is attached to prescribed possibilities.	Learning is flexible and open to possibilities.
Trainer is seen as the sole expert and the learning is limited to the trainer's knowledge.	Participants are seen as valued and valuable to the learning of others and share in the responsibility of the learning experience.
Knowledge is transferred from "trainer-as-teacher" to "participant-as-student."	Skills and knowledge are developed via hands-on learning experiences.
Learning occurs through memorization and is monitored and assessed by the trainer.	Learning occurs through real-world experiences and is self-assessed by personal mastery.
The learning experience translates to antiquated leadership understandings emphasized by power, position, and prestige as well as leadership practices that encourage waiting to be told what to do and when to do it.	The learning experience translates to leadership understandings emphasized by authentic personhood and meaningful leadership pursuits and practices that encourage enacting leadership when personally called to create change.
Learning is anti-equity and assumes all of the participants are ready and able to receive the same message.	Learning is rooted in equity, and participants are individually able to learn what is most salient to them.

with Plato and Aristotle (J. Roberts, 2012). While White men have dominated this space as the scholarly authorities, Indigenous knowledge systems detailed the importance of experience in learning and development. To highlight and emphasize the importance of Indigenous wisdom, J. Roberts (2012) cites Barnhardt (2008) to emphasize that Indigenous people traditionally acquired their knowledge through direct experience in the natural environment. A story is recounted in his text from Charles Eastman (1858–1939), a Santee Sioux, who wrote about his life and experiences. In this story, Eastman describes a child of 5 or 6 who, of his own accord, determined what he was to do that day. Nobody told the child where to go, what to avoid, when to return, or what to do when he got tired. Prior to his adventure, though, the boy's uncle asked him to "look closely at everything you see."

Upon the boy's return, the uncle had questions. The elder asked. The boy answered. This back-and-forth process of questions and detailed responses filled their evening conversation, with the boy describing the elements of his day.

The Eastman story highlights an Indigenous notion of experiential learning that is holistic in nature. It is not compartmentalized into separate subjects and disciplines. It is practical and relational. Experiential learning, much like what the boy experiences on his adventure, is grounded in careful observation, experimentation, and localized personal experiencing (J. Roberts, 2012). And it is followed by a leadership educator hosting an intentional reflective dialogue, much like the uncle.

Experiential learning spans beyond traditional Western educational systems. Confucianism, for instance, is known for its emphasis on experiential learning (Beard & Wilson, 2018). Confucius's famous aphorism "I hear I forget, I see I remember, I do I understand" illuminates the core construct of experiential learning from an Eastern learning orientation.

David Kolb (2015) is understood to be the contemporary forefather of experiential learning, due to his germinal work, _Experiential Learning: Experience as the Source of Learning and Development_ and the development of his experiential learning theory (ELT) and experiential learning cycle. These were originally designed to integrate the common themes of his experiential learning influencers into a systemic framework that would serve to address contemporary problems of learning.

Kolb's (2015) experiential learning influencers include many historical scholars who touched upon various facets of experiential learning from diverse disciplines: John Dewey (education), Mary Parker Follett (learning relationships), Paulo Freire (critical pedagogy), William James (psychology), Kurt Lewin (organizational development), Jean Piaget (cognitive development), and Lev Vygotsky (social development theory)—among others. Experiential learning is not simply having experiences and assuming something is learned. It takes serious and significant work and should be strategically facilitated by a skilled and savvy educator. In Kolb's (2015) words:

> Through a synthesis of works of the foundational scholars . . . truth is not manifest in experience; it must be inferred by a process of learning that questions preconceptions, tempers the vividness and emotion of experience with critical reflection, and extracts the correct lessons from the consequences of action. (p. xxi)

Kolb (2015) defines *learning* as the process whereby knowledge is created through the transformation of experience. To unpack this understanding, he articulates six core characteristics of learning. First, *learning is conceived as a continuous process, not outcomes*. When we engage in experiential learning, our focus is on the experience and learning journey, not on data acquisition.

Second, *there is no formal endpoint to learning, development, or skills enhancement*. Learning is a cyclical process of engaging in experiences, critically reflecting on them, applying the learning, and repeating.

Third, *learning requires the resolution of conflicts of prior knowledge or understanding*. Namely, our objective is to assist leadership training participants in (a) recognizing their current understanding of the phenomena in question, (b) acknowledging its flaws, and (c) resolving the conflict by internalizing the new way of understanding the phenomena. For example, you are facilitating a training and a group of participants are displaying a demeaning communication style. First, they need assistance in recognizing that their leadership communication practice is demeaning. If they don't see this as problematic, it is not going to change. Once that recognition occurs—through their participation in hands-on experiential learning activities and the subsequent reflective dialogue—they can honestly and authentically acknowledge that their communication methods are flawed and detrimental to this training experience. If that is their communication habit beyond the training bubble, it is most likely limiting their leadership effectiveness in practice. Finally, they can strategically and tactically make changes to their communication practice.

One approach of thinking about this process is the unlearning–learning Hegelian dialectic model. The formula consists of a triad: thesis, antithesis, synthesis. The thesis is our current perspective or understanding. This is how we know the world and ourselves within the world. The antithesis is a contradiction to our thesis. It is novel and it stands in opposition to our perspective, understanding, how we know the world, and see ourselves within the world. The synthesis is the resolution between the thesis and antithesis. It is an integration between the old perspective and our new way of understanding the phenomenon.

Fourth, *learning is a holistic process of adaptation*. To return to our previous communication example, if shifting from a demeaning communication practice to a more compassion-centric approach does not occur, especially after being alerted to the problematic nature of our communication style, it is safe to assume that my communication practice will continue to cause me, my colleagues, and my organization problems— ultimately limiting effectiveness. It is for this reason that during our leadership trainings, we purposefully utilize experiential learning to create experiences that enable our participants to adapt. We include reflective opportunities for participants to strategize about action planning for post-training changes. This is preparatory for their leadership learning applications beyond the training bubble.

Fifth, *learning involves transactions between people and their environments*. When we engage in experiential learning, we recognize how the influence of others and of the environment shapes our learning. Experiential learning activities remove participants from their conditioned mind-space—and often physical environment—as a way to enhance learning opportunities. Even if we utilize the same physical space for a training as a regular weekly meeting, the design of the room (i.e., shifting the table and chair setup) or structure of participant engagement expands learning opportunities because these differing interactions challenge their modus operandi. The alternative, most notably in conventional learning, is a static experience void of external influence. A traditional lecture on communication can be replicated over and over and over again regardless of the space and attendee engagement. The result is going to be similar across the board. Most likely, limited change (at best) to one's behavior or leadership practice. Yet, if we want to magnify learning opportunities and the application of leadership skills, capacities, and healthy habits among our participants, experiential learning activities (and reflective dialogue) that harness their engagement are substantially better to get the result we and they desire.

Finally, *learning is the process of creating knowledge.* We do this by encouraging participants to experience the experiences, internalize what has occurred, and utilize that data to change leadership practices. Of course, if we refer back Kolb's (2015) first characteristic, it is an ongoing, cyclical process. Once we have our new knowledge, we test it through experiences, internalize it, and apply that learning to our practice. Repeat.

Kolb's (2015) experiential learning cycle (see Figure 11.1) is a popular and easily understood four-stage framework that illuminates what this looks like in our training practice. We begin with concrete experiences (facilitating experiential learning activities) and then host reflective observations and abstract conceptualizations—what we consider reflective dialogue. We then release the participants into the wild so they can engage in actively experimenting with applying their leadership learning.

Experiential learning in a leadership training and development context is a cyclical and recursive process. As an overview, our participants engage in an immediate and concrete experience. This experience—facilitated as an activity—is the basis for their reflections and observations. These observations and insights get processed and distilled through our facilitation of reflective dialogue into abstract concepts. These abstractions are the seedlings from which new actions derive. The actions are tested through experimentations. New experiences then occur—replicating the cyclical experiential learning processes.

The experiential learning cycle. The cycle consists of four stages:

Stage 1—concrete experience. Participants actively experience an activity to drive their learning.

Stage 2—reflective observation. Participants consciously reflect upon on that experience.

Stage 3—abstract conceptualization. Participants attempt to articulate what is observed—in ways that makes sense for themselves.

Stage 4—active experimentation. Participants implement their learning into new experiences—with the plan of internalization and synthesis.

Tactically, as leadership educators, our work is in four general domains. We first establish an environment where the participants are willing (ideally, eager and enthusiastic) to be engaged in the leadership learning experience. This is a leadership learning container or holding environment—a bubble—that is characteristically different from what they consider normal or routine. A holding environment should be considered

Figure 11.1. The experiential learning cycle.

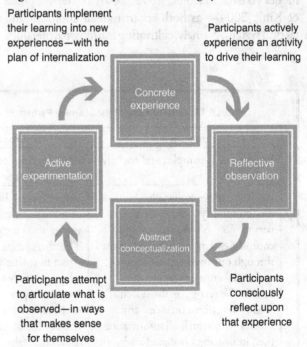

Participants implement their learning into new experiences—with the plan of internalization

Participants actively experience an activity to drive their learning

Participants attempt to articulate what is observed—in ways that makes sense for themselves

Participants consciously reflect upon that experience

Note. Adapted from *Learning: Experience as the Source of Learning and Development* (2nd ed., p. 51), D. Kolb, 2015, Pearson. Reprinted with permission.

a container that fosters growth—specifically one in which we focus less on empowering our participants and more on encouraging them to access their innate power (Chace, 2019).

Next, we infuse an exciting experiential learning activity (or sequence of activities) to provide a hands-on, immersive learning opportunity for our participants. This is then followed by—always followed by—reflective dialogue. The reflective dialogue is enabled by an introspective atmosphere for the participants to reflect—and share—about their experience(s) as well as to conceptualize about how the learning from this experience(s) is applicable to their "real-world" contexts. Specifically, we conclude the reflective dialogue by posing the question, *How does this apply to life outside of our leadership learning bubble?* Finally, before concluding the training, we purposefully draw connections and encourage action planning on how they will incorporate their learning into enhanced leadership practices. (These processes and mechanisms are described in more detail in the next chapter as we seek to create a *training story* that serves as an organizational and planning force for our training experience.)

As we design leadership learning laboratories for our participants, we should utilize the learning partnerships model (Baxter Magolda, 1992, 2001; Baxter Magolda & King, 2004)—as both an attitudinal approach and tactical system. Namely, cultivating learning partnerships with our leadership training participants will expand the opportunity for them to *access* the training message and material, *internalize* their leadership learning, and then *apply* the learning to their practice beyond the training bubble.

Marcia Baxter Magolda and Patricia King (2004) describe learning partnerships as a method that empowers individuals to develop self-authorship—an essential conduit for effective leadership. Leadership educators facilitate this developmental growth by supporting participants as they synchronize their beliefs, values, and interpersonal loyalties while challenging them to see reality as complex. Our balancing of guidance along with empowerment enables our participants to shift from authority dependence to self-authorship. Rather than see us, leadership educators, as the sole authority on leadership and the solitary conduit to their leadership learning, as learning partners, we embolden them to become authorities and authors of their own leadership development.

Learning partnerships are guided by three assumptions, summarized in Table 11.2. First, *knowledge is complex and socially constructed*. Often, our leadership training participants see knowledge dichotomously—either-or, right-wrong, yes-no. For example, they sometimes believe, fiercely, there is only one right way to lead or only those in positions of authority and power are the leaders. Others believe that leadership is tethered to birthrights—that some people are born

TABLE 11.2: A Detailing of the Learning Partnership Assumptions and a Brief Description of Each Assumption

Assumption 1	*Assumption 2*	*Assumption 3*
Knowledge is complex and socially constructed.	Our identities play a central role in crafting what we know.	Knowledge is mutually constructed by sharing power.
Rather than see knowledge dichotomously—either-or, right-wrong, yes-no—we recognize its complexity. Knowledge is composed through our lived experiences and social engagements with others. We recognize the systems, interconnections, nuances, and spectra with which all information (i.e., knowledge) is shared and gleaned.	Who we are—how we identify (all of our identities!)—informs how we see and engage in the world. This then labels, categorizes, and structures what we know to be true, false, or somewhere in between. By knowing our authentic selves, we become more comfortable and confident in what we know to be true, false, or somewhere in between.	We cocreate learning by sharing power and authority. Rather than dictate, leadership trainers open the space and engage in experiential learning and reflective dialogue so that the collective, trainers and participants alike, can coconstruct a leadership learning experience that is "hands-on," engaging, and designed to promote knowledge acquisition.

with the leadership skills and capacities that others will simply never attain. With these perceptions, there is no middle ground. People are born leaders—or not. My way of leading is the right way—others are wrong. Leadership educators know, though, that knowledge is complex and socially constructed. Our leadership knowledge, wisdom, and insight are composed through our lived experiences and social engagements with others. We recognize the systems, interconnections, nuances, and spectra with which all information (i.e., knowledge) is shared and gleaned. As leadership educators, when we approach our leadership trainings with the notion that knowledge is complex and socially constructed, we craft experiences for our participants to intentionally engage with others and wrestle with diverse perspectives.

Second, *our identities play a central role in crafting what we know.* Who we are informs how we see and engage in the world—we label, categorize, and structure what we know to be true, false, or somewhere in between based upon our identities. Our identity is composed of multiple notions of self. I'm not just a leadership educator. I am a leadership educator who identifies as a scholar-practitioner (not just an academic), uncle, White, cisgender, able-bodied, healthy (and on and on and on). All of these identities and notions of self inform and influence what I know, how I see myself in the world, and how I engage with others—including training participants. When leadership educators craft trainings with this assumption, we intentionally leverage our identity as an interpretative instrument of reality—which enables us to realize how our thoughts, feelings, and actions shape our beliefs, values, and expectations (Chunoo, 2020). We become much more conscious and cognizant of infusing opportunities for participants to safely bring their whole selves and share their whole selves as they engage in our cocreated leadership learning experience. (For a fantastic overview of the intersection between leadership learning and the learning partnerships model, explore Vivechanand Chunoo's 2020 chapter in the New Directions for Student Leadership publication *Evidence-Based Practices to Strengthen Leadership Development* [2020].)

The third learning partnership assumption is that *knowledge is mutually constructed by sharing power.* As leadership educators, we cocreate leadership learning opportunities by sharing our authority. Rather than lecture and dictate, we craft our leadership trainings as holding environments infused with hands-on experiential learning activities and reflective dialogue. In this way our participants can coconstruct their leadership development experience and acquire knowledge as empowered and engaged participants. These assumptions are the attitudinal approach that we bring to our leadership training experiences.

If the three assumptions of the learning partnerships model are our mental framework and positioning, the following three principles are our practices. As savvy leadership educators, these assumptions manifest into our facilitation of leadership learning experiences by validating our participants' capacity to know, situating the leadership learning in participants' experiences, and learning by mutually constructing meaning. These three principles are summarized in Table 11.3.

Validation is essential to leadership learning. *We validate our participants' capacity to know about leadership.* Leadership educators celebrate the contributions and voices of participants. Regardless of the depth of one's exposure to the leadership literature and scholarship, we have all experienced—and possibly practiced—outstanding leadership. The same is true for destructive and terrifying leadership. We all know about leadership from witnessing and practicing it every day of our lives. By validating the experiences and wisdom of our participants, we apply the attitude that knowledge is complex, rooted in lived experiences, and constructed through social engagements—rather than owned and authored solely by leadership educators as experts. In practice, we validate our participants' capacity to know not by lecturing about leadership. Rather, we strategically pose questions and facilitate experiential learning activities—along with reflective dialogue—to draw out the voices of our participants. We then offer our authentic gratitude and celebration of their contributions.

Our second practice is to *situate learning in participants' experiences.* Whose training is it? As leadership educators, we craft leadership learning experiences that meet our participants where they are at. Our task is to ensure that the whole of the training experience, including the topic or theme, experiential learning activities and reflective dialogue, the physical environment, and every other design and facilitation element of the training, resonates with participants. This resonance encourages the internalization of their learning and, ultimately, the infusion of their leadership

---

TABLE 11.3: A Detailing of the Learning Partnership Principles (Practices) and a Brief Description of Each Principle (Practice)

Principle (Practice) 1	*Principle (Practice) 2*	*Principle (Practice) 3*
We validate our participants' capacity to know.	We situate the learning in participants' experiences.	We learn by mutually constructing meaning.
As leadership educators, we celebrate the contributions and voice of participants. We have all experienced exceptional leadership and terrifying leadership. By validating the experiences and wisdom of our participants, we apply the attitude that knowledge is complex and rooted in both lived experiences and social engagements—rather than owned solely by the trainer.	As leadership educators, we craft leadership trainings that meet our participants where they are. Our task is to ensure that the whole of the training experience—including the topic or theme, experiential learning activities, and reflective dialogue—resonates with participants so they can internalize the learning and infuse it into their leadership practice.	As savvy and skilled leadership educators, we relinquish control so that all of those in the leadership training experience can—individually and collectively—make sense of the material. This collaborative coconstruction of meaning enables everyone to understand and internalize leadership learning—resulting in enhanced operationalization of leadership practice.

---

learning into their leadership practice. Think about it in this way: If I am charged with facilitating a leadership training for a broad swath of positional student leaders, it is antithetical to cultivating leadership learning partnerships (i.e., we do not meet our participants where they are) by hosting it in the midst of midterm examinations or shortly before their interviews for formal leadership roles such as resident assistant, orientation leader, or peer advisor. As advantageous and important as the training might be, their minds are appropriately elsewhere—focusing on their studies or preparations for the interviews. Similarly, if the particular group with whom I am facilitating a leadership training is struggling with an internal trust matter and I plow straight through with the original training topic, I am doing everyone a disservice. This is *their* training. It would be most advantageous to focus on trust building—to meet them where they are—rather than whatever was previously thought as the most appropriate and essential theme.

Our third leadership learning partnership practice is to *mutually construct meaning with our participants.* It is often quite difficult, yet exceptional leadership educators relinquish control so that our participants can—individually and collectively—make sense of the leadership message and material. This collaborative coconstruction of meaning enables everyone to understand and internalize leadership learning—resulting

in the enhanced application and operationalization of leadership in practice. Again, much of this occurs when we shape our trainings around experiential learning activities and reflective dialogue. If we lean on lecturing, we are the ones who are constructing the meaning and then attempting to impart it to the minds of our participants. The subliminal expectation is for them to internalize *our* meaning and replicate it in their experiences. This is considered a banking approach to learning (Freire, 1970/2002).

Freire's (1970/2002) explanation of the banking approach to teaching and learning has relevance for our work in a training context. Here participants are treated as repositories of information to whom trainers and facilitators make deposits. Leadership trainings approached in this way not only severely limit the mutual construction of meaning, they often perpetuate oppressive, degrading, and dehumanizing actions (Mullen, 2009). Leadership educators need to be mindful of banking practices because of the structural and mechanical aspects of traditional leadership training practices that naturally establish and provoke deposits. Namely, when leadership educators position themselves as experts (those who are certain about their knowledge) and relegate participants as novices—we are making harmful deposits. When leadership educators solely lecture at participants—we are making limiting deposits. When leadership educators facilitate trainings without examining and engaging in purposeful identity work—we are making toxic deposits.

Reflective Dialogue

Woven into the fabric of experiential learning is reflection and dialogue. In the context of Kolb's (2015) experiential learning cycle, we guide our leadership training participants through strategically structured concrete experiences. These structured experiences provide the fodder for learning because they enable the training message to become accessible. The actual learning will not occur, though, until our participants have an opportunity to process and *internalize* their experiences through reflection and dialogue.

Experience alone is insufficient in experiential learning. It is the reflection and dialogue that transforms the experience into an educative one (Joplin, 1995). Reflective dialogue is the crux of the leadership learning experience. Without the reflective dialogue, the engaging and enjoyable experiential learning activities do not serve their intended purpose. They just become a form of entertainment. Experiential learning activities leverage their symbolism, metaphors, and lessons as opportunities for growth and behavior change far beyond the training bubble when complemented with reflective dialogue. Without the reflective dialogue, wisdom and insight garnered from the experience may lay dormant in our participant's subconscious. Processing the experience through a masterfully hosted reflective dialogue serves like a highlighter on this book's pages—it illuminates and calls attention to the most important elements of the training.

Leadership scholars Cameron Beatty and Kathy Guthrie (2021) articulate that "leadership development requires facilitation from educators and advisors to reinforce how knowledge gained from educational experiences and skills obtained from training are strengthened through reflection" (p. 86). They go on to share that it is this introspection that prompts participants to develop meaning around their experiences. This is due to the reflective experiences serving as a process for participants to gain clarity on their identities, on their identity as a leader, healthy leadership habits, and changes to their leadership practice.

Leadership educators host reflective dialogue immediately following every experiential learning activity. Reflective dialogue is a combination of reflection and intentional, empowering dialogue. It is this dyad of reflection and intentional, empowering dialogue that enables this learning experience to be transformative. *Reflective dialogue* is also commonly referred to as *processing, debriefing*, or *unpacking conversations*.

Reflection

Reflection is an integral element of leadership learning. The reflection component of a training is an intentional moment for participants to cognitively process and increase their understanding of the experience. Reflection offers space for participants to question the integrity of their deeply held assumptions and beliefs (Taylor, 2009). Through reflection, our participants make meaning of their experiences and reconsider their actions and beliefs (Volpe White et al., 2019). Often, reflection is perceived as touchy-feely, lacking rigor, too subjective, and unnecessary (Ash & Clayton, 2009).

Participants tend to want to move straight from the engaging and entertaining activities to more of the same or to magically apply their learning. Yet they don't realize that the secret sauce of leadership learning is the reflection.

To take our participants deeper in their leadership learning journey, we can engage in *critical* reflection. Julie Owen, (2016, 2020) a leadership scholar, expresses that critical reflection goes beyond thinking so that we can purposefully address issues connected to the nature and sources of power. In our reflective dialogue with participants, we should purposefully consider who really benefits and who is silenced; which actions result in real change versus only the appearance of change; and the systemic and institutionalized nature of oppression.

Ash and Clayton (2009) articulate that critical reflection is generative, deepening, and documentary. As a generative process, critical reflection engages our leadership training participants to articulate questions, confront biases, examine causality, connect theory to practice, and examine the interconnections and systems at play. As a deepening process, critical reflection encourages our participants to challenge simplistic conclusions, invite alternative perspectives, and ask "why" question iteratively. And critical reflection also documents learning by producing outcomes and new expressions of evaluation. As you can imagine, learning through critical reflection does not manifest automatically. It must be intentionally designed, carefully prepared, and masterfully facilitated.

Reflection can be facilitated in a variety of ways and via diverse mediums. A selection of these includes artwork, blogs and electronic postings, formal presentations, journaling, mind-mapping, multimedia, role play, service-learning, simulations, one-to-one or group engagements, vision boards, and traditional written reflections. In Volpe White et al.'s (2019) *Thinking to Transform: Reflection in Leadership Learning*, the authors present six categories for reflection methods. These include the contemplative, creative, digital, discussion, narrative, and written.

Contemplative reflection practices assist our leadership learning participants in focusing attention inward. These practices quiet our minds and cultivate our capacities for deep concentration and insight. They might be facilitated through mindfulness exercises, meditation, walking a labyrinth, intentional journaling, yoga, or deep listening.

Through the creation and interpretation of the arts, broadly, our participants partake in reflective practice. Creative expression encourages the juxtaposition of ideas, which spurs deep thinking and analysis.

Our digital engagements also provoke critical reflection. When we view controversial material within the digital landscape, we can be aroused into a critical reflective space. Leadership educators can utilize this as a strategic medium for leadership learning.

Discussion and dialogue promote reflection, as does narrative material. These storied sources prod us to reflect on what we perceive. Finally, writing serves as an important forum for reflection. When we write, we are able to harness our energy and attention toward what we put on paper.

Regardless of how it is facilitated, there are three foci of reflection: content, process, and premise (Mezirow, 1991). When reflecting on content, we invite our leadership training participants to reflect upon their thoughts and feelings, and about the material or theme of experiential learning activities. Process reflections hone in on perceptions of performance during the experiential learning activities. Premise reflections explore why we think and feel the way we do as well as why we believe we performed in a certain way during the experiential learning activities.

Exceptional leadership educators don't just haphazardly pose questions and call it reflection. No. We are deliberate and intentional. In the words of A. Kolb and Kolb (2017):

> Reflection requires space and time for it to take place. It can be inhibited by impulsive desires and/or pressures to take action. It can be enhanced by the practices of deliberately viewing things from a different perspective, and empathy. Stillness and quieting the mind foster deep reflection. (p. 129)

Dialogue

Dialogue is the other essential medium through which transformative leadership learning and meaning-making are fostered. It is this collective experience—the conversational back-and-forth—that enables our participants to interpret the meaning of their experiences, examine the validity of their prior understanding, and introduce changes to their practice. Dialogue, compared to debate and discussion, seeks understanding across difference grounded in personal storytelling and sharing, empathic listening, and interpersonal inquiry (Nagda & Maxwell, 2011). In dialogue, we seek an understanding of our own and others' perspectives along with an appreciation of our life experiences that inform those perspectives. Debate is an imposition of a singular perspective with no interest in understanding or appreciation. Discussion can be considered a combination of serial monologues—also void of sincere understanding or appreciation. Dialogue, though, affects and alters the trajectory of our becoming (Daloz Parks, 2000). Simply, some aspects of who we are remain undiscovered or hidden until we engage in purposeful dialogue with others.

Dialogue is infused into our leadership trainings as a partnering methodology with reflective observation. This is where the participants' experiences are reflected on, assumptions and beliefs are questioned, and habits of mind are ultimately transformed (Taylor, 2009). The type of dialogue we seek and facilitate is not approached as an analytical or point–counterpoint exercise. Rather, we emphasize healthy inquiry, relational engagement, collaborative communication, and the pursuit of new ways of leading—new ways of *being*.

Although the nature of this kind of dialogue is important for all leadership training participants, it is essential for developmentally younger ones. Daloz Parks (2000) suggests that young adults are particularly open to cultivating dialogue because of the way it honors one's growing curiosity about self and the world.

> When one speaks and then is heard—but not quite, and therefore tries to speak yet more clearly—and then listens to the other—and understands, but not quite, and listens again—one becomes actively engaged in sorting out what is true and dependable within oneself and about one's world. How one makes meaning is composed and recomposed in that process. (p. 142)

Dialogue is the dynamic interaction between speaking and listening. Otto Scharmer's theory U and his four fields of conversation (speaking) and listening are an important starting point. (More on these four fields can be found in chapter 9. More on theory U can be found in chapter 5.) When we open our minds, hearts, and wills and deepen our engagements with speaking and listening, in the words of Adam Kahane (2004):

> Every one of us gets to choose, in every encounter every day, which world we will contribute to bringing into reality. When we choose the closed way, we participate in creating a world filled with force and fear. When we choose an open way, we participate in creating another, better world. (p. 132)

This *open way* manifests when we purposefully practice healthy and engaging ways of speaking and listening. Kahane (2004) suggests certain practices. As leadership educators, during our leadership trainings—and beyond the training bubble—we create the conditions and hold fast to expectations of our participants where these practices are not simply espoused but enacted.

First, we need to invite ourselves and our participants to notice and pay attention to our state of being and how we practice speaking and listening. With this awareness, we should share authentically about what we are thinking, feeling, and wanting. We remember that our wisdom and insight is important—yet not more important than the wisdom and insight of others. We are all valued and valuable to each other's leadership learning and development.

During our dialogue, we each reflect on our role in the challenges we face and opportunities to overcome these obstacles. We listen with empathy. And we listen to more than just the words being spoken. We listen to what is attempting to be generated through our collective engagement in this conversation. We listen to the change yearning to emerge—spurred from this dialogue. "Listening moves us closer; it helps us become more whole, more healthy, more holy. Not listening creates fragmentation, and fragmentation is the root of all suffering" (Wheatley, 2007, p. 219).

We also purposefully pause. We stop talking. We relax, lean into the conversation, and engage with full presence. And when the dialogue is coming to a close, we make commitments for next steps and action plans. Then we go and do. We enable the dialogue to come to life through our actions.

Jack Mezirow (1991), a preeminent scholar of adult learning, suggests that in this type of discourse, under optimal conditions, our participants should be free from coercion and distorting self-perceptions. They should be open to alternative perspectives and encouraged to assess differences of opinion objectively. Each participant should have equal opportunities to share their voice—including challenging, questioning, refuting, and reflecting—while also welcoming others to do the same. When engaged in this way, in dialogue,

> I create a space inside myself where I can hear you, where I can feel what you are saying. I create a space inside myself where I can hear myself, where I can listen to and feel my own reactions to what you say . . . dialogue is essentially an attitude. It is a radically different attitude toward oneself, toward others, toward knowledge and problems. (Zohar, 1997, pp. 142, 144)

Reflective dialogue includes both the internal exploration and the external conversation between participants. This type of leadership learning is near impossible without reflective dialogue. We devise experiential learning activities to serve as a vehicle to engage participants in purposeful, reflective conversation. The activities themselves serve as a window into our participants' personal beliefs, underlying philosophies, and rationale for their actions.

As leadership educators, we utilize reflective dialogue as a tool for participants to uncover their personal beliefs, underlying philosophies, and rationale for their actions. This is the opportunity in the training to suss out what may not have been observed by the participants and to illuminate these hidden interpretations. Furthermore, reflective dialogue assists participants in applying the learning from the experiential activities to their contexts beyond the training.

Tactically, as leadership educators, our work, with regard to reflective dialogue, is in three domains: observation, posing questions, and assisting participants in applying their learning.

Before facilitating reflective dialogue, we need to observe the experiential learning activities and actions of the participants. While facilitating, we have a keen eye on who is participating—and who is not; what is being said—and what is not; what are the perceived or actual attitudes, feelings, and vibes in the space; and how each individual is contributing to the goal—or not.

Once the activity has come to a close, we utilize our observations to pose questions, mindfully, that encourage the participants to critically reflect upon their actions and opportunities for leadership learning. Once the questions are posed, we step back and allow the participants to respond and drive the direction of the conversation.

The conclusory practice of hosting this reflective dialogue is to engage participants in ruminating on the ways they can practically apply their learning to life beyond the training. This application component of the reflective dialogue is indispensable. Unless participants can translate their learning into leadership practices, the experiential learning activity and reflective dialogue's value is limited.

Conclusion

Leadership educators who desire impacts will craft learning experiences that engage learners in activities that help them discover the learning and retain it through practice. They will be comfortable with asking questions rather than always offering an answer, knowing learners have the resources to almost always find those answers. They will plan lots of practice to ensure the skills are developed and remembered. They will avoid the typical presentation in favor of activities. . . . It's all about retrieval—learners need to play with the content, wrestle with it, try it (Halls, 2019, p. 26).

Extraordinary leadership educators facilitate leadership learning experiences that enable participants to see themselves and their actions in new ways. During our training experiences, the focus should be less on what I do as a facilitator and more on the learning opportunities for our participants. We should relentlessly be pondering about what the participants are engaging in—and how they are processing that experiential engagement—to cultivate new knowledge and to enhance their skills.

We do this by facilitating experiential learning in tandem with reflective dialogue. This combination enables participants to enthusiastically engage in a hands-on learning experience where they can critically reflect and dialogue about adaptations to their leadership practice. This method encourages participants to *access* the training message and material and then *internalize* their leadership learning. From there, they can *apply* and infuse healthy leadership habits into their practice.

CHAPTER 12

Creating a "Training Story"

As LEADERSHIP EDUCATORS, OUR objective is to transport our participants to a different mental space than what they experience in their day-to-day lives. In our normal operations, rarely do we create opportunities to reflect upon and tactically enhance our leadership practice. This is why and how our leadership trainings serve as the gateway for leadership development. Powerful, effective leadership educators frame trainings as stories to amplify the impact of our participants' leadership learning.

Effective leadership educators author engaging, dynamic, and potent training stories that captivate our audience—the participants. It is critical that we craft a cohesive and resonant story so that our participants feel a connection to it and, at the conclusion, are moved by it such that they enact change beyond the training bubble. Like all stories, our leadership training story has an important flow and essential elements.

Based upon my years of experience facilitating leadership trainings and developmental experiences, I've crafted a training story methodology based upon the German playwright Gustav Freytag's dramatic structure. This is Leadership Trainer's Narrative Approach to facilitating leadership trainings. Freytag recognized the dramatic elements (i.e., exposition, rising action, apex, falling action, and resolution) as the building blocks of a narrative structure. These elements can be visually depicted as a pyramid diagram, hence the name *Freytag's Pyramid* (Harun et al., 2013). Freytag's pyramid is widely applied to all narrative forms, and found to characterize most successful fiction (Rolfe et al., 2010). Leadership educators can utilize this narrative structure to serve as a grounded framework for our training experience—our training stories.

Just like in theater and literature, our training story has an exposition, rising action, apex, falling action, and resolution. The *exposition* sets the tone for the whole training experience as our welcoming to the engagement. The *rising action* gathers the participant's energy and attention by providing an overview of the training theme and hinting at what's to come. The *apex* is the pinnacle of the leadership training experience. Here we immerse our participants in the hands-on experiential learning activities. This is immediately—and always—followed by the *falling action*. In the context of leadership trainings, this is when we host a reflective dialogue. Following the reflective dialogue, we have the *resolution*. Finally, we bring all the learning together and clarify the opportunities for implementation. See Figure 12.1 for a visual of Leadership Trainer's Narrative Approach for crafting a training story.

Exposition

The *exposition* of a story refers to the formal opening. As leadership educators, this relates to setting the tone for the training experience, introducing the characters, and laying the foundation for the rest of our training story. Our exposition needs to be compelling. This is the first taste for our participants. If our participants are engaged and intrigued, they will release inhibitions, reduce fear, and acknowledge this training experience as an opportunity for learning

Figure 12.1. Leadership Trainer's Narrative Approach.

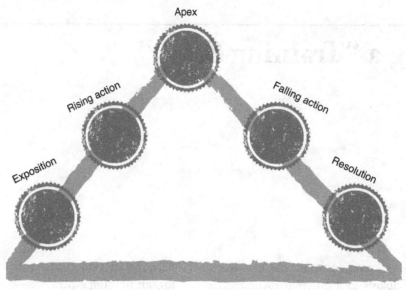

Note. Reprinted with permission.

and development. If not, we can assume they will be standoffish, fearful, questioning, checked out, and/or doubtful that this training will provide them with the leadership learning and development they are yearning for.

The word *welcome* comes from a combination of two Old English words—*willa* meaning "pleasure" and *cuma* meaning "guest." Together, they are understood to mean "to pleasure guests." We create a pleasing environment and pleasurable opening as a way to engage and entice the attention of our participants. Tangibly, there are five elements that create a pleasant and engaging welcoming: (a) We prepare ourselves mentally, emotionally, tactically, and physically for the training experience; (b) we prepare the physical environment and ensure it is organized and situated fittingly well in advance of participants' arrival; (c) we verbalize their entry into the training space and offer a welcoming gesture; (d) we offer a start warning so as to prepare participants for the impending formal launch of the training; and (e) then we begin.

Preparations

Exceptional leadership educators never just *show up* and, poof, they are ready to go. We have work to do well before the clock strikes and it's *go time*. Long before any training begins, we need to go on a reconnaissance mission. We collect data on the participants' interests and desires so we can craft a training experience that meets their needs and can be

translated from the training to their real-life leadership practice.

The reconnaissance mission is focused on assessing the training needs of our participants. Basic and core considerations for this investigation include the following:

- Who are our participants? (What are their descriptive features—age range, gender, and other identities? What are their professional or leadership roles, nature of their work, rationale for participating, and relationships to one another?)
- How many participants are expected?
- What is the participants' level of familiarity with this training topic or theme—and what are their attitudes toward the training and training theme?
- If this is a compulsory training experience, what are the desires, expectations, and intended outcomes of the coordinating, supervising, or mandating force?
- Where is the training space, and what are the environmental dynamics for that space? What are the technological considerations? (This is often an opportunity for leadership educators to clarify—possibly dictate—what type of space would be optimal and what might be needed for experiential learning activities, reflective dialogue, and technology use.)

We conduct this assessment because a training intervention may not actually address the developmental concerns being raised. Or, our particular knowledge, skills, and interests may not actually be a good fit for what is desired and expected. There is no greater waste of time for leadership educators than to facilitate trainings that are ultimately not needed. There is no greater waste of time for participants than to sit through a training led by an ill-equipped and poorly prepared facilitator.

Once we have confidence that we're an incredible match and our plan will meets participants' expectations, we need to diligently prepare for it—and then practice. The master trainer, Jonathan Halls (2019) shares his reflections.

> In my experience working with trainers across the globe, most folks agree that practice is important. But I see many pay lip service to this simple truth rather than incorporating it into their work. How? I see half-day training sessions with two and a half hours' worth of PowerPoint slides. I see learning plans for one-day workshops with 10 learning objectives, which are impossible to deliver unless they are being presented and not practiced. I've lost track of how many training sessions I've seen that are little more than a performance by the trainer, where learners listen and watch but don't engage in practice. The notion that training is a delivery of information is so entrenched. . . around the world [they] are little more than information dumps. (pp. 15–16)

As part of our preparations, we focus inwardly so we can be our best selves when it comes time for the training experience. We set our intention for the training experience and our facilitation of it. We can ask a series of overarching questions to focus our attention: How do I want to show up to this training experience? How do I want to engage and interact with the participants? How can I best serve these participants? What do I hope to accomplish through this training experience? Once our intention is set, our personal preparation happens in multiple domains: emotionally, mentally, physically, and tactically.

Emotionally, we ensure that we are fully present and focused on this particular training and these particular participants. *Mentally*, we have a deep knowledge of the training theme, learning outcomes, and material. We have thought through potential obstacles, questions, and concerns that might be raised by the participants. *Physically*, we are well fed and hydrated and dressed appropriately for the audience and experience. Tactically, we have confidence in the flow of the training. We have included engaging experiential learning activities and reflective dialogue in our training—and we have confidence in our ability to facilitate and host them for optimal leadership learning.

Environmental Preparations

Once we are feeling personally settled, the training environment needs to be prepared. We arrive early so that we can dedicate time and energy to establishing the space as a leadership learning laboratory—one in which participants feel safe, courageous, and able to experiment within the leadership learning experience. We center our attention around what design and structure will enable our participants to learn best. Here we have two primary considerations: engagement and safety.

For engagement, we want to consider what design and structure of the training environment will enable our participants to be fully immersed in the experience, contributory, and prepared to learn best. For safety, we want to consider what design and structure of the training environment will enable our participants to feel at home, secure in their contributions, and emotionally empowered.

Our trainings may incorporate technology (e.g., slide decks projected onto a screen), physical activities, varying types of dialogue opportunities, space for meals, and many other components. All of this should be organized prior to the first participant arriving. There are few things more unsettling—for leadership educators and our participants—than to be setting up and preparing the space when participants arrive. I always aim to be completely set up and ready to go at least 30 minutes in advance of the official start time. This gives me plenty of time to navigate unforeseen circumstances and adapt to unexpected changes, use the facilities, refocus on my personal preparation after the space is prepared, and greet the participants when they arrive.

As part of our preparations, it is important to have several experiential learning activities planned that can be utilized in various space configurations and with various technological or equipment needs—all of which align with the training vision and theme. Even with the most meticulous plans and ideal physical environments, we need to be prepared for spur-of-the-moment changes.

Opening the Training

Ideally, participants enter our trainings feeling calm, secure, relaxed, open to learning, and ready to apply their new ideas and skills to their leadership practice. Many do. However, it is wise to assume that a number of participants will not—they will be anxious about participating. These hesitancies are often rooted in nervousness that they might be called on to speak in front of others, worried about not measuring up to the other participants, concerned that work is piling up while they are at the training, or cautious about why they were sent—possibly forced or "voluntold"—to attend the training. They may wonder if their participation is a reward or a punishment (Bolton & Bolton, 2016).

Instead of entering the training with an open-minded approach to their leadership learning, Bolton and Bolton (2016) offer that many participants feel guarded. Their cautiousness is often felt and on display until the training experience provides them with positive answers to one or more of three crucial, yet usually unspoken questions: Will I be safe—not be put on the spot or otherwise made vulnerable? Will it be worthwhile—something I can really use? Will it be reasonably engaging—or will I be bored?

When our participants feel unsure of the answers to these questions, they tend to be closed to learning. Their defensiveness is often expressed by being uninvolved and emotionally distant, forming exclusive—sometimes resistant—subgroups, and explicitly questioning the applicability of what is being taught. When we do not purposefully defuse these anxieties, the resulting defensive behavior can transform what was meant to be a positive learning experience to a nightmarish experience for leadership educators and participants alike (Bolton & Bolton, 2016).

These first moments of the training are particularly important for leadership educators. Often, participants will provide a grace period where overt hostility and antagonism will be on pause. There is a veneer of politeness, watchfulness, and reserve as participants decide their feelings about the training, how they want to show up, and the ways they will engage with us and the other participants (Silberman & Biech, 2015).

Tactically, we can defuse participant nervousness and hesitancy by focusing on a five-pronged opening process: (a) welcome participants, (b) offer a "start warning," (c) invite introductions, (d) explore learning outcomes and community agreements, and (e) host initial Q's and A's.

We know that our participants—like all of us—want to be seen and valued. They want to be acknowledged for dedicating time, energy, and (potentially) resources to this training experience. As participants arrive, we express our gratitude and recognize them for being with us for this training opportunity. If appropriate, we might offer a physical gesture. The four "H's of acknowledgment" include a hello, handshake, high-five, or a hug. Or we might engage these participants with small talk. It is suggested to have a few go-to questions to build rapport (Oberstein, 2020). These might be connected to the training experience: Why did you sign up for this training, or What are you most looking forward to about this training? To build rapport, we might also ask questions that are more personal in nature: Where are you coming from? What is the best restaurant in this neighborhood for lunch or dinner? What was—or what will be—your weekend highlight?

This allows them to be seen, recognized, confirm they are in the right place, and loosen possible tensions that may exist.

As our participants are entering, we offer a prestart warning—maybe 2 minutes or 5 minutes before the program is about to begin. This encourages participants to find a seat, reduce chatter, and set their intention for the training. It is also confers to them that you are serious about this experience and paying attention to facilitating a rewarding experience.

Once the stated warning time has been reached, we begin the training. If someone else is providing a formal opening and introduction, we should request they add a statement to indicate why *you*, of all the possible leadership educators, were selected to provide this particular training—and why they are excited about it. These introductory statements, even more than reading one's biographical information (which often feels very scripted), are intended to generate enthusiasm and buy-in from the participants. It gives a personal touch to the introduction and shares with the participants that you were personally selected for very specific reasons rather than your name chosen off a random list.

When it is our turn to offer the opening to the training, it should be clear and robust. With this training launch, we convince participants that this is the right place for them to be—especially with all of the other competing factors in their lives. We should begin with an introduction of ourselves as leadership educators. This includes our professional background and expertise on the subject matter, elements of our biography that have resonance with our participants, and our delight in facilitating *this* leadership learning opportunity. We then provide an introduction to the training—including the theme or topic and a general plan for the training.

This is also an appropriate time to offer a land acknowledgment. Land acknowledgments are formal statements of recognition and respect. Indigenous Peoples' land—on which the vast majority of us now reside and work—was stolen and colonized—and continues to be. Although land acknowledgments may feel and sound different depending on the training context and facilitator, we express them as a way to raise awareness for and honor the traditional stewards of the training site. Native Land provides a tremendous resource to assist us in finding information on the ancestral homes of where we live and work (https://native-land.ca).

Here I provide a sample land acknowledgment that I utilize when facilitating a virtual training from my home. Of course, after verbalizing this message and having the words on my screen, I create a purposeful pause for a moment of reflection. This should not be rushed. Otherwise, it feels insincere. I also invite participants, if they feel comfortable, to share a personally meaningful land acknowledgment for their locale:

> We acknowledge that the land each of us live on and is nourished by is the traditional, ancestral, and unceded homelands of Indigenous and tribal nations. For over 500 years, in what we understand as North America, systems of oppression have dispossessed Indigenous people of their lands and livelihoods. We take a moment, now, to honor these individuals, communities, and nations. I reside in the Roslindale neighborhood of Boston, Massachusetts, on the original homelands of the *Massa-adchu-es-et* and *Paw-tuck-et* tribal communities.

As part of the introductions, we want to create an opening for participants to introduce themselves. This is designed and structured as a way for the folks in the room to learn names and draw connections among the participants. If the group is small enough, the whole collection can offer their introductions. If the audience is too large for that, participants can share brief statements with neighbors or in small groups.

A note about icebreakers. Icebreakers and name games can derail a training before it actually gets started.

This is because they are often facilitated in ways that make participants feel incredibly uncomfortable or completely miss the objective of drawing connections across participants. Ice breakers should be facilitated with intentionality and should be designed to initiate connections of meaning and depth. For example, when we have to memorize 13 things about someone else—and then share them with the group—the focus is on memorization and sharing these 13 things correctly. In this scenario, our participants are not focused on learning anything substantial about their partner, nor are they focused on listening to other participants share about their partners.

My favorite ice breaker is called Shoe Stories. With Shoe Stories, participants are provided the choice of sharing one thing that feels comfortable and has resonance for them. They can share something about their shoes from the past—either literally or metaphorically—or something in the future—either literally or metaphorically. What makes this a wonderful ice breaker is that it gives participants choice and flexibility. They get to decide how they want to show up and share. They are choosing for themselves what they want to offer to the training community—rather than memorize other people's stuff. Shoe Stories also enables participants to focus on a singular detail per person. This opens opportunities to draw connections across participants. I often share that my shoes have been to Nicaragua (past, literal) or are going to transform the landscape of leadership training and development (future, metaphorical). If someone else in the training community has been to or is going to Nicaragua, there is a connection point that we can leverage to deepen our relationship. These connections—especially among participants—help them feel at ease as they formally enter into the training experience. A free downloadable resource of 90 icebreaker questions for connections of meaning and depth can be found at the Leadership Trainer website (https://leadershiptrainer.org/ice-breaker-questions).

Following the introductions, it is essential to offer the learning objectives and community agreements—affectionately known as LOCA. We offer our learning objectives to make it clear what we hope our participants will be able to access, internalize, and apply to their own leadership practice. These are utilized to ensure for our participants that the training has been thoroughly thought through. It also provides a mental agenda to assist our participants in understanding where in the training we're at, at any particular time during the training experience. Our learning objectives should be written and shared in a style that is easy to understand, direct, and connected to specific actions that can be evaluated (Silberman & Biech, 2015). Using jargon, acronyms, or terms that can be misinterpreted should be avoided. Finally, our learning objectives should be a narrow list. This is for two core reasons. First, a long list of outcomes can be overwhelming and cause our participants to become disengaged about how extensive this training experience is going to be. Second, we want our trainings to focus on a particular theme or topic. By crafting narrow learning objectives we can stay focused on just the essential elements of that training topic. Otherwise, we might become distracted by trying to incorporate too much into any one training experience. For our participants to *access* that training message and material, *internalize* leadership learning, and *apply* that learning to their practice, our learning objectives need to be narrow and focused.

Our community agreements are intended to be group-designed-and-agreed-upon behavioral expectations. There are often referred to as *expectations* or *ground rules*. Leadership educators will have a selection of ideas in mind to begin the exercise and include expectations that were not offered by the training community. These might include respectful and honest communication, confidentiality, participatory engagement, asking questions, using "I" statements, and starting/ending on time.

Most importantly, though, we also want to give power and authority to the group so that participants themselves can begin to cocreate the training experience. This is also an opportunity to set a tone around participant involvement and engagement before the experiential learning activities and reflective dialogue. Before moving on, the training community will need to acknowledge their agreement with a simple head nod, verbal statement, or signature on a cocreated list. As the training gets underway, we can reference these if we believe the training community is not abiding by them. Although we are the facilitators of the training experience, the group should be invited to collectively hold one anther accountable for monitoring and enforcing the community agreements.

Before moving into the rising action of our training story, we welcome questions from participants. But *Q's and A's*, in this context, are really about leadership educators asking participants questions about how they are feeling and getting an acknowledgment from our participants that they are ready to proceed. We utilize this information to best prepare ourselves and participants for success in what's to come. For example, if the energy is quite low, we might infuse an activity into the experience to get participants moving around. Or if there is a sense that we need time to use the facilities, we take that time so participants can be fully engaged for a deeper exploration into the theme of the training. Figure 12.2 details the core features of the Exposition of the training story.

Figure 12.2. Exposition of Leadership Trainer's Narrative Approach, highlighting key features.

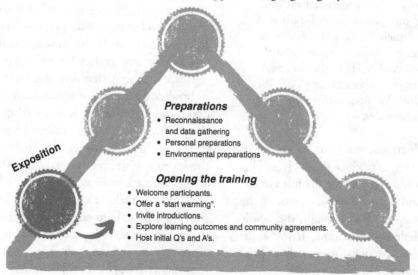

Note. Reprinted with permission.

Rising Action

Our leadership training participants, it can be assumed, want to make a change or an enhancement to their current leadership practice. The conflict is that their current skill set or competencies are insufficient. Our task, before the training experience concludes, is to assist them in illuminating their growth area(s) and either draft action plans or, at a minimum, strategically think through ways to enhance their skills and capacities once they are beyond the training bubble. The *rising action* makes clear what the conflict (i.e., theme or topic of the training) is as well as how we will navigate through this challenge (i.e., utilizing experiential learning and reflective dialogue) to resolution.

The rising action, of the entire training, is the most conventional of the leadership learning experience. This is when we leverage our expertise and briefly offer to participants our wisdom and knowledge. Structurally, this is the part of the training where participants are situated in a state of prolonged passive learning. Because we know that learning is not best received from lecturing, we want to be concise and offer just the essential information. This typically involves the data from the field to bolster interest and provide a grounded foundation for what we offer. For example, if our training theme is "compassion in leadership," we'll use this time—the rising action—to indicate the financial strain organizations face due to aggressive and ill-tempered managers. We can also share insight about the personal benefits and positive implications of practicing compassion as part of their leadership regimen. It is this information that builds a foundation while also establishing credibility for both ourselves and the topic.

If we are facilitating a training with layers of information, we want to scaffold the learning. This is also understood as *chunking* the content. Essentially, we want to reduce the complexity of the training material to bite-size messages. This enables our participants to process the information and utilize that new knowledge as they move forward to continue their learning. Often with each chunk, we facilitate an experiential learning activity or another engagement tool to assist our participants in grappling with the content in a hands-on fashion. Once they've demonstrated comprehension—usually through the reflective dialogue—we can move on to the next chunk.

Delivering a Training Message

When delivering our training message, our preparations focus exclusively on the question, What do the participants *need* to know about this training topic? In other words, we've focused our energy on narrowing all the things we could share to just the essentials. We want to be brief. Our particpants *need* us to be brief. When delivering the training message, we want it to be sharp, to the point, and relevant to the lives of the participants.

Our training message should be *sharp*. We want our training message to have an edge. (As I like to quip, *if we are not living on the edge, we're taking up too much space!*) Leadership themes and topics can be generic. Communication, for example, is, well, highly communicated as a leadership training topic. It is so broad and popular. We want to differentiate our training from others by providing a message that is novel and exciting for our participants. The topic isn't going to change. Our message and delivery of it is what makes it edgy. We offer a new way to explore the topic, ask provocative questions about the theme, and share data that are sexy and intriguing. This is how we get our participants engaged—rather than participating in just another communication training.

For some examples, depending on the audience and context, I might use a song for the group to listen to or a movie clip to watch as an entry point as we explore the topic, rather than the traditional approach of just me, as the facilitator, offering my reflections about healthy communication habits. Alternatively, I might share a personal story—or better yet, ask participants to think back on a time when they were poor communicators. By inviting a selection of participants to share their stories, both serious and comical ones—before asking the whole participant body to offer reflections on what they heard about poor communication behaviors—we center the training experience in the lives, wisdom, and insight of our participants while preparing them for immersive, participatory engagement with the material in the soon-to-be facilitated experiential learning activity.

We can also use data to make a bland or overdone topic both sexy and intriguing. To continue with this communication example, I might use data from Project Worldwide's 2019 study of 471 survey respondents. They found that 74% of people have stopped dealing with a company and moved to a competitor due to feeling the company was disorganized, 92% have had to repeat a piece of information to two or more people within an organization, 85% find it annoying to have to repeat information when working with other organizations, 96% think the organizations they deal with could improve when it comes to communication, and even though 89% believe that effective communication is extremely important, 80% of the respondents rate their own organizations' communication as either average or poor (Project Worldwide, 2020). These data highlight intriguing information about communication that can be packaged and offered to our participants to spur dialogue and spice up our training experiences.

Our training message should be *concise*. We don't want to ramble. Learning happens best when we are immersed in the learning experience. Listening to a lecture or presentation, no matter how spectacular the leadership educator is, is not immersive. We want to share what they need to know as a precursor—and opening act—before doing the headline performance of the experiential learning activities and reflective dialogue.

Finally, we meet our participants where they are by ensuring our training message has *relevancy* to our participants. We utilize data and stories and experiences that have resonance with *these* particular participants. The theme, in general, and the examples utilized during our rising action should be directly connected to the work and life experiences of our participants. This resonance enhances the opportunities for participants to be engaged. The greater their engagement with the training material, the more likely they will be to *access* it, *internalize* the learning, and then *apply* the learning to their leadership practice.

Regarding technical delivery, Bolton and Bolton's (2016) pointers will ensure the message lands as intended. *First, we establish a home base.* This is where we stand and can have control over the room. From our home base, we can see and engage with the whole lot of participants—and they can see and engage with us. In this position, if we are using a screen for slides, video, or other resources, our positioning will not block participants from seeing it. And from our home base, we have the training materials easily accessible. This way, we are not trying to sprint to the other side of the room to get worksheets or an experiential learning prop. Additionally, our materials should be arranged and organized based upon when their use will be needed. When we do move away

from our home base, which can be a powerful engagement tactic when implemented purposefully, we're not meandering without purpose through the audience or dashing from one side of the room to the other. We do it strategically—and then return to our home base.

Second, we use healthy body language. This includes the utilization of relaxed power postures to indicate our expertise and skill. When our bodies are feeling loose yet engaged, our minds respond in positive ways. When we are physically tense, that tension is where our minds revert to. We also incorporate hand and facial gestures to exaggerate the most important points and engage participants. We want to emphasize, authentically, our expressions. This proves to our participants that we are listening intently to them. It also allows participants further away to get a sense of what is going on even if they are not close enough to fully hear the exchange. With this in mind, we always repeat questions before answering them and, if there is even the slightest concern, we ask the participants if they heard the participant comments or want them repeated. Eye contact is essential. When we utilize eye contact effectively our participants feel deeply connected and valued. They feel seen, literally and figuratively.

The third tactic is to bring the energy. When we are authentically excited and energized about the content, the participants are invited to be as well. This should be genuine and natural; otherwise it is easily identified as fake and forced.

A fourth tactic is to involve participants. The next segment of the training—the experiential learning activities and reflective dialogue—will surely involve them. Yet there is no reason why they shouldn't be involved in the rising action. When we include participants through the use of strategic questioning and dialogue, they are much more likely to be engaged and present during this portion of the training experience and for what is to come. We can elucidate stories from their own experiences to center the training in their relevancy. This also heightens the excitement when they share examples of leaders who lack compassion or communicate poorly. Their responses and stories are also incredibly beneficial for us. As we move through the training, we can refer back to them to highlight how the new leadership practices that they are experimenting with and (hopefully) acquiring for their own healthy leadership habits are major shifts from the faulty examples shared during the rising action. These two practices of strategic questioning and inviting participant stories also reinforces our acknowledgment of the varying levels of chunked material that we have included in this section of the training. With each chunk, we can pause, engage, assess, and then move forward—or, if needed, revisit the concept to ensure participants have access to the message.

If we are going to use PowerPoint or another design presentation software—Canva (my preference), Prezi, Google Slides, or others—we want our slides to support us, rather than becoming the main attraction. Often, the presentation becomes a crutch that leadership educators lean on to help them get through the training. When this happens, participants are quick to notice and often perceive the leadership educator as ill-prepared and/or not knowledgeable about the training topic or the flow of their own training.

Our slides should be reference points for us. Visibly, they should have graphics or images. Words should be kept to a minimum—just the key points—and typed in large, bold fonts. Excessive text limits the impact of the presentation and causes us to rely too heavily on trying to read and reiterate what is there. When the slides are designed well, participants are better able to focus on the message we are delivering. This makes the experience more memorable and leadership learning more accessible. Figure 12.3 details the core features

of the Rising Action of Leadership Trainer's Narrative Approach.

Apex

The *apex* is the turning point of the leadership training story. It is the peak of the training experience. This is the most physically and emotionally intense portion of the training because our participants are provided immersive, hands-on opportunities to explore and experiment with the training theme. This is when we relinquish control and give ownership of the training experience to our participants. Here we facilitate experiential learning activities with creativity and dynamism so that our participants can maximize their leadership learning opportunities. By doing so, we create the conditions for the internalization of leadership learning—and then the application of it into their leadership practice. As Silberman and Biech (2015) suggest, experiential learning not only enhances understanding of concepts, it is the gateway to skill development.

There are two general types of experiential learning activities: *physically engaged* activities and *reflective exercises*. With both styles of experiential learning, our activities should have an objective, method, and

Figure 12.3. Rising action of Leadership Trainer's Narrative Approach, highlighting key features.

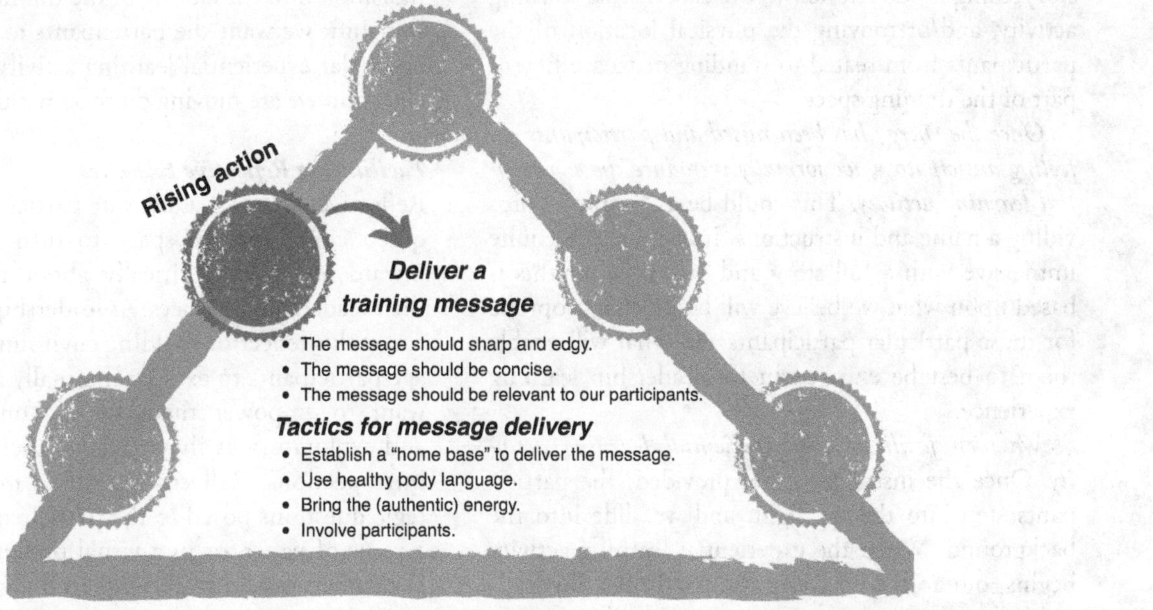

format (Silberman & Biech, 2015). The objective is the goal—what is to be accomplished by the participants. The method expresses what the participants need to do to accomplish the goal. And the format is the structure of the experience and environmental considerations for the activity.

Facilitating Physically Engaged Activities

Physically engaged activities do not necessarily mean rigorous military-style boot-camp training—although it could depend on the theme, context, and participants. Physically engaged activities include those experiential learning opportunities that involve some semblance of bodily movement. Here we want participants moving and doing something to navigate a challenge or accomplish a task—either individually or in a group. Our hope is to physically immerse them into an experience where they can experiment with the leadership concept. There are five general processes for facilitating physically engaged experiential learning activities:

We raise the energy of the participants. Physically engaged experiential learning activities typically follow a conventional learning (lecture)-style presentation during the rising action—when we present the leadership theme or topic for the training. We want to raise the participants' energy so it matches the level of investment needed for the experiential learning activity. We can do this by increasing our own level of engagement and energy, shifting into a fantasy or storytelling mode relevant to the experiential learning activity, and/or moving the physical location of the participants from seated to standing or to a different part of the training space.

Once the energy has been raised and participants are feeling anticipatory, we formally introduce the experiential learning activity. This could be as simple as providing a name and instructions. It could also be quite immersive with a full story and props. All of this is based upon what we believe will be most appropriate for those particular participants and what will enable them to best be engaged in the leadership learning experience.

We then facilitate the experiential learning activity. Once the instructions are provided, the participants step into the spotlight, and we slide into the background. When the experiential learning activity begins, our role is to create the conditions for leadership learning and to ensure safety. Ideally, once we

offer the instructions, the participants will be fully engaged and immersed in the experience. We are too. This is not a moment for us to check out. Our role shifts to that of monitoring progress, serving as gatekeeper, asking questions, offering strategic commentary, shifting rules, and tracking time. Besides that, we allow and encourage the participants to fend for themselves as they navigate the experiential learning activity toward goal accomplishment. During the activity, we are also observing the actions and comments of the participants so we can lead an informed reflective dialogue following the experiential learning activity. Furthermore, we ensure physical and emotional safety. If need be, we remove participants or end the activity entirely if we believe it could be harmful to one or more participants.

We bring the group back together once the experiential learning activity has come to a close. This is when we slide into the reflective dialogue (falling action) to process the experience. Here we want to capitalize on the energy so that a rich and fulfilling reflective dialogue can take place. In bringing the participants back together, we could form a circle (sitting or standing) or return to their seats. Generally, we want to use this opportunity to shift from the experience itself to the reflective dialogue where we can unpack what happened.

Once the reflective dialogue has been facilitated, we seamlessly shift to the next part of the training. This could be to another experiential learning activity or transition into the closing of the training. As we make this shift, we want the participants to know that this particular experiential learning activity has come to a close and we are moving on to something new.

Facilitating Reflective Exercises

Reflective exercises allow our participants to have a quiet, contemplative space to turn their attention inward and think critically about themselves and their leadership practices. As leadership educators, we create this reflection-holding environment to encourage participants to explore internally and deeply. We want to empower them to be honest, authentic, and exploratory as they navigate their thoughts and introspections. Reflective exercises manifest as strategic questions posed to the participants verbally, on a piece of paper, or in a visual presentation (slides). Reflective exercises are also arranged as worksheet activities or journaling exercises. They can be more physical in nature and include going on a stroll, walking a labyrinth, or meditating on a particular topic. As the facilitator of this experience, we provide the questions or prompts as well as the guidelines and instructions so that explicit exercise boundaries can help engage and focus the participants. In order to effectively facilitate reflective exercises, we need to ensure the conditions and process are designed for the reflective journey.

We begin by settling the energy. In order for participants to effectively engage in reflective work, there needs to be a sense of calm and quiet. With reflective exercises, we are creating a moment for our participants to purposefully pause. To do this, we can facilitate a brief breathing exercise or pose a reflective question whereby the participants are instructed to draft a response on a notecard or Post-It note. These energy-settling activities promote enhanced calm and stillness in both our participants' bodies and minds.

Once the energy is settled, we formally introduce the reflective exercise, using clear, calming language. Here we share expectations for the activity and any guidelines (e.g., write in a journal, take a stroll, utilize a particular worksheet) as well as the time allotted for the reflections. It should also be plainly expressed whether participants will be keeping their reflections to themselves or sharing them with small groups or large groups—as this will impact how they proceed with their reflections.

As the reflective exercise unfolds, we provide ample time and space for reflecting. Due to the quiet in the room, we often feel like we need to do something or say something. Don't. After delivering the instructions and expectations, let it be. We are most effective when we provide the participants ample time and space to engage in the reflective inquiry. Note that it may take some time for participants to get into a reflective rhythm. This is often the most difficult time for facilitators because of the silence in the training space. Welcome the silence. Allow participants to dig deeply into their reflections. This does not mean that we check out. Rather, we utilize this time to review the next phase of the training as well as to stay present to the needs of the participants while they engage in their reflective exercise. Leadership educators can engage in one-to-one conversations with participants to assist them in digging deeper into their reflections or just by strolling around the room to hint to the participants we are available and engaged. Of course, we don't want

the participants to feel suffocated or distracted by our presence so we need to balance our engagement with the perceived needs of the participants. Additionally, if we are not engaging in the reflective exercise along with our participants in this moment, we should have personally engaged in it prior to the training so we can contribute to the forthcoming reflective dialogue by sharing our own reflections.

When the appropriate amount of time has elapsed, we bring the group back together. We gently remind them that the time during the training has closed for the reflective experiential learning activity. Of course, we encourage them to continue their reflections on their own accord during another appropriate segment of the training or following the training.

Once the reflective dialogue has been facilitated, we seamlessly shift to the next part of the training. This could be to another experiential learning activity or a transition into the closing of the training. As we make this shift, we want the participants to know that this particular experiential learning activity has come to a close and we are moving on to something new.

Regardless of the nature of the experiential learning activities—physically engaged or reflective—there are six core preparatory questions for us to consider. These questions ensure the experiential learning activities will be relevant and fruitful for our participants. We begin by asking, *Do the activities align with the outcomes of the training experience?* If it does not, we should not be facilitating it. Everything about the training experience, especially the experiential learning activities, should be integrated as a way to the learning outcomes and unified as a way to realize the learning outcomes.

Next, we consider the knowledge base and skill set of our participants. *Are the experiential learning activities healthy challenges for our participants?* If they are considered too easy a challenge, participants will be bored, and their focus of attention will wane. If the activities are too challenging, participants will get frustrated or angry—limiting their ability to learn due to attachment to these limiting emotions. To answer this question, it is imperative we have a solid understanding of our participants. We do this as part of our preparations.

In addition to reconnaissance about the participants, we also want to scout details about the training space. *Is the training space conducive for these experiential learning activities?* A surefire way to derail a training experience is to try to incorporate experiential learning activities into a training environment that is not fitting. If we are facilitating physically engaged activities, participants need space to move around and get fully immersed. If it is a reflective activity, participants need a quiet and comfortable space to support their reflections. The design of the training space matters significantly.

The fourth question we consider when planning experiential learning activities asks, *How much time will the experiential learning activities take?* The experiential learning activities should fit seamlessly into the training program. When considering the time, we also want to reserve enough time for the reflective dialogue, not just participating in the experiential learning activities. Of course, having backup plans for experiential learning activities to add or which ones to remove is important.

We also want to ensure the experiential learning activities are well suited for the size of the group. We ask, *Are these experiential learning activities aligned—or have I structured these experiential learning activities— for the size of participant body?* Sometimes, we have an amazing idea for an experiential learning activity that only works with a large group of participants. If our training only includes a dozen participants, we'll need to reserve that amazing experiential learning activity idea for another training. The reverse is also true. Some activities only work with smaller group sizes.

When this occurs, we do have the flexibility to break the entire participant body into smaller units, but that takes some strategizing to ensure it is deployed and facilitated appropriately.

The last question we ask is internal—about our preparations. *Have I practiced facilitating these experiential learning activities—and the follow-up reflective dialogue questions?* We should never facilitate experiential learning activities for the first time live during a training program. We also want to have dry runs and practice opportunities to think through how we will deliver the instructions, what materials we'll need, what obstacles we might encounter, what the space considerations are and if they align with the group size, and whether these experiential learning activities support the training's learning outcomes.

These questions are critical because the experiential learning activities are the feature of our training program that enables our participants to wrestle with the theme. As they seek to develop new skills or enhance their leadership capacities, they will need structure that can illuminate their current practice— as well as growth opportunities, an environment that is conducive for this type of learning, and time to practice in an immersive way. This is that time. This time to experiment through the experiential learning enables them to access the training message and material. Then in the reflective dialogue, we create

Figure 12.4. Apex of Leadership Trainer's Narrative Approach, highlighting key features.

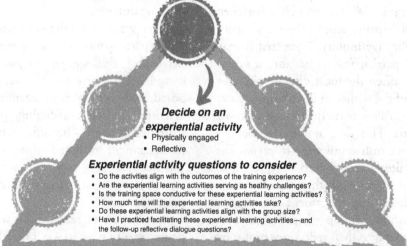

Note. Reprinted with permission.

the conditions for them to unpack the experience, reflect on what was learned, and internalize that learning. Figure 12.4 details the core features of the training story.

Falling Action

Just as every powerful story moves from the apex toward the resolution, every transformational leadership training includes reflective dialogue as a follow-up to experiential learning activities. During our reflective dialogue, our participants are safely guided to critically analyze their individual (and if applicable, group) performance during the experiential learning activity. As discussed in the previous chapter, leadership educators focus on three domains of reflection as we host these dialogues: content, process, and premise (Mezirow, 1991).

When asking questions, we can tether them together to get a complete picture—a holistic reflection on their experience immersed in the activity. Of course, we aim for the reflective dialogue to be a dialogue—a robust conversation among the participants rather than an analytical, point–counterpoint, or blaming style of discourse. When this occurs, people feel shut down and silenced. Rather, we emphasize healthy inquiry, relational engagement, collaborative communication, and the pursuit of new ways of being—new ways of leading.

Based upon research conducted by Anna Yeakley (2011), a scholar and facilitator who focuses on intergroup dialogue, there are five overarching facilitation skills essential to promoting positive outcomes from reflective dialogue. These include (a) creating a safe space, (b) recognizing signs of negative processes, (c) encouraging and supporting depth of personal sharing, (d) engaging conflicts as teachable moments, and (e) attending to identity differences in awareness and experience.

Tactically, during the reflective dialogue, our role as leadership educator-hosts of the conversation is in three capacities: We pose questions, we observe, and we assist our participants in translating their learning from the experiential activities to their leadership practice beyond the training bubble.

As hosts of the reflective dialogue, *we pose questions*. We are strategic in what we ask, how we ask it, and to whom it is asked. We want to encourage our participants to think critically about their actions and

opportunities for leadership learning. These questions should be relevant to the experience and formulated to be one at a time so participants can respond and build upon others' reflections. Our role, once the questions are posed, is to step back and allow the participants to respond and drive the direction of the conversation. As this is their training experience, our reflections are structured to repeat and emphasize what participants are offering, rather than take ownership over the messaging. By serving in this capacity, we can strategically encourage and support the personal sharing of participants, create the necessary space to utilize conflicts as teachable moments, and attend to identity differences being offered in the reflections.

Before leadership educators facilitate reflective dialogue, we need to *observe the actions of our participants* during the experiential learning activities. While facilitating, we have a keen eye on who is participating—and who is not; what is being said—and what is not; what are the perceived or actual attitudes, feelings, and vibes in the space; and how each individual is contributing to the goal—or not. This information is utilized as fodder for our questions when it comes time for the reflective dialogue. And during the reflective dialogue, we utilize the same observation skills and questions to get a sense of what is going on and how all of this information can be strategically utilized to enhance the leadership performance of our participants—both individually and collectively. This observational lens enables us to ensure a safe space is maintained as well as to recognize any signs of negative processes undertaken by the participants.

As savvy leadership educators, we always close the reflective dialogue by posing a *now what?* question to the participants. Now that we've had this experiential learning activity and reflective dialogue, what do we do with our learning? *How do we apply our leadership learning to our leadership practice?* We want to encourage our participants to make tangible agreements and tactical plans so that their leadership learning can be applied as a healthy leadership habit. Our work is only as good as our participants' abilities to infuse their leadership learning into practice. A free downloadable resource of 18 go-to reflective dialogue questions—bracketed into three groups (i.e., content, process, and premise) can be found at Leadership Trainer's website (leadershiptrainer.org/reflective-dialogue-questions).

Figure 12.5. Falling action of Leadership Trainer's Narrative Approach, highlighting key features.

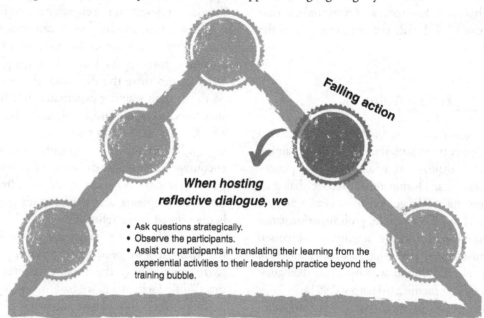

Falling action

When hosting reflective dialogue, we

- Ask questions strategically.
- Observe the participants.
- Assist our participants in translating their learning from the experiential activities to their leadership practice beyond the training bubble.

Note. Reprinted with permission.

There are several models that can be implemented to facilitate reflective dialogue. Each of these should be determined based on a number of factors, including the size of the training group, the energy and engagement levels of the participants, the learning style of the participants, and time allotted for the reflective dialogue, among others factors. These models can also be stacked to go from smaller to larger—or vice versa, larger to smaller.

In a one-to-one structure, participants will match up in pairs and engage in dialogue with their partner. With small groups, participants can organize in a group of three or four and engage in dialogue. With a large group, participants will gather as an entire entity and engage in dialogue.

The World Café (Brown & Isaacs, 2005) is another engaging dialogue structure that encourages whole-group dialogue in small-group configurations. It is identified as a social technology for engaging people in conversations that matter. In summary, the process unfolds by asking participants to join in groups and think about a question of significance. After the participants have had some time to collectively reflect and vocally process, the participants are instructed to find a new group to continue that same dialogue—albeit with new group members. The idea here is that each participant is expected to not only bring their own

perspectives, thoughts, and ideas to the new group but the insights of their previous group members. This process continues for several rounds until there is a sense that the whole "world" has participated in a single conversation (more can be found at www.theworldcafe.com). Figure 12.5 details the core features of the Falling Action of Leadership Trainer's Narrative Approach.

Resolution

The only way to conclude a training is with intention and purpose. Often, due to many factors—including time constraints, low energy, interest in the "next thing"—leadership educators rush to close up the training with limited intention. The *resolution*, though, if prepared well and facilitated with meaning, serves to wrap the entire training together while solidifying the leadership learning of our participants and propelling them to infuse their leadership learning into healthy leadership habits. When participants leave with positive feelings about the leadership learning experience and the accomplishment from their time in the training, they are more likely to implement their new ideas and skills in their leadership practice (Bolton & Bolton, 2016).

Exceptional leadership educators plan for and effectively close training sessions in order to bring together all of the learning points, create a space for final reflections, answer questions, and emphasize the most significant leadership messages. There are six steps to an effective leadership training closure:

We are intentional in the planning of the closing. Often, we think we can just close the training with a simple goodbye and recap of the training message. This is *not* how it is done. Rather, we purposefully incorporate time in the schedule for the closing. We make it an intentional feature so as to set the expectation for ourselves—and our participants.

When facilitating the closing, we review the theme and learning points articulated by the participants. This usually occurs during the reflective dialogue. However, we emphasize the learning points they raised throughout the entire training. We also utilize their insight to begin their action planning. We ask and guide them to think purposefully about the practical application of their leadership learning into their leadership practice. The more our participants acknowledge and celebrate their learning, the greater the likelihood that it will be transferred into practice (Oberstein, 2020).

We conclude the training by reiterating what was learned. Here, we reinforce the major themes and takeaways for participants and highlight what they should know moving forward. Once the material has been reemphasized, we begin to strategize with the participants ways to infuse their learning into practice outside of the training context. This might mean we offer a space for participants to draft a commitment list or to vocalize action plans or create accountability buddies—something to reinforce the importance of moving from the training to their beyond-the-training bubble leadership contexts.

Once clear plans have been devised, we provide space for general questions and comments. Often, participants want to follow up with questions or comments about the topic or theme, experiential learning activities, something that was triggered during the reflective dialogue, or other training opportunities. In our closing, we offer time and space for these questions and comments so participants feel seen and valued.

We don't want to close out a training before offering an evaluation of the training—or indicate an evaluation will be forthcoming. We always want to be in a position of making improvements and enhancing the experience for our future participants. By receiving feedback,

we will be in a better-informed position as we shape the next leadership training opportunities. This could be a formal written evaluation provided at the conclusion of the training experience—if we've built in enough time for this while ending on time—or simply as a notice about a forthcoming electronic evaluation. Evaluations and assessments are two separate entities, although usually combined into one document. An evaluation is about enjoyability and technical aspects of the training experience, for example, "On a scale of 1–5, how engaging was Jonathan?" Or, "Was the physical space conducive for this training?" An assessment is about learning. The assessment should be tethered to the learning outcomes. If we are serious about assessing learning, we might want to consider a preassessment to understand prior training knowledge and then a postassessment following the training—although not immediately following. Participants will need some time and space to apply their learning and implement their new skills into their practice. I suggest at least a week, if not longer. Of course, we could always invite participants to longer-term follow-up assessments to really gauge learning over 6 months, a year, or longer.

While highlighting resources pertaining to the themes and learning points from this training, we share with our participants how else they can find information to enhance their leadership practice on this topic or anything else of relevance to the training experience. Leadership learning is a lifelong pursuit. "No formal training program, by itself, can lead to long-lasting learning and change. . . . Really effective training may provide a solid *start* in a process of learning and change, but it doesn't represent its *end*" (Silberman & Beich, 2015, p. 319). This may include opportunities for future trainings.

As a last measure, we always want to remind our participants that the effectiveness of this training—and any training experience—is what they do beyond the bubble. Our last words in the training hold significant weight. The recency effect suggests that the most recently presented instructions or experiences will be remembered best, which means that we ought to be strategic with how we close—literally the last thing we offer. If we want our participants to apply their learning to practice, then as our final gesture we want to explicitly and formally encourage our participants to apply their learning from this training to their leadership practice. During the training, they *accessed* a message and material by participating in experiential learning

Figure 12.6. Resolution of Leadership Trainer's Narrative Approach, highlighting key features.

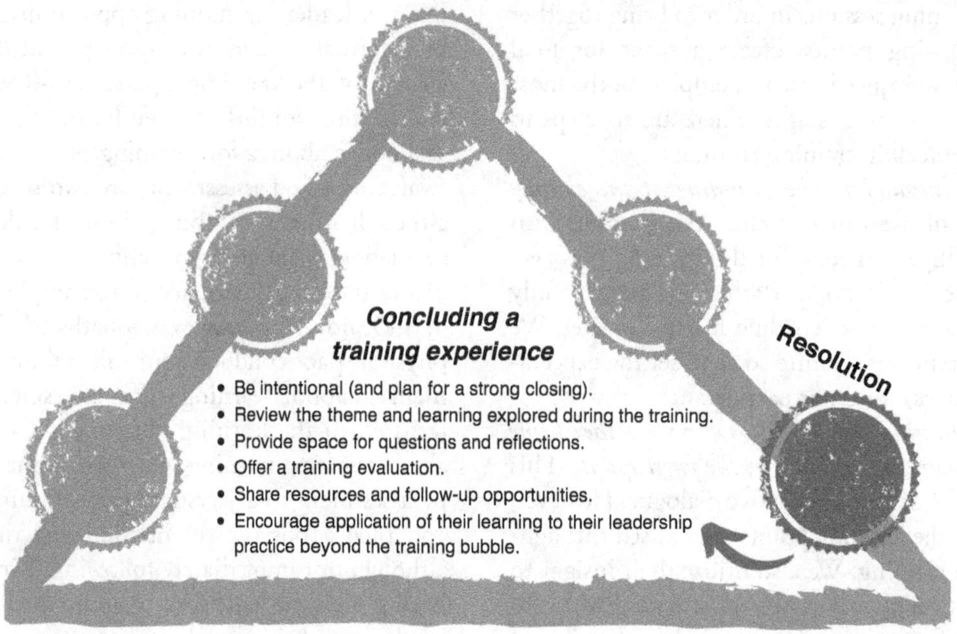

Concluding a training experience

- Be intentional (and plan for a strong closing).
- Review the theme and learning explored during the training.
- Provide space for questions and reflections.
- Offer a training evaluation.
- Share resources and follow-up opportunities.
- Encourage application of their learning to their leadership practice beyond the training bubble.

Resolution

Note. Reprinted with permission.

activities, *internalized* it through the reflective dialogue, and now they are prepared to *apply* practice.

Finally, a personal plea—conclude the training at the designated and labeled time. When offering leadership trainings, we make a commitment to offer a robust, dynamic leadership learning experience in the time allotted. We always end on time. Even if participants are late and we begin 30 minutes behind schedule, we end at the scheduled time. This is a matter of respect and respecting the commitment we've made to ourselves and our participants. Figure 12.6 details the core features of the training story.

Conclusion

As leadership educators, when we craft training stories, we are able to organize our thoughts, attention, and energies to design and then deliver amazing and impactful training experiences. Leadership Trainer's Narrative Approach is one such methodology. There are many other ways to construct and coordinate

trainings. If you are seeking resources to assist you in planning your next training experience, Leadership Trainer has two free resources that you might find valuable. The Training Checklist offers three dozen items—organized by six categories—to assist you in focusing your attention as you prepare your next leadership training. Visit this website to learn more and download the checklist: leadershiptrainer.org/preparation-check-list.

Additionally, if you are seeking a template that will offer you countless opportunities to plan amazing and impactful training experiences that utilize this training story as a structure and methodology, the Training-Planning Template may be of value. Leadership Trainer's Training-Planning Template is arranged by the five training story components to best focus your attention. Each dimension of the Narrative Approach is explored with numerous questions so your trainings experiences can be planned for strategically and comprehensively. Visit this website to learn more and get access to the Training-Planning template: leadershiptrainer.org/training-planning-template.

CHAPTER 13

Training and Facilitation Practices

IN THE PREVIOUS CHAPTER, we explored Leadership Trainer's Narrative Approach—a methodology for facilitating amazing and impactful leadership trainings. Our *training story* establishes a clear flow from preparations through the live training experience to the formal conclusion. Although each part is essential, the critical features of our training story for the internalization and application of participants' leadership learning is the experiential learning activities (apex) and reflective dialogue (falling action). In this chapter, we explore a selection of training and facilitation best practices that bring the story to life. To be clear, though, the Narrative Approach and these best practices are not intended to be strict rules. Rather they intended to provide a structure and formula for facilitating amazing and impactful training experiences.

Trainer Presence

When facilitating leadership trainings, we are essentially providing a public performance. Participants are particularly sensitive to a trainer's presence. They "will be looking at you more than anything or anyone else . . . your every move will be scrutinized. . . . Everything you do has meaning for them" (Skills Converged, 2016, p. 149). Yikes!

Our *presence* is about connecting to the experience so we can engage in sensing, tuning in, and acting from our highest future potential (Hayashi, 2021)—it is not charisma. Our presence enables us to create the conditions and environment for our participants to *access* information, *internalize* leadership learning,

and *apply* it to their leadership practice. Commanding and dynamic leadership educators are engaging. We empower our participants by assisting them in recognizing their magic. When tapping into our presence,

> we can collectively perceive and experience the present moment without the limitation of our habitual concepts, opinions, or projections. In doing so, we contact our innate intelligence, tender caring, and courage—three qualities that manifest as the true moves we make as we cocreate with each other the systems in which we live and work. (Hayashi, 2021, p. 6)

Our leadership training presence is less about us and more about how we can shine to illuminate our participants' greatness—and our collective greatness. We know, from our own experiences, that participants more easily integrate their leadership learning into practice when they feel a healthy, positive emotional connection to their leadership educators.

Our presence is the combination of our energy and pace. When trainer energy is low and pace is slow, it is a clear indication of boredom and lack of interest. Rather, leadership educators leverage their positive attitudes and an engaging pace to show excitement, care, and dedication to the training experience, participants, and topic being addressed. Timothy Koegle (2007), a presentation consultant and author of *The Exceptional Presenter*, suggests we find a healthy rhythm of speaking, pausing, breathing, and speaking. Speak. Pause. Breathe. Speak. Essentially, we want to deliver a message, offer an instruction, ask a question, or provide a response statement. Then we take a moment to pause and attend to the energy in the space and verbal and nonverbal communication from the participants. We consciously breathe to enhance our vitality and calm any nerves, and then move on to the next thing we want to deliver, offer, ask, or provide.

Leadership training presence is having the ability to connect authentically with the thoughts and feelings of others (Halpern & Lubar, 2004). Our presence is about how we show up to our training experiences and use our voice and body to influence our participants to learn and ultimately make behavioral change (Szelwach, 2020). This *showing up* and connection needs to be real. Yet there is a performative quality to facilitating leadership trainings. We bring our full authentic selves while also amplifying our energy and authority. By expressing our authentic voice and fully embodying this role, our participants will feel at home and encouraged to bring their full selves to the training.

Facilitating trainings with this depth of authenticity may initially feel uncomfortable. There is often internal resistance. We feel compelled by our protective patterns of behavior and limiting beliefs to curb our vulnerability and honesty. When we facilitate with presence, we push beyond self-limiting attitudes. We amplify our own dynamism and magnetism, which enhances the experience for our participants.

Leadership educators model effective communication so we can cultivate synergistic connections with and between participants. Cultivating presence as a facilitator of leadership learning requires increased self-awareness and confidence so that our authentic selves can be projected. How we show up, how we connect, how we speak and listen all combine to create the impact we have on the leadership development and application of our participants (Halpern & Lubar, 2004). Our presence manifests in three ways: internal disposition, physical body, and vocal engagement.

Internal Disposition

Cultivating outward presence begins with a focus internally. We begin with our breath. Nurturing internal presence begins by taking control of our breathing. Deep, full breaths.

Deep. Full. Breaths.

Quick, shallow breaths can make us anxious—which elicits fear and activates our nervous system's fight-or-flight response. This type of breathing impacts our ability to make sound decisions and act from a place of calm and clarity (DeMarsay, forthcoming). This is not how we want to approach our leadership trainings. Intentional breathing with deep and long breaths can make us feel calm and collected and operate from a place of steadiness and awareness. When we breathe deeply in this manner, we naturally readjust our mindset and discharge our nervous energy (Nelson et al., 2020).

When we are calm and collected, we are present. We begin internally because participants will subconsciously mimic our breathing patterns. In this way, leadership educators profoundly influence our participants' ability to learn and engage with the leadership material being presented.

Physical Body

Once we have control over our breathing, we support our presence by physically holding ourselves in power poses. According to Koegle (2007), there are four ways to appear relaxed, confident, and professional. We want to reduce our swaying, rocking, shuffling, and leaning; keep our heads and eyes forward to connect with our participants; smile sincerely; and move with purpose, energy, and enthusiasm. These tactics subconsciously communicate a remarkable amount to our participants—namely, that we are courageous, capable, and confident—and that this role, leadership educator, is one for which I am primed. We are expressing to our leadership training participants that, of all the people, *I* am the one who is equipped to develop your leadership skills and capacities by facilitating this amazing and impactful training experience.

Technically, by engaging our body in this way, we instigate our brain to respond in a feedback loop—releasing chemicals that reinforce those feelings of poise, self-assurance, strength, and energy. The opposite is also true: When we are feeling weak or depleted, we naturally slump, face away from our participants, fold our bodies, or fidget. This is inhibiting. Our brains respond by activating self-protective measures. Our participants can sense it and may feel discomfort leading to disengagement.

Vocal Engagement

What and how we vocalize has significant implications. Ideally, our participants will value our insights and ideas regardless of how they are expressed. Unfortunately, when we have unpleasant vocal engagement and communication styles, our participants will simply stop listening to whatever it is that we are expressing—no matter how valuable it is (Kaner, 2014).

Vocal engagement is about utilizing our authentic, powerful voice because it is natural, compelling, and draws our participants in (Nelson et al., 2020). Our vocal presence should be clean, straightforward, and poised. Filler words, such as *like* or *um*, should be removed from our vocabulary. Our vocal presence should also be at an appropriate volume and tempo. This takes practice, as does the utilization of a microphone. Mic checks are not just for technology preparation. We can utilize that time strategically to regulate our voice so that we're not sounding too soft or blaringly loud.

When speaking, we want to be engaged and looking at our participants, rather than the clock or other distractions. Looking away—avoiding our participants—communicates a lack of confidence and authority. Strong vocal projection, clear enunciation, and purposeful eye contact command attention.

When feeling grounded in our own embodied presence, we are able to tune into our surroundings, listen with equanimity, speak with clarity, lead with a larger perspective (Hayashi, 2021)—and facilitate trainings that enact what they espouse. Our presence conveys an incredible amount of information to our participants, namely, that we care about them and this experience, that we have diligently prepared, and that we actually know what we are doing and how to do it. Our presence ensures for our participants that we are the conduit for their leadership learning and that by facilitating this training experience they will be able to *access* the training message and material, *internalize* leadership learning, and *apply* it to their leadership practice.

Communicating Effectively as a Leadership Educator

The trainings we facilitate may evoke fears, doubts, or other limiting emotions in our participants. This evocation reduces their ability to listen. If they're not able to attend to the information being presented, they most certainly will not be able to internalize or incorporate healthy leadership habits into their leadership practice. It is for this reason we need to communicate

effectively—to ensure the intended message is received and that the leadership development and application can occur following the training. In order to communicate effectively we need to understand our rationale for what needs to be expressed.

Communication, in the broadest sense, is utilized to give and get—to deliver as well as to receive—information. We communicate to change behavior. We raise concerns, offer advice, provide challenge, and deliver praise with the hope that there is a behavioral response.

We communicate to ensure understanding. Leadership educators utilize communication techniques to ensure the acquisition and understanding of the leadership message or that learning has occurred. Typically, this is engaged through asking questions and then listening for response or watching for body language cues.

Communication, as we all already know, is not limited to what we say or what we hear from others. Communication is happening all the time, internally—from our subconscious. It is internalized through our senses. In essence, communication is rooted in how well we can sense what is going on around us. The more we can objectively and accurately sense, the more effective we can be in communicating. For example, our ability to objectively and accurately understand others—and vice versa—is much greater when we are in the physical presence of others—compared to when we speak over video—which is more complete than a phone conversation—which is more enhanced than an email correspondence—which has greater objectivity and accuracy than a text message.

The same is true with the objective understanding and accuracy of identifying our emotions—and their causes. When we are influenced by anger, frustration, disappointment, or depression, our objectivity and accuracy falter. This limits our abilities to communicate as effectively as we would like—or to receive and internalize communications from others.

Our human nervous system is designed to use our subconscious sensory systems as much as possible to navigate our normal day-to-day routines that keep us alive—breathing, heart beating, and so on—with limited engagement from our conscious brain. To put it in perspective, our unconscious mind processes 11 million pieces of information per second (Coyle, 2009)—what amounts to 200,000 times more than our conscious processing (Hurwitz & Hurwitz, 2015). We are deeply influenced by this feedback—albeit mostly unaware of it. It is for this reason we need to, as leadership educators, create the calming conditions and enjoyable environments for participants (and ourselves) to maximize as much of these data bits as possible.

Tactically, the way to engage our participants is to diversify our training experience with multiple learning modalities. For example, we might include music, creative or artistic expressions, video clips and multimedia resources, reflective exercises, physically engaged activities, small-group and large-group dialogue, and even purposeful pauses to encourage processing of the training experiences.

Our ability, as leadership educators, to communicate effectively and in diverse modalities is what enables our participants to access the training message and material, internalize leadership learning, and apply that learning to their practice. We need to practice healthy communication and ensure we communicate in ways that have resonance with our participants.

Asking Powerful Questions

A best practice for leadership educators is to strategically utilize questions to stimulate the reflection and action of participants. Our questions are purposeful. We carefully assess the training dynamic and use a variety of types of questions to elicit responses that can assist our participants in (a) uncovering their subconscious motivations, (b) learning something new, (c) connecting their thoughts to actions, and (d) providing a moment of healthy challenge.

Although we have a specific leadership message to share with our training participants, rarely do we dictate to participants what they should believe or do. This is because we know that leadership learning occurs when the opportunity to wrestle with new ideas is presented along with the occasion to author a response. Questions powerfully provoke this kind of wrestling. Questions are the foundation of thinking about leadership in new ways. Questions encourage participants to pursue dynamic responses. Questions provide motivation to move from thinking to acting. And questions shift authority and expertise from the facilitator to the participants.

More specifically, we know that our participants have wisdom, knowledge, and important information about leadership—from their own personal experiences. Questions allow them to be seen and valued for their wisdom, knowledge, information, and experiences. Our participants are seeking to be validated. Questions encourage validation and buy-in, increasing their levels of engagement in the training—and thus their leadership learning. Lastly, our participants are seeking opportunities to develop their leadership skills and capacities—that's why they are in the training. Questions establish a safe space for this pursuit and development to occur.

Leadership educators craft questions as a way to direct our participants' energy and focus their attention in five directions: future, past, purpose, foundation, and present (Nelson et al., 2020)

Future questions are employed to imagine possibilities, set trajectories, and inspire action.

Past questions are employed to celebrate, highlight, and honor past contributions.

Purpose questions are employed to illuminate why we are here.

Foundation questions are employed to identify our shared values.

Present questions are employed to access our internal states and present-moment awareness.

There are four types of questions available to leadership educators: closed, factual, open, and process, as shown in Table 13.1.

In addition to strengthening the level of engagement of our participants through the use of strategic questions, there are significant benefits for leadership educators. Asking questions enables us to assess the energy level and presence of the participants. Asking questions allows us to monitor the space as a way to measure how the participants are doing and what shifts or changes are necessary. Asking questions can also be implemented to emphasize a training topic or lesson. When engaged in this way, asking questions serves to highlight the most important aspects of the training or leadership learning we hope the participants take from the experience. Berger (2014) suggests that, to ask powerful questions, we must step back to assess what is missing or being silenced. Leadership educators utilize observation skills—getting on the balcony—as suggested by Heifetz (1994), from the adaptive leadership model (see chapter 5), to gauge the dynamic in the training. We also challenge assumptions—including our own. As the facilitators of leadership learning, we bring to light those assumptions that drive one's leadership practice. We question the questions that

TABLE 13.1: A Description of the Four Types of Questions Leadership Educators Can Utilize When Facilitating Trainings—Along With Types of Responses and Some Examples

Question	Response	Training Example
Closed	Closed questions have one of two responses: "Yes" or "No."	• Are you with me? • Does this make sense? • Did you learn an important leadership skill today?
Factual	Factual question answers are brief and rooted in personal truth, feeling/emotion, or experience.	• The agenda for today's training includes . . . How does that sound? • Are leaders born or developed? • What are one or two leadership skills that you learned today?
Open	Open questions require reflection, creativity, and substance in their responses.	• What interests you in this particular leadership training? • Where are the gaps in your (or your organization's) leadership practice(s)? • How does this leadership topic/skill connect or resonate with your situation or context?
Process	Process questions are open questions that necessitate purposeful time and space for reflection. Process questions utilize "quiet time" for personal reflection before answering.	• What has been a defining moment in your leadership development? • How do you define/understand *leadership*? • What is your action plan to implement your leadership learning from this training into your leadership practice? • How might this leadership training be improved?

are asked. Are the right questions being asked? Who is asking the question? What questions are not (possibly purposefully) being asked that should be? Essentially, our work is to focus the questions on themselves to ensure that the right questions are being pursued. We utilize questions to gain a deeper understanding of the problem at hand. Leadership educators illuminate the situation—for ourselves and the participants—by posing questions that serve to clarify what is really going on. Finally, we take ownership. We lean into our role as leadership educators by posing questions with confidence—and own the direction that the ensuing dialogue takes.

A selection of powerful questions for personal exploration and project/work settings are provided in the following. These can also be utilized to add depth to icebreaker activities.

Personal

- Who am I?
- What sort of life do I want to live?
- What excites my curiosity, wonder, and delight?

- How can I fill my next hour?
- What provides me with emotional nourishment?
- What story is limiting me/holding me back?
- What am I trying to prove? And to whom?
- If I were in your shoes and asked for advice, what would you say?
- Is what I am doing helping me follow my joy?
- What can I learn from the challenges and struggles I face?
- What is one small step I can take that gets me closer to realizing my vision?
- What am I ready to change? What am I not ready to change?
- What brings me closer to the home of my highest self?
- How do I want to be known?
- How do I want to be remembered?

Project/Work

- How would my ideal self create a solution?
- If not me, who? If not now, when?

- Just because it happened in the past, why must it be repeated?
- Just because it has not happened yet, why can't it?
- Why should I settle for what currently exists?
- What question has not been asked that needs to be?
- If there was an extra hour in the day, what would I do with it?
- If I had unlimited resources, what would I do?
- How much energy is this worth?
- If I could not fail, what would I do now?
- What drains my energy? What recharges my energy?
- How can I better infuse all of my intelligences into my work/project?
- Who do I need to include? Why is that person essential?
- What is something I ought to unlearn to perform better?
- What is my next step?

One of the most common fears of budding leadership educators is what to do when a question is asked and nobody responds. First, we need to develop our capacity to be comfortable with silence. Once we become comfortable with the crickets, we can more easily assess and understand the reason for the silence. For one, it could simply be the participants processing our questions—engaging in the all-important personal reflective inquiry. In this case, silence does not mean surrender. The quiet is part of the participant's quest to process their leadership learning and share a response that is authentic and true. Jumping in prematurely will not provide them the time and space to adequately engage in the reflective process.

It might, however, be that the dynamics of the group are a clue. Is a supervisor or manager there? Could people be waiting for her to respond? Could it be the supervisor or manager has intentionally—or unintentionally—silenced the group? In this scenario, participants could be fearful of responding to questions with that person in the room.

In another scenario, the silence could be due to our own facilitation. Were we speaking too quietly? It is possible the participants did not hear the question. Was our question somewhat mumbled and jumbled? It could be the participants did not understand the question. Our comfort with silence will allow us to properly gauge the situation and negotiate the quiet so as to have an informed and impactful response.

Several leadership theories presented in this book are grounded in questions of meaning and depth. Quinn and Spreitzer (2005; see chapter 5), when engaging individuals to shift from the normal state of leadership to the fundamental state of leadership, initiate the process with questions. They articulate that the question structure is important because it stimulates people to action. Their rationale is straightforward: Asking questions enhances mindfulness and asking questions moves us from a passive state to a more active state.

As we shift from comfort centered to purpose centered, we ask, *What result do I want to create?* As we shift from externally driven to internally driven, we ask, *Am I internally driven?* As we shift from self-focused to other focused, we ask, *Am I other focused?* And as we shift from internally closed to externally open, we ask, *Am I externally open?*

Scharmer's (2007) theory U (see chapter 5) includes two questions at the foundation: *Who is my Self?* and *What is my Work?* Only by wrestling with these questions can we move through the "U." These queries are the energizing force behind an open mind, open heart, and open will. By asking, *Who is my Self?* as leadership educators, we encourage participants to explore their personal visions and values. There are other ways to ask this. *What brings me joy? What lights my fire?* By asking, *What is my Work?* as leadership educators, we encourage participants to explore what kind of future we're called to bring forth. Other ways to engage this question ask, *What work makes me come alive? What would be missing from the world if I did not pursue this?*

In a third example, D. Roberts's (2007) conviction in action model (see chapter 5) is framed within the question, *Where does my deepest passion connect with my communities' greatest need?* As leadership educators, we encourage participants to explore both their *in*vironment as well as the environment. We reflect on our convictions and match those to the pressing concerns of our community. This work is not possible without, first, asking this question, then engaging in the contemplative work to uncover responses, and finally moving into action.

Asking powerful questions is an important facilitation skill for leadership educators. Doing so not only allows us to intentionally connect theory to practice, it structures the training experience with the participants at the fore. Asking questions engages participants and keeps them engaged.

Time Management

Only through the effective use of time are we able to manifest a leadership learning experience that develops the leadership skills and capacities of our participants. From the moment our trainings begin, leadership educators masterfully manage time so that we can include everything we've planned for, our participants stay engaged, and we conclude at the exact right time. When leadership educators ineffectively manage time, participants may feel like something was missing, that they did not get their money's worth, the program is too boring or too rushed, or they're frustrated about rushing to the next thing because they are running late.

Time management begins with skillful and deliberate program planning. During our preparations, we strategically allocate time parameters for each segment of the training. When we practice, we hold fast to those parameters. Yet when it comes time for the actual training, we recognize the potential need to relinquish some aspects of the training (if time is tight), and we design it with a few extra additions that we can incorporate into the training (if we need to fill more time). I recall from my early days of facilitating training experiences that when I practiced, I would share with myself (when solo) and with collaborators (when cofacilitating), "Next I'll do this . . . then I'll do that." Essentially, I would narrate what I would do rather than actually practice my facilitation. This did not allow me to accurately decipher how much time was necessary for each segment. Only by actually rehearsing our scripts and deliberately practicing our messaging will we sufficiently predict the flow and accurately determine the appropriate time allocation.

Even the most experienced leadership educators cannot definitively know how any one training will unfold. Participants are unpredictable. For instance, we may believe and plan for one segment of a training to take 30 minutes to complete. Yet it may wrap up in 12 minutes—or at the 54th minute, the dialogue is going strong with no end in sight. Adapting and staying nimble are important attributes of exceptional leadership educators.

Too Much Time . . . Not Enough Content!
Rarely do people complain when they have met their goal and have a few extra minutes and can leave early. End too soon, though, and this could result in feelings of resentment. Participants may believe that they did not get their money's worth, that the program content was not comprehensive enough, or that their vision of the program didn't match the reality of it.

What do we do when we have extra time? Leadership educators need to assess (a) the amount of time left for that particular segment of the training or the training as a whole, (b) the energy level of the group to determine what might be the next best steps, (c) the type of programmatic infusion that makes the most sense—an additional experiential learning activity, a dialogue, a purposeful pause, or something else. We always plan for secondary "go-to" icebreakers, experiential learning activities, or reflective dialogue questions that can be included with little preparation or props.

Too Much Content . . . Not Enough Time!
Too much content and not enough time is a bit trickier to manage. When participants sense we are running late or are crunched for time, there is a general sense of nervousness with the collective energy. People begin to check out and gather their belongings, interrupting the flow of the training and the opportunity for leadership learning. We should always be willing to let go of segments in order to end on time. Additionally, we sometimes need to act boldly to end a conversation (even in the middle of a participant speaking) so we can move to the next phase or element of the training or conclude the training at the designated time. Remember, continuing the dialogue can always take place informally once the training has come to a formal close.

What do we do when we have too little time? During our planning and preparation, it is often wise to plan for the experiential learning activities and reflective dialogue to take more time than expected. Additionally, when training programs include purposeful pauses (breaks), it is wise to initially design for longer breaks. If necessary, these can be reduced or completely eliminated if more time is needed.

When eliminating components of our training, the content and experiential learning activities should be prioritized based on their centrality and connectedness to the learning objectives of the training. Keep what is essential. Remove what does not directly relate to the intended outcomes. Of course, cutting the closing is not an option.

An important strategy for leadership educators is to provide general notions of how the program will unfold rather than specific time allotments for participants. This way, the program, structurally and curricularly, progresses as planned (in the minds of the participants) even if we are continually adding and removing elements of the training experience rooted in our effective time-management skills.

Obstacle Management

Obstacles are impediments for us in creating exceptional leadership learning experiences. Undoubtedly, leadership trainings will be rife with obstacles. How we navigate them will determine how well participants receive and appreciate the training. Savvy leadership educators can shift these obstacles into opportunities—usually without participants even knowing.

Training obstacles are varied. Yet they are practically included in every training. Typically, they emerge in the form of technology issues, space dynamics, or in connection with our experiential learning activities.

Technology Obstacles

Did you bring your computer? Do you have an adapter? Do you need a projector? Are your materials on a thumb drive? Is your clicker working? Is the screen fuzzy? Is the projection too close and big . . . too far and small? Is there a microphone . . . a microphone for the participants? Are the lights working? Is there electricity?

Any one of these technology obstacles can be significantly problematic. Yes, we should absolutely take advantage of the technological resources if they are available. However, during our preparations, we need to prepare as though when the time for the training arrives, we will not use the technology.

Space Obstacles

The physical environment for the training is a significant factor, and often an obstacle to the leadership learning of our participants. Think of the most recent training of which you were a part: Was the physical space the right size for the group—or did the space cause the training to feel too crowded or cavernous? Did it have the structure needed for the participants to be successful—space for dynamic experiential learning activities and reflective dialogue? Was a bathroom close? Was the kitchen and catering team next door making too much noise? Were the chairs comfortable—too comfortable and informal for the training? Were more chairs available if necessary—close to the training space? Was the furniture moveable or permanent? Where does the extra furniture go to create some space? How was the furniture used as part of the experiential learning props—was it as intended or a problem due to a space obstacle? Were there columns blocking some participants from seeing? Is the space inclusive and equipped for participants of all abilities—who was (or could have been) restricted or limited by the space dynamics? Were there tables or did people have to write with paper on their lap? Was the air conditioner blasting—was it making too much noise? Was the heat overwhelming? Was the training outside—was it supposed to be but the rain made that untenable? Was there wall space for Post-It notes? There are lots of space and potential structural obstacles to consider.

The physical environment of our training greatly impacts our ability to facilitate the leadership learning and development of our participants. Ideally, we would design the space that works perfectly for our intended training and participants. The only problem is that most of the time, our trainings are located in spaces out of our control—hence, an obstacle.

Detailed in Figure 13.1 are a sampling of space-design options and configurations for your next leadership training. Be creative. When planning for trainings, think critically about the learning objectives. What information do we want participants to access, internalize, and then apply? With this information, we can craft an experience and design our training environment to accomplish this goal. For example, if we want to infuse multiple opportunities for small-group conversations into the training, the "classroom" structure would not be ideal.

When thinking about these space arrangements, what might be the benefits and challenges of each one—depending on varying dynamic of your training programs?

My preference is to utilize a "multipurpose room" because of the ability to have multiple setups within the same physical environment. At the front can be

Figure 13.1. Room setup options for leadership educators. Space setup options for leadership training experiences.

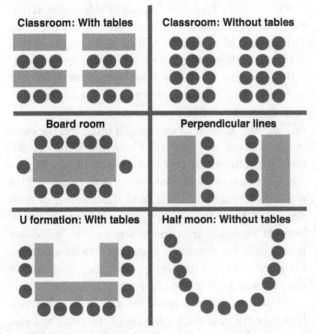

traditional seating while the back or side can be open space for experiential learning activities.

If we are facilitating worksheet-based activities, it is best to have tables. This provides the participants with a hard surface on which to write. It is a best practice during the reflective dialogue for the whole group to be engaged. For this to smoothly occur, it is suggested that the participants should be in a circle. The "half moon" or "U" formation best lend themselves for that aspect of the training. Of course, if participants are going to be in small groups for certain experiential learning activities, "circles" or "board room"–style arrangements lend themselves well for that type of engagement.

Experiential Learning Activity Obstacles
Leadership development and capacity-building happens best, as we know, when participants are immersed in the learning experience itself. This is why experiential learning activities are so important to leadership trainings. They are not without obstacles, though: Do we have enough materials and props for the number of participants? Do we have enough participants for the intended activities? Is the space conducive for these activities? Can the activities be facilitated only indoors or outdoors? What if we can't be in that environment—do we have back-up plans? If we are outside, is it too windy for our props . . . are they blowing

away? If we are indoors, is the activity too noisy for the space . . . are we interrupting others who are not part of the training? Are the experiential learning activities in the same space as the rest of the training—can we set up and prep in advance or will the props be a distraction? If not, will it take too long to set up in the middle of the training? Do I need volunteers—do I have confidence they know what they are doing when the time comes for them to perform?

At the intersection of experiential learning activity obstacles and people obstacles is recognizing the level of risk involved for our participants. Remember, each participant has a different threshold and tolerance for risk. Although some may believe an activity is very low risk, others may see a serious stretch or threat to participation.

Risk levels can be identified by a traffic light metaphor. See Figure 13.2 for a visual representation and key constructs of this metaphor. Low-risk activities

Figure 13.2. Levels of risk associated with a traffic light metaphor.

Red light *High risk*	Yellow light *Medium risk*	Green light *Low risk*
Activities yield serious concerns and a significant amount of thought energy.	Activities yield slight concerns and a decent amount of thought energy.	Activities yield little to no concerns or thought energy.
Examples include sharing vulnerably and exertion beyond physical comfort levels.	Examples include personal sharing, large-group dialogue, and some physical activities.	Examples include name sharing, journaling, and brainstorming.

are synonymous with a green light. These experiential learning activities yield little to no concerns or thought energy. These activities necessitate surface-level sharing of oneself and often do not include physical exertion—for example, sharing our names at the introduction of a leadership training, journaling, or participating in a brainstorming session.

Medium risk is correlated with a yellow light—move forward cautiously. These experiential learning activities yield slight concerns and a decent amount of thought energy. These activities encourage deeper levels of sharing but provide participants the option of sharing as much or little as they desire. They may also include physical exertion that may include public speaking, writing on a whiteboard, or certain experiential learning activities. An example would be a leadership educator asking, "What has been an important leadership-developmental experience in your life?" For some, this question is easy to answer. For others, it may be a serious stressor because of limited formal leadership experiences. There might be deeply rooted embarrassment by not having had opportunities to experiment with leadership while growing up. Alternatively, some participants may have heightened levels of anxiety around public speaking. Being asked to vocalize something to a large group of participants may manifest as angst, apprehension, and nervousness. The Four Corners activity can be considered a medium-risk activity. For some, moving to their respective corner and sharing about why comes naturally. For others, it is anxiety inducing. We may also find as this activity (or any other experiential learning opportunity) progresses, those who expressed it as low risk find it more challenging—and vice versa. Of course, the last thing to consider is that the outward display of our participants may not be their internal reality.

High risk is equated with a red light—take serious precautions and monitor the environment diligently. With these experiential learning exercises, serious concerns and a significant amount of thought energy are needed on the part of our participants. These activities are intended to purposefully draw participants out of their comfort zone and tend to be physically engaging. For example, if I were to ask a group of budding leadership educators, "What do you fear most about facilitating a leadership training?" we're asking for our participants to be vulnerable. These are important questions to ask and should be included in our experiential learning activities and

the follow-up reflective dialogue. We just need to fully recognize the implications and foresee the obstacles they might manifest. Experiential learning activities that should be recognize as high risk are the Rope Pull and the Mine Field activities. With the Rope Pull activity, participants need to exert themselves physically. They begin on the floor, seated, and need to use the strength of the group to pull each member to a standing position—at the same time. Those who self-identify as weak or overweight often feel the most concern about this activity. The Mine Field necessitates participants to be blindfolded and needing to rely on others to move from one area to another. This is a red-light activity because of the amount of trust needed. Additionally, although small, there is risk of hurt. If someone mistakenly steps on a "mine"—a tennis ball, for example—they could twist an ankle. Or if they are moving too quickly, they might bang their shin or knee into a chair—another mine.

As leadership educators, we can utilize this risk lens, internally, at the beginning of trainings to assess our participants' level of engagement and risk. Then, we stagger our training components to continually heighten the level of risk as we move from the welcome exposition through to the closing resolution. Clearly, we want to design trainings that avoid high-risk activities at the beginning—even if all the participants know one another—so that we can effectively ease into those experiences that might cause more resistance and caution. By staggering these experiences, we develop trust among the participants and establish an emotionally safe environment to explore leadership. Of course, we always have secondary and tertiary options available to us in case we find the planned experiential learning activities are too risky or not risky enough for our participants.

A final note regarding risk is that an effective training utilizes the participants with the most fear as the barometer. Leadership learning is best engaged in an environment that challenges participants but does not make them so uncomfortable that they are stressed and unable to grow (Perruci & Warty Hall, 2018). If an activity is going to exclude participants—either physically or emotionally—leadership learning is lost. That activity needs to be scrapped in favor of one that is inclusive of the group in its entirety. I can recall during an outdoor adventure course team-building day with my department, the assistant director was deathly afraid of heights and had a low tolerance for risk. In one activity, the whole group needed to get from one side of a raised platform to the other. To me, this did not evoke fear, but excitement. I lived, and still do, for these types of team-building experiential activities. We needed to use a rope a couple feet off the ground (for our feet) and another 5 or 6 feet above the ground (for our hands) to shimmy across to the other platform. If anyone touched the ground, the whole group needed to start from the beginning. As you can imagine, it had enough give that the ropes would move and sway as we tried to slide across. After half the group accomplished the task, it was the assistant director's turn. He was visibly shaken and was literally shaking. His hands would not physically grip the rope. He was sweating profusely and his shirt was in need of a good wringing. Although the group provided healthy amounts of encouragement and praise, this was too high-risk of an activity for him. After several attempts, it became clear he was not going to be able to make the crossing. We engaged in a short reflective dialogue about the activity. It was evident that while we were dialoguing, the facilitator was moving on to plan B or C because his original experiential learning activity plans were going to be too risky for our assistant director and our particular group as a whole.

Insightful leadership educators think through these obstacles—and many others—during our preparations, when we arrive at the training space, and as we are immersed in the training experience itself. We are constantly thinking through the potential obstacles so we can navigate them with confidence and in ways that often go unnoticed by the participants. This necessitates trainer presence so that we can consistently tweak—in the moment—the level of challenge for our participants. Although we need to be mindful of how various activities might be exclusive and limiting for certain participants, we also know that the more difficult or challenging the experience is, the deeper the opportunity for learning.

People and Group Management

A primary task of leadership educators is to effectively manage people and group dynamics during our training experiences. What happens when a question is raised and nobody answers? Silence. Or when everyone has something to say—sometimes offering to share something completely irrelevant to the conversation at hand and the theme of the training?

What do leadership educators do when participants get enraged, frustrated, disappointed, or defiant? What if some participants display these emotions while others are elated and celebratory? These are some of the questions leadership educators need to wrestle with and prepare for in advance of trainings so that we can navigate people and group-related quandaries.

Silent and Talkative Participants

The most common people-related obstacle during leadership trainings is related to our participants' level of investment—specifically how that translates into their interest in sharing thoughts, ideas, and opinions. Leadership educators can engage participants to bring voices into the fore as well as limit—in a healthy, productive way—voices that overpower the conversations.

Sometimes we get silent participants. These individuals may be disengaged or fearful of sharing. There may also be power dynamics between the participants that discourage people from sharing. These individuals could also just take a bit longer to process information and questions and need some extra moments to consider their best response.

A best practice when noticing silent participants is to begin with a reflective exercise using Post-Its, index cards, or a worksheet to get their juices flowing. Once individual and personalized ideas are drafted, it may be easier to include the quieter participants in the dialogue. Additionally, once drafted, these could be shuffled and shared with other participants so it becomes a mystery as to whose ideas are being shared. Another strategy is to begin with one-to-one pair-sharing. This allows for a safer environment for participants to potentially partner with a trusted individual with whom they can share more intimately. From there, the pairs can be offered an opportunity to summarize their conversation or offer a key point to the larger group. Or you can scale up from the pairs to a small group to a bit larger group to the whole room. Remember, every voice is valuable and should be valued. It may take some time, but including every participant's voice is essential for a meaningful, impactful leadership training.

Sometimes we get participants who won't quit. They have something to offer about everything—related or otherwise. We should celebrate that they are engaged and invested in the training. Yet if we do not stop them, other participants may become disengaged. Or other participants may feel like they don't have an opportunity to contribute. In other training scenarios, the whole group is chatty and it is impeding our ability to move the training along.

When dealing with a single talkative participant, we need to remember that as the facilitator of the training experience, we have responsibility for managing the flow of the program. We can pick and choose who we want to respond to a question and include in the dialogue. We should have comments at the ready like, "I'd like to hear from someone who we have not heard from in a while," or "What about someone from this side of the room," or we can live on the edge and call someone out by name—all with the plan of including others so the dominant talkative person's voice has less of a presence. If need be, during a break, it is sometimes appropriate to invite the talkative person to a one-to-one conversation and ask for their assistance in bringing people's voices into the conversation. We can utilize them as an ally and advocate rather than scolding them or making them feel like they are disturbing the training—which they very well may be doing.

When the entire training group is chatty, it is important for us to share this with the group. Typically they are receptive. We can acknowledge the time it is taking for everyone to share their ideas and we need to reduce the comments so we can fully engage in the complete training experience. We can also institute a "no repeat" rule—so that if a comment was already shared, nobody else needs to offer the same sentiment. As the training facilitators, we can also set time limits—which can be offered publicly or just for our own reference—for particular discussions. Once the time has reached its limit, we can offer an extension—recognizing that something else may need to get cut. The group can then make an informed decision on how they want to proceed. Lastly, utilizing one-to-one pair-sharing or smaller groups may help in managing time associated with chatty participants.

Disruptive and Resistant Participants

Disruptive and resistant participants are difficult. They are often challenging and demanding of our attention because they may be causing friction among other participants in a training. Before responding, we want to be sure we understand the underlying reason for their disruptive behavior and resistance. This is sometimes obvious—they have been forced or "voluntold" to participate. They simply do not want to be there and are

acting out accordingly. Other participants may not even recognize their disruptive behavior. For example, they are on their phone responding to email or text messages, not realizing the impact it is having on others. Similarly, they could be acting during an experiential learning activity or sharing their insight through the reflective dialogue in a way that is making participants uncomfortable—or worse. Once we have an idea of the root cause of their disruptive or resistant behavior, we can proceed with managing that behavior.

One strategy is to set group norms and expectations at the beginning of the training. As leadership educators, we can include our own so as to limit disruptive and resistant behaviors. For example, what is the collectively agreed-upon policy regarding appropriate phone usage or side conversations? Then, if those expectations are broken, we can refer back to them and hopefully reduce further issues. Similarly, at the start of the training, we can offer an icebreaker question: "What would you be doing if you were not here?" We can then offer a meditative exercise for them to release that activity. Then return to the theme. "We are here . . . how can we make the best of our time together?"

One of the best ways to change the behavior of disruptive or resistant participants is to enable them to "win." By celebrating the progress and accomplishment of an experiential activity or their time in the training, we may see a shift in their attitude and the way it manifests. Of course, if nothing else seems to be working, it is entirely appropriate and expected to have a side conversation with the participant. You can offer your reflections and perceptions of their behavior and ask if they are noticing it as well. You can offer them options as to how they want to proceed. Then, finally, if behavioral change still does not occur, as a way to save the sanctity of the training program, you can ask them to leave—noting that their disruptive or resistant behavior is causing a significant disturbance in the training and to the other participants. If, though, the disruption is causing physical or emotional hazard to other participants, it is critical to intervene and remove the disruptors from the training experience with immediacy. If this does occur, be sure to pause the planned training experience to check in with the participant body to assess how the group is doing. At this time, it may be more appropriate to shift to what is needed by the participants at that particular time than to continue with the original training plan. Remember, it is our *partici-pants'* training and learning opportunity—even if that means the learning is disconnected from the theme of the prepared training.

Facilitating Trainings in Virtual Environments

Before 2020, most of us would not believe that leadership trainings could be facilitated in virtual environments. Now we know that it is possible. Not only is it possible, leadership trainings facilitated over the internet can be just as effective as face-to-face experiences. Yet many of us have hesitancy with facilitating training experiences in any context except for face-to-face engagements. When digitally training, we often revert back to conventional learning structures where we lean on lecturing and slide decks. Not only does this impair our participants' leadership learning, it results in a disappointing training experience and disengaged training culture.

A virtual training is understood as a highly interactive synchronous online training with defined learning objectives, participants who are individually connected from geographically dispersed locations, and a web-based platform for their training engagement (Huggett, 2013). A virtual training is different from a webinar, class, video conference, or other type of online learning experience. It is taking place live with the intentional inclusion of highly interactive experiences.

When facilitating trainings in virtual environments, leadership educators should utilize the Narrative Approach to create the five-pronged training story. Although the training is behind a screen, it is still a leadership training we are facilitating. It still needs to be engaging to be a meaningful, worthy, and transformative leadership learning opportunity. "If training event facilitators are expecting rich training outcomes—changed behavior and improved performance—they need to design live online training in a way that enables such results" (Laborie & Stone, 2015, p. xx). To be clear, these leadership trainings should include experiential learning activities and reflective dialogue—just as they would in face-to-face engagements. Yes, it is possible to facilitate experiential learning activities in virtual environments. And, yes, it is possible to host reflective dialogue in virtual environments.

I regularly I facilitate Preparing *Leadership Trainers: Tactics and Techniques for Experiential Learning and Reflective* Dialogue, a no-cost virtual workshop that highlights how to facilitate experiential learning activities and reflective dialogue in virtual environments. More details and registration information can be found within the Leadership Trainer website (leadershiptrainer.org/preparing-leadership-trainers-signup).

John Chen, author of *50 Digital Team-Building Games* (2012) suggests several preparatory measures for virtual trainings. First, understand and test the technology. Although our technological advancements can lead to incredible training experiences, they can also fail and lead to training disruptions. Chen (2012) highlights that more than 80% of webinar presenters, as an example, used the webinar platform for the first time when conducting a webinar. It is always a wise move to test the systems and facilitate a trial experience in advance of your virtual leadership training.

It is also important to prepare the participants. A good habit is to send out instructions, notices, and reminders for what the virtual experience will involve and the technical details for participating. Participants should be invited to download the necessary software in advance as it may take some time—potentially causing them to be late and miss information or for you, as the leadership educator, to begin later than expected. In one technology failure example, I had crafted an automated system to automatically send a reminder with the Zoom link to participants. Yet I did not doublecheck the link. Inevitably the automated reminder email sent an old, defunct link. The training needed to be canceled because nobody could access the platform. Yet there were a dozen prospective participants who had registered and were ready for the leadership training experience.

Just as we do in face-to-face trainings, we want to prepare backup plans so we can effectively navigate obstacles and challenges. This includes having extra experiential learning activities to add into the training experience or to swap with an originally planned activity. It also includes having extra reflective dialogue questions. We may also need to cut components of our training if we start late due to technology issues or in the case of highly engaged participants. In addition to back-up plans, we will also navigate group dynamics and people-related considerations. Sometimes, this is easier to do than in face-to-face trainings. For example, if one participant is determinately and deliberately disruptive, we have the power to mute that participant and remove them from the training experience—something much more difficult to do in a face-to-face environment.

During the virtual training experience a best practice is to utilize a training partner (generally recognized as a producer) and a participant map. Sometimes, our virtual training experiences have more participants than we can see on our screen. A training producer would have the responsibility of monitoring engagement as well as the chat box as a way to keep you abreast of what is occurring beyond what you are able to see on your screen. The participant map enables us to document whose voices have been included—and the insight they offer—as well as who has been quieter, disengaged, or silenced. This could be a formal document or a scratch pad. Essentially, you would detail the participant names on the left column with plenty of space for check marks and notes to the right. Whenever a participant speaks, draft a check mark and note to get a sense of participant engagement and contributions to the leadership learning experience. Those notes can be referenced during reflective dialogue or as part of the training resolution as we shift to thinking about the application of the participants' leadership learning in practice.

Laborie and Stone (2015) articulate that well-designed virtual training experiences should be facilitated with intention by "technically agile" trainers. Technically agile trainers engage in the following practices: attend to raised hands, chats, and whiteboard in a timely manner; use tools strategically while not letting them become the focus of the experience; inform participants when and how questions will be addressed; and remain calm during unexpected situations. Being technically agile also means that leadership educators in virtual trainings recognize that their voices are the most important tool for maintaining engagement. This is about having an on-air facilitator presence.

In addition to being technically agile, there are important tactical approaches to consider when engaging in the virtual training environment. Howles (2022) utilizes the BLEACH acronym to be mindful of our background, lighting, expressions, angle, clothing, and headroom. Like it or not, our *background* is a critical feature of the training environment. Participants will closely examine everything within the frame of reference of our virtual training box. We need to be mindful and strategic when selecting our background so that it becomes a supportive mechanism and not a distraction.

Lighting is the second consideration. We need to ensure that our training environment is not too dark or that the light is not creating too many shadows. We should always have the light source—whether that is a lamp or window—in front of our faces.

Emphasizing our *expressions* is the third component of these tactical suggestions. We ought to ensure our facial expressions, eye contact with the camera, and hand gestures are coordinated to create an engaging virtual presence. This is especially true if we are utilizing multiple screens. Our expressions and engagement can be perceived incorrectly if our participants are seeing as though we are looking away from the camera lens.

The *angle* with which we engage is also of paramount concern. Our camera should be level with our face. It should not be positioned to look up at our face and ceiling. Nor should it be facing down toward the floor.

Our *clothing* and accessories also matter when facilitating virtual trainings. For example, thin stripes can appear wavy or shimmery on camera. When we wear a white shirt with a white background, we may become washed out. Similarly, if we are utilizing a green screen, be sure to avoid green clothing as you become part of the background. With accessories, it is advised to avoid anything that might be flashy and distracting or that make loud noises when using the keyboard or mouse.

Similar to the camera angle, we want to cognizant of our *headroom*. Our head should be centered within the frame. We do not want too much space above our head or on either side of our head. This means we may need to adjust our camera or either move closer or further from the camera so that we have the correct amount of headroom. With all of these suggestions, carving out time for set-up and checks before the virtual training experience is the responsible approach.

Scott Allen, a leadership scholar and educator, has fluency with engagement through digital mediums. He is the host of two podcasts—*Phronesis* found at his website scottallen.net and *Captovation*, taglined as presentation coaching for the digital age and found at captovation.ai. One of his *Captovation* blog posts, coauthored with Maria Soriano Young, is entitled "What's Your Signal Strength When Presenting Online (Hint: We Don't Just Mean Your Wi-Fi)?"

(Allen & Young, 2021). To focus on on-air presence, they suggest visualizing a Wi-Fi image at full strength. This has a dot at the bottom and several curved lines as indicators of strength that fan out from the bottom dot.

As the leadership educator, we are at the bottom—the dot. Our objective is to connect with our participants at full strength. Anything less than that is frustrating. The service is disrupted and the message is not received in its entirety. Allen and Young (2021) suggest that at one bar of signal strength, leadership educators are consumed within their nerves. They are just going through the motions to get to the end of the training experience. With two bars of service, the message is being delivered, but not at the level desired for our participants. It feels choppy. Here leadership educators may feel robotic and automated. This can often happen when delivering the same training over and over again without acknowledging that the training is a novel experience for the participants. Finally at full force—three bars of signal strength—leadership educators find a balance and groove. When this happens, we are technically proficient, feeling at home in this digital training environment, and able to shine.

I suggest that to engage at a three-bar level, we emphasize the use of experiential learning activities and reflective dialogue, not shy away from them because we are behind a screen. Experiential learning activities for virtual environments are critical to maximizing participant engagement because they provide structure and purpose to the participants' interactions and collaborations. When facilitating experiential learning activities and hosting reflective dialogue, technically agile trainers encourage the voices of many participants, probe with questions that elicit deeper thought and responses from participants, ensure the content is relevant for the participants, demonstrate empathetic listening rather than just listening to respond, encourage interaction and collaboration, and manage time effectively. Otherwise, leadership educators can become captive to the features of the online platform. For example, we should avoid dropping in a poll to an otherwise lecture-driven training just because the tool is available to us. Leadership educators should take advantage of these tools so long as they support the goals of the training experience.

For virtual trainings, it is also suggested that the participant count should be limited to a reasonable number (a maximum of 16 to 24 participants); that the participants should engage in smaller breakout groups; that virtual trainers should engage via audio, chat, and whiteboarding; and that planners should think of the event in the same way as an in-person training event (Laborie & Stone, 2015).

Our goal as leadership educators, although we are in a virtual environment, is to enhance the experience for participants in ways that motivate them to learn (Huggett, 2013). There are certainly differences and nuances to facilitating leadership trainings virtually, yet, on the whole, everything we do in face-to-face trainings should be replicable in virtual trainings so that our participants can access the training message and material, internalize the leadership learning, and apply that learning to their leadership practice beyond the (virtual) training bubble.

Conclusion

In this chapter, we explored a selection of training and facilitation best practices that enable leadership educators to shine as we bring our training story to life. When we strategically incorporate these into our facilitation practice, our participants are better positioned to be captivated, engaged, and participatory throughout the training experience. More, with these practices, we enhance our confidence to navigate challenges and shift obstacles into learning opportunities.

Leadership Training Facilitation— Part Four Conclusion

When we reflect on the terrible training experiences of which we have been a participant, it is safe to assume they were disturbing because of the conventional lecture-style approach or because the trainer was poor at facilitating the experience. Part Four of *Preparing Leadership Educators* was written so we can eradicate terrible training experiences.

These three chapters were drafted to provide you—and all leadership educators—with tactics, techniques, a proven methodology, and best practices for facilitating amazing and impactful training experiences. We can (and should) utilize experiential learning and reflective dialogue, the Narrative Approach to craft a training story, and these healthy facilitation habits to design and deliver leadership trainings that enable participants to *access* the training message and material, *internalize* learning, and then *apply* their learning beyond the training bubble.

CHAPTER 14

Conclusion

WE NEED NO REMINDER of our organizational and global challenges. They are numerous, immensely complex, and daunting. And they continue to unfold at seemingly unprecedented rates. We barely navigate through one before another, more formidable and massive in scale, emerges. To navigate these challenges, we will need bold action from leaders who are skilled and savvy.

This is *our* moment to shine. As leadership educators, our worthy work is grounded in enhancing leadership insights and effectively developing the leadership skills and capacities of our participants. To do this, we need to be intentional in acquiring leadership theoretical knowledge, practicing healthy leadership habits, and utilizing time-tested facilitation tactics and techniques—particularly experiential learning and reflective dialogue. When we do, it will be through our leadership training experiences that our participants will be challenged and supported to become the agents of change our organizations and communities desperately need. It is through the facilitation of these training experiences that out participants will gain more clarity, act more wisely, and perform more admirably. Without us, how will the next generations of leaders have the wisdom, competencies, and dispositions to overcome these obstacles? They won't (at least not effectively).

Leadership educators have a role to play in each individual's *human becoming*. It is through our leadership trainings and development that we encourage our participants to become more humane and

humble—reflective and resonant—gritty and grateful. What we do emboldens them to become the emotionally intelligent visionaries we seek. Our work results in hopeful, mindful leaders who thrive and enable their organizations to flourish. We challenge the status quo of the leadership landscape by assisting them in shifting from understanding leadership guided by position, power, prestige, and personal reward to leadership grounded in authentic personhood and the intrinsic purpose for our work.

Leadership educators have a role to play in *humanities becoming*. When our participants' notions and practice of leadership deepens we contribute to the developmental processes that enable these leaders to nourish our organizations and communities. It is this type of nurturing that enables systemic and structural change rather than the surface-level approaches that fail to live up to their potential. And, collectively, we become more connected to one another and the home of our highest possibilities.

I am inspired by the potential of intentional leadership training and development. I believe you should be, too. I firmly believe that when individuals gather to expand their leadership knowledge, cultivate their leadership capacities, and strengthen their leadership skills, both personal transformation and progressive organizational and communal change can occur. This is only possible, though, if we, leadership educators acquire the knowledge base, skill set, and dynamism to ensure our leadership training experiences are amazing *and* impactful.

214

Finally, now that we've reached the last paragraph of this book, let us take a moment to purposefully pause and breathe, recognize our leadership educator potential, relish in our superhero status, and develop the best trainings of our participants' lives—ones in which they can *access* the message and material, *internalize* leadership learning, and *apply* that learning to their leadership practice. Let's be exceptional leadership educators. Let's be extraordinary at facilitating the leadership training and development of our participants.

Afterword

When you walk with purpose, you collide with destiny.

—Bertice Berry

The opening epigraph is one that I have turned to throughout my professional life as a student affairs practitioner and leadership educator. It not only grounds my practice in intention, but it also offers space for dynamic iterations of what will ultimately emerge. Perhaps like me, you jumped into the world of leadership training and development due to your interest in supporting the growth and development of others. My educational path taught me the *what* of student affairs by exposing me to the history of higher education, the legal frameworks that guide our policies, and a host of leadership and development theoretical models—all of what Jonathan Kroll calls the "stuff of leadership education."

What more could a new professional need to be successful as they enter the field? Well, apparently a lot! In fact, nearly 60% of student affairs practitioner programs fail to prepare us for *how* to be effective leadership educators. As practitioners, the *how* is perhaps the most critical aspect of our leadership education work because it enables us to effectively develop the leadership skills and capacities of others. The *how* of our leadership educator practice is in how we curate inclusive environments to meet learners where they can thrive; the *how* of our leadership educator practice is in how we facilitate scaffolded opportunities for learners to try out (and sometimes fail in) diverse ways of knowing through experiences; and, perhaps most important, the *how* of our leadership educator practice is in how we involve learners in critical reflection that makes way for personal growth. The *how* is our purpose as leadership educators, but for far too long our preparation programs have not equipped us to walk with that purpose.

In *Preparing Leadership Educators: A Comprehensive Guide to Theories, Practices, and Facilitation Skills* Kroll masterfully brings together the theoretical (the what) and the practical (the how) of leadership education that our practice, *our field* desperately needs. He encourages readers to engage with the text as a resource rather than a novel. This is critically important because like our students, we are all at different places in our learning and development. While some practitioners may need to brush up on leadership theory to strengthen the intention behind their work, others (ahem, most of us) could greatly benefit from incorporating experiential learning and reflective dialogue into their training and facilitation practice. By crafting 'training stories' to structure our training experiences, to deploying the dozens of experiential activities described herein, to using the tips on facilitating reflective dialogue, practitioners at any point in their career can gain from the wisdom of this text.

We live in a world with complex and wicked problems. Our collective work as leadership educators is to help learners develop the skills and capacities to address these pressing demands using critical, intentional, and socially just modalities. This approachable text provides practitioners with a framework for addressing the knowledge gap that holds us back from maximizing our impact on the growth and development of others. By folding in the approaches described in this text into our practice we can strengthen the meaning and impact that validate our purpose—in doing so, we cultivate better pathways for learners to collide with their destinies.

Sarah Kutten
Assistant Vice Provost of Students and Belonging
University of Oregon, Portland
Board Chair, Leadership Trainer

Appendix A

Praxis Grid (Theories and Practices in Relationship to Experiential Learning Activities)

Leadership Theories and Themes	Name of Activity	Type of Activity	Page Number for Overview and Instructions
What Is Leadership?	Four Corners	physically engaged	22
Trait Approach	Line Up!	physically engaged	29
Skills Approach	Trade Me a Skill?	physically engaged	31
Behavioral Approach	Extraordinary Leader	reflective (worksheet)	33
Situational Approach	The Great Card Race	physically engaged	35
Path-Goal Theory	Pebble in the Shoe	physically engaged	38
Leader–Member Exchange	Assessment (e.g., DISC, MBTI or Strengths)	reflective (worksheet)	40
Transformational Leadership	Shrinking Islands	physically engaged	44
Servant Leadership	The Great Balloon Grab	physically engaged	45
Leadership Challenge	Bridge Build	physically engaged	48
Social Change Model of Leadership (7Cs)	Intersections	physically engaged	50
Relational Leadership Model	House Drawing	physically engaged	52
Connective Leadership Model	Rope Pull	physically engaged	57
Bad Leadership	Collage	reflective (artistic/creative)	59
Adaptive Leadership	ABCs Challenge	physically engaged	63
Fundamental State of Leadership	The Most Delicious Meal	physically engaged	65
Complexity Leadership	Object Toss	physically engaged	69
Theory U (Presencing)	Haiku	reflective (artistic/creative)	73
Conviction in Action	Values Exploration	reflective (worksheet)	75

(Continues)

(Continues)

Leadership Theories and Themes	Name of Activity	Type of Activity	Page Number for Overview and Instructions
Spiritual Leadership	Personal Flags	reflective (artistic/creative)	78
Authentic Leadership	How Do I Occur?	reflective (partner and dialogic)	80
Followership	Pirate's Booty	physically engaged	84
Gender and Leadership	Labyrinth	physically engaged	87
Culture and Leadership	Thoughts in a Minute	reflective (personal engagement)	90
Socially Just and Culturally Relevant Leadership	Tower Build	physically engaged	94
Leading and Other Developmental Relationships	Shoe Swap	physically engaged	99
Leadership Ethics	Up, Down, and All Around	physically engaged	101

Leadership Practices	Name of Activity	Type of Activity	Page Number for Overview and Instructions
Visioning	Tombstone and Obituary	reflective (worksheet)	110
Thinking Systemically	Keep Me in the Middle	physically engaged	113
Practicing Mindfulness	Grape Meditation	reflective (personal engagement)	116
Integrating Reflection and Action	Monument Build	physically engaged	121
Cultivating Emotional Intelligence	Feeling Words	reflective (personal engagement)	124
Offering Compassion	Metta	reflective (personal engagement)	127
Offering Compassion	Naikan	reflective (personal engagement)	127
Offering Compassion	Tonglen	reflective (personal engagement)	127
Offering Compassion	Right Speech and Intentional Listening	reflective (personal engagement)	127
Being Hopeful and Optimistic	Ideal Me/Real Me	reflective (worksheet)	132
Displaying Gratitude	Gratitude ABC List	reflective (group engagement)	135
Communicating	Mine Field	physically engaged	140
Engaging With Groups and Teams	Lava Lake	physically engaged	143

Leadership Practices	Name of Activity	Type of Activity	Page Number for Overview and Instructions
Motivating Others Toward Goal Accomplishment	Library Design	reflective (group engagement)	146
Navigating Dissonance and Toxicity	Number Cross	physically engaged	149
Nurturing Self-Efficacy and Confidence	Pillars of Power	reflective (worksheet)	152
Demonstrating Grit and Resilience	Four-Minute Scan	reflective (personal engagement)	155
Applying Strengths and Principles of Positive Psychology	Me at My Strongest	reflective (partner and dialogic)	158
Tapping Into Flow States	Peaks and Valleys	reflective (worksheet)	160
Embracing and Extending Cultural Humility	Identity Mapping	physically engaged	163

References

Abe, J. (2020). Beyond cultural competence, toward social transformation: Liberation psychologies and the practice of social humility. *Journal of Social Work Education, 56*(4), 696–707.

Adair, R. (2008). Developing great leaders, one follower at a time. In R. Riggio, I. Chaleff, & J. Lipman-Blumen (Eds.), *The art of followership: How great followers create great leaders and organizations* (pp. 137–154). Jossey-Bass.

Adriasola, E., & Lord, R. (2021). From a leader and a follower to shared leadership: An identity-based structural model for shared leadership emergence. In Z. Jaser (Ed.), *The connecting leader: Serving concurrently as leader and follower* (pp. 31–66). Information Age.

Allen, K., & Cherrey, C. (2000). *Systemic leadership: Enriching the meaning of our work.* University Press of America.

Allen, S., & Roberts, D. (2011). Our response to the question: Next steps in clarifying the language of leadership learning. *Journal of Leadership Studies, 5*(2), 65–70.

Allen, S., & Young, M. (2021, August 12). What's your signal strength when presenting online (Hint: We don't just mean your Wi-Fi)? [Blog post]. *Captovation.* https://www.captovation.ai/blog/signalstrength

Alvesson, M., & Robertson, M. (2016). Money matters: Teflonic identity-maneuvering in the investment banking sector. *Organization Studies, 37*(1), 7–34.

American College Personnel Association & National Association of Student Personnel Administrators. (2015). *ACPA/NASPA professional competency areas for student affairs practitioners* (2nd ed.).

American College Personnel Association & National Association of Student Personnel Administrators. (2016). *ACPA/NASPA professional competencies rubrics.*

Anthony-Gonzalez, M., & Roberts, D. (1981). A comprehensive leadership program model. In D. Roberts (Ed.), *Student leadership programs in higher education* (pp. 19–28). Southern Illinois University/American College Personnel Association.

Armstrong, K. (2010). *Twelve steps to a compassionate life.* Knopf.

Ash, S., & Clayton, P. (2009). Generating, deepening, and documenting learning: The power of critical reflection in applied learning. *Journal of Applied Learning in Higher Education, 2009*(1), 25–34.

Ashford, S., & DeRue, D. (2012). Developing as a leader: The power of mindful engagement. *Organizational Dynamics, 41*, 146–154.

Ashkenaus, R., & Hausmann, R. (2016, April 12). Leadership should focus on experiments. *Harvard Business Review.*

Association of American Colleges. (1986). *The campus climate revisited: Chilly for women faculty, administrators, and graduate students.* Author.

Avolio, B. (2011). *Full range leadership development* (2nd ed.). SAGE.

Bandura, A. (1977). *Social learning theory.* Prentice Hall.

Barasch, M. I. (2009). *The compassionate life.* Berrett-Koehler.

Bariso, J. (2018). *EQ applied: The real-world guide to emotional intelligence.* Borough Hall.

Barnhardt, R. (2008). Indigenous knowledge systems and Alaska native ways of knowing. *Anthropology & Education Quarterly, 36*(1), 8–23.

Baron-Cohen, S. (2011). *The science of evil.* Basic Books.

Bass, B. (1985). *Leadership and performance beyond expectations.* Free Press.

Baumister, R. (1995). Self and identity: An introduction. In A. Tesser (Ed.), *Advanced social psychology* (pp. 51–98). McGraw-Hill.

Baxter Magolda, M. (1992). *Knowing and reasoning in college: Gender-related patterns in students' intellectual development.* Jossey-Bass.

Baxter Magolda, M. (2001). *Making their own way: Narratives for transforming higher education to promote self-development.* Stylus.

Baxter Magolda, M. B., & King, P. M. (2004). *Learning partnerships: Theory and models of practice to educate for self-authorship.* Stylus.

Beard, C., & Wilson, J. (2018). *Experiential learning: A practical guide for training, coaching, and education* (4th ed.). Kogan Page.

Beatty, C., & Guthrie, K. (2021). *Operationalizing culturally relevant leadership learning.* Information Age.

Beatty, C., & Manning-Ouellette, A. (2018). The role of liberatory pedagogy in socially just leadership education. In K. Guthrie & V. Chunoo (Eds.), *Changing the narrative: Socially just leadership education* (pp. 229–244). Information Age.

Beatty, C., & Manning-Ouellette, A. (2022, January). Exploring leadership learning through short-term study abroad experiences. *Journal of Leadership Education*, 1–15.

Beatty, C., Manning-Ouellette, A., & Wiborg, E. (2021). Addressing White fragility in leadership education. In K. Guthrie & V. Chunoo (Eds.) *Shifting the mindset: Socially just leadership education* (pp. 257–270). Information Age.

Beerel, A. (2009). *Leadership and change management.* SAGE.

Ben-Shahar, T., & Ridgway, A. (2017). *The joy of leadership: How positive psychology can maximize your impact.* Wiley.

Bennett, M. (1986). A developmental approach to training intercultural sensitivity. *International Journal of Intercultural Relations, 10*(2), 179–186.

Bennett, M. (2013). *Basic concepts in intercultural communication: Paradigms, principles, and practices.* Intercultural Press.

Berger, W. (2014). *A more beautiful question: The power of inquiry to spark breakthrough ideas.* Bloomsbury.

Berkley, R., & Kaplan, D. (2020). *Strategic training and development.* SAGE.

Bertrand Jones, T., Guthrie, K., & Osteen, L. (2016). Critical domains of culturally relevant learning: A call to transform leadership programs. In K. Guthrie, T. Bertrand Jones, & L. Osteen (Eds.), *Developing culturally relevant leadership learning* (pp. 9–22). Wiley.

Blake, R., & Mouton, J. (1964). *The managerial grid.* Gulf.

Blake, R., & Mouton, J. (1978). *The new managerial grid.* Gulf.

Blake, R., & Mouton, J. (1985). *The managerial grid III.* Gulf.

Blanchard, K., Zigarmi, P., & Zigarmi, D. (1985). *Leadership and the one-minute manager: Increasing effectiveness through situational leadership.* William Morrow.

Blumen, L. (2008). Bystanders to children's bullying: The importance of leadership of "innocent bystanders." In R. Riggio, I. Chaleff, & J. Lipman-Blumen (Eds.), *The art of followership: How great followers create great leaders and organizations* (pp. 219–236). Jossey-Bass.

Bolton, R., & Bolton, D. (2016). *What great trainers do.* AMACOM.

Bordas, J. (2012). *Salsa, soul, and spirit: Leadership for a multicultural age.* Berrett-Koehler.

Boyatzis, R., & McKee, A. (2005). *Resonant leadership: Renewing yourself and connecting with others through mindfulness, hope, and compassion.* Harvard Business School Press.

Brah, A., & Phoenix, A. (2004). Ain't I a woman? Revisiting intersectionality. *Journal of International Women's Studies, 5*(3), 75–86.

Brookfield, S., & Hess, M. (2021). *Becoming a White antiracist.* Stylus.

Brown, J. (2013, November 15). *Fire.* Breathing Space. https://www.judysorumbrown.com/blog/breathing-space

Brown, J. (2016). *The sea accepts all rivers & other poems.* Trafford.

Brown, J., & Isaacs, D. (2005). *The world café: Shaping our futures through conversations that matter.* Berrett-Koehler.

Buechner, F. (1993). *Wishful thinking: The seeker's ABCs.* HarperOne.

Bunting, M. (2016). *The mindful leader.* Wiley.

Burch, G., Giambatista, R., Batchelor, J., Burch, J., Hoover, J., & Heller, N. (2019). A meta-analysis of the relationship between experiential learning and learning outcomes. *Decision Sciences Journal of Innovative Education, 17*(3), 239–273.

Burgess, H., & Butcher, J. (1999). To challenge or not to challenge: The mentor's dilemma. *Mentoring & Tutoring: Partnership in Learning, 6*(3), 31–47.

Burns, J. M. (1978). *Leadership.* HarperPerennial.

Butcher, J. (2002). A case for mentor challenge? The problem of learning to teach post-16. *Mentoring & Tutoring: Partnership in Learning, 10*(3), 197–220.

Butler Bass, D. (2018). *Grateful: The subversive practice of giving thanks.* HarperOne.

Cabral, A. (1974). National liberation and culture. *Transition, 45,* 12–17.

Cannato, J. (2010). *Field of compassion.* Sorin Books.

Carter, B. (2011). *Untamed leadership.* Enso Books.

Cashman, K. (2008). *Leadership from the inside out: Becoming leaders for life.* Berrett-Koehler.

Cashman, K. (2012). *The pause principle: Step back to lead forward.* Berrett-Koehler.

Chace, S. (2019). Uses of a holding environment as a container for stepping up and stepping back in the context of truth and reconciliation. In H. E. Shockman, V. Hernández, & A. Boitano (Eds.), *Peace, reconciliation and social justice leadership in the 21st century: The role of leaders and followers* (pp. 49–66). Emerald.

Chaleff, I. (2009). *The courageous follower: Standing up to and for our leaders* (3rd ed.). Berrett-Koehler.

Chaleff, I. (2019). Leading and following for transformation in a racialized society. In H. E. Shockman, V. Hernández, & A. Boitano (Eds.), *Peace, reconciliation and social justice leadership in the 21st century: The role of leaders and followers* (pp. 11–22). Emerald.

Chan, L., & Reece, A. (2021). Positive cultural humility in organizations. In S. Donaldson & C. Chen (Eds.), *Positive organizational psychology interventions: Design and evaluation* (pp. 125–140). Wiley.

Chen, J. (2012). *50 digital team-building games: Fast, fun meeting openers, group activities and adventures using social media, smart phones, GPS, tablets, and more.* Wiley.

Chen, L., & Kee, Y. (2008). Gratitude and adolescent athletes' well-being. *Social Indicators Research, 89*(2), 361–373.

Chodron, P. (2009). *Taking the leap: Freeing ourselves from old habits and fears.* Shambhala.

Chunoo, V. (2020). Leadership learning partnerships: Self-authored leadership through the learning partnerships model. In K. M. Soria & M. R. Johnson (Eds.), *Evidence-Based Practices to Strengthen Leadership Development* (New Directions for Student Leadership, no. 168, pp. 97–108). Wiley.

Chunoo, V., & Guthrie, K. (2021). Now more than ever: The imperative for socially just leadership education. In K. Guthrie & V. Chunoo (Eds.), *Shifting the mindset: Socially just leadership education,* (pp. 1–8). Information Age.

Cilente, K. (2009). An overview of the social change model of leadership development. In S. Komives & W. Wagner (Eds.), *Leadership for a better world: Understanding the social change model of leadership development* (pp. 43–78). Jossey-Bass.

Clutterbuck, D. (2008). What's happening in coaching and mentoring? And what is the difference between them? *Development and Learning in Organizations, 22*(4), 8–10.

Collins, P., & Bilge, S. (2020) *Intersectionality* (2nd ed.). Polity Press.

Cosgrove, S. (2010). *Leadership from the margins: Women and civil society organizations in Argentina, Chile, and El Salvador.* Rutgers University Press.

Council for the Advancement of Standards in Higher Education. (2020). *CAS professional standards for higher education* (10th ed.). CAS.

Coyle, D. (2009). *The talent code: Greatness isn't born, it's grown.* Arrow Books.

Cox, J., & Simpson, M. (2020). Cultural humility: A proposed model for a continuing professional development program. *Pharmacy, 8*(214), 1–9.

Crenshaw, K. (1989). Demarginalizing the intersection of race and sex: A Black feminist critique of antidiscrimination doctrine, feminist theory and antiracist politics. *University of Chicago Legal Forum, 1989*(1), 139–167.

Csikszentmihalyi, M. (1990). *Flow: The psychology of optimal experience.* HarperCollins.

Csikszentmihalyi, M. (2006). Introduction. In M. Csikszentmihalyi & I. Csikszentmihalyi (Eds.), *A life worth living: Contributions to positive psychology* (pp. 3–18). Oxford University Press.

Daloz, L. A. (1986). *Effective teaching and mentoring: Realizing the transformational power of adult learning experiences.* Jossey-Bass.

Daloz Parks, S. (2000). *Big questions worth dreams: Mentoring young adults in their search for meaning, purpose, and faith.* Jossey-Bass.

Day, D., Harrison, M., & Halpin, S. (2009). *An integrative approach to leader development: Connecting adult development, identity, and expertise.* Routledge.

Delucca, G., & Goldstein, J. (2020). *Positive psychology in practice: Simple tools to pursue happiness and live authentically.* Rockridge Press.

DeMarsay, T. (2020). *A qualitative study exploring the lived experience of organizational leaders with a contemplative practice* [Doctoral dissertation, Fielding Graduate University]. ProQuest.

DeMarsay, T. (forthcoming). *An invitation to contemplative leadership: How to live mindfully in times of crisis and uncertainty.* TGH International.

DiCicco, T., & Hacker, C. (2002). *Catch them being good.* Viking.

Duckworth, A. (2016). *Grit: The power of passion and perseverance.* Scribner.

Dugan, J. (2017). *Leadership theory: Cultivating critical perspectives.* Jossey-Bass.

Duhigg, C. (2014). *The power of habit: Why we do what we do in life and business.* Random House.

Dunn, A., Moore, L., Odom, S., Bailey, K., & Briers, G. (2019, October). Leadership education beyond the classroom: Characteristics of student affairs leadership educators. *Journal of Leadership Education, 18*(4), 94–113.

Dunn, A., Moore, L., Odom, S., Briers, G., & Bailey, K. (2021, April). Necessary leadership educator competencies for entry-level student affairs leadership educators. *Journal of Leadership Education, 20*(2), 43–62.

Durkheim, E. (1982). *The rules of sociological method.* The Free Press. (Original work published 1895)

Dutton, J., & Heaphy, E. (2003). The power of high-quality connections. In K. Cameron, J. Dutton, & R. Quinn (Eds.), *Positive organizational scholarship* (pp. 263–278). Berrett-Koehler.

Dweck, C. (2006). *Mindset: The new psychology of success.* Random House.

Eagly, A., & Carli, L. (2007). *Through the labyrinth: The truth about how women become leaders.* Harvard Business School Press.

Earnshaw, G. (1995). Mentorship: The students' views. *Nurse Education Today, 15,* 274–279.

Emmons, R., & McCullough, M. (2003). Counting blessings versus burdens: An experimental investigation of gratitude and subjective well-being in daily life. *Journal of Personality and Social Psychology, 84*(2), 377–389.

Erkut, S. (2001). *Inside women's power: Learning from leaders* (CRW Special Report No. 28). Wellesley Center for Women/Wellesley College.

Extejt, M., & Smith, J. (2009). Leadership development through sports team participation. *Journal of Leadership Education, 8*(2), 224–237.

Farrelly, D., Kaplin, D., & Hernandez, D. (2021, January 29). A transformative approach to developing cultural humility in the classroom. *Teaching of Psychology.* Advance online publication.

Ferrucci, P. (2006). *The power of kindness.* Penguin.

Fink, L. D. (2013). *Creating significant learning experiences: An integrated approach to designing college courses, revised and updated.* Jossey-Bass.

Fisher, E. (2020). Cultural humility as a form of social justice: Promising practices for global school psychology training. *School Psychology International, 4*(1), 53–66.

Foronda, C. (2020). A theory of cultural humility. *Journal of Transcultural Nursing, 31*(1), 7–12.

Foster, M., Taylor, V., & Walker, J. (2021). *Experiential exercises in the classroom.* Edward Elgar.

Freedman, J. (2019). *At the heart of leadership: How to get results with emotional intelligence* (4th ed.). Six Seconds.

Freire, P. (2002). *Pedagogy of the oppressed.* Continuum International. (Original work published 1970)

Gardiner, M., Tiggemann, M., Kearns, H., & Marshall, K. (2007). Show me the money! An empirical analysis of mentoring outcomes for women in academia. *Higher Education Research & Development, 26*(4), 425–442.

Garvey, B., Stokes, P., & Megginson, D. (2018). *Coaching and mentoring: Theory and practice* (3rd ed.). SAGE.

Garvey Berger, J. (2019). *Unlocking leadership mindtraps: How to thrive in complexity.* Stanford University Press.

Garvey Berger, J., & Johnston, K. (2015). *Simple habits for complex times: Powerful practices for leaders.* Stanford University Press.

George, B. (2003). *Authentic leadership: Rediscovering the secrets to creating lasting value.* Jossey-Bass.

George, B., & Baker, D. (2011). *True north groups: A powerful path to personal and leadership development.* Berrett-Koehler.

Gillihan, S. (2018). *Cognitive behavioral theory made simple: 10 strategies for managing anxiety, depression, anger, panic, and worry.* Althea Press.

Goldman, A. (2009). *Transforming toxic leaders.* Stanford University Press.

Goldstein, J. (2008). Conceptual foundations of complexity science: Development and main constructs. In M. Uhl-Bien & R. Marion (Eds.), *Complexity leadership: Part I: Conceptual foundations* (pp. 17–48). Information Age.

Goldstein, J., Hazy, J., & Lichtenstein, B. (2010). *Complexity and the nexus of leadership: Leveraging nonlinear science to create ecologies of innovation.* Palgrave MacMillan.

Goleman, D. (1997). *Emotional intelligence. Why it can matter more than IQ.* Bantam Books.

Goleman, D. (1998). *Working with emotional intelligence.* Bantam Books.

Goodwin, D. (2018). *Leadership in turbulent times.* Simon & Schuster.

Gostick, A., & Elton, C. (2020). *Leading with gratitude: Eight leadership practices for extraordinary business results.* HarperCollins.

Graen, G., & Uhl-Bien, M. (1995). Relationship-based approach to leadership: Development of leader-member exchange (LMX) theory of leadership over 25 years: Applying a multi-level, multi-domain perspective. *The Leadership Quarterly, 6*(2), 219–247.

Graham, L. (2018). *Resilience: Powerful practices for bouncing back from disappointment, difficulty, and even disaster.* New World Library.

Greenleaf, R. (1970). *The servant as leader.* Greenleaf Center for Servant Leadership.

Greenleaf, R. (1977). *Servant leadership: A journey into the nature of legitimate power and greatness.* Paulist Press.

Guthrie, K., Beatty, C., & Wiborg, E. (2021). *Engaging in the leadership process: Identity, capacity, and efficacy for college students.* Information Age.

Guthrie, K., Bertrand Jones, T., & Osteen, L. (2016). Editor's notes. In K. Guthrie, T. Bertrand Jones, & L. Osteen (Eds.), *Developing culturally relevant leadership learning* (pp. 5–8). Wiley.

Guthrie, K., Bertrand Jones, T., Osteen, L., & Hu, S. (2013). *Cultivating leader identity and capacity in students from diverse backgrounds.* Wiley.

Guthrie, K., & Chunoo, V. (2018). Opening up the conversation: An introduction to socially just leadership education. In K. Guthrie & V. Chunoo (Eds.), *Changing the narrative: Socially just leadership education* (pp. 1–8). Information Age.

Guthrie, K., Chunoo, V., & Teig, T. (2021). Leadership education: Teaching resilience for future success. *Journal of Higher Education and Leadership Studies, 2*(3), 58–75.

Guthrie, K., & Jenkins, D. (2018). *The role of leadership educators: Transforming learning.* Information Age.

Guthrie, K., & Osteen, L. (2016). *Reclaiming higher education's purpose in leadership development.* Jossey-Bass.

Gwinn, C., & Hellman, C. (2019). *Hope rising: How the science of hope can change your life.* Morgan James.

Haber-Curran, P., & Owen, J. (2013). Engaging the whole student: Student affairs and the national leadership education research agenda. *Journal of Leadership Education, 12*(3), 38–50.

Halls, J. (2019). *Confessions of a corporate trainer: An insider tells all.* ATD Press.

Halpern, B., & Lubar, K. (2004). *Leadership presence. Dramatic techniques to reach out, motivate, and inspire.* Avery.

Hammel, K. (2013). Occupation, well-being, and culture: Theory and cultural humility. *Canadian Journal of Occupational Therapy. Revue Canadienne d'Ergotherapie, 80,* 224–234.

Hanson, R., & Hanson, F. (2018). *Resilient: How to grow an unshakeable core of calm, strength, and happiness.* Harmony.

Harper, J., & Kezar, A. (2021). *Leadership for liberation: A framework and guide for student affairs professionals.* USC Pullias Center for Higher Education.

Hart, W. (1987). *The art of living: Vipassana meditation as taught by S. N. Goenka.* HarperCollins.

Harun, A., Razeef, M., Abd Razak, M. R., Nasir, M. N. F., Nasir, M., & Ali, A. (2013, June). *Freytag's Pyramid: An approach for analyzing the dramatic elements and narrative structure in Filem Negara Malaysia's first animated cartoon* [Conference paper]. IEEE Symposium on Humanities, Science and Engineering Research, Penang, Malaysia.

Hassan, Z. (2006). *Connecting to the source: The U-process.* Systems Thinker.

Hawkins, P., & Shohet, R. (2020). *Supervision in the helping professions* (5th ed.). McGraw-Hill.

Hayashi, A. (2021). *Social presencing theater: The art of making a true move.* PI Press.

Heifetz, R. (1994). *Leadership without easy answers.* Belknap Press of Harvard University.

Heifetz, R., Grashow, A., & Linsky, M. (2009). *The practice of adaptive leadership: Tools and tactics for changing your organization and the world.* Harvard Business School Press.

Hickman, G., & Sorenson, G. (2014). *The power of invisible leadership: How a compelling common purpose inspires exceptional leadership.* SAGE.

Higher Education Research Institute. (1996). *A social change model of leadership development.* Author

House, R., & Mitchell, T. (1974). Path-goal leadership theory. *Journal of Contemporary Business, 3,* 81–97.

House, R., & Mitchell, T. (1975). *Path-goal theory of leadership* (Technical Report 75-67; Contract M 170-761, N00014-67-A-O103-0032). Organizational Effectiveness Research Programs, Office of Naval Research.

Houston, P., & Sokolow, S. (2006). *The spiritual dimension of leadership: Eight key principles to leading more effectively.* Corwin Press.

Howles, D. (2022). *Next level virtual training: Advance your facilitating.* ATD Press.

Huggett, C. (2013). *The virtual training guidebook: How to design, deliver, and implement live online learning.* ATD Press.

Hurwitz, M., & Hurwitz, S. (2015). *Leadership is half the story: A fresh look at leadership, followership, and collaboration.* University of Toronto Press.

Iannello, K. (1992). *Decisions without hierarchy: Feminist interventions in organization theory and practice.* Routledge.

International Leadership Association. (2021). *General principles for leadership programs: 2021 concept paper.*

Isaacson, M. (2014). Clarifying concepts: Cultural humility or competency. *Journal of Professional Nursing, 30*(3), 251–258.

Jaser, Z. (2021). *The connecting leader: Serving concurrently as a leader and a follower.* Information Age.

Jaworski, J. (1998). *Synchronicity: The inner path of leadership.* Berrett-Koehler.

Jaworski, J. (2012). *Source: The inner path of knowledge creation.* Berrett-Koehler.

Jenkins, S., & Owen, J. (2016). Who teaches leadership? A comparative analysis of faculty and student affairs leadership educators and implications for leadership learning. *Journal of Leadership Education, 15*(2), 98–113.

Jewell, L. (2017). *Wire your brain for confidence: The science of conquering self-doubt.* Famous Warrior Press.

Johnson, C. (2018). *Meeting the ethical challenges of leadership: Casting light or shadow* (6th ed.). SAGE.

Johnson, C. (2019). *Organizational ethics: A practical approach* (4th ed.). SAGE.

Johnson, W. B., Rose, G., & Schlosser, L. Z. (2010). Student-faculty mentoring: Theoretical and methodological issues. In T. D. Allen & L. T. Eby (Eds.), *The Blackwell handbook of mentoring: A multiple perspectives approach* (pp. 49–70). Wiley-Blackwell.

Jones, S., & Bitton, A. (2021). Applying the lens of intersectionality to leadership learning. In K. Guthrie & V. Chunoo (Eds.), *Shifting the mindset: Socially just leadership education* (pp. 163–174). Information Age.

Joplin, L. (1995). On defining experiential education. In K. Warren, M. Sakofs, & J. Hunt (Eds.), *The theory of experiential education: A collection of articles addressing the historical, philosophical, social, and psychological foundations of experiential education* (3rd ed., pp. 15–22). Kendall Hunt.

Kahane, A. (2004). *Solving tough problems: An open way of talking, listening, and creating new realities.* Berrett-Koehler.

Kaner, S. (2014). *Facilitator's guide to participatory decision-making* (3rd ed.) Jossey-Bass.

Kanov, J. M., Maitlis, S., Worline, M. C., Dutton, J. E., Frost, P. J., & Lilius, J. M. (2004). Compassion in organizational life. *American Behavioral Scientist, 47*(6), 808–827.

Katz, R. (1955). Skills of an effective administrator. *Harvard Business Review, 33*(1), 33–42.

Kegan, R. (1994). *In over our heads: The mental demands of modern life.* Harvard University Press.

Kellerman, B. (2004). *Bad leadership: What is it, how it happens, and why it matters.* Harvard Business School Press.

Kellerman, B. (2008). *Followership: How followers are creating change and changing leaders.* Harvard Business Press.

Kellerman, B. (2018a). *Barbara Kellerman—Standards (#ILA2018WPB Plenary 27 October)* [Video]. YouTube. https://www.youtube.com/watch?v=urhs49eQQBE

Kellerman, B. (2018b). *Professionalizing leadership.* Oxford University Press.

Kelley, R. (1998, November–December). In praise of followers. *Harvard Business Review, 66,* 142–148.

Kelley, R. (2008). Rethinking followership. In R. Riggio, I. Chaleff, & J. Lipman-Blumen (Eds.), *The art of followership: How great followers create great leaders and organizations* (pp. 5–16). Jossey-Bass.

Kendi, I. (2019). *How to be an antiracist.* One World.

Kets de Vries, M. F. R. (2004). *Lessons on leadership by terror.* Edward Elgar.

Kezar, A. J., Carducci, R., & Contreras-McGavin, M. (2006). *Rethinking the "l" word in higher education: The revolution of research on leadership.* Wiley.

Kielburger, C., & Kielburger, M. (2004). *Me to we: Finding meaning in a material world.* Simon & Schuster.

Klau, M. (2017). *Race and social change: A quest, a study, and call to action.* Jossey-Bass.

Koegle, T. (2007). *The exceptional presenter: A proven formula to open up and own the room.* Greenleaf Book Group Press.

Koestenbaum, P. (1991). *Leadership: The inner side of greatness.* Jossey-Bass.

Kolb, A., & Kolb, D. (2017). *The experiential educator: Principles and practices of experiential learning.* EBLS Press.

Kolb, D. (2015). *Experiential learning: Experience as the source of learning and development* (2nd ed.). Pearson.

Komives, S., Lucas, N., & McMahon, T. (2013). *Exploring leadership: For college students who want to make a difference* (3rd ed.). Jossey-Bass.

Kotler, S. (2014). *The rise of superman.* New Harvest.

Kouzes, J., & Posner, B. (2017). *The leadership challenge* (6th ed.). Jossey-Bass.

Kouzes, J., & Posner, B. (2018). *The student leadership challenge* (3rd ed.). Jossey-Bass.

Kroll, J. (2016). What is meant by the term group mentoring? *Mentoring & Tutoring: Partnership in Learning, 24*(1), 44–58.

Kroll J., & Guvendiren, J. (2021, October 14). Student affairs practitioners as leadership educators? A content analysis of preparatory programs. *Journal of Student Affairs Research and Practice.* Advance online publication.

Kroll, J., & Moreno, M. (2022). Training leadership trainers: Cultivating the next generation of leadership educators in Nicaragua. *Journal of Leadership Education.*

Kusy, M., & Holloway, E. (2009). *Toxic workplace: Managing toxic personalities and their systems of power.* Jossey-Bass.

Kutten, S. (2020). *#AdultingWhileBlack: Encountering in the campus climate and the formation of racialized adult identity among traditional-age black college students* [Doctoral dissertation, Portland State University]. PDX Scholar.

Laborie, K., & Stone, T. (2015). *Interact and engage: 50+ activities for virtual training, meetings, and webinars.* ATD Press.

Ladson-Billings, G. (1995). Toward a theory of culturally relevant pedagogy. *American Educational Research Journal, 32*(3), 465–491.

Lawler, E. (2006). What makes people effective? In J. Gallos (Ed.), *Organization development* (pp. 545–564). Jossey-Bass.

Laing, R. D. (n.d.). *Quotable quotes.* goodreads. https://www.goodreads.com/quotes/90551-the-range-of-what-we-think-and-do-is-limited

Leavitt, H., & Lipman-Blumen, J. (1995, July–August). Hot groups. *Harvard Business Review.*

Le Bon, G. (2009). *The crowd* (5th ed.). Transaction. (Original work published 1895)

Lencioni, P. (2002). *The five dysfunctions of a team.* Jossey-Bass.

Lencioni, P. (2005). *Overcoming the five dysfunctions of a team: A field guide.* Jossey-Bass.

Lewis, S. (2011). *Positive psychology at work: How positive leadership and appreciative inquiry create inspiring organizations.* Wiley-Blackwell.

Liden, R., Panaccio, A., Hu, J., & Meuser, J. (2014). Servant leadership: Antecedents, consequences, and contextual moderators. In D. Day (Ed.), *The Oxford handbook of leadership and organizations* (pp. 357–379). Oxford University Press.

Liden, R., Wayne, S., Zhao, H., & Henderson, D. (2008). Servant leadership: Development of a multidimensional measure and multi-level assessment. *The Leadership Quarterly, 19,* 161–177.

Lilius, J. M., Worline, M. C., Maitlis, S., Kanov, J., Dutton, J. E., & Frost, P. (2008, September). The contours and consequences of compassion at work. *Journal of Organizational Behavior, 218,* 193–218.

Lindahl, K. (2008). *The sacred art of listening.* SkyLight Paths.

Lindqvist, E. (2012). Height and leadership. *The Review of Economics and Statistics, 94*(40), 1191–1196.

Lipman-Blumen, J. (1996). *The connective edge: Leading in an interdependent world.* Jossey-Bass.

Lipman-Blumen, J. (2005). *The allure of toxic leaders: Why we follow destructive bosses and corrupt politicians—and how we can survive them.* Oxford University Press.

Lipman-Blumen, J., & Leavitt, H. J. (1999). *Hot groups.* Oxford University Press.

Loehr, J. (2007). *The power of story: Rewrite your destiny in business and in life.* The Free Press.

Loehr, J., & Groppel, J. (2008). *The corporate athlete advantage.* Human Performance Institute.

Loehr, J., & Schwartz, T. (2003). *The power of full engagement.* The Free Press.

Mahoney, A. (2016). Culturally responsive integrative learning environments: A critical displacement approach. In K. Guthrie, T. Bertrand Jones, & L. Osteen (Eds.), *Developing culturally relevant leadership learning* (pp. 47–60). Wiley.

Marion, R. (2008). Complexity theory for organizations and organizational leadership. In M. Uhl-Bien & R. Marion (Eds.), *Complexity leadership: Part I: Conceptual foundations* (pp. 1–17). Information Age.

Maslow, A. (1943). A theory of human motivation. *Psychological Review, 50*(4), 370–396.

McCullough, M., Emmons, R., & Tsang, J. (2002). The grateful disposition: A conceptual and empirical topography. *Journal of Personality and Social Psychology, 82*(1), 112–127.

McDonald, M. L., & Westphal, J. D. (2013). Access denied: Low mentoring of women and minority first-time directors and its effects on appointments to additional boards. *Academy of Management Journal, 56*(4), 1169–1198.

Mcnally, P., & Martin, S. (1998). Support and challenge in learning to teach: The role of the mentor. *Asia-Pacific Journal of Teacher Education, 26*(1), 39–50.

McNeill, D. P., Morrison, D. A., & Nouwen, H. J. M. (1982). *Compassion: A reflection on the Christian life.* Doubleday.

Meadows, D. (2008). *Thinking in systems: A primer.* Chelsea Green.

Mertz, N. (2004). What's a mentor anyway? *Educational Administration Quarterly, 40*(4), 541–560.

Mezirow, J. (1991). *Transformative dimensions of adult learning.* Jossey-Bass.

Middlebrooks, A., Allen, S., McNutt, M., & Morrison, J. (2020). *Discovering leadership: Designing your success.* SAGE.

Morgan, G. (1997). *Images of organization.* SAGE.

Mosher, D., Hook, J., Farrell, J., Watkins, C., & Davis, D. (2017). Cultural humility. In E. Worthington, D. Davis, & J. Hook (Eds.), *Handbook of humility: Theory, research, and applications* (pp. 92–104). Routledge.

Müceldili, B., Erdil, O., Akgün, A., & Keskin H. (2015). Collective gratitude: Positive organizational scholarship perspective. *International Business Research, 8*(8), 92–102.

Mullen, C. A. (2009). Re-Imagining the human dimension of mentoring: A framework for research administration and the academy. *The Journal of Research Administration, 40*(1), 10–31.

Mullen, C. A., English, F. W., & Kealy, W. A. (2014). *The leadership identity journey: An artful reflection.* Rowman & Littlefield.

Mumford, M., Zacaro, S., Harding, F., Jacobs, T., & Fleishman, E. (2000). Leadership skills for a changing world: Solving complex social problems. *The Leadership Quarterly, 11*(1), 11–35.

Murphy, W., & Kram, K. (2014). *Strategic relationships at work: Creating your circle of mentors, sponsors, and peers for success in business and life.* McGraw-Hill.

Museus, S., Lee, N., Calhoun, K., Sánchez-Parkinson, L., & Ting, M. (2017). *The social action, leadership, and transformation (SALT) model.* National Institute for Transformation & Equity & the National Center for Institutional Diversity.

Nagda, B., & Maxwell, K. (2011). Deepening the layers of understanding and connection: A critical-dialogic approach to facilitating intergroup dialogues. In K. Maxwell, B. Nagda, & M. Thompson (Eds.), *Facilitating intergroup dialogues: Bridging difference, catalyzing change* (pp. 1–22). Stylus.

Ndalamba, K., Caldwell, C., & Anderson, V. (2018). Leadership vision as a moral duty. *Journal of Management Development, 37*(3), 309–319.

Neff, K. (2011). *Self-compassion: The proven power of being kind to yourself.* William Morrow.

Nelson, K., Ronka, D., Lang, L., Korabek-Emerson, L., & White, J. (2020). *Life-changing workshops: Creating the conditions for transformation in your groups, trainings, and retreats.* Cliffhouse Press.

Nemeth, C., & Nemeth-Brown, B. (2003). Better than individuals? The potential benefits of dissent and diversity for group creativity. In P. Paulus & B. Nijstad (Eds.), *Group creativity* (pp. 63–84). Oxford University Press.

Newman, A. (2019). *Building leadership character.* SAGE.

Northouse, P. (2021). *Leadership: Theory and practice* (9th ed.). SAGE.

Oberstein, S. (2020). *Troubleshooting for trainers.* ATD Press.

Osland, J. S., Kolb, D. A., Rubin, I. M., & Turner, M. E. (2007). *Organizational behavior: An experiential approach* (8th ed.). Pearson.

Owen, J. (2016). Fostering critical reflection: Moving from a service to a social justice paradigm. In W. Wagner & J. Pigza (Eds.) Innovative Learning for Leadership Development. (New Directions for Student Leadership, No. 145, pp. 49–55). Jossey-Bass

Owen, J. (2020). We are the leaders we've been waiting for: Women and leadership development in college. Stylus.

Owen, J., Devies, B., & Reynolds, D. (2021). Going beyond "add women then stir." In K. Guthrie & V. Chunoo (Eds.) *Shifting the mindset: Socially just leadership education.* (pp. 88–100). Information Age Publishing.

Owens, B., Johnson, M., & Mitchell, T. (2013). Expressed humility in organizations: Implications for performance, teams, and leadership. *Organization Science, 24*(5), 1517–1538.

Palmer, P. (2000). *Let your life speak: Listening for the voice of vocation.* Jossey-Bass.

Payscale. (2022). *Gender pay gap report.* https://www.payscale.com/data/gender-pay-gap

Perruci, G., & Warty Hall, S. (2018). *Teaching leadership. Bridging theory and practice.* Edward Elgar.

Priest, K., & Jenkins, D. (2019). Developing a vision of leadership educator professional practice. In K. Priest & D. Jenkins (Eds.), *Becoming and Being a Leadership Educator* (New Directions for Student Leadership, no. 164, pp. 9–22). Wiley.

Project Worldwide. (2020). *Communications statistics 2020.*

Quinn, R. (2004). *Building the bridge as you walk on it: A guide for leading change.* Jossey-Bass.

Quinn, R. (2005, July–August). Moments of greatness: Entering the fundamental state of leadership. *Harvard Business Review.*

Quinn, R., & Quinn, R. (2015). *Lift: The fundamental state of leadership* (2nd ed.). Berrett-Koehler.

Quinn, R., & Spreitzer, G. (2006). Entering the fundamental state of leadership: A framework for the positive transformation of self and others. In R. Burke & C. L. Cooper (Eds.), *Inspiring leaders* (pp. 67–83). Routledge.

Rath, T., & Clifton, D. (2004). *How full is your bucket?* Gallup Press.

Rath, T., & Conchie, B. (2008). *Strengths based leadership: Great leaders, teams, and why people follow.* Gallup Press.

Ready, D., & Conger, J. (2003, Spring). Why leadership development efforts fail. *MIT Sloan Management Review, 44*(3), 83–88.

Rego, L., Mohono, K., & Peter, G. (2019). Beyond ubunto: What the world can learn about building community from Africa. In H. E. Shockman, V. Hernández, & A. Boitano (Eds.), *Peace, reconciliation and social justice leadership in the 21st century: The role of leaders and followers* (pp. 11–22). Emerald.

Rendón, L. (2014). *Sentipensante (sensing/thinking) pedagogy. Educating for wholeness, social justice, and liberation.* Stylus.

Rest, J. (1986). *Moral development: Advances in research and theory.* Praeger.

Rest, J. (1993). Research on moral judgment in college students. In A. Garrod (Ed.), *Approaches to moral development* (pp. 201–211). Teachers College Press.

Rezaei, R. (2018). Creating brave spaces in leadership education. In K. Guthrie & V. Chunoo (Eds.), *Changing the narrative: Socially just leadership education* (pp. 213–228). Information Age.

Riggio, R. (2020). Why followership? In M. Hurwitz & R. Thompson (Eds.), *Followership Education* [Special Issue] (New Directions for Student Leadership, no. 167, pp. 15–22). Wiley. https://doi.org/10.1002/yd.20395

Riggio, R., Zhengguang, L., Reichard, R., & Walker D. (2021). Everyday leadership and engaged followership: Two sides of the same construct. In Z. Jaser (Ed.), *The connecting leader: Serving concurrently as a leader and a follower* (pp. 245–261). Information Age.

Rinpoche, S. (1993). *The Tibetan book of living and dying.* HarperCollins.

Ritscher, J. (1986). Spiritual leadership. In J. Adams (Ed.), *Transforming leadership: From vision to results.* Miles River Press.

Roberts, D. (2007). *Deeper learning in leadership: Helping college students find the potential within.* Jossey-Bass.

Roberts, D., & Ullom, C. (1989). Student leadership program model. *NASPA Journal, 27*(1), 67–74.

Roberts, J. (2012). *Beyond learning by doing: Theoretical currents in experiential education.* Routledge.

Rogers, J., & Dantley, M. (2001). Invoking the spiritual in campus life and leadership. *Journal of College Student Development, 42*(6), 589–603.

Rolfe, B., Jones, C., & Wallace, H. (2010, September 6–10). *Designing dramatic play: Story and game structure* [Paper presentation]. Proceedings of HCI 2010, University of Abertay, Dundee, United Kingdom.

Ropers-Huilman, R. (2013). Engaging Whiteness in higher education. In L. Landreman (Ed.), *The art of effective facilitation: Reflections from social justice educators* (pp. 81–100). Stylus.

Rost, J. (1993). *Leadership for the twenty-first century.* Praeger.

Sanchez, N., Norka, A., Corbin, M., & Peters, C. (2019). Use of experiential learning, reflective dialogue, and metacognition to develop cultural humility among undergraduate students. *Journal of Social Work Education, 55*(1), 75–88.

Sanford, N. (1967). *The student in the total learning environment.* Wiley.

Sawyer, K. (2007). *Group genius: The creative power of collaboration*. Basic Books.

Scharmer, O. (2007). *Theory U: Leading from the future as it emerges*. Society for Organizational Learning.

Scharmer, O. (2018). *The essentials of theory U: Core principles and applications*. Berrett-Koehler.

Scharmer, O., & Kaufer, K. (2013). *Leading from the emerging future: From ego-system to eco-system economics*. Berrett-Koehler.

Seemiller, C., & Crosby, B. (2019). Exploring and enhancing leader, educator, and leadership educator professional identities. In K. Priest & D. Jenkins (Eds.), *Becoming and Being a Leadership Educator* (New Directions for Student Leadership, no. 164, pp. 71–86). Wiley. https://doi.org/10.1002/yd.20359

Seemiller, C., & Priest, K. (2015). The hidden "who" in leadership education: Conceptualizing leadership educator professional identity development. *Journal of Leadership Education*, *14*(3), 132–151.

Seemiller, C., & Priest, K. (2017). Leadership educator journeys: Expanding a model of leadership educator professional identity development. *Journal of Leadership Education*, *16*(2), 1–22.

Seligman, M. (1991). *Learned optimism: How to change your mind and your life*. Knopf.

Senge, P. (1990). *The fifth discipline: The art & practice of the learning organization*. Currency Doubleday.

Senge, P., Scharmer, O., Jaworski, J., & Flowers, B. S. (2004). *Presence: Human purpose and the field of the future*. Society for Organizational Learning.

Shapiro, R. (2006). *The sacred art of lovingkindness*. SkyLight Paths.

Silberman, M., & Biech, E. (2015). *Active training: A handbook of techniques, designs, case examples, and tips* (4th ed.) Wiley.

Silsbee, D. (2018). *Presence-based leadership: Complexity practices for clarity, resilience, and results that matter*. Yes! Global.

Skills Converged. (2016). *Train the trainer: The art of training delivery* (2nd ed.). Author.

Smutney, M. (2019). *Thrive: The facilitator's guide to radically inclusive meetings*. Civic Reinventions.

Solomon, R. C. (1977). *The passions*. Anchor Books.

Soria, K., & Johnson, M. (2020). A conceptual framework for evidence-based leadership development practices. In K. Soria & M. Johnson (Eds.), *Evidence-Based Practices to Strengthen Leadership Development* (New Directions for Student Learning, no. 168, pp. 9–17). Wiley.

Southwick, S., & Charney, D. (2018). *Resilience: The science of mastering life's great challenges* (2nd ed.). Cambridge University Press.

Stech, E. (2008). A new leadership-followership paradigm. In R. Riggio, I. Chaleff, & J. Lipman-Blumen (Eds.), *The art of followership: How great followers create great leaders and organizations* (pp. 41–52). Jossey-Bass.

Stroh, D. (2015). *Systems thinking for social change: A practical guide to solving complex problems, avoiding unintended consequences, and achieving lasting results*. Chelsea Green.

Suarez, C. (2015). Never created with nosotros in mind: Combating colorblind leadership education with cultural competency and intersectionality of identities. In A. Lozano (Ed.), *Latina/o college student leadership: Emerging theory, promising practice* (pp. 29–44). Lexington Books.

Szelwach, C. (2020). Embodied leadership: Skills for the fourth industrial revolution. *Body Studies Journal*, *2*(6), 53–65.

Tangney, J. (2000). Humility: Theoretical perspectives, empirical findings, and directions for future research. *Journal of Social and Clinical Psychology*, *19*(1), 70–82.

Taylor, E. (2009). Fostering transformative learning. In J. Mezirow & E. Taylor (Eds.), *Transformative learning in practice: Insights from community, workplace, and higher education* (pp. 3–17). Jossey-Bass.

Teig, T. (2018a). *Higher education/student affairs master's students' preparation and development as leadership educators* [Doctoral dissertation, Florida State University]. ProQuest.

Teig, T. (2018b). Integrating social justice in leadership education. In K. Guthrie & V. Chunoo (Eds.), *Changing the narrative: Socially just leadership education* (pp. 9–26). Information Age.

Tervalon, M., & Murray-García, J. (1998). Cultural humility vs cultural competence: A critical distinction in defining physician training outcomes in multicultural education. *Journal of Health Care for the Poor and Underserved*, *9*, 117–125.

Thompson, S. (2004). Leading from the eye of the storm. *Educational Leadership*, *61*(7), 60–63.

Trungpa, C. (2005). *Training the mind*. Shambhala.

Tuckman, B. (1965). Developmental sequence in small groups. *Psychological Bulletin*, *63*(6), 384–399.

Uhl-Bien, M., & Marion, R. (2008). Complexity leadership—A framework for leadership in the twenty-first century. In M. Uhl-Bien & R. Marion (Eds.), *Complexity leadership: Part I: Conceptual foundations* (pp. xi–xxiv).Information Age.

Urry, J. (2003). *Global complexity*. Polity.

van Dierendonck, D. (2011). Servant leadership: A review and synthesis. *Journal of Management*, *37*, 1228–1261.

van Vugt, M., & Ahuja, A. (2011). *Naturally selected: The evolutionary science of leadership*. HarperCollins.

Vaill, P. (1989). *Managing as a performing art: New ideas for a world of chaotic change.* Jossey-Bass.

Vasquez, M. (2016). The value of promoting womanist and mujerista leaders. In T. Bryant-Davis & L. Comas-Díaz (Eds.), *Womanist and mujerista psychologies: Voices of fire, acts of courage* (pp. 263–275). American Psychological Association.

Velott, D., & Forté, K. (2019). Toward health equity: Mindfulness and cultural humility as adult education. In E. Tisdell, K. Gupta, & K. Archuleta (Eds.), *Meditation and mindfulness in adult education* (pp. 57–66). Wiley.

Villalobos, J. (2015). Applying White followership in campus organizations. In A. Lozano (Ed.), *Latina/o college student leadership: Emerging theory, promising practice* (pp. 167–184). Lexington Books.

Viscott, D. (1993). *Finding strength in difficult times.* Contemporary Books.

Volpe White, J., Guthrie, K., & Torres, M. (2019). *Thinking to transform. Reflection in leadership learning.* Information Age.

Vongalis-Macrow, A. (2016). It's about the leadership: The importance of women leaders doing leadership for women. *NASPA Journal About Women in Higher Education, 9*(1), 90–103.

Vroom, V. (1964). *Work and motivation.* McGraw-Hill.

Wallerstein, I. (2004). *World systems analysis: An introduction.* Duke University Press.

Watt, S. (2016). The practice of freedom: Leading through controversy. In K. Guthrie, T. Bertrand Jones, & L. Osteen (Eds.), *Developing culturally relevant leadership learning* (pp. 35–46). Wiley.

Wells, R. (2020). Pedagogy: Identifying and leveraging institutional entry points. In J. Bruce & K. McKee (Eds.), *Transformative leadership in action: Allyship, advocacy, & activism* (pp. 239–254). Emerald.

West, M. (2003). Innovation implementation in work teams. In P. Paulus & B. Nijstad (Eds.), *Group creativity* (pp. 245–276). Oxford University Press.

Wheatley, M. (1999). *Leadership and the new science: Discovering order in a chaotic world.* Berrett-Koehler.

Wheatley, M. (2007). *Finding our way: Leadership for an uncertain time.* Berrett-Koehler.

Wilkerson, I. (2020). *Caste: The origins of our discontents.* Random House.

Williams, K. D. (2010). Dyads can be groups (and often are). *Small Group Research, 41*(2), 268–274.

Yeakley, A. (2011). In the hands of facilitators: Student experiences in dialogue and implications for facilitator training. In K. Maxwell, B. Nagda, & M. Thompson (Eds.), *Facilitating intergroup dialogues: Bridging difference, catalyzing change* (pp. 23–36). Stylus.

Zohar, D. (1997). *Rewiring the corporate brain: Using the new science to rethink how we structure and lead organizations.* Berrett-Koehler.

About the Author

Jonathan Kroll is a leadership educator and entrepreneur. He began his career in higher education (student affairs) by focusing on leadership development, community engagement, and reflection initiatives. He has cofounded two leadership training businesses and, during the past decade, has facilitated hundreds of leadership workshops, retreats, trainings, and conference presentations to tens of thousands of participants across four continents.

Jonathan serves as the program director and assistant teaching professor in the Professional Leadership Studies program at the University of Rhode Island. He also founded and serves as the executive director and a master trainer for Leadership Trainer—a Boston-based 501(c)(3) nonprofit organization that focuses exclusively and explicitly on trainer preparation.

Jonathan earned a PhD from Fielding Graduate University in leadership, with a focus in group mentoring. He consults, writes, teaches, and trains about leadership, mentoring, and training and facilitation. Contact Jonathan by email (Jonathan.Kroll@ LeadershipTrainer.org).

About the Leadership Trainer Organization

Leadership Trainer, a 501(c)(3) nonprofit organization, aspires to be the undisputed authority in trainer preparation. We are cultivating culture change within the leadership landscape by providing exceptional trainer preparation programming and resources for those who are responsible for and charged with the leadership training and development of others. We believe that every training ought to be facilitated by amazing and impactful facilitators who can design and deliver training experiences that enable their participants to *access* the training material and message, *internalize* the learning, and then *apply* that learning to their practice.

Leadership Trainer offers a range of no-cost downloadable resources and programming. We provide one-to-one leadership training-coaching to individuals at all facilitation skill levels as well as organizational consulting to organizations of all types (higher education, nonprofit, corporate) to assess training programs and enhance training knowledge and facilitation capacities of team members. Our Mastery Course is a 12-module self-paced virtual program designed to provide you with the knowledge and skills to facilitate informed and lively training experiences.

Our flagship experience is the Leadership Trainer Certification Program. It is a one-of-a-kind, immersive, engaging, hands-on trainer preparation experience that will (a) prepare you to facilitate amazing and impactful trainings rooted in dynamic, culturally relevant, and learning-oriented facilitation techniques—including experiential activities and reflective dialogue; (b) empower you to purposefully engage in critical self-reflection and identity exploration; and (c) enable you to utilize leadership scholarship to enhance your own understanding and practice of leadership.

Explore all of Leadership Trainer's offerings at our website (LeadershipTrainer.org).

Index

A Guide for Leaders in Higher Education, Second Edition

Concepts, Competencies, and Tools

Brent D. Ruben, Richard De Lisi, and Ralph A. Gigliotti

Foreword by Jonathan Scott Holloway

"After an award-winning first edition, Brent Ruben, Richard De Lisi, and Ralph Gigliotti are back with a second edition of *A Guide for Leaders in Higher Education: Concepts, Competencies, and Tools*. This book could not come at a better time given the leadership challenges facing society like COVID-19 and issues of equity and social justice. The authors not only address higher education's role in meeting these challenges, but they expand their treatment of the book's core concepts and tools. As a result, they bridge theory and practice and underscore the communicative foundation of academic leadership in sophisticated fashion. The continuing importance of their work cannot be underestimated. It is a resource that all academic leaders need—and will thoroughly enjoy."—*Gail T. Fairhusrt, Distinguished University Research Professor, University of Cincinnati*

"This book is unique in providing both frameworks and vital information needed for successful leadership in higher education. I recommend it to all of our department chairs and use it in our leadership development program. Coverage of essential topics such as the changing landscape of higher education, perspectives on leadership, and communication strategies for academic leaders, makes this an essential resource for aspiring and current academic leaders."—*Eliza K. Pavalko, Vice Provost for Faculty and Academic Affairs; and Allen D. and Polly S. Grimshaw Professor of Sociology, Indiana University Bloomington*

Implementing Sustainable Change in Higher Education

Principles and Practices of Collaborative Leadership

Brent D. Ruben

Foreword by Doug Lederman

"Leaders with skills to help their teams and ultimately higher education organizations harness the richness of diverse individuals, ideas, and talent will be critical for future innovation and transformational change. These leadership competencies matter, whether engaging diverse colleagues in establishing shared aspirations and goals or addressing inequities or fostering inclusive environments. The more the people feel included, the more they are likely to be satisfied and the more likely they are to engage and collaborate—all of which ultimately lifts individual and organizational performance. The value of these ideas is incorporated in this book through the excellence in higher education framework, particularly on issues of culture, inclusion, diversity, and community."—**Sangeeta Lamba**, *MD, MS-HPEd, Vice Chancellor for Diversity and Inclusion at Rutgers Biomedical and Health Sciences*

"*Implementing Sustainable Change in Higher Education* is a compelling book that will guide and inspire all leaders at all levels in your institution. Brent Ruben, using long standing principles and practices, has put together excellent resources that will assist leaders in moving through their journey to success. If you are unsure about how to move your organization forward, this book will help you find the way."—**Cindy Taylor,** *Assistant Vice-President for Human Resources, Carleton University*

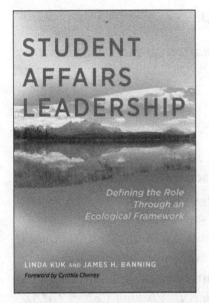

Student Affairs Leadership

Defining the Role Through an Ecological Framework

Linda Kuk and James H. Banning

Foreword by Cynthia Cherrey

Kuk and Banning offer readers a new lens for viewing leadership, one that goes beyond a focus on the behavior and values of leaders as individuals to examine how positional leaders interact with their environments to engage in leadership "in context."

This book is addressed to aspiring and senior student affairs officers and offers a new "ecological" framework that recognizes that today's leaders are affected by factors they may not control, and work within an environment they cannot expect to mold solely through their execution of skills and strategies.

Based on research supported through a grant from the National Association of Student Personnel Administrators (NASPA) Foundation, this book explores leadership as an interactive process within varied environmental contexts, and through an analysis of the transactional process between the leader, the organizational members, and the various components of the organizations environment.

It describes how leaders deploy differing competencies, skills, and strategies in varied contexts, and how they choose to use past experiences, their training, and personal characteristics to set priorities and navigate the cultural, social, physical, legal and political, resource, and ethical environments of their organizations.

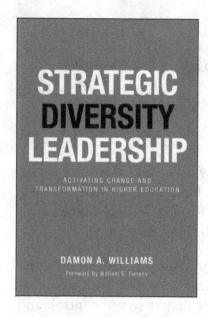

Strategic Diversity Leadership

Activating Change and Transformation in Higher Education

Damon A. Williams

Foreword by William G. Tierney

"*Strategic Diversity Leadership* is a president's 'how to' guide for making excellence inclusive in the academy in the 21st century. This book provides the fundamental building blocks for defining your campus diversity and inclusion agenda, while creating meaningful strategies and establishing a foundation of accountability. It is one of the most significant books ever published on diversity in the academy, and one that will remain pivotal reading for years to come."—**Ronald A. Crutcher**, *President, Wheaton College (MA)*

"*Strategic Diversity Leadership* makes the assumption that diversity is central to a successful country, but for diversity to succeed necessitates 'strategy'—it does not just organically happen. The book is a moral compass for how we are to proceed in the 21st century, necessitating that we take risks into uncharted territory. The text helps us prepare for the trip, offers a rationale for why the trip must be taken, provides a sense of what we are to accomplish on the trip, explains the benefits of undertaking the trip, and finally suggests initial paths that we might take. With Williams as our guide, the odds are pretty good we will get where he wants us to go. But first we need to read the book."—**William G. Tierney**, *University Professor and Wilbur-Kieffer Professor of Higher Education; Director of the Center for Higher Education Policy Analysis, University of Southern California*

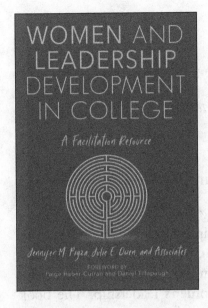

Women and Leadership Development in College

A Facilitation Resource

Jennifer M. Pigza, Julie E. Owen, and Associates

Foreword by Paige Haber-Curran and Daniel Tillapaugh

As leadership educators shift from teacher- to learner-centered environments, from hierarchical to shared responsibility for learning, and from absolute to constructed ways of knowing, a desire for new inclusive and creative pedagogies is also emerging. This text includes over 40 easy-to-follow modules related to women and leadership development crafted by experienced leadership educators and practitioners. Each module includes learning objectives, detailed instructions, and ideas for adapting the module to diverse learning spaces and audiences. Here are but a few of the critical questions that are addressed in the modules:

- How do we make explicit the complexities of power in leadership and in the stories we tell ourselves about feminism and gender in leadership?
- How can we interrogate and deconstruct dominant narratives and invite intersectionality? Whose voices are missing or silenced in content and process?
- What practices build leadership efficacy and habits of critical self-reflection?
- What are the effects of stereotypes, prejudice, and discrimination in leadership?
- How are learning and leadership both individual and collective processes?
- How do we develop critical consciousness and maintain hope in the face of the long arc of structural change?

This text is a detailed resource for anyone interested in women and leadership education, whether through a full-length course, a weekend workshop, or a one-time topical session. It also serves as a companion to the book *We Are the Leaders We've Been Waiting For: Women and Leadership Development in College* (Owen, 2020).

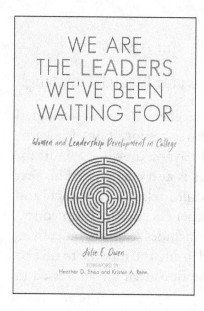

We Are the Leaders We've Been Waiting For

Women and Leadership Development in College

Julie E. Owen

Foreword by Heather D. Shea and Kristen A. Renn

"*We Are the Leaders We've Been Waiting For* is a compelling and necessary contribution to the scholarship on leadership and gender. Julie Owen integrates foundational and contemporary concepts and frameworks with powerful narrative in thoughtful and critical ways to advance our understanding of women's leadership. The book will undoubtedly transform students, educators, and our world. I can confidently say this is the book I've been waiting for."—*Paige Haber-Curran, Associate Professor, Texas State University*

At this time of social flux, of changing demographics on campus and the world beyond, of recognition of intersectional identities, as well as the wide variety of aspirations and career goals of today's women undergraduates, how can colleges and universities best prepare them for the demands of modern leadership?

This text speaks to the changing context of today's women students' experiences, recognizing that their work–life goals may go beyond climbing the corporate ladder to include social innovation and entrepreneurial goals, policy and politics, and social activism.

This book is a product of multiple collaborations and intellectual contributions of a diverse group of undergraduate and graduate women who helped shape the course on which it is based. They provided research support, critical readings, as well as the diverse narratives that are included throughout the book, not as an ideal for readers to aspire to but as an authentic expression of how their distinct and sometimes nonconforming lived experiences shaped their understandings of leadership. It goes beyond hero/she-ro person-centered approaches to get at the complex and intrapersonal nature of leadership. It also situates intersectional identities, critical consciousness, and student development theory as important lenses throughout the text.

22883 Quicksilver Drive
Sterling, VA 20166-2019

Subscribe to our email alerts: www.Styluspub.com

DATE DUE

6/14/23	
6/16/23	
	PRINTED IN U.S.A.